COLLINS GUIDE TO

CATHEDRALS, ABBEYS AND PRIORIES

of England and Wales

HENRY THOROLD

Photographs by
PETER BURTON

Foreword by John Piper C. H.

COLLINS
8 Grafton Street, London W1
1986

William Collins Sons & Co. Ltd
London · Glasgow · Sydney · Auckland
Toronto · Johannesburg

BRITISH LIBRARY CATALOGUING IN PUBLICATION DATA

Thorold, Henry
Collins guide to cathedrals, abbeys and
priories of England and Wales.
1. Churches – England   2. Church architecture
– England
I. Title
246.9′0942   NA5461

ISBN 0-00-217241-0

First published 1986
Copyright © Henry Thorold 1986

Picture origination by Gilchrist Bros. Leeds
Maps by Leslie Robinson
Set in Linotron Ehrhardt by
Rowland Phototypesetting Ltd, Bury St Edmunds, Suffolk
Made and printed in Great Britain by
William Collins Sons & Co. Ltd, Glasgow

To
John Barratt
Peter Burton
Mervyn James
John Stevens-Guille
Basil Wilks

sodalibus in nonnullis itineribus

CONTENTS

WALES

John Piper's Baptistery window at Coventry Cathedral

FOREWORD

I have always regarded John Betjeman's introduction to *Collins Guide to English Parish Churches* (1958) as one of his very best pieces of prose. It was the mainstay of the book, which has had several editions. I remember gratefully many happy laughs and animated discussions during its making, about churches that were 'winners' or 'too dim' for inclusion, and whether illustrations were 'musts' or 'not quites', and so on. So I was delighted when the present author asked me to write a few words to bless this new book, which I now recognize as a wholly worthy younger relation of the *Guide to English Parish Churches*.

Henry Thorold is an old friend of mine as he was of John Betjeman and is no stranger to churches large and small. I have had the pleasure of visiting a good many with him, and can recommend him as an undeterrable explorer and sound chronicler of old (and sometimes unwanted) churches, also a stout enemy of despoilers, destroyers and redundancy promoters. Also that he has knowledge, tenacity and sensibility to add to his gifts as an architectural and topographical writer. Five of the best of the *Shell County Guides* are his work. Driving about in one of his counties, I often think, 'What does Henry say about this place?' And there, if one stops and looks, is an admirable little prose-poem about it – short, informative and original.

In this new book he is vividly perceptive about the atmosphere of buildings: whether admiring or critical, the remarks are always clear and worth remembering. So it is very good to have his authoritative and up-to-date descriptions of the great cathedrals, which could not be better done, while Peter Burton with his sympathetic eye backs him up with his photographs, nearly all of which have been taken on their recent visits.

I much admire the shorter descriptions and pictures of the lesser abbeys and priories. These are done with an immediate feeling for the atmosphere of each place, and the excitement of discovery. Whoever can have visited them all in a short time, like these two have? Merevale Abbey, Lapley Priory, Knaith Priory, Tilty Abbey, Owston Priory, Pamber Priory – whoever has even heard of some of them? The answer is only the readers of very local guides or learned County Society volumes. Sometimes these monastic sites have little to show but a fairly unnoteworthy church in a dull village. But there are a lot of surprises. At Brinkburn, for instance: a well-restored 12th-century church beside a big house in a beautiful wooded combe on a low cliff (Northumberland). Or Letheringham, in 'a wonderfully remote and inaccessible spot, approached by back lanes . . . a church in a spacious setting of old walls, meadows and copses, with a farmyard close at hand' (Suffolk). And Ewenny: a beautiful ruin three miles from the sea in the flat land south of Bridgend in South Wales. This priory was painted by Turner, who also did some beautiful drawings of it in one of his travelling sketchbooks. I hope to visit these and a lot more mentioned in this book before long. Who could resist them? And because I have enjoyed Henry Thorold's monastic miniatures so much I looked out again another miniature piece of which I was reminded by his writing. It is from Henry James' *English Hours* (1905):

> In so far as beauty of structure is beauty of line and curve, balance and harmony of masses and dimensions, I have seldom relished it as deeply as on the grassy nave of some crumbling church, before lonely columns and empty windows where the wild flowers were a cornice and the sailing clouds a roof.

JOHN PIPER
December 1985

ACKNOWLEDGEMENTS

It was my old friend Mr Richard Ollard who first wrote to me proposing this book: Collins, he said, were contemplating a guide to cathedrals and abbeys, a sequel to John Betjeman's *Guide to English Parish Churches* – and Sir John Betjeman had suggested me. From the very first Mr Ollard has fostered this book, and I am most grateful to him for his suggestions, criticisms, and unfailing encouragement. In the same breath I must thank Mr John Piper, C.H., for the most delightful and generous Foreword which he has written. He was closely associated with the *Parish Churches:* it is an immense pleasure to have his support in this work.

Every cathedral, abbey and priory described in these pages has been visited or revisited for the purpose: it has been a great task, but an extremely pleasurable one. Cathedrals I have been 'collecting' since the age of four – but as the book progressed more and more little-known priories have turned up in unsuspected places, necessitating further forays into distant parts of England or Wales. I must record my gratitude to many friends for their hospitality on these journeys, and in particular to Mrs Edward Croft-Murray who entertained both author and photographer on numberless occasions at Croft Castle in Herefordshire – on that strategic borderland of England and Wales.

Grateful thanks are due to many cathedral dignitaries, incumbents, architects, librarians, vergers, custodians and other friends. A special debt of gratitude is due to the Bishop of Ely and Mrs Walker, the Provost of Blackburn, the Dean of Chichester, the Dean of Exeter, the Provost of Newcastle, the Dean of Peterborough, the Dean of St Albans, the Provost and Chapter of Southwell, the Dean of Wells, the Dean of Winchester, Canon Henry Stapleton of Rochester, Canon Ingram Hill of Canterbury, the Vicar of Tewkesbury, Prebendary Gerard Irvine, Dr Geoffrey Barnard, Mr Robert Crayford, and Mr Peter Foster, Surveyor of Westminster Abbey; the late Mr David Verey treated me to a memorable tour of Gloucester Cathedral a few months before his untimely death.

Mr Peter Burton has worked tirelessly as photographer for the book; nothing has ever been too much trouble for him, and he has driven many thousands of miles on its behalf. Most of the churches described here I have visited in his company. I am also most grateful to Mr Harland Walshaw, who took the following photographs: p. 2, Wells Cathedral; p. 35, 'Bell Harry'; p. 63, Bishop Sherborne's tomb; p. 80, Jarrow Priory; p. 126, Lichfield Cathedral; p. 150, St Paul's Cathedral; pp. 156 and 157, St John's Priory; p. 206, the crypt at Rochester; p. 207, West Malling Abbey; p. 236, Southwark Cathedral; p. 239, Dr Lockyer's tomb; pp. 264 and 265, Romsey Abbey; p. 278, vault at York Minster; p. 288, Old Malton Priory; and p. 289, Selby Abbey. Grateful thanks are also due to the National Trust for allowing us to reproduce the old watercolour of Llandaff Cathedral on p. 302.

Finally I must thank Mr Dan Franklin of Collins for his most able work in knocking the book into its final shape, and Miss Vera Brice for its accomplished and beautiful design.

HENRY THOROLD

Marston Hall, Grantham

St Thomas the Apostle, December 1985

INTRODUCTION

The bell is ringing for Evensong; under the medieval gateway the path slopes gently down to the west front. Smooth lawns, interrupted here and there by an old tomb or headstone, prebendal houses behind us and on our left, the many gables of the Bishop's Palace on our right, the looming silhouette of the cathedral ahead – and we are at the west door. It is twenty to six, and the bell stops ringing: Evensong is at 5.45. The Norman nave is in darkness, but lights at the crossing illuminate the screen, and behind the organ, erect in its classical case, the chancel is brightly lit. Hither we hasten. The choir is assembled in the north transept, choristers, lay clerks, clergy. So to our stalls: we are in time.

The introit is sung, the procession moves in, and Evensong begins. Psalms, lessons, canticles, collects, anthem, prayers: the poetic language of the Prayer Book, the chants, the settings; the unemotional, sedate form of Anglican worship is deeply moving; but for weekday Evensong the congregation is small.

Yet here, day after day, the cathedral is fulfilling its function: the worship of Almighty God. Day after day, winter or summer, Evensong is offered – sung by the choir during term-time, recited antiphonally by the clergy during the holidays.

This is what the cathedrals were built for – the abbeys, the priories. It was a deep, irrepressible, irresistible, religious impulse that drove men to build these churches – the nave at Gloucester, the octagon at Ely, the spire at Salisbury, the fan vault at Westminster, the chantry chapels at Tewkesbury: here the worship of God was to be offered. The vision of Heaven, the near presence of angels and saints, demanded that for a time every day mortal man should detach himself from the cares, the pleasures, of this life, and concentrate on Him. It was faith that built these churches, raised these vaults and towers, faith that moved the masons, carpenters and glaziers to cut the stones, carve the stalls, fill the windows with jewel-like glass – the faith which moves mountains. These buildings were designed to bring Heaven to men, and men to Heaven. That is the only purpose of the cathedrals, abbeys and priories of England and Wales.

The Cathedrals

There are forty-two cathedrals in England, and six in Wales. It is sometimes imagined that the word 'cathedral' denotes a very large church: this is not so. A church is a cathedral when it contains the throne of a diocesan bishop – the Latin word *cathedra*, the Greek word Καθέδρα, means throne or seat – and it need not be of enormous size. Christ Church at Oxford, for instance, is not large, but it is a cathedral because it holds the throne of the Bishop of Oxford; St Asaph in Wales is even smaller, but a cathedral it is because it holds the throne of the Bishop of St Asaph. On the other hand very large churches such as Westminster, Tewkesbury, Selby, Beverley – all described in this book – are not cathedrals, despite their size and grandeur, for they contain no episcopal throne. Of the forty-two English cathedrals, twenty-six are ancient, four are modern, and twelve are parish churches which in the course of the past century or so have become the cathedrals of new dioceses.

It is the twenty-six ancient cathedrals which must engage our attention first. They are all different – different in size, different in style, and different in foundation. There are giants like York and Lincoln, smaller cathedrals like Hereford and Chester. Every style of English architecture is to be found within their walls, from Saxon in the crypt at Ripon to Perp fan vaulting in the 'New Building' at Peterborough; and so to the classical baroque of St Paul's. Some of the cathedrals were in origin monastic churches also, some were served by secular canons.

There are seventeen medieval cathedral foundations: of these eight were monastic. Canterbury, Rochester, Winchester, Worcester, Durham, Norwich and Ely were all Benedictine, Carlisle was

Augustinian. The other nine, York, London, Lichfield, Hereford, Wells, Exeter, Lincoln, Chichester and Salisbury were 'secular' foundations, and from the time of Henry VIII have been known as cathedrals of the Old Foundation; after the Dissolution of the monasteries Henry founded five new dioceses: the cathedrals of Chester, Gloucester and Peterborough were all former Benedictine churches, Bristol and Oxford Augustinian. These are the cathedrals of the New Foundation. Thereafter no new diocese was founded till Ripon in 1836. Here, as at Southwell nearly half a century later, a grand collegiate church which had for centuries served as an extra 'bishopstool', an auxiliary cathedral in the enormous Archdiocese of York, became the cathedral of the new diocese. The diocese of St Albans was founded in 1877, the former Benedictine abbey becoming the cathedral; Southwark followed in 1904, and there the former Augustinian priory became the cathedral.

14th-century boss in the cloisters at Norwich

Of the four new cathedrals, Truro, by J. L. Pearson, and Liverpool, by Sir Giles Gilbert Scott, were built for those new dioceses, founded in 1877 and 1880 respectively; Guildford, by Sir Edward Maufe, for the diocese formed in 1927, and Coventry, by Sir Basil Spence, for the diocese founded in 1918, to take the place of the former parish church, destroyed by bombing in 1940.

The remaining twelve are all glorified parish churches – some more glorified than others; the new nave at Portsmouth is still (1985) unfinished.

In Wales the picture is much the same; there are four ancient cathedrals – St David's, Llandaff,

Bangor and St Asaph; at Brecon the ancient priory became the cathedral of the new diocese of Swansea and Brecon (1923); at Newport the parish church of St Woolos became the cathedral for the new diocese of Monmouth (1921).

The Abbeys and Priories

The abbeys and priories are far more numerous than the cathedrals, and far more varied. This book describes only the monastic churches of England and Wales that are still in use for worship. Only a handful survived the Dissolution in their complete state, through some stroke of good fortune: Westminster, Tewkesbury, Selby, Bath, Christchurch, Malvern, Romsey, Sherborne; for the rest it is a nave here, a chancel there, an aisle or a mere chapel. They stand on the edge of a town, perhaps, or in a village or remote hamlet, or lost in a meadow – gaunt but beautiful fragments, bereft of their cloisters, refectories, chapter houses, or accompanied by their roofless ruins; bereft of their monks or nuns or canons – but still, in their fragmentary state, used as parish churches, still echoing on Sundays with the praises of God. The following pages describe their state and tell their tales.

The Religious Orders

Something must be said about the religious orders which built these amazing churches. The founder of Western monasticism was St Benedict, who in 529 established at Monte Cassino his first monastery, and composed his Rule based on the vows of poverty, obedience and chastity; the monks' day was divided between the worship of God in the celebration of the Mass and the recitation of the Canonical Offices, the work of the cloisters in meditation and the copying, translating and illuminating of manuscripts, and the work of the fields, to provide the necessary food and clothing. St Augustine, on his arrival in 597, brought this noble Rule to England and established the first Benedictine monastery at Canterbury. The movement spread rapidly: as has been said, seven of the monastic cathedrals were Benedictine, and most of the greatest abbey churches which survive today – Westminster, Tewkesbury, Bath, Selby, Sherborne, Romsey, Malvern – were Benedictine also.

By the time of the Norman Conquest there were thirty-five monasteries in England, and nine nunneries, all Benedictine.

The Cistercian Order was established at the end of the eleventh century at Cîteaux (whence it took its name), and its Rule was drawn up by St Stephen Harding, Abbot of Cîteaux, an Englishman from Sherborne. Based on St Benedict's, it was more austere, forbade unnecessary decoration in its churches, and insisted that its houses should be founded in remote, wild places, far from towns and civilization. It was to St Stephen, and his disciple St Bernard, Abbot of Clairvaux, that the whole inspiration of the Cistercian movement was due, the spiritual ideals of its Rule, the intellectual prowess of many of its leaders, and the calm beauty and simplicity of its churches – reflecting so powerfully the peace and serenity of its life. But most of these churches, built in remote dales and valleys, are now mere romantic ruins like Rievaulx and Fountains, and do not fall within the compass of this book: only Abbey Dore and Holm Cultram have survived in use, and their survival seems almost miraculous.

The most austere order of all was the Carthusian, founded by St Bruno at La Chartreuse in 1084. St Bruno's rule was based on the hermit ideal of each monk living almost entirely by himself in his own tiny house. Grouped round the central cloister, these little cells afforded almost complete isolation for the brethren, who only met in church, or for occasional gatherings in the chapter house or refectory. There were only nine Carthusian houses in England: the most complete remains are at Mount Grace in Yorkshire – but the church is a ruin, and is therefore outside the scope of this book. The only Carthusian church to survive is the lay brothers' chapel at Witham in Somerset, and here nothing remains of the conventual buildings.

The Augustinian Canons, or Black Canons, first appeared in England about 1100: they were quite different from the other orders, being a preaching order, who, though living under Rule and in communities, worked in the world. Their Rule was based on the Rule of St Augustine of Hippo, and their more liberal ideals and more sociable way of life commended them to the people at large. They were never as rich as the Benedictines, but their influence was widespread. Carlisle Cathedral (as has been said) was Augustinian; so was Christchurch Priory, so was Cartmel, so was Lanercost,

so was Dorchester. The Premonstratensians, or White Canons, were a more austere offshoot of the Augustinians, taking their name from Prémontré, where the order was founded by St Norbert in 1123; in England, only the Abbey at Blanchland survives in use.

There was only one English order – the Gilbertines, named after St Gilbert of Sempringham (in Lincolnshire), who in the twelfth century founded a double order of men and women – the men following the Rule of St Augustine, the women that of St Benedict. They occupied adjacent houses and had separate cloisters, but worshipped in the same church, albeit divided by a high wall, so that they could but hear each others' voices. Twenty-six such houses were established, but only one church survives in use: Old Malton in Yorkshire.

As for the women's orders, few of their churches survive. For the most part small and poor, they mainly followed the Benedictine Rule: only Romsey attained any size or importance. That church survives – as do Elstow and St Radegunda's at Cambridge, Nun Monkton in Yorkshire, and Usk in Wales.

Today

It is hard for us today, except with the eye of faith, to see these great churches as they were at the height of their medieval splendour, ablaze with colour, echoing with prayer and plainsong, shrines and altars glittering with lamps and candles; but even now a medieval cathedral is one of the wonders of the world. Here as nowhere else the genius of the Middle Ages can be seen: in its building every skill, every science, was employed. Even today it is amazing how much survives. Despite the Reformation, despite the Civil War, despite the lack of appreciation of Gothic architecture in the eighteenth century, despite the over-zealous restorations of the nineteenth, despite apathy and ignorance and the tyranny of changing fashion, the cathedrals survive. Up and down the country, the English cathedral, serene in its close, surrounded by lawns and ancient houses, stands there, waiting to receive us. It is a very English institution – its setting uniquely so, for in the rest of Europe a cathedral close is unknown.

Never have our cathedrals been more visited, never more loved. Skilled and scholarly architects,

Stoking up at Hereford: these magnificent Victorian stoves – Gurney's Patent, the London Warming and Ventilating Co. – have heated many draughty cathedral naves and transepts, as they still do at Hereford

bands of dedicated masons, guard the fabric; the Friends of the Cathedral support it with their offerings and their prayers; the devoted ladies of the close adorn it with wonderful displays of flowers and foliage – or with their needles make new cushions or hassocks (indeed ten thousand new embroidered hassocks have appeared in recent years throughout the land). The standard of music is everywhere superb – but this is nothing new: the Three Choirs Festival, at Hereford, Gloucester and Worcester, was founded in the maligned eighteenth century (1724); now, as then, precentors and organists, lay clerks and choristers, fill the church with music and with song; loyal vergers are in continual attendance; devoted deans and canons pray and preach without ceasing.

The dangers which beset the cathedral today are subtle: the first is commercialism. There are some cathedrals which seem over-conscious of the tourist trade: 'Toilets', 'Gift Shop', 'Restaurant' proclaim the notices; these are inappropriate. A cathedral is the House of God, the house of prayer: nothing should be allowed to detract from its religious, its supernatural atmosphere. Here it must be admitted with regret that certain cath-

edrals now charge for admission: the memory of turnstiles at one, of ropes and queues at another is depressing. But at too many there is what can only be described as a 'welcoming' epidemic: every notice is entitled 'Welcome to so-and-so Cathedral', every leaflet headed with that same hollow greeting. Some fresh thoughts seem called for here.

The second menace is clutter: in some cathedrals the aisles, or transepts, are strewn with placards, posters, of purely secular and passing interest; the nave perhaps littered with cheap furnishings around a brash 'kitchen table' altar, out of keeping with the building, unworthy of its setting: the tyranny of passing fashion. The appeal of a great cathedral lies in its silence and its emptiness. The very stones cry out proclaiming the power and majesty of God. Let them speak. *Dat Deus incrementum.*

If I may end on a personal note, cathedrals have dominated my life. When I was a small child, born into an Army family, we lived at Chester. Every Sunday, sixty years ago, I attended Children's Service at Chester Cathedral, taken by that much-loved Dean, F. S. M. Bennett. Here I learned much of my religion. We moved to Salisbury, and every Sunday till I went to my preparatory school I attended Mattins with my mother at that cathedral – then still resplendent with its Victorian furnishings. On holiday at our family home on the borders of Lincolnshire and Nottinghamshire I came to know Lincoln and Southwell. At Oxford I was a member of the college whose chapel is also a cathedral. Ordained in Scotland, I served my title at Gilbert Scott's cathedral at Dundee. Most of my ordained life, as a master at Lancing College, I served that school chapel which in size and splendour is all but a cathedral. And living now once more at the family house I am within close reach of Southwell, where the bell rings daily for Evensong at 5.35, and the peals ring out on Sunday for Mattins or Sung Eucharist – a summons to which I often respond. Here, as in so many cathedrals, the great legacy of prayer and praise is gloriously maintained, and the bells and the very stones cry out *Ad Majorem Dei Gloriam.*

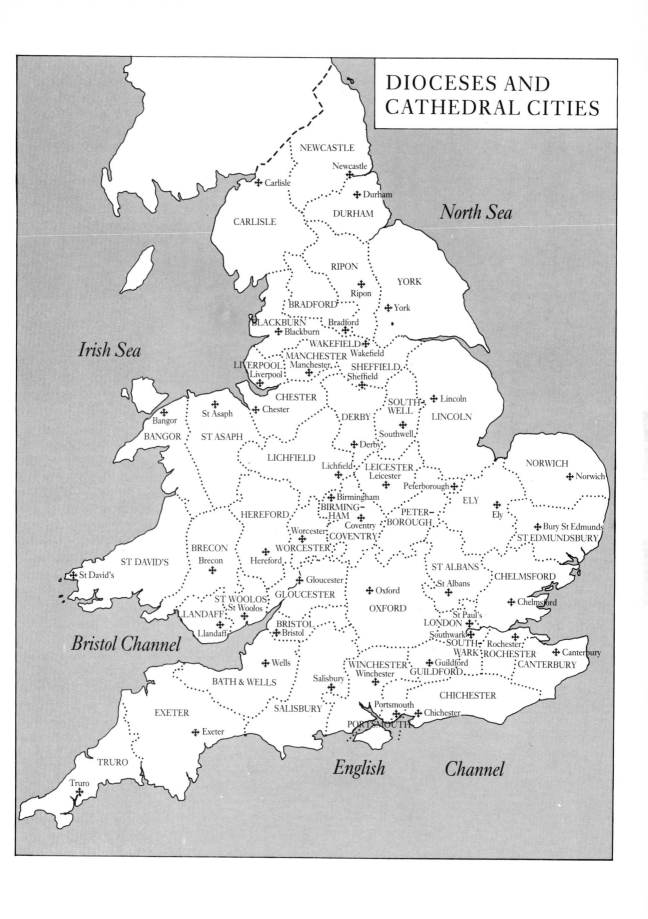

DIOCESES AND CATHEDRAL CITIES

North Sea

Irish Sea

Bristol Channel

English Channel

NEWCASTLE
Newcastle
✠ Carlisle
✠ Durham
CARLISLE
DURHAM
RIPON
YORK
Ripon
BRADFORD
✠ York
BLACKBURN
Bradford
✠ Blackburn
WAKEFIELD
MANCHESTER
Wakefield
LIVERPOOL
Manchester
SHEFFIELD
Liverpool
Sheffield
CHESTER
St Asaph
✠ Chester
SOUTH-
WELL
✠ Lincoln
Bangor
DERBY
LINCOLN
BANGOR
ST ASAPH
Southwell
LICHFIELD
✠ Derby
NORWICH
LEICESTER
✠ Norwich
Lichfield
Leicester
✠ Birmingham
Peterborough
BIRMING-
ELY
HEREFORD
HAM
PETER-
Ely
Worcester
Coventry
BOROUGH
BRECON
WORCESTER
COVENTRY
Bury St Edmunds
Brecon
Hereford
ST EDMUNDSBURY
ST DAVID'S
ST ALBANS
St Albans
CHELMSFORD
✠ St David's
Gloucester
✠ Chelmsford
ST WOOLOS
GLOUCESTER
Oxford
LLANDAFF
St Woolos
OXFORD
St Paul's
Llandaff
BRISTOL
LONDON
✠ Bristol
Southwark
Rochester
SOUTH-
✠ Canterbury
WINCHESTER
WARK
ROCHESTER
Wells
Guildford
CANTERBURY
BATH & WELLS
Salisbury
Winchester
GUILDFORD
EXETER
SALISBURY
Portsmouth
CHICHESTER
✠ Exeter
PORTSMOUTH
✠ Chichester
TRURO
Truro

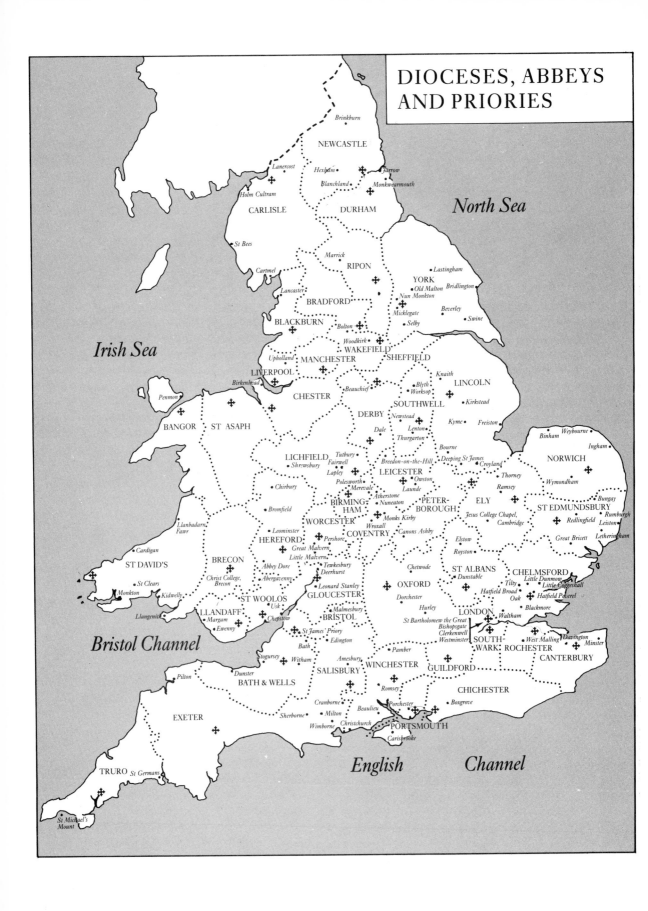

DIOCESES, ABBEYS AND PRIORIES

North Sea

Irish Sea

Bristol Channel

English Channel

NEWCASTLE
Brinkburn
Lanercost
Hexham *Jarrow*
Blanchland *Monkwearmouth*
Holm Cultram
CARLISLE
DURHAM
St Bees
Marrick
Cartmel RIPON *Lastingham*
Lancaster YORK
Old Malton *Bridlington*
BRADFORD *Nun Monkton*
Micklegate *Beverley*
BLACKBURN *Bolton* *Selby* *Swine*
Upholland *Woodkirk*
WAKEFIELD
MANCHESTER SHEFFIELD
LIVERPOOL *Knaith*
Birkenhead *Beauchief* *Blyth* LINCOLN
CHESTER *Worksop*
Penmon SOUTHWELL *Kirkstead*
DERBY *Newstead*
BANGOR ST ASAPH *Dale* *Lenton* *Kyme* *Freiston*
Thurgarton
Bourne *Binham* *Weybourne*
Deeping St James *Ingham*
LICHFIELD *Tutbury* NORWICH
Shrewsbury *Fairwell* *Breedon-on-the-Hill* *Croyland*
Lapley LEICESTER *Thorney* *Wymondham*
Chirbury *Polesworth* *Owston* *Ramsey*
Merevale *Laund* *Bungay*
Bromfield BIRMING- *Atherstone* ELY ST EDMUNDSBURY
HAM *Nuneaton* *Rumburgh*
Llanbadarn WORCESTER *Monks Kirby* *Jesus College Chapel,* *Redlingfield* *Leiston*
Fawr *Wroxall* COVENTRY *Canons Ashby* *Cambridge* *Letheringham*
Leominster *Pershore* *Elstow* *Great Bricett*
Cardigan HEREFORD *Great Malvern* *Royston*
BRECON *Little Malvern* *Chetwode* ST ALBANS CHELMSFORD
ST DAVID'S *Abbey Dore* *Tewkesbury* *Dunstable* *Little Dunmow*
Christ College, *Deerhurst* OXFORD *Tilty* *Little Coggeshall*
St Clears *Brecon* *Abergavenny* *Hatfield Broad* *Hatfield Peverel*
Monkton *Leonard Stanley* *Dorchester* *Oak*
Kidwelly ST WOOLOS GLOUCESTER *Hurley* *Blackmore*
Llangenith LLANDAFF *Usk* *Malmesbury* LONDON
Margam *Chepstow* BRISTOL *St Bartholomew the Great* *Waltham*
Ewenny *St James' Priory* *Bishopsgate*
Bath *Edington* *Clerkenwell* SOUTH- West Malling* *Davington*
Stogursey *Witham* *Westminster* WARK ROCHESTER *Minster*
Pilton *Pamber* GUILDFORD CANTERBURY
Dunster SALISBURY WINCHESTER
BATH & WELLS *Amesbury* *Romsey* CHICHESTER
Cranborne *Beaulieu* *Porchester* *Boxgrove*
EXETER *Milton* PORTSMOUTH
Sherborne *Christchurch*
Wimborne *Carisbrooke*

TRURO *St Germans*

St Michael's
Mount

ENGLAND

The chapter house vault at Southwell

DIOCESE OF
BATH & WELLS

Wells Cathedral

WELLS IS THE perfect cathedral city, small and secluded and set in delectable Somerset countryside against the long green ridge of the Mendips. Narrow streets lead into the Market Place, which is dominated by two medieval gatehouses – the Bishop's Eye which leads to the Palace, and Pennyless Porch which leads to the Cathedral, whose three towers stand grandly over the roof-tops of the surrounding houses. There is a row of shops on the left, with little Georgian bay windows above, and, on the right, a small classical Town Hall. Pennyless Porch brings us into the close, and the path leads us towards the west front. But we should turn left, walk across the smooth lawns to the farthest corner where another medieval gatehouse leads into the outside world, stand back, and survey the scene. Although less spectacular than Salisbury, this close is in its own way of almost equal charm. We can walk slowly up the north side, and admire the grand houses which stand here. There is the Old Deanery, with its buttressed and turreted and embattled 15th-century front, but with the sash windows introduced by an early-18th-century Dean; the Chancellor's House, another Tudor house but with 18th-century Venetian windows (now the Wells Museum); then the former Archdeaconry, another ancient house, with oriel window and other early features, which is now the music school of the Cathedral School. Here the Chain Gate crosses the road, providing a covered way from the north transept and Chapter House to the Vicars' Hall and Vicars' Close: it was built by that great builder Bishop Bekynton in 1459. Here we must turn in, and walk the length of Vicars' Close, a unique medieval street, with houses for the Vicars Choral, with their Chapel at the north end, their Hall at the other. It was built

in the 14th century: small gardens line the street; sash windows have in most cases replaced the original mullions, but tall chimneys and other medieval features survive to adorn these enchanting houses. And having walked their full length, we can return, gazing all the time upon the north side of the Cathedral, the octagonal Chapter House close at hand, the many-pinnacled central tower above us – one of the most lovely of all Somerset towers – and, passing the splendid E.E. north porch, we can stand before the west front.

This is not only one of the special glories of Wells: it is also the most spectacular west front of any cathedral in England. It was built in the mid

OPPOSITE *Wells Cathedral from the south-east;* ABOVE *Vicars' Close, built in the mid 14th century to provide houses for the Vicars Choral*

13th century, and represents the finest display of medieval sculpture in the country, with row upon row of figures of saints and apostles, priests and bishops, kings and queens – not only covering the whole façade, but also enveloping the sides of the towers and rising to the figure of Our Lord in the central gable. This is much mutilated, but most of the other figures are in a remarkable state of preservation. The buttresses, the shafts of Purbeck marble, the arched niches, the deep recesses, the gabled arcades, the carved quatrefoils, the stiff-leaf capitals, the crockets, finials and pinnacles, all provide high relief and a magical display of contrasts and deep shadows, of light and shade, to the whole composition. Three doorways and three long lancet windows are extra, essential, features; and, at either end, the twin towers, completed in the 15th century, with their blunt panelled tops complete this amazing frontispiece.

The see of Wells was founded in 909: two hundred years earlier a collegiate church had been established here, and this small Saxon church became the first cathedral, to be replaced by a Norman cathedral, which was consecrated in 1148. As is described under Bath Abbey (q.v.) tussles between Bath and Wells lasted for 200 years, and for a time Bath maintained its supremacy; but in the end Wells regained first place as the cathedral, though bishops ever since have been entitled Bishops of Bath and Wells. The Cathedral which we see today was begun at the end of the 12th century by Bishop Reginald de Bohun; the three western bays of the chancel were built by him, together with the transepts and the four eastern bays of the nave; the nave was completed by his successor Bishop Jocelin (brother of Hugh of Lincoln); Chapter House and central tower were completed in the early 14th century, and the Lady Chapel, eastern bays of the chancel, and retrochoir were added later in the century. Western towers and cloisters were completed in the early 15th century.

Inside, the E.E. nave is of serene perfection, with its clustered columns and delicate stiff-leaf capitals, its closely spaced continuous lancet triforium, lofty clerestory and simple sexpartite vault.

Wells Cathedral BELOW *the north porch: double arcading and stiff-leaf capitals (c. 1230);* OPPOSITE *the nave (early 13th century), with the strainer arches added a century later to strengthen the crossing*

The celebrated inverted arches at the crossing terminate the view; they were built in the early 14th century to strengthen the piers after the completion of the central tower. Above the inverted arch the rood, by Sir Charles Nicholson (1920) to replace the original destroyed at the Reformation, is a powerful aid to devotion. The Perp chantries to Bishop Bubwith (1424) and Treasurer Sugar (1489), on either side of the crossing arch, are special delights; and to stand in the south transept and absorb the vista through these three inverted arches is a unique experience.

In the north transept is the famous astronomical clock (1390), where above the dial little figures of armed horsemen perform their tournament every hour, and Jack Blandiver kicks his bell at every quarter; and in the N.E. corner a door gives access to the double-branching staircase which leads to the Chapter House and, across the Chain Gate, to the Vicars' Hall. These well-worn steps are often photographed: they ascend gently, then turn off steeply to the right, and then also ascend straight on to encompass the bridge of the Chain Gate. The Chapter House was completed in the early 14th century and must rank with those at Southwell or Salisbury as among the most beautiful in England, with its central clustered column branching into a hundred slender ribs, and its eight traceried windows (with fragments of old glass in the tracery) pouring daylight upon the seats round every wall.

The chancel is entered under the stone pulpitum, and is a wondrous creation of panelled, traceried stonework – the earlier western bays merge almost imperceptibly with the three eastern bays, unified by the delicate canopied tabernacle work of the triforium, the elaborate traceried 14th-century windows, and the lofty vault composed of unusual patterned lierne ribs. Golden light pours through the 14th-century glass in the east and four other windows, and the three narrow arches at the east end provide a glimpse into the vaulted retrochoir and Lady Chapel beyond. There are medieval misericords in the stalls, but the stone canopies are by Salvin, emulating the 14th-century stone episcopal throne; on the right of the sanctuary is the chantry of Bishop Bekynton, with its canopied altar and iron railing enclosing the tomb.

What can be said of the retrochoir and Lady Chapel except that they are exquisite work of the Dec period? The Lady Chapel is polygonal, and

Wells: the chapter house, completed in the early 14th century; the central clustered column branches into a hundred slender ribs

glows with golden, jewelled, medieval glass; the retrochoir connects it with the chancel by means of a complex antechapel of free-standing clustered columns, supporting a forest of delicate vaults. Here there are vistas across the eastern chapels of remarkable beauty: medieval tombs, beautifully furnished altars (one by Sir Ninian Comper) and much ancient glass combine to create a wonderful climax to a numinous interior.

A doorway in the south transept leads into the spacious three-sided cloisters, built in the first half of the 15th century: the Library, furnished with 17th-century bookcases, is built over the East Walk, and contains rare manuscripts and printed books; the walks below are lined with 18th-century monuments. And a door at the south end leads to the Palace, where the 14th-century gatehouse and its attendant walls still surround the bishop's residence, and where the swans in the moat still ring the bell when desiring to be fed. And the walk eastwards along the moat provides an unforgettable view of the east end of the Cathedral, where flying buttresses support the clerestory, and the noble tower is reflected in the calm waters of the moat – the moat fed by the springs or wells from which the city takes its name.

Bath Abbey

It is a great experience to arrive at Bath by train – to speed along Brunel's Great Western line high above the Avon Valley, and to slow down as the train approaches the city. From the carriage window there is a wonderful panorama of Georgian terraces, streets, crescents and churches, the monolithic pile of the Abbey with its tall pinnacled tower presiding over all. One of the pleasures of Bath is to explore the city on foot. It is but a short walk from Bath Spa station to the very heart of things, to Parade Gardens, Orange Grove and the Abbey itself. Beyond, the smart shops of Milsom Street lead to the Assembly Rooms, the Circus and Royal Crescent, and Robert Adam's Pulteney Bridge crosses the Avon to the splendours of Pulteney Street and Bathwick.

But the first pleasure of all must be to make for the west front of the Abbey and stand in the Abbey churchyard with the Pump Room on our right. There was once a Saxon church here, a Benedictine priory founded in the 10th century. But in 1088 John of Tours, Bishop of Wells, transferred the see to Bath, and a Norman cathedral was built.

Bath Abbey from the south: vast Perp windows in the clerestory, smaller windows in the aisle

Tussles between Wells and Bath continued; in 1245 a settlement was reached, by which it was agreed that the bishop should return to Wells, but that his title should be Bath and Wells. So it has continued.

We are standing before the Perp west front, built in the very earliest years of the 16th century. Bath was the last complete monastic church to be built in England before the Dissolution. In 1499 Oliver King, Bishop of Bath and Wells, was on a visitation: he was perturbed at the dilapidated state of the Norman cathedral. That night he had a dream in which angels appeared ascending and descending a ladder set between heaven and earth, and a voice cried, 'Let a King rebuild My church.' So he set to work, employing the King's masons, Robert and William Vertue (who were responsible for Henry VII's Chapel at Westminster, and St George's Chapel, Windsor). On either side of the west window are lofty pinnacled buttresses, and carved on these are long ladders with little figures of angels ascending and descending, commemorating Bishop King's dream. Above the window, and surrounded by more angels, is the figure of Christ. Above the doorway is the figure of Henry VII, together with the Royal Arms; the door itself was given in 1617 by Sir Henry Montagu, and bears his arms and those of his brother James, Bishop of Bath and Wells and subsequently of Winchester.

The interior is like an enormous lantern: the vast spreading fan vault, reaching from end to end, the great sense of height, with lofty crossing arches and clerestory with tall traceried windows, the arcades themselves with their four-centred arches – it is all a design of the strictest uniformity. The transepts are aisleless and narrow, further accentuating the sense of height; the aisles are also narrow, and their vaults carry pendants.

Under the N. arcade stands the tomb of Bishop Montagu (d.1618) with his recumbent effigy lying between four Corinthian columns, and bearing his arms as Bishop, first of Bath and Wells, then of Winchester. At his express wish he is buried here: it is to him that we owe the completion of the church. The dissolution prevented the vaulting of this nave (1539), which stood roofless until the early 17th century. 'Walking with Sir John Harington,' runs a contemporary account, 'overtaken by a sharp shower, and invited into the roofless nave, the Bishop remarked on the want of shelter; Sir John replied "If the church does not keep us safe from the waters above, how shall it save others from the fire below?"' Thanks to the Bishop's liberality, the nave was vaulted in plaster – to be replaced by the present stone vault erected by Sir Gilbert Scott in his restoration between 1864 and 1870, imitating the chancel vault. In the vestry, on the S. side of the chancel, there is still an example of Bishop Montagu's plaster vaulting.

Close to the sanctuary is the Chantry of Prior Byrde, who was prior at the time of Bishop King's

Bath: fan vaulting in the nave: a remarkable copy by Gilbert Scott of the original vault in the chancel

rebuilding, and his accomplice. He died in 1515, and his chantry is a feast of Perp carving and fan vaulting. In the S. choir aisle there survives in the E. wall one relic of the Norman cathedral – a round-headed arch which would have led into the S. transept: it is now filled with a Perp traceried window.

But the greatest feature of the interior – other than the building itself – is the fascinating collection of monuments to those who came to take the waters, or to live and die in this most fashionable of resorts. We can stand in the S. aisle and lament, as we are bidden, the death of Beau Nash (1761): *'Adeste, O cives, adeste lugentes! Hic silent Leges Ricardi Nash, Armig: nihil amplius imperantis.'* ('Draw near, fellow citizens, draw near in mourning! The laws of Richard Nash Esqre do not apply here: he delivers his commands no more.') Smith Callis, Esqre, Rear Admiral of the Blue, died the same year: 'In every instance of Tryal (many of the utmost danger) his steady courage prevailed . . .' We can enjoy his long epitaph here. 'In this chancel lie the remains of Sir Marmaduke Wyvill Bt. of Constable Burton in Yorkshire . . .' Sir Marmaduke died in Bath in 1774. A Derbyshire baronet, Sir Nigel Gresley, died here the same year, and another Sir Nigel Gresley in 1808. And there is the intriguing monument to 'James Tamerz Grieve, Esqre of Moscow', who died here in 1787, and one to Robert Walsh, Esqre, who died in 1788: 'by the death of this gentleman an ancient and respectable family in Ireland became extinct'. From the previous century there is the monument to the Royalist Sir Philip Frowde (1674), with his distinguished bust: 'Sir Philip Frowde, Knt. who served his Matie Charles ye First in ye qualities of Collonel of horse during the whole late war . . .' The monuments are an afternoon's entertainment, redolent of Bath, and of the history of the time.

Nothing whatever remains of the monastic buildings, but to the S. of the church is a sweet sequestered little square called Abbey Green, sheltered by a great plane tree. This occupies their site. Here we can sit, or refresh ourselves in a nearby café, and contemplate.

The aisle walls are adorned with monuments to those who came to take the waters, or to live and die in Bath

Dunster Priory

The castle of the Luttrells – they have been there since 1376 – standing romantic on its wooded hill; the village street with its old houses, the Yarn Market, the octagonal gabled market cross built in 1589 by George Luttrell; the Folly Tower on Conygar Hill to the N. – Dunster is rightly celebrated for its beauty and its charm, and for its setting on the edge of Exmoor, with the sea not far away. The Priory of Dunster, a Benedictine cell of Bath, was founded at the end of the 11th century, and the monks' church, half monastic, half parochial, stands back from the street in its churchyard, externally all Perp, with its tall central tower.

Inside, there are wagon roofs and elegant Perp arcades, but the whole interior is dominated by the magnificent late-15th-century screen of West Country type, which, canopied and richly carved, extends the full width of this grand wide church.

It will be noticed that the N. aisle is two bays shorter than the S. – the monastic buildings abutted here – and that the crossing is narrow. Indeed, on inspection, it will be seen that the lower half of the Perp crossing arches is Norman work – a surviving fragment of the original 12th-century church. The high altar of the parish church stands here, with an 18th-century candelabrum of great magnificence suspended above. Beyond stands the chancel, screened off, mysterious, inaccessible.

The chancel was the monastic church, and it is still a church apart. It is approached by the S. transept, through an extraordinary E.E. arch, whose shafts are curiously bent outwards, just below the capitals, as though to allow for a wider passage. It is unique. After the Dissolution, the chancel became the property of the Luttrells, just as at Arundel, where the chancel fell to the Norfolks. The Luttrells used the chancel simply as a place of burial; here stand their tombs: 15th-century alabaster effigies, a grand Jacobean tomb, and later, smaller, monuments. After long neglect, it was restored sympathetically by G. E. Street in

The 15th-century screen at Dunster: distinguished West Country workmanship

1875, and is now used as the Lady Chapel, furnished with Street's stalls, like a monastic choir.

Little remains of the monastic buildings – but the N. door in the nave leads into a charming garden, which marks their site.

Stogursey Priory

'Out of the world into Stogursey,
Out of Stogursey into the sea.'

So the old saying goes. Or as A. K. Wickham has described it, 'Stogursey lies in that strange forgotten country, between the Quantocks and the sea.'

The Priory stands at the end of the village street, a cruciform church with central tower and lead spire. The exterior, so large, so seemingly inexplicable, is exciting: Perp windows, grand embattled chancel aisles. The tower does not at first sight appear Norman, because of the Victorian windows and parapet, but the herringbone masonry prepares us for antiquity within. And the interior is indeed still more exciting.

The aisleless Perp nave leads to the Norman crossing, as wonderful as it is spacious: there are sturdy round arches on simple round columns with remarkable carved capitals – with animals or leaves or human faces: they are all different. This is work of *c.* 1100. The crossing makes a splendid setting for a beautiful nave sanctuary. And, beyond, steps lead up to the Norman chancel, with gently sloping floor, and, marked in the floor, the line of the three original eastern apses – to the transept chapels, and the original apsidal chancel. Here Norman arches (*c.* 1180) date from the time when the chancel was extended, and the spacious aisles formed, to N. and S. More steps lead up to the high altar, behind which is a neo-Norman east end (1865, by John Norton). Looking back from here there is a wonderful view westwards, through the chancel and crossing to the aisleless nave beyond.

The chancel chapels are wonderful, too: to the N. a beautifully furnished Lady Chapel, to the S. the Verney Chapel, with its early Verney tombs and excellent later monuments – to Peregrine Palmer (1684), with garlands and cherubs' heads, and Nathaniel Palmer (1717), with more cherubs and flowers; to Sir Thomas Wroth (1717) and Thomas Palmer (1724) – another distinguished monument. It is unfortunate that the sculptors of these monuments are as yet unidentified.

Stogursey: the Norman crossing, with an 18th-century candelabrum and the tomb of John de Verney (1472) in the foreground

The history of the Priory may be briefly told: Stogursey was founded as a Benedictine priory, a cell of the abbey at Fonlay in Normandy, *c.* 1100. It was supressed as an alien priory in 1414, on the eve of Agincourt, and in 1440 the property was bestowed by Henry VI on his new foundation of Eton, and formed part of the original endowment of the college. The Provost and Fellows of Eton College are still Patrons of the living.

Witham Priory

Deeply sequestered in the enchanting Somerset countryside S. of Frome lies the little village of Witham Friary, close to the River Frome and the Great Western main line: the occasional roar of a passing train is the only sound from the outside world to disturb its peace. Meandering lanes lead

Witham Priory, the only surviving medieval Carthusian church in England

to the village: a break in the thick foliage reveals a glimpse of a small but imposing apsidal church with a tall gabled bellcote, decidedly French in its appearance. This is all that remains of Witham Priory, the earliest Carthusian monastery, or charterhouse, to be founded in England, established by Henry II *c.* 1170. There were early setbacks, but in 1179 St Hugh, urgently sent for by the King, arrived here from the Grande Chartreuse, to become third Prior and virtual founder of the house, finally established by Royal Charter in 1182. Hugh became Bishop of Lincoln in 1186, but it was he who built this church – the lay brothers' chapel – which survived as the parish church after the Dissolution. Nothing is left of the other conventual buildings, which lay to the S.

But this little church is a jewel, with its steep-pitched roof, small round-headed windows and heavy flying buttresses, which were added by William White who restored the church in 1876 and rebuilt the west end and added the bellcote. The interior is solemn, dark and mysterious, with its simple rib vaulting, triple lancets at the E. end, Jacobean pulpit, and homely Victorian furnishings. There are fragments of ancient glass, and several Comper windows. A romantic, holy, spot.

DIOCESE OF
BIRMINGHAM

Birmingham Cathedral

'HIS MOST EXCELLENT MAJESTY King George upon the kind application of Sir Richard Gough to the Rt Honourable Sir Rob Walpole Gave £600 toward finishing this CHURCH A.D. 1725.' So proclaims the inscription above the inner door of the S.W. porch. This grand new church of St Philip was consecrated in 1715, and the tower was completed ten years later, thanks to the King's gift. The little town of Birmingham had begun to grow during the 17th century, but life was still centred round the old parish church of St Martin in the Bull Ring. As industry developed and the town began to expand up the hill, there was need for a new church in the High Town; an Act of Parliament of 1708 created the new parish, and Thomas Archer, a Warwickshire gentleman, was appointed architect. Archer, one of the great exponents of English Baroque, had spent four years on the Continent as a young man, and had studied the work of the great masters Bernini and Boromini; he designed the north front of Chatsworth, Heythrop House in Oxfordshire, the Pavilion at Wrest; among his churches are St John's, Smith Square, and St Paul's, Deptford. St Philip's became the cathedral of the new diocese of Birmingham in 1905.

Here at St Philip's he designed a grand rectangular building with a shallow apsidal sanctuary and a capacious galleried nave to seat the large congregation of a growing town. Sir Richard Gough, who interceded with the Prime Minister, was Lord of the Manor of Edgbaston: the King's generous gift was a rare compliment to the increasing importance of Birmingham.

Doric pilasters, round-headed windows, an entablature above, a balustraded parapet capped with urns – such is the side façade of the church; at the west end there is a projection under the tower, with a curved pediment: on either side there are pedimented doorways, with oval windows above with luxuriously carved surrounds. The tower sails

above: twin Corinthian pilasters adorn the corner buttresses, and carved scrolls support the lead dome, which is capped with a lantern and a gilded weather vane (which incorporates a boar's head, the crest of Sir Richard Gough). The church was enlarged in 1883 by J. A. Chatwin; his is the chancel, built in strict harmony with Archer's design. The interior is dignified with five-bay arcades of square fluted columns and round-headed arches with scrolled key stones; the nave leads up to the more elaborate chancel added by Chatwin, with its free-standing Corinthian columns, and (as in Archer's original design) shallow apsidal sanctuary.

But the interior is made by the glass: there are three gorgeous windows in the sanctuary, and another at the west end, designed by Burne-Jones and made by Morris & Co. – the Ascension at the east end, the Judgement at the west, the Nativity and Crucifixion on either side in the sanctuary. The designs are dramatic, and the great splashes of red and green and blue illuminate the whole church. The scale of Burne-Jones' figures, the composition of each scene, the grouping, the dark backgrounds, the angels' wings or the soldiers' banners are all magnificently appropriate to the large windows; the many vivid details rivet the attention.

There is, alas, little original furnishing, apart from the handsome organ case (by Thomas Schwarbrick, 1715) in the chancel, and another of similar date (which came from another church) in the north gallery. Unfortunately the altar has been removed from the sanctuary: Tijou's beautiful iron railing now merely encloses a chair, and a wretched little table, covered with a carpet, stands at the chancel step – altogether pathetic and unworthy, a pandering to modern liturgical fads. So splendid an interior calls for a splendid High Altar – in the holy of holies at the east end.

Pigeons and starlings flutter ceaselessly among

the trees of the surrounding square – their screech-ings echoing against the high office buildings standing around. Below, in the churchyard, stands the bronze figure of Charles Gore, first Bishop of Birmingham, by Stirling Lee (1914), which is arresting and highly appropriate to the great man.

Merevale Abbey

Merevale Hall, seat of the Dugdales, castellated and turreted, stands like a fairy castle on the hills to the S. in a secluded park, protected by thick woods. The house is a rebuilding of *c.* 1840 by Edward Blore and Henry Clutton. Below are the fragments of a Cistercian abbey, built into farm buildings – but a little farther to the W., and approached by an imposing gatehouse built by Clutton, is the Chapel of Our Lady, the medieval *capella ante portas*, which survives as the parish church. It is a building of special charm and interest.

The exterior is unassuming, with a little wooden bell turret; inside, a very short nave, with two (blocked) 13th-century arches, leads into a Perp chancel, rebuilt *c.* 1500, with the most delicate arcades of four bays, a grand E. window, and windows with Perp tracery in the N. aisle, Dec windows in the S. Moreover, the E. window is filled with sumptuous glass of the 14th century (probably from the Abbey itself), and there are further fragments in the aisles. There is a brass to Robert Earl Ferrers (d. 1412), descendant of an earlier Robert Ferrers who founded the abbey in 1148; and there are 18th-century monuments (and hatchments) to the Stratford family, whose heiress married Richard Dugdale in 1767 – descendant of Sir William Dugdale, the celebrated antiquary and genealogist, and author of *Monasticon Anglicanum*. At the W. end a remarkable 15th-century oak screen, complete with loft, is reputed to have come from the Abbey – but in fact it is a perfect fit in its present setting. In the chancel is a Snetzler organ of 1777.

Polesworth Abbey

The countryside here, on the borders of Warwick-shire, Staffordshire and Leicestershire, close to No Man's Heath, has been scarred by open-cast

Merevale. The medieval capella ante portas, *all that survives of the Cistercian abbey*

The chancel at Merevale, and the east window with 14th-century glass from the destroyed abbey church

mining, and there is a large sprawl of miners' houses on the S. of the village, itself much muti-lated by unattractive modern building. But in the main street stands the 15th-century timbered gate-house to the Abbey: the impressive fragment of the church lies beyond, the church of a Benedictine nunnery, founded here in the 9th century by St Modwena and King Egbert, with St Editha (King Egbert's daughter) as the first Abbess. There is a sturdy 14th-century tower at the E. end of the N. aisle, and, inside, a magnificent Norman arcade of eight bays, with the plainest of unmoulded arches resting on round columns with scalloped capitals.

OPPOSITE *Birmingham Cathedral: Thomas Archer's new church, completed in 1725*

The 15th-century gatehouse to Polesworth Abbey

G. E. Street restored the church in 1869, and built the present chancel; there are two ancient tombs – one of the 14th century carries the early-13th-century effigy of an abbess holding a crozier, the other an early-15th-century figure of a lady; and on a bracket in the Lady Chapel is a fragment of a 14th-century sculpture of the Crucifixion.

On the S. side of the church the vicarage garden with its square lawn marks the site of the cloisters, and the vicarage itself is a charming brick and timber house of 1868, which incorporates ancient materials from the conventual buildings: there is a large Elizabethan fireplace in the big room adjoining the church, and in the garden a tall column, a fragment of a 17th-century sundial. Below, meadows slope down to the River Anker.

DIOCESE OF
BLACKBURN

Blackburn Cathedral

THERE IS REALLY VERY LITTLE to see in Blackburn, for all its size and industrial importance. The middle of the town is curiously village-like, with endless streets of small houses climbing the hills on all sides. But there is grand open country not far away, and northern Lancashire, when industry is left behind, has undoubted character and individuality. Blackburn grew large and prosperous on cotton all through the 19th century, but apart from the big railway station and the classical St John's Church (1789) with its domed tower, there is really very little else of note, except of course, for the Cathedral, whose east end is opposite the station.

Approaching it from the west, the building is attractive, standing in a big open churchyard with its trees and a few old tombs. There is a bold pinnacled west tower and a long clerestoried nave; outwardly it is a big Commissioners' type church of the early 19th century. The diocese of Blackburn was created in 1927, formed out of the diocese of Manchester, and St Mary's Parish Church became the Cathedral. A medieval church stood on the site, but by the early 19th century it had become dilapidated, and in 1818 a new church was built to the design of John Palmer, architect of Manchester. This is the nave and tower which

Blackburn Cathedral: the west tower

we see today. Plans were laid for enlarging the church when it became the cathedral, and in 1933 Mr W. A. Forsythe was appointed architect. He designed spacious transepts, a central tower and a long chancel. Work began in 1938, but on the outbreak of war building was abandoned. It was resumed in 1950, and north and south transepts were built. In 1961, on the death of Mr Forsythe, Mr Laurence King was appointed architect, and to him was committed the task of completing the extensions on a more modest scale.

Walking round the outside, Mr King's octagonal central lantern tower and tapering fleche will be seen. The idea of this is excellent, but the details are stark: it is not a happy blend with the Gothic stonework of nave, transepts and eastern chapel. Inside, John Palmer's nave is charming. It is vaulted in plaster – as are the aisles – and now that it has been cleaned and the galleries have been removed, it will be seen what a scholarly architect John Palmer was, and how spacious and well-proportioned his church is. Now, delicately gilded and coloured, the walls and background glistening white, this nave is pure delight. Light shines down on the crossing through the lantern tower on the High Altar; beyond, high up on the east wall, there is a coloured rood with attendant figures, and behind the altar a screen divides the eastern ambulatory from the Lady Chapel. There are dramatic and unexpected vistas across the transepts, with their spacious aisles, into the nave, or the eastern chapels. It is a brilliant transformation.

Lancaster Priory

Lancaster is the county town of Lancashire, and although there are large, spreading and uninteresting suburbs, the old town is compact, historic and interesting. There are steep streets of Georgian houses leading up to the Castle, some of them still cobbled, and on the quay, where the Lune Navigation made a thriving port in the 18th century – Lancaster was the chief port of Lancashire until Liverpool eclipsed it – stands the charming Custom House, built by Richard Gillow (of the cabinet-making family) in 1764; and there are old warehouses along the water front. The Old Town Hall is a handsome, almost Vanbrughian, building of 1781 (designed by Major Jarrat); there is a much grander Edwardian Town Hall of appropriate municipal splendour built in 1906 (by E. W. Mountford); and conspicuous on its hill to the E. is the Ashton Memorial, with its green dome, built by the first Lord Ashton in memory of his wife – an incredible Baroque building by Sir John Belcher.

But for us it is to climb the hill to the Castle and the Priory. The Castle keep is Norman (early 12th century), and many of the other buildings are medieval; Thomas Harrison added to them, and adapted them, in the early 19th century, to serve as Shire Hall and prison. The Priory stands hard by, with its long embattled nave and chancel, and its tall W. tower, embattled and pinnacled, rebuilt in almost Gothic survival style in 1759 by Henry Sephton. Steps lead up to the church: '15th-century Priory Church, OPEN DAILY' proclaims a notice by the bottom step. This is welcoming. Lancaster Priory was bestowed on the Benedictine Abbey of Seez in Normandy in 1094 by Roger of Poitou, a cousin of the Conqueror, and continued as a cell of Seez until 1414, when upon the suppression of alien monasteries by Henry V it was given to the Brigittine convent of Syon in Middlesex – the only house in England of the Order of St Brigit of Sweden – and so continued until the Dissolution. An imposing two-storeyed porch of 1903 (by Austin and Paley) leads to a 13th-century doorway, and so into the church – a particularly grand parish church with a long nave and an almost equally long chancel; both are clerestoried, and the arcades lead into spacious aisles; a chancel arch with clustered columns divides nave from chancel, and there is an even more spacious outer aisle on the N. side, with a polygonal apse, built in 1903 as the memorial chapel of the King's Own Royal Lancashire Regiment, all bedecked with colours and standards.

But the best thing of all is the remarkable set of canopied choir stalls in the chancel. There are ten on either side – 14th century in date, with tall, traceried, pinnacled canopies, flamboyant in style, with an amazing wealth of carvings and misericords. They may have been brought here from Cockersand or Furness; alternatively they may have been made for this church. They were admired by Ruskin. There is decent Victorian glass everywhere (E. window by Wailes), a number of interesting 18th-century monuments, and magnificent brass candelabra of the 18th century adorn chancel and nave.

Blackburn: John Palmer's nave (1818) with its plaster vaulting

From this hilltop there are wide views of Morecambe Bay and the Lune estuary, and towards the
hills of the Lake District; and, from below, Castle
and Priory form a remarkable group of buildings
when seen across the River Lune.

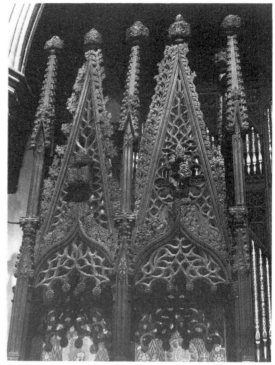

Lancaster Priory: the 14th-century canopied stalls

DIOCESE OF
BRADFORD

Bradford Cathedral

BRADFORD BECAME PROSPEROUS on cloth: from medieval times its cloth merchants thrived, and built their sturdy stone houses round the town and in the neighbouring valleys. Some of these houses survive, submerged perhaps in suburbia or industry. But it was never a big town. The 19th century changed all that: within the hundred years from 1801 to 1901 the population leapt from 6000 to 180,000; so most of what we see in the middle of Bradford is Victorian, sometimes splendid, often sombre. The best building is undoubtedly the Town Hall, whose chimes echo across the streets: built by Lockwood and Mawson, local architects, in 1878 in a kind of Florentine Gothic, its tower

Bradford Cathedral: the nave and chancel, and the Lady Chapel (1963) by Sir Edward Maufe

seems inspired by the Palazzo Publico in Siena. And a stone's throw from Forster Square, in the heart of the city, stands the Cathedral, until 1919 the parish church of Bradford.

It is very much a parish church: extensions and embellishments have been made since 1950, but a parish church it remains, squat, sturdy, stocky, with a low clerestoried nave, low transepts no higher than the aisles, and the strong, square, low W. tower, generously pinnacled and battlemented – all 15th-century Perp work. Since 1950 Sir Edward Maufe has added low extensions to the west end, to contain vestries, choir rooms and so on; and more recently a low central lantern tower with a pyramid roof, and an apsidal E. end, with one of his characteristic bell turrets on the S. side. It is by no means unattractive.

Inside, there are low 14th-century arcades, and a tall tapering Perp font cover. The Victorian chancel arch leads up into the chancel, under the lantern tower. Maufe's narrow pointed, slightly odd-shaped arches separate the sanctuary from the ambulatory, and beyond the High Altar there is a vista to the Lady Chapel, with its three apsidal windows filled with Morris glass (1862) of the highest quality and charm: this originally filled the E. window. All the fittings and furnishings are by Maufe, including the organ case at the W. end.

Throughout the Cathedral there are monuments of interest: the best are the tablets to Abraham Sharpe by Sheemakers (1742), and to Abraham Balme by Flaxman (1796). And the inscription on the monument to Joseph Priestley is worth quoting: 'This marble is inscribed by the company of the proprietors of the Canal Navigation from Leeds to Liverpool, to the memory of Joseph Priestley, Esq. as a mark of regard for his able, zealous and assiduous attention to the interests of that great undertaking ... in the most important and arduous situation of Superintendent, which he held under the Company for nearly half a century. Died 14th August, 1817, aged 74'. And at the base of the tablet (by William Pistell) is a relief of the construction of a canal.

The see of Bradford was founded in 1919, and formed out of the diocese of Ripon.

'Instruct the ignorant' – Flaxman's monument to Abraham Balme in Bradford Cathedral

Bolton Priory

Bolton Priory is almost universally known as Bolton Abbey – which in fact it never was. But the romantic sight of the ruins of the church in their incomparable setting somehow, in the popular imagination, conferred the fictitious title on the place. The Priory here was founded in 1151 by Alicia de Romilly for Augustinian Canons. The chancel is a ruin – but here there are fragments of the Norman church: blank arcading and round-headed arches, on to which was grafted the important 14th-century work which is so prominent. The large traceried windows stand empty now, little is left of the transepts, and nothing of the central tower; all has crumbled away since the Dissolution (1539).

But the nave survives, and this is the parish church. Approaching it across the smooth grass, the appearance of the west end is puzzling. This is the west tower, begun in 1520, but never completed at the time of the Dissolution. Ornate buttresses, an elaborate west door, a grand traceried Perp window with ogee top – all stands open to the sky. The nave itself dates from the mid 13th century: on the south side some of the blank arcading of the cloister survives; above is a row of six double-light windows with little quatrefoils in the spandrels. The entrance to the church is now by the N.W. door: it is a capacious nave, with the

Bolton Priory: the long 13th-century nave windows above the arcading and ruins of the cloister court on the south side

north aisle separated by an arcade of alternately octagonal and circular piers. Opposite, the six double-light windows are filled with splendid, colourful, Pugin glass (1860), which brings warmth into the interior. G. E. Street restored the church in 1880: he was responsible for the blind arcading on the wall above the altar – the wall which blocks the crossing arch – which was decorated at this time by A. Bottomley. Lilies for the Virgin, wild roses to denote the Crown of Thorns, vines the Blessed Sacrament – each panel is painted with some symbolic flower. It is simple and effective. But it is the Pugin glass which makes the church.

To the west stands the gatehouse: to its 14th-century centre mid-19th-century wings were added (by Sir Joseph Paxton, according to Howard Colvin), to make it an occasional residence for the Dukes of Devonshire. To the south stands the rectory, a charming house of the 17th century, incorporating fragments of the monastic buildings. And the setting, of course, is legendary, with the sweeping meadows bordering the River Wharfe, the Stepping Stones, and the tree-hung hills beyond. It has always been a haunt of painters – Turner, Ruskin, Sutton Palmer. But in summer now the place is over-run by tourists and trippers: a beautiful winter day mid-week is recommended for a visit to Bolton Priory.

DIOCESE OF
BRISTOL

Bristol Cathedral

To John Betjeman Bristol was 'the most beautiful, interesting and distinguished city in England'.
'It is a town,' he wrote, 'associated with rich men
in the tobacco, wine, and chocolate trades . . .
There is the old city, the port on the Avon, with
narrow streets, old churches, timber-framed
houses and an 18th-century theatre . . . and a
second city, Clifton, like Bath a late Georgian spa,
on the heights of the Avon Gorge. The Gorge is
crossed by Brunel's Suspension Bridge, which is
a delicate balanced structure, like an insect of
enormous size, pausing astride the rocks and
trees.' Despite bombing, despite so many terrible
modern buildings, out of scale and out of sympathy
with the place, despite unceasing traffic swirling
along the new 'relief roads' which have in some
places torn apart the guts of the city, beautiful,
interesting and distinguished Bristol remains.

And in the heart of the old city stands the
Cathedral, full length in its splendour on College
Green – three towers, long traceried windows the
full height of the building, pinnacled, embattled
parapets, pinnacled, embattled transept, with a
lower, clearly earlier, chapel extending on its east
side. At first sight it appears all of a piece; then it
becomes apparent that the two west towers, earlier
in style but newer in texture, are in fact Victorian,
indeed that the whole nave, though so close in
style to the chancel, is Victorian too. What has
happened?

Bristol was created a diocese by Henry VIII in
1542, at the same time as Gloucester, Chester,
Oxford and Peterborough: in all these cases a
great existing abbey church became the cathedral.
So it was here: the abbey church of Augustinian Canons, suppressed in 1539, became Bristol
Cathedral. It had been founded in 1140 by Robert
FitzHardinge, and a grand Norman church was
built, of which important parts remain. In the early
13th century the Elder Lady Chapel was built,
opening out of the north transept, in the E.E. style:
at the end of the 13th century rebuilding of the

entire chancel began, starting with an entirely new
Lady Chapel at the east end. It is this new chancel
which makes Bristol unique and superlative among
English cathedrals. Rebuilding of the transepts
and central tower, a big, square, pinnacled Perp
tower, followed in the 15th century. In the 16th
century work began on rebuilding the nave; the
outer walls were built up to the sills of the windows,
and most of the Norman nave had been pulled
down, when the Dissolution took place. Work was
abandoned, the west arch of the crossing was
walled up, two bays of the Norman nave were left
to act as buttresses, and the church continued
shorn of its nave till 1868, when G. E. Street was
appointed architect to build the nave, begun over
three hundred years earlier; the towers were completed in 1888, after Street's death. With its rose
window and enormous central porch, the west
front wears a decidedly French look.

Enter by the N.W. porch and stand in Street's
nave – and look on, past the stone screen to the
medieval chancel, past the chancel to the Lady
Chapel beyond that. We can only gasp at the sight:
great wide nave, great lofty aisles as high as the
nave, long aisle windows flooding the nave and the
aisles with light, the absence of triforium and
clerestory, the wide spreading vault above, like the
spreading branches of a beech wood in summer.
Street, bravely and humbly, carried on where the
medieval builders had perforce to leave off. Yet
his nave is not a slavish copy of their chancel. The
vaulting of the nave is simpler and (as it were)
earlier, and the vaulting of the aisles follows a
different pattern; the nave piers have elaborately
carved stiff-leaf capitals. We can now walk up the
nave into the chancel, built between 1298 and
1330.

The chancel, with the Lady Chapel beyond, is
unique in England: it is what the Germans call a
'hall church' – a building in which the roofs of
nave and aisles are of the same height. Indeed
Bristol Cathedral is the earliest church of this

*Bristol Cathedral: the early 14th-century aisle vault, with little bridges providing internal flying buttresses to support the
chancel vault*

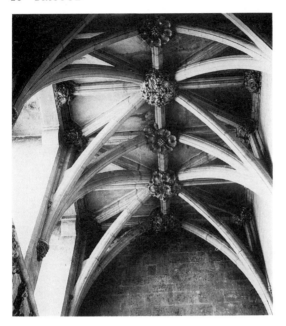

ABOVE *Vaulting in the ante-chapel of the Berkeley Chapel*
BELOW *'Stellate' recesses for medieval effigies and marble tablets in the Lady Chapel*

type in Europe. 'Its architect,' wrote Sir Nikolaus Pevsner, 'was a man of great and singular genius ... a man of supreme inventiveness in matters of decoration as well as of space.... No man then alive could compete with him;' and he goes on: 'his work at Bristol is superior to anything else built in England, and indeed in Europe, at the same time.' We can only stand and stare – at the chancel vault, the earliest lierne vault in England, at the design of the aisle vaults, where little bridges provide internal flying buttresses to support the chancel vault, at the great sense of space contrived, at the cool, airy elegance and the gay spontaneity of the whole design. It is a masterpiece.

The furnishings and fittings of the chancel have been much moved about and altered; the choir stalls, in origin early 16th century, were extensively restored by Pearson; the misericords are original; the reredos is by Pearson too (1899), and the open stone chancel screen is also his (1904). After the destruction of the original nave, a stone pulpitum stood in the second bay of the chancel, thus contriving a short nave of two bays, which, with the transepts and crossing, must have seemed like the ante-chapel of a college chapel; the High Altar then stood where the Lady Chapel now is. The organ case is of 1682, and very fine: it originally stood on the pulpitum.

The Lady Chapel to the east is all part of the 'hall church', and the reredos and sedilia, the big traceried windows and the unusual 'stellate' recesses containing tombs of 14th-century dignitaries, are all part of the design: sedilia and reredos were delightfully and gaily regilded and recoloured by Professor E. W. Tristram; the glass in the east window is medieval, but somewhat renewed and restored in 1847. On the altar is a noble pair of silver candlesticks dated 1712, a thankoffering for the safe return of two ships, the *Duke* and the *Duchess*, from a trip round the world – a reminder of the importance of the port of Bristol.

The same rich decoration is to be found in the Berkeley Chapel (south side of chancel) and its ante-chapel; in the Berkeley Chapel is a very rare 15th-century brass candelabrum. The Newton Chapel (south transept) was the last work to be done at this stage: it contains important tombs to the Newtons of Barrs Court, and other monuments.

In a comparable position, opening out of the north transept, is the Elder Lady Chapel, the early-13th-century E.E. chapel which we noted

Bristol Cathedral: G. E. Street's nave, J. L. Pearson's screen and High Altar reredos

outside. Here there are triple lancets, Purbeck shafts, stiff-leaf capitals and a rib vault; it is known that the abbot of the day asked the Dean of Wells for the loan of his masons for its erection – so the connection with Wells is established. At the east end of the north choir aisle is an interesting late-17th-century window, said to have been the gift of Nell Gwyn. Here and throughout the Cathedral are notable monuments of every century to past citizens of Bristol.

A narrow door in the south transept leads down to the cloisters, of which only the east and part of the north walks survive. These are Perp, but the east wall is Norman, and a splendid Norman vestibule leads into the Norman chapter house, one of the most magnificent Norman interiors in Eng-land: lofty, vaulted, its walls arcaded and intricately carved and ornamented (c. 1150). The cloisters lead into a diminutive precinct: to the south stands the Cathedral School (incorporating the Abbot's House), to the west the Abbey gatehouse, with its robust Norman arch and, above, the house itself built c. 1500, with its mullioned windows and panelled, pinnacled parapet. Through this we return to the bustle of College Green.

Bristol: late Norman decoration in the chapter house

St James' Priory, Bristol

St James' Priory stands in the very heart of Bristol, surrounded by new office blocks and old warehouses – a new dual carriageway to the S. with endless traffic streaming by, and old lanes to the N. Yet St James' is not quite obliterated. It stands on rising ground in its own large churchyard, which is filled with ancient tombs and protected by trees. There is a 14th-century tower of West Country type at the E. end of the S. aisle, and a Norman west front adorned with interlacing blind arcading, a trio of round-headed windows and a small wheel window above.

The Benedictine priory was founded in 1139 by Robert Earl of Gloucester (illegitimate son of Henry I) as a cell of Tewkesbury Abbey. After the Dissolution the nave was purchased by the parishioners to serve as the parish church; the monastic buildings and the choir passed into private hands and were pulled down. The nave is still used as a parish church (1984), but is to be declared redundant and used for diocesan purposes – retaining a chapel for worship. Inside, the Norman nave survives – with its five imposing bays of round piers with attached shafts and scalloped capitals; there is a Victorian 'Norman' east end, and beyond the N. aisle a large outer aisle of 1864 with an

St James' Priory: the Norman west front and 14th-century tower

elaborate Victorian arcade of polished marble columns. There is a hefty 19th-century pulpit, an 18th-century sword rest, a Stuart Royal Arms, and an interesting collection of monuments, ranging from the elaborate tomb of Sir Charles Somerset (1599) to the bust of the Revd. Thomas Biddulph (by E. H. Bailey, 1842): he was Vicar of St James' and one of the founders of the Church Missionary Society.

Samuel Wesley, musician, was baptized here in 1766; in the register his father Charles is described as 'preacher in the Horsefair'. Both Charles and his more famous brother John often worshipped and preached in this church at the time of the founding of their Methodist mission in Bristol.

Malmesbury Abbey

Main roads from Cirencester or Chippenham, from Cricklade or Tetbury, all lead into the town, with its old streets, its Market Cross, and its bustle. But the thing to do first is to leave the main roads and seek out the country lanes, towards Foxley perhaps, or the back lane to Corston, leave the car, and walk along the water meadows to the S.W. of the town. From here there is a wonderful view – of the huddle of houses with their stone roofs, the spire of St Paul's, the long line of the nave of the Abbey. And, if there is time, do not leave it at that: take the footpath to Daniel's Well: from here it is possible to see everything close up – the ruined west front of the mighty church, and the details of St Paul's steeple in the foreground. And then, on the N. side, there is another wonderful view from the Abbey Mill – the view which Turner painted in 1826 – which should not be missed, with the gaping arch of the ruined crossing at one end, the empty windows of the west end at the other. From here it is possible to walk back under the very shadow of the Abbey into the Market Place. Here stands the Market Cross (built *c.* 1500), comparable with those at Chichester or Salisbury; here, through the late-18th-century Gothicky gatehouse, we enter the churchyard.

The south front of the church stands before us – such as it is: the rump of the nave, with its prominent, awe-inspiring porch, its lofty clerestory, flying buttresses, the ruined S. transept to the E., gaping clerestory to the W., a single, solid, Norman buttress beyond that, a solitary relic of a great west front. The Benedictine abbey was originally founded in the 7th century by an Irish hermit, and grew in importance under St Aldhelm, its first Abbot, who died in 709. It was his shrine which made Malmesbury a place of pilgrimage during the Middle Ages, and the Abbey became famous as a place of learning. The present church was begun in the second half of the 12th century, and originally a tremendous central tower was crowned with a spire taller than Salisbury's: but this collapsed in a storm in 1479, ruining much of the eastern half of the church. After the Dissolution (1539), William Stumpe, a wealthy Malmesbury clothier who had purchased the monastic

Malmesbury Abbey: the fragmentary west end of the nave and the south porch

property, presented the church to the town to serve as the parish church; but the west tower fell soon after, damaging the last three bays of the nave. What survives is what we see today.

Its great glory is the porch, which contains some of the finest Norman sculpture in England. The outer arches in themselves are intricately and gloriously carved: the inmost with the story of the Creation, the middle with the stories of Old Testament figures – Noah, Abraham, Moses and David – the outer with scenes from the life of Our Lord. Over the actual door is a tympanum with the figure of Christ in glory, attended by two winged angels, and the jambs and surrounds are carved with elaborate bands and patterning. But it is the sides of the interior of the porch which are the most thrilling of all. Here under the vault are seated the figures of the twelve apostles, six on either side, an angel flying above their heads: their pose, the folds of their draperies, the spirited features of their faces, form a most remarkable composition.

The nave itself – the six surviving bays, with their round columns, slightly pointed arches, the elaborate Norman triforium, the elaborate Perp clerestory above that, and the 14th-century lierne vault – is tantalizingly beautiful. But the blocked-up E. wall, the stone pulpitum at the crossing now serving as a reredos, the blocked-up west wall with its large traceried 19th-century window, tell the story of disaster and destruction. Above the third bay on the S. side is a little stone balcony or watching chamber, its precise purpose unknown. St Aldhelm's Chapel is in the S. aisle – but his shrine has disappeared, his place of burial unknown. The 14th-century tomb of King Athelstan is in the N. aisle: Athelstan died in 940, and the erection of this monument to Malmesbury's greatest benefactor was an act of 14th-century *pietas*.

It is worth walking round to the E. end to survey the three surviving columns of the crossing, and the two surviving Norman arches – and then round to the N. side to contemplate the site of the cloisters and the other monastic buildings. To the E. stands Abbey House, built by William Stumpe, and incorporating part of the Reredorter. At the S.W. corner of the churchyard stands solitary the tower and broach spire of St Paul's church, once the parochial church, its steeple, now that both abbey towers have fallen, now acting as its bell tower.

The south porch at Malmesbury contains some of the finest Norman sculpture in England. ABOVE *Scenes from the Old Testament in bands on the exterior of the porch.* BELOW *Detail of apostles and angel from the interior walls of the porch*

DIOCESE OF
CANTERBURY

Canterbury Cathedral

THE MOTHER CHURCH of England, the mother church of the Anglican Communion: the Cathedral stands majestic above the roof-tops of the city – majestic and romantic from the low green Kentish hills which surround it. It was on the brow of the hill at Harbledown, on Watling Street, that Chaucer's pilgrims halted before descending into the town, and fell on their knees in prayer at the first sight of the Cathedral. Much survives of the medieval city walls: from London we can enter the ancient city through the Westgate, with its two round towers (*c.* 1350). This is now a museum, and it is worth climbing to the top to obtain the finest view of the Cathedral – of the west front with its two low towers, and 'Bell Harry' rising behind in all its glory. Canterbury was the victim of 'Baedeker' raids in 1942, and whole areas were flattened by the German bombs. Mercifully the Cathedral survived. There has been some commonplace rebuilding, but much remains of the old town. From the High Street, Mercury Lane leads to the Buttermarket, and here stands Christ Church Gate, built in 1517, magnificent and turreted, with splendid doors bearing the arms of Archbishop Juxon: he attended Charles I on the scaffold, and became Archbishop at the Restoration. This is the entrance to the Precincts.

The Cathedral rises above us, with its towers, its lofty nave and transept, elaborate S.W. porch; all this is Perp. And then, as we walk east, we find earlier work beyond: a Norman eastern transept, with shallow apsidal chapels, and then the long apsidal retrochoir with lancet windows, and, accompanying this, an oddly placed extruding chapel at its side; beyond again, and most puzzling, is the Corona, or Becket's Crown, the mysterious round chapel at the east end. It is worth taking note of all this, because it explains much of what we shall see within.

Only a tradition remains of the first little basilica which King Ethelbert gave to St Augustine on his arrival in 597, and of the Saxon cathedral which replaced it. It was destroyed by fire in 1067, and replaced by a new cathedral built by Lanfranc, the first Norman Archbishop: this, too, has disappeared, though the present nave and transepts stand on Lanfranc's foundations. The choir was rebuilt by Lanfranc's successor, Anselm, to accommodate the growing monastery, and this was consecrated in 1130. Part of this rebuilding survives – but the choir itself was destroyed by another fire in 1174. The timing seemed providential, for the martyrdom of Becket occurred in 1170, and the opportunity was taken to rebuild both choir and retrochoir to accommodate a worthy shrine for St Thomas Becket. The cult of the murdered archbishop grew so tremendously, and the income from the pilgrims' offerings became so immense, that in the 14th century the nave and transepts, S.W. tower and central tower were all rebuilt in glorious Perp. So here is the vast cathedral we see today.

We must return to the S.W. porch. The new nave was begun in 1391, and completed in 1405, and the south transept was completed in 1414; the S.W. tower was built between 1424 and 1434 – though for some reason Lanfranc's Norman N.W. tower was not rebuilt, until in 1832 George Austin, the cathedral architect, built in its place a replica of the S.W. tower. There was hesitation about rebuilding the north transept – hallowed as the scene of the martyrdom – but this was carried out in 1468; finally 'Bell Harry' was built at the very turn of the century, and completed in 1503. Henry Yevele was master mason of the nave, John Wastell of 'Bell Harry'. It is this slender, soaring, central tower that pulls the whole building together: the lofty nave, the long straggling choir and retrochoir,

Canterbury Cathedral: 'Bell Harry' rising above the north transept and chapter house roof

Canterbury: the view west through the chancel to the crossing and nave

the corona, the double transepts. The Cathedral is sometimes criticized for its lack of architectural unity: this may be true. On the other hand its remarkable complexity gives the building tremendous character and extraordinary charm.

Inside, there can be no doubt about the wonder of the nave: the soaring height, the immense arcades, the clerestory windows far above, with the most delicate of lierne vaults in nave and aisles – the aisles themselves of great height with long traceried windows – and the eastward view to 'strainer' arch, added by Wastell to strengthen the crossing piers when 'Bell Harry' was built; and so to the pulpitum behind, with its flight of steps ascending – and, beyond that, mystery and darkness: the nave is one church, the chancel beyond another.

And so to the crossing: it is all steps – steps up to the chancel, steps down to the transepts – and, above, the delicate fan vault of the lantern, the lofty vault of the narrow transepts. From the south transept leads St Michael's Chapel, the Warrior Chapel, stacked with splendid tombs and monuments; from the north the Lady Chapel, fan vaulted, and entered by an elaborate stone screen. And on the south wall a tablet proclaims

THOMAS BECKET
Archbishop Saint Martyr
died here
Tuesday 29th December
1170

And now, up, up, up those steps through the pulpitum into the chancel. We are in a different world, a different church – a building indeed so different that there is nothing like it in all England. This is the choir built by William of Sens, the Frenchman chosen to take charge of the rebuilding after the fire. It is half Romanesque, half Gothic, yet so remote from the English Transitional that it has been dubbed by Francis Bond as 'made in France'. The lancet windows, the coupled columns, the Corinthianesque capitals, rich zigzag ornament, all seem French in inspiration; yet there are English features, too, in the use of brown or grey Purbeck marble, in shafts or string courses. It is solemn, numinous; steps again lead up and up, and in the sanctuary the arcades curve inwards, and the retrochoir is narrower and extends to the eastern apse. It was so built to preserve those small extruding chapels – relics of Anselm's choir – observed outside; but the effect is masterly. The retrochoir, or Trinity Chapel, was the site of

ABOVE *View up into 'Bell Harry' from the crossing*
BELOW *'Corinthianesque' capitals in William of Sens' apsidal chapel*

Becket's shrine. Nothing survives: twenty-six cartloads of gold and jewels were removed to Henry VIII's treasury in 1538. But there is compensation in what survives: the tomb of the Black Prince, eldest son of Edward III, hero of Crécy and Poitiers (1370), his recumbent figure in gold armour, his surcoat, gauntlet, shield and scabbard suspended above. Opposite is the tomb of Henry IV (1413) and his Queen, Joan of Navarre (1437); the King's little chantry is nearby, on the other side of the ambulatory. And at the east end is the Corona, or Becket's Crown, the round chapel which until recently held the 13th-century Purbeck marble throne in which archbishops are enthroned; it has been removed, and placed at the top of the sanctuary steps, where it stands in isolation and looks absurd: what is worse, the High Altar has been demoted to the lower stage – and that marvellous ascent to the Holiest Place, to God's Altar as to Heaven itself, now leads merely to a prelate's throne. A grave mistake.

And another French feature of this choir is the glass. In the Trinity Chapel, in the ambulatories, in the Corona and the eastern transepts, is the finest 13th-century glass in England, that rich-toned medallion glass so reminiscent of Chartres, and made perhaps in France. This creates tremendous 'atmosphere'. And on either side those earlier Norman chapels, relics of Anselm's choir, still hug the later chancel: St Andrew's Chapel on the north side, St Anselm's on the south; and here, high up in the apse, is the 12th-century wall painting of St Paul shaking off the viper in Malta.

And then, underneath all this, is a third most wonderful church: the crypt at Canterbury is the largest and most remarkable of any cathedral in England. The major crypt is under the chancel, and is part of Anselm's building (early 12th century): steps lead down from the crossing on north and south sides into an enormous undercroft, with 'nave' and double aisles, where a forest of pillars uphold a spreading groin-vault. The pillars are adorned with carved capitals, some purely decorative with leaves or foliage, some with the most entertaining carvings of human figures or animals – some playing musical instruments. And in the centre is the Chapel of Our Lady Undercroft, divided from the rest by delicately carved stone screens (14th century). At the sides are smaller chapels: St Gabriel's is adorned with 12th-century wall paintings; the Black Prince's Chantry is (somewhat unexpectedly) reserved for Huguenot

A capital in the Norman crypt at Canterbury

worship, as it has been, indeed, for several centuries. And beyond, under the Trinity Chapel, is the later, larger and loftier crypt, which is light and spacious, and almost a complete church in itself.

The cloisters are approached from the north transept; they were rebuilt at the same time as the nave, and are extremely decorative with large

The cloisters at Canterbury

traceried windows and a Perp lierne vault adorned with heraldic bosses, all recently repainted. On the east side stands the large rectangular chapter house (14th–15th century): here T. S. Eliot's *Murder in the Cathedral* was first performed. And in the N.E. corner of the cloisters a doorway leads out into the charming labyrinth of the conventual buildings: in the small Infirmary Cloister is the Lavatory Tower, Norman below, Perp above, which supplied water for the monastery. Many of the buildings round Green Court (to the north) are part of the King's School; on the east side is the imposing Deanery, part medieval, part Tudor: the last Prior, at the Dissolution, became the first Dean.

Walking round Green Court, or back to the south side through the ruins of the Infirmary, past the Corona, it is possible to appreciate the scale and splendour of the Cathedral and its monastic buildings, of the precincts with the medieval and Georgian houses standing around, and, gazing up, repeat Erasmus' words on first beholding the Cathedral: *'Tanta majestate sese erigit in coelum'* – 'With what majesty does it rise to the sky.'

Minster Abbey

Minster Abbey

The Isle of Sheppey is an odd little world: Kingsferry Bridge connects it with the mainland, and off the A249 (to Sheerness) a minor road leads to Minster, a steep hill bringing us to the Abbey, which was founded as a Benedictine nunnery on the highest point in Sheppey by Queen Sexburga, widow of King Ercombert, *c.* 674. It is an odd, squat, venerable church, with a broad low western tower crowned with a timber belfry. This tower was still incomplete at the time of the Dissolution, and the little belfry is a later addition. To the west of the tower and at right angles to the church is a large detached gatehouse which led to the conventual buildings; it is an indication of the grandeur and importance which once belonged to the Abbey.

The church itself is two churches side by side, the monastic church to the north, the parish church alongside it to the south. Sexburga's original foundation was sacked by the Danes in the 9th century: after many vicissitudes it was re-

founded by William de Corbeil, Archbishop of Canterbury, *c.* 1130. He rebuilt the nuns' church and the conventual buildings and gatehouse (this was enlarged in Perp style in the 15th century); the church was dedicated to SS Mary and Sexburga. The parochial nave was built in the 13th century, but a walk round the outside will reveal Saxon features, Roman tiles and much early masonry, all re-used in the rebuilding.

Inside, the nuns' church has the proportions of a Saxon building; the chancel was rebuilt in the 14th century, and there is a somewhat rough-hewn fragment of a reredos here. A 13th-century arcade divides the nuns' church from the parochial: this is equally spacious, and the south doorway is late Norman, the porch rebuilt by Ewan Christian, who restored the church in 1879. But the monuments are the outstanding feature. There is the tomb of Sir Robert Shurland, Lord of Sheppey (d. 1300), with its elaborate canopy whose shafts rest on lions couchant; the figure of the knight lies on one side, gazing up with his legs crossed, his shield beneath him. At his feet is the little figure of his squire, and the head of his horse – the horse that saved him from drowning in the sea; the story is told in the *Ingoldsby Legends*. In the floor nearby are the exceptional brasses of Sir John de Northwode and his wife (*c.* 1330), and in the Nuns' chancel the alabaster effigy of an unknown knight, sometimes said to be that of the Duke of Clarence (of Malmsey wine fame), who was Constable of Queenborough Castle nearby; but Tewkesbury also claims him. Sir Thomas Cheyne, Lord Warden of the Cinque Ports, Treasurer of the Household to Henry VIII and Edward VI, to whom the monastic property was granted at the Dissolution (1536), has a grand Renaissance tomb of 1558.

The village of Minster is an odd little place too: the street lies below the church – a public house or two, a shop or two – with no buildings of note; beyond, there are long roads of suburban semis. But from the churchyard there are wonderful views across the Thames Estuary to the north, of industry round the mouth of the Medway to the west, and to the east and south over desolate flat meadows where sheep graze. Minster should certainly be visited for its atmosphere – and as one of the most ancient cradles of English monasticism.

Davington: the Norman west front. The many-gabled Priory House incorporates part of the monastic buildings

Davington Priory

Faversham is an ancient town, with a wide creek of the River Swale connecting it with the estuary and the outside world. A prosperous port in the Middle Ages, it is still busy on its riverside with wharves and small boat-building yards. There are streets, wide and narrow, lined with houses of many dates: the Guildhall in the Market Place has an open ground floor with timber arcades of 1574 and a cupola-crowned late Georgian upper storey;

the parish church has a late-18th-century tower and steeple inspired by St Dunstan-in-the-East. Away to the west on rising ground is Davington, now a suburb; here, accompanied by roads of modern semis, stands Davington Priory.

Davington Priory, founded in 1153 for Benedictine nuns by Fulk de Newenham, is not only a church of great delight: it is also of exceptional interest for having been rescued and restored from 1845 onwards by Thomas Willement, the stained-glass artist. He bought church and priory house that year – both in a near derelict condition, and although much of his decoration in the church was swept away in the 1930s, it is to him that we owe the very existence of the building.

By 1536 the small community here had dwindled to nothing, so there was nothing to dissolve; but the buildings, of course, became Crown property. During the course of the next two centuries the nave of the church was used as a parish church, but all was more or less derelict, and services had lapsed, by the time of Willement's arrival. Of two western towers, the north-west had disappeared, and the south-west was decapitated. The many-gabled house, built round the converted cloisters, was divided into tenements, occupied by many families. All was *ichabod*.

We do not know what architect assisted Willement: it may have been L. N. Cottingham, with whom he often worked. The south-west tower was repaired and given its tiled cap, the church was restored, and the house converted into a residence for himself, adorned with his own stained glass and painted decoration.

The church is of simple austere beauty with arcades of round arches and square piers, round-headed windows in the nave, lancets in the north aisle. There is a badly weathered Norman west doorway; at the east end, on either side of the altar, is a blocked doorway: this was the pulpitum between nave and monastic choir. There is a magnificent Norman-revival font of 1847, decorated with the symbols of the evangelists, executed by John Thomas, and presented by friends of Willement to celebrate his achievements here. There is a black oak pulpit, made up of continental carved panels of the 17th century. Willement filled all the windows with his own glass, and decorated the walls with his paintings. His house adjoins the church on the south side, and a window from an upper room looks down into the nave.

In 1934 the Church reacquired the property

and a further restoration took place: the entire interior was whitewashed, and Willement's glass removed from the west windows. It is sad that his decoration has disappeared; even so, the interior, glistening white, and lit by the clear glass in the west windows, has charm and distinction.

The garden of the Priory House makes a lovely setting, with a wide meadow on the west grazed by Jacob's sheep. There is a long gabled front facing west, and, round the corner, a small garden with box-edged parterre in what was the cloister court, with more timber-framed stuccoed gables enclosing the courtyard. The house is private, and not open to the public, but the church is in regular use as the parish church.

The austere Norman nave of the Benedictine Priory at Davington, rescued in 1847 by Thomas Willement, the stained-glass artist

DIOCESE OF
CARLISLE

Carlisle Cathedral

CARLISLE IS frontier country: the border is only seven miles away – with Gretna Green beyond, where the accommodating blacksmith would oblige those who wished to take advantage of the different marriage laws in Scotland. And the city is a frontier city, with fragments of the city walls, and a castle originally built by Rufus, its keep and curtain wall built by Henry II. Hadrian's wall runs through the outer suburbs of the town. All through the Middle Ages Scottish raids were made across the border, and the Cathedral itself wears the scars inflicted in the Civil War.

The Cathedral stands in the middle of the town: traffic rushes by on one side, the railway – the main west coast route to Scotland – on the other. A line of shops, and the east end of the Cathedral is upon us: iron gates lead into the Abbey – the cathedral precinct – where remains of the monastic buildings press hard upon the church. The long chancel, short transepts, a squat central tower – all of red sandstone – and beyond all this the rump, the lowly rump, of the nave.

The see of Carlisle was founded by Henry I in 1133: eleven years earlier Henry had brought Augustinian Canons here, and refounded a small community which had originally been established *c.* 1100; he was patron of this new order, and transferred Adelulf, Prior of Nostell in Yorkshire, to be its first prior. Adelulf was his confessor, and Henry appointed him first Bishop of Carlisle in 1133. Building began here *c.* 1130, and what remains of the Norman church must date from the middle of the 12th century. Outside, the chancel must be absorbed first. It is of great size and splendour, with the largest Dec curvilinear traceried east window in England (51 ft high). The aisles are earlier – E.E. – with lancets in pairs, and blind lancets to left and right with narrow shafts; but the clerestory windows are Dec. E.E. work carries on

in the eastern aisle of the transept – but there are Norman windows above, and on the west side of the transept all is Norman too. The rump of the nave is Norman, with later traceried windows in the aisle. This all explains its history and prepares us for what we shall see inside.

We enter by the porch in the south transept (by Ewan Christian, and modelled, it is said, on the chapter house door at Southwell). The first impression is one of loftiness, the narrowness, of transepts and crossing. The eye is carried up: the Norman piers have been extended upwards to carry the later tower (early 15th century). The curious spectacle of the empty traceried window on the north side of the crossing is explained by the fact that the roof of the north transept has been raised – this was originally a window above the transept roof. The enormous pipes of the organ surmounting the screen conceal the chancel arch. To the west are the sad remains of the nave – a mere two bays, of the former eight. The rest was destroyed by the Scottish troops in 1645, to repair the fortifications of the city. The arches are low, and the piers large and round: the triforium is composed of the simplest of arched openings, the clerestory of small Norman windows. It is a severe composition, but beautiful in its simplicity. The nave is now furnished as the Chapel of the Border Regiment – with excellent, dignified fittings and ornaments by Mr Stephen Dykes-Bower. The sight of the deformed Norman arches – such as the arch from the south transept, and the triforium arch above – due, apparently, to a depression in the ground at a time of severe drought, is entertaining.

We enter the chancel – much wider than the nave, and therefore oddly aligned. It is, without doubt, spectacular. After the confined space of the crossing, the transepts and the nave, their stark

OPPOSITE *Carlisle Cathedral: view into the chancel, with the Dec arcades (the capitals carved to illustrate the labours of the month) and the choir stalls, some of the finest medieval stalls in England*

simplicity and severity, the chancel bursts upon us with its glorious tracery, its medieval glass above, Hardman's admirable Victorian glass below, Sir Charles Nicholson's High Altar and canopy (1934), the Antwerp pulpit, the Salkeld screen, the magnificent array of early-15th-century canopied stalls – all these are outstanding. The pulpit, which is a memorial to Dean Mayne (d. 1962), is of *c.* 1560, and came originally from Antwerp; the Salkeld screen (of much the same date) was the gift of Lancelot Salkeld, last Prior and first Dean, and displays wonderful Renaissance decoration; the choir stalls constitute, with those at Chester and Lincoln, the finest medieval stalls in England. In addition to all this, the Dec arcades themselves are remarkable: the capitals are carved, and illustrate the labours of each month – March digging, April pruning, September reaping, and so on. And above us is the wooden barrel-vaulted roof, all gaily painted.

There are earlier screens at the entrance to St Catherine's Chapel in the south transept, erected by Prior Gondibour (*c.* 1490); and in the north

transept is the Brougham Triptych, serving as a reredos in St Wilfrid's Chapel. This is early 16th century, made in Antwerp for a church in Cologne; it was brought to England in the 19th century by Lord Brougham for his chapel at Brougham near Penrith. Splendidly restored recently at the Victoria and Albert Museum, it is now on loan to the Cathedral.

As for the monastic buildings, nothing survives of the cloisters or chapter house, except for a few shafts. The Fratry, however, is an important survival, with a Great Hall above to serve as Cathedral library and chapter house, and a vaulted undercroft below, which is used as the Cathedral bookshop and restaurant. The Abbot's House is now the Deanery; and there are several charming 18th-century canons' houses. At the west end stands the gatehouse, erected in 1527 by Abbot Slee: '*Orate pro anima Christopheri Slee*', the ·inscription runs, '*qui primus hoc opus fieri incipit A.D. MDXXVII.*'

Cartmel Priory

A remote part of England: Morecambe Bay almost cuts off the Cartmel Peninsula from the mainland. Cartmel itself is a little town in miniature, the priory gate leading into a tiny market square: there are houses and cottages closely packed, all somewhat dwarfed by the priory church which stands at the end of a narrow street, presiding over all. The sea is only two miles away to the east: Holker Hall a mile to the south-west.

The Priory stands fortress-like on the eastern edge of the village. It is cruciform in plan, and a short nave and choir, wide transepts, rise cliff-like to uphold a squat central tower, with a second upper tower above set diagonally upon it. This tower is unique in England, and of special charm. Outwardly the church looks all Perp. But come inside.

Cartmel Priory was founded for Augustinian Canons in 1188, by William Marshall, Earl of Pembroke. The south doorway is of this date, but the door on the north side is earliest E.E. The interior is amazingly lofty and spacious. It will be seen at once that the chancel was built first: here the arcades have round arches – but the triforium is formed of a continuous arcade of little E.E. lancets, and here and there are pointed arches: the choir, transepts and crossing must have been

Carlisle: the most spectacular Dec east window in England, filled with medieval glass above and Hardman's glass below

Cartmel Priory

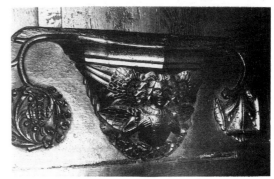

LEFT *George Preston's 17th-century screen*
ABOVE *a medieval misericord*

built at the very end of the 12th century. The north choir aisle, which is vaulted and called the Piper Choir, is of this date, but the more spacious south choir aisle, called the Town Choir and always reserved for the parish, was rebuilt in the early 14th century.

The very grand Perp east window was inserted in the 15th century: here there are fragments of contemporary glass; the three central lights are filled with figures of saints, as are some of the tracery lights. For the rest, the glass is clear, and the spreading branches of an ancient tree outside supplement the tracery of the long straight Perp mullions. At this stage, too, the upper part of the tower was added, and set diagonally in order not to overburden the foundations in the spongy ground; the nave was completed then, too, and many Perp windows inserted throughout the church. The cloisters and monastic buildings, which were originally on the south side, were moved to the north – apparently on account of the spongy ground. They must have been cold and dark on the north, lying under the shadow of the enormous church. But all have disappeared, except for the gatehouse which now stands detached, as we have seen, in the middle of the village.

The Priory was dissolved in 1537; the church was purchased by the parish, but only the Town Choir remained in use. Stripped of its lead, the rest of the building became a roofless shell, and so remained till 1618, when George Preston of Holker Hall, whose family had acquired much of the monastic property, restored the main church and built the new roof. He was the second founder of the church, and its greatest benefactor.

The glory of the church now is the remarkable woodwork installed by him in the choir. The screen, the canopies of the stalls, and the screens in the sanctuary, are most unusual. Slender columns, crowned with Corinthian capitals and carved with trailing vine stems and instruments of the Passion, form the canopies to the medieval stalls with their misericords: between them elaborate open-work panels provide the backs, and in the screen these are on hinges, so that they can be opened or closed as may be required.

In the nave is Preston's painted memorial, recording his work of restoration; the property passed by marriage to the Lowther family, to whom there are monuments in the Town Choir, including Sir William, 1st Bt. (1705) and Dame Catherine his wife, *née* Preston, (1700); the 2nd Bt. married a daughter of the 2nd Duke of Devonshire, and the Cavendish family eventually inherited the property. The Cavendishes still hold Holker.

There are a number of medieval tombs to priors or canons, and near the altar is the important tomb of the first Lord Harrington (1347), under an elaborate canopy: little figures of saints and mourners stand above, weeping or praying. The monument seems to have been reassembled during the 17th-century restoration. Near the north door a 17th-century brass plate commemorates Rowland Briggs of Swallowmire, who bequeathed a charity to provide bread for 'the most indigent householders of this parish every Sunday for ever'. It is attached to his bread cupboard, on which loaves are often displayed. In the nave is the tomb with recumbent effigy (by Thomas Woolner) of Lord Frederick Charles Cavendish, Chief Secretary for Ireland, who was murdered in Phoenix Park, Dublin, within a few hours of his arrival from England in 1882.

'My soule hath a desire and longing to enter into the Courts of the Lord. I had rather be a doore keeper in the House of my God than to dwell in the tabernacles of wickedness': so reads George Preston's inscription on his screen. It is due to him that we can enter into the courts of the Lord, here in Cartmel.

Holm Cultram Abbey

Abbey Town, where Holm Cultram Abbey stands, suggests a prim settlement of elegant 18th-century terraces and squares, polite society, erudite neighbours. Not so. It is a gaunt village of old farms, rough cottages and council houses, in a bleak, flat, cold stretch of country close to Solway Firth. The lanes twist and turn, there are stunted trees bent by the prevailing wind, an occasional unexpected grander house in an enclosed garden – and views across the Firth to Dumfriesshire. And in the midst of all this stands the abbey church, stark and beleaguered in the centre of the village, surrounded by a large churchyard. It is hard to comprehend that this rump of a building was once the church of a Cistercian abbey. Cistercian houses were always built in remote situations – Fountains, Rievaulx – which is why so few of them survived as churches after the Dissolution. Holm Cultram is the rare exception. Abbey Town grew up round the church: the parishioners petitioned to retain it: what was more, it was not merely a place of worship – it was the only building which could serve as a protection against the marauding Scots.

Rievaulx was founded from Clairvaux in 1132; Melrose was a daughter of Rievaulx, founded two years later, Holm Cultram a daughter of Melrose, founded in 1150. To the visitor today this fragment of a Cistercian church, sitting here in the middle of dull houses, towerless and shorn of all its buildings, has a rare presence. There is a curious squat

Holm Cultram Abbey, a holy, haunting spot

double bellcote in the apex of the 18th-century gable on the west front; below, the early-16th-century porch, built by Abbot Chamber in 1507, with Georgian Gothic windows in its upper storey, leads to a sumptuous Norman doorway: push the door open (and it needs a good push), and we are in the nave of the late-12th-century church. Six bays survive: aisles, transepts, chancel, central tower – all are gone. The Norman arcades are blocked, Georgian windows inserted in the walls, the roof (of ancient timber) sits low above the arches where triforium and clerestory once stood; there is a 17th-century Gothic-survival east window, some gaudy Victorian glass, and modern furniture. It is all rather odd – but decidedly a holy, haunting spot.

Lanercost Priory

Lanercost stands in as beautiful a setting as could be found: meadows surround it, the River Irthing passes by, on an escarpment a mile or so away stands the medieval castle of Naworth. The most spectacular approach is past the Castle, down the road bordering the park, to Lanercost Mill and the medieval bridge over the Irthing; from here it is a short step to the gatehouse. At first sight the church looks intact, complete with its monastic buildings to the right; a second glance shows that only the nave is intact and roofed, and that tower, transepts and chancel are a shell. A curious little bellcote on the tower holds a single bell.

Lanercost was founded *c.* 1169 by Robert de Vaux for Augustinian Canons. Most of the church which we see is in purest E.E. style. There is a long nave, and the west front of almost perfect

Lanercost: the E. E. west front and the surviving monastic buildings

symmetry has a grand, deeply splayed doorway, with a frieze above of trefoil-headed arcading, and, above that, three tall lancet windows; in a niche beneath the gable is a statue of St Mary Magdalen, with a canon kneeling at her side: it is wonderfully preserved (mid 13th century).

Inside, the nave is lofty, narrow, a trifle bleak with its scraped walls and much pitch pine furnishing. There is a lofty arcade on the north side, with a most decorative arcaded clerestory above; this is repeated on the south side, but there is no arcade here, only a row of tall lancet windows high up – for the cloisters ran below on this side. The crossing arch is blocked, and here an odd sub-Gothic window affords a glimpse of the ruined parts beyond. There is Morris glass in the north aisle: one little window depicts Abraham sacrificing Isaac, the latter lying on what looks like a Victorian kitchen range.

Walking round to the east end we find transepts, tower and chancel, wonderfully preserved, but roofless – everywhere the differing shades of stone, red sandstone or white, everywhere delightful E.E.

details. The aisles are still vaulted, and here are the monuments of the Dacres – the family who acquired the property after the Dissolution – and their descendants the Howards, Earls of Carlisle, of Naworth.

On the south side it is possible to make out the foundations of cloisters and chapter house. Further west there is a whole range of buildings, which were converted into a house by Sir Thomas Dacre in the 16th century; these include the Prior's House, which incorporates a Pele Tower. Beyond again is the vicarage, which was also part of the monastic quarters. Apart from all this, there are few signs of human habitation: it is all seclusion, solitariness, separation from the outside world.

St Bees Priory

Standing exposed on the wild Cumberland coastline, St Bees seems as remote in its situation as any monastic church in England. The small town – or large village – lies on the south side of the wide valley, the Priory and St Bees School on the north. The school was founded by Archbishop Grindal in 1583, making use of the chancel of the church as a schoolroom: in the early 19th century the pretty little open quadrangle was built on the opposite side of the road, with later buildings beyond. The playing fields sweep down to the little river, where the railway line turns in from the coast.

Though deprived of most of its chancel, the Priory is grand and spacious, with a magnificent Norman west door, and E.E. nave and transepts. Butterfield heightened the low central tower during his restoration of 1858. Inside it will be seen that it is his work which is the making of the church: the blank east wall he decorated with strongly, simply patterned stonework in his own inimitable style, and at the crossing he erected the tall wrought-iron screen – a masterpiece. There are good Victorian furnishings in the present chancel.

The Priory was founded as a Benedictine nunnery *c.* 1120 by William de Meschines, on the site of a 7th-century foundation which had been destroyed by the Danes. In the wall opposite the west door are fragments of early sculpture which may go back to earliest times; there is a 14th-century effigy in the north transept, and a number of 18th- or early-19th-century monuments elsewhere. Apart from Butterfield's work, it is the situation which is most memorable, with the prevailing wind blowing in from the sea, and the roar of the waves pounding on St Bees Head.

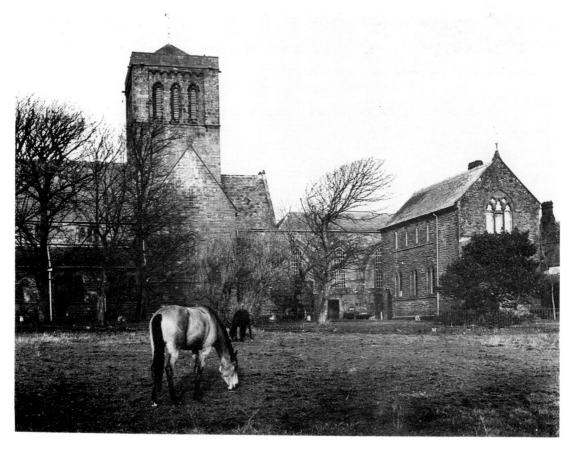

St Bees Priory, as remote in its situation as any monastic church in England

DIOCESE OF
CHELMSFORD

Chelmsford Cathedral

CHELMSFORD IS the ancient county town of Essex, but much modern industry (Marconi, for instance) has transformed it into a great sprawling place, with large new office buildings in the centre and vast housing estates round the periphery. There is still some feeling of antiquity round the Cathedral – but there are few buildings of note. The handsome Shire Hall, by John Johnson (1791), is an exception.

Chelmsford was created a new diocese in

Chelmsford Cathedral: the 15th-century tower and south porch

1913, and St Mary's Parish Church became the Cathedral. It is a good Perp town church of East Anglian type, but it is disappointing that in the course of the past seventy years so little has been done to give it in any way the dignity of a cathedral. What is more, it has in recent years been the victim of a wholesale 'reordering' – that is a massacre of the interior – so that there is really very little to see inside.

The S. porch and W. tower are the most notable features of the building – mainly built in the 15th century, of stone and flint, and attractive in their East Anglian way. The tower is crowned with an open cupola and slender lead spire of 1749; the two-storeyed porch is an excellent example of flint 'flushwork'. In 1873 an outer N. aisle was added, and in 1923 Sir Charles Nicholson rebuilt the east end, adding two extra bays, and also designed the Chapter Room and vestries which form, as it were, a large north transept. All this is decent work, but of no special interest. The building remains very modest for a cathedral.

Inside, it is interesting to find that the nave was rebuilt in 1801–3 by John Johnson, then the County Surveyor (see Leicester). The earlier nave had collapsed without warning, on the opening of a vault under the south arcade. It is an excellent rebuilding; Johnson used Coade stone for the south arcade, and the charming plaster ceiling is by him. There is little of note otherwise, except for a number of monuments: a grand standing wall monument to Thomas Mildmay and his wife (1571); another to Benjamin Mildmay, Earl Fitz-walter (1756), by James Lovell – Lovell was a protégé of Horace Walpole, and this is his most important work; another to Matthew Rudd (1615), ascribed to Epiphanis Evesham; and so on. Otherwise the whole interior has been swept bare: the High Altar has been banished from the east and replaced by a jazzy hanging; a new altar of the 'butcher's block' kind has been erected at the chancel step. So much for 're-ordering'.

Blackmore Priory

Blackmore is unique among English monastic churches for its wonderful 15th-century timber bell tower, which rises like an enormous squat pagoda above the meadows and old brick walls of Jericho, and the priory church itself. This was

Blackmore: the exterior and BELOW *the interior of the bell tower*

founded in the 12th century by the de Samford family for Augustinian Canons: it stands at the end of an Essex village street of timbered, or later, houses. A wide 'cat-slide' tile roof, dormer windows, flint walls, Perp tracery: outwardly the church looks anything but monastic. As is apparent within, it is but the nave: the north aisle is 14th century, the south with its unusual brick arcade is 16th, and was built after the Dissolution, when the Canons' choir was pulled down. Of special interest are the two Norman west bays of the nave and the west wall with its Norman doorway and twin windows above. Onto this original west front the bell tower was built *c.* 1480, and it is a thrill to pass through the door and gaze up at this marvel of timber construction, with its massive posts, arched braces and cross-beams – a labyrinth of woodwork. There is an alabaster tomb with the effigies of Sir Thomas Smyth and his wife (it was his father who acquired the monastic property in 1540), and there are many ledger stones in the sanctuary. Doorways on the south side must have led to the cloisters and priory buildings. Jericho Priory (alias Blackmore House), with its sash windows and walled gardens, occupies part of the monastic grounds.

Little Coggeshall: early lancet windows dressed with brick

Little Coggeshall Abbey

Nothing remains of the church of the Cistercian abbey, founded by King Stephen *c.* 1140. But the monastic chapel of St Nicolas survives, the *capella ante portas*, now the parish church, standing in a field down a bumpy muddy lane which leads off the road from Feering to Great Coggeshall, in the village signposted COGGESHALL HAMLET. It is a building of utter simplicity, with little lancet windows dressed with brick – a very early instance of the use of brick. Inside, there is a striking east window of the Crucifixion. There are fragments of the monastic buildings incorporated in a 16th-century house nearby; Long Bridge, too, incorporates many medieval monastic bricks.

Little Dunmow Priory

Stane Street runs cross country east to west from Colchester to Braintree and Great Dunmow; between Braintree and Great Dunmow a minor road leads off south to Little Dunmow. And on the edge of the small and scattered village of Little Dunmow there appears an ancient little church, with what appears to be a spiky minaret attached to its N.W. corner. This is all that remains of Little Dunmow Priory, founded for Augustinian Canons in 1106 by Geoffrey Baynard. In its day this was a large cruciform church, with transepts and central tower: what remains is the Lady Chapel, which formed a sumptuous south aisle to the chancel of the monastic church. At the Dissolution (1536) all else was destroyed. The comic little minaret for the bell was added in the restoration of 1872.

What remains is of considerable beauty: on the north side, now walled off, there is an arcade of five bays of *c.* 1200, with shafted columns, carved capitals and moulded arches; this originally led into the chancel. The rest of the chapel is a rebuilding of *c.* 1360 in the Dec style, merging into Perp, with a great east window, and four others on the south side, filled with Dec or Perp tracery and flooding the church with light. The walls between and below are adorned with niches and carved stone panelling, with delightful little figures of animals or saints. There is the tomb of Walter Fitzwalter and his wife, with their alabaster effigies (*c.* 1460), and, among other monuments, one by Thomas Adye of 1753 to Sir James Halley, with a mourning female figure holding a medallion portrait of the deceased (Adye's favourite conceit). And in the sanctuary is the famous Dunmow Flitch chair. According to tradition (of Norman or Breton origin, introduced here by the Fitzwalters) a flitch of bacon was presented to a married couple who, a year and a day after their marriage, could vow that never for one moment had they regretted their marriage (the happy husband was then carried aloft in the chair). It does not appear to have been claimed or presented very often.

Hatfield Broad Oak Priory

A delightful village on the edge of Hatfield Forest, and a grand Perp church with an immense west tower: this was the nave of the Benedictine Priory founded here *c.* 1135 by Aubrey de Vere; the monastic chancel has vanished, and only the 12th-century crossing piers, built into the outside of the east wall, remind us of what has disappeared. The recumbent effigy of Robert de Vere, 3rd Earl of Oxford (d. 1221), occupies the centre of the pre-

Little Dunmow: 14th-century traceried windows set in a wall of stone and flint

Hatfield Broad Oak: the parochial nave, now shorn of its monastic chancel

sent chancel, and the reredos and sanctuary panelling are distinguished early-18th-century work by John Woodward, who worked at Trinity College, Cambridge – to which foundation Henry VIII granted the property here after the Dissolution. There is a magnificent 18th-century brass candelabra, a notable George III Royal Arms and a fine array of 18th-century monuments.

Hatfield Peverel Priory

The heavy traffic on the A12 between Chelmsford and Colchester rushes by along the new dual carriageway, bypassing the village: the Priory stands to the south, on the edge of the parkland which surrounds the 18th-century Priory House. It is the nave of the Benedictine Priory founded

Hatfield Peverel: 16th-century continental glass in the south aisle

here by a Peverel in the 12th century as a cell of St Albans. The west door is Norman, as is the blocked arch of the crossing; this is now the east end of the church. Central tower, chancel, transepts – all have disappeared. North aisle and arcade are Perp, the south aisle of 1873 – but at its east end stands the fascinating fragment of a Tudor brick building which was once the apple store of the prior's house and is now the vestry. After the Dissolution a many-gabled house was built along this south side, of which pictures exist. It was pulled down when the 18th-century Priory House was built, but its great brick garden walls survive. The best thing in the church is the old glass in the south aisle: here two windows are filled with fragments of richly coloured, largely foreign, glass of the 16th or 17th century, ingeniously and sometimes rather oddly pieced together. There are fragments, too, of ancient English glass in the north aisle, with some later heraldic panels.

Tilty Abbey

The Cistercian Abbey was founded in this green valley in 1153: nothing remains save a few fragments of masonry. But nearby, with a handful of cottages for company, stands the monastic chapel of St Mary, the *capella ante portas* of the Abbey, now the parish church. It is a precious relic. The nave is small and simple with E.E. lancets, but at the east end is a much grander chancel, added in the early 14th century, an addition of the greatest beauty, with a magnificent traceried east window and carved niches in the adjoining buttresses. The

nave is stuccoed and yellow-washed, the chancel glistening flintwork. And at the west end of the nave there is a small 18th-century belfry – yellow-washed also – crowned with a white-painted cupola. The interior is brilliantly white, with daylight streaming in through the clear windows, and beautifully furnished with sedilia and piscina, small monuments and important brasses, a hatchment (of the Maynard family) and woodwork bleached by the sunlight. From the churchyard gate there is a view up the valley to Thaxted spire.

At Tilty E. E. lancets in the nave lead to a grander Dec chancel

Waltham Abbey

Although dangerously close to the spreading suburbia of N.E. London, Waltham Abbey remains an Essex town: open countryside and Epping Forest are nearby; a pleasant group of buildings in the market place, and the timbered Welsh Harp Inn, accompany what remains of the great Abbey of Augustinian Canons, which in its time was one of the most important monastic foundations in England. A college of secular canons was established here in 1030. This was rebuilt *c.* 1060 by King Harold, and it was here that he was buried after his defeat at Hastings. It was refounded as an abbey of Augustinian Canons by Henry II in 1177, one of his acts of expiation after Becket's murder, and a vast new church was built east-wards, with central tower, transepts and chancel. The conventual buildings stood to the N., but nothing, or almost nothing, remains of these – and nothing of the 12th- and early-13th-century church. Only the earlier, Norman, nave survives, walled off at the W. end of the crossing. Even this is of considerable magnificence. After the

Tilty crowned with its homely 18th-century cupola

Conquest the Bishops of Durham acquired the manor: the interior of the church bears unmistakable evidence of this connection.

To the N.W. of the church the Abbey gateway survives, with its bridge over the stream, and walking round the exterior it is possible to appreciate the W. tower (built by the parish after the Dissolution) and the 14th-century W. front which the tower partly conceals; the Norman windows and the slightly pointed windows of the clerestory – and then the one remaining pillar of the crossing. This blocked-up W. archway was remodelled by William Burges in 1859. On the S. side is the 14th-century Lady Chapel, standing on an undercroft, built of stone and flint, with its Dec windows and its own stairway leading up to a door at its W. end. This much remains of Waltham Abbey.

The majestic interior makes up for any disappointment: here is a nave of Norman splendour, with enormous round pillars, wide lofty triforium, and clerestory. This nave is of seven bays, and the pillars, carved with chevron or spiral ornament, at

Waltham Abbey: William Burges' east end

The Norman nave of Waltham Abbey is an echo of Durham

once bring Durham to mind: it is a remarkable display of Norman grandeur. The flat Victorian timber ceiling, painted by Sir Edward Poynter, in lozenge shapes with emblems of the signs of the zodiac, brings Peterborough to mind. At the W. end a lame attempt was made in the 14th century to transform Norman into Gothic – but after hacking out one Norman arch the attempt was given up: it nearly brought the whole nave tumbling down. There is a 17th-century pulpit, with suspended sounding board, and the narrow aisles are hung with monuments and hatchments – but it is Burges' E. end which arrests attention. A rose window, a triplet of pointed windows below, richly sculptured carvings and stocky clustered columns, with an ornate reredos below – all this provides an appropriate and successful climax to the nave,

bold, original, and unmistakably Victorian. The reredos is painted and gilded; marble and warmly coloured tiles provide a worthy sanctuary – and the windows are filled with sumptuous glass by Burne-Jones. This E. end is a triumph.

The Lady Chapel provides a perfect foil for all this Norman toughness, all this Victorian assertiveness. Here is a building of 14th-century charm: traceried windows, whitened plastered walls, an 'English' altar with riddells – and, above the altar, the upper half of the bare wall is adorned with a faded but moving mural of the Last Judgement.

As has been said, little remains of the monastic buildings – except, inexplicably, one 12th-century entry into the cloister. Vaulted and impressive, it stands quite by itself, remote and far from the church, in a distant corner of the graveyard.

DIOCESE OF
CHESTER

Chester Cathedral

RED SANDSTONE, black-and-white houses, the city walls, the Rows – Chester is a very individual city. The Welsh border is close, and the River Dee, flowing wide and magnificent, makes a grand sweep along the south edge of the town. There are grand views across the river from the south-east, grand views across the Roodee from the south-west – the Roodee since the 16th century the Chester Racecourse, laid out on what was once the Roman harbour. From here Chester stands apparently compact, protected by its city walls, with houses big and small, the towers and spires of the churches, the tall tower of the Victorian Town Hall, and the Cathedral with its square tower and prominent battlemented pinnacles. It is a great misfortune that several 'tower blocks' have been allowed to rear their ugly heads to disfigure this enchanting prospect.

Chester is a Roman city – the city of Deva – an important Roman town, and the headquarters of

Chester Cathedral: the central tower, chancel and chapter house

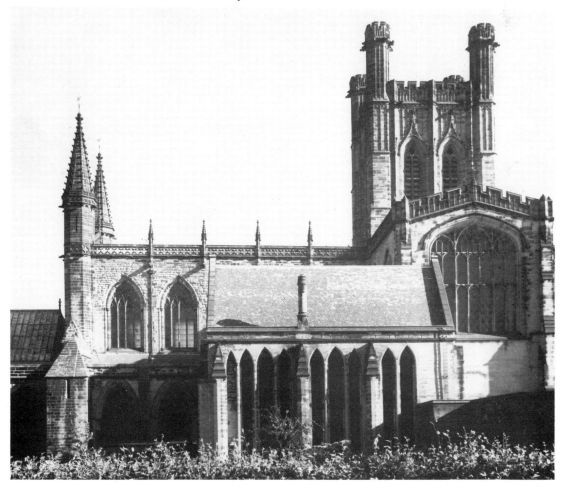

the XXth legion. It was also an important medieval city, and a port until the Dee silted up in the 16th century. It is the only town in England to have preserved its medieval walls complete.

The best thing to do is to enter Chester from the south, across the Dee Bridge (dating from the 14th century), park the car, climb the walls, by the Bridgegate (1791) perhaps, and (if there is time) make a complete circuit of the walls. From them we can survey the city: its streets, its houses great and small, the Castle (in origin medieval, but rebuilt in pure Greek Revival by Thomas Harrison at the end of the 18th century), the towers round the walls – the Water Tower, King Charles' Tower, the Goblin Tower, the Clock Tower over the Eastgate. All are landmarks on the way. From the east walls we get a view of the Cathedral standing quite close to the wall here. And having made the circuit, we can walk up Bridge Street, admiring the wealth of old houses, and the Rows – that upper gallery of shops at first-floor level – to the Cross; from here St Werburgh Street leads up to the Cathedral, standing hemmed in by shopping streets. And St Werburgh Street, with its black-and-white houses, like so many imposing timbered houses all around, is a 19th-century creation by the Chester architect John Douglas, almost as splendid as the 16th-century originals.

Before entering the Cathedral we should walk round the exterior. Beyond the west front, the medieval Abbey Gate leads into Abbey Square, an enclosed precinct of 18th-century houses, and into Abbey Street, narrow and cobbled. From here there is an excellent view of the Cathedral, with the monastic buildings occupying its north side – the refectory, chapter house, and the smaller buildings surrounding the cloisters. We can go through the churchyard, past the Lady Chapel, and round to the south side again. The entire church is built of red sandstone, warm in colour, but friable in texture – and much of the exterior is the result of 19th-century refacing and restoration, by Harrison (c. 1820), Hussey (c. 1840), Scott (c. 1870) and Blomfield (c. 1890). There are lancets in the Lady Chapel, Dec Geometrical windows in the choir and transept aisles, Perp windows in the clerestory; and, again in the nave, Dec windows below, Perp above. The central tower is Perp, but the embattled pinnacles are by Scott. We can enter by the Perp south-west porch.

Chester Abbey was founded in 1092 by Hugh Lupus, Earl of Chester, for Benedictine monks. After the Dissolution in 1540, Henry VIII founded the Diocese of Chester (1542), and the abbey church became the cathedral. Fragments remain of the original Norman building, but what we see as we enter is the result of the rebuilding which began with the Lady Chapel (c. 1280), continued with the choir (c. 1300), the south transept (c. 1340), and finally the nave (1360–1460). At first sight the interior is one of remarkable uniformity: the orderly procession of nave arches with the big clerestory windows above – in place of a triforium there is a stone gallery below the windows – leads on to the lofty arches of the crossing, and on to the choir beyond: the wooden lierne vault is Scott's, and a masterpiece. Scott, as he was inclined to do, removed the stone pulpitum, and substituted the present wooden screen, which repeats the pattern of the canopies of the return stalls behind: at the centre, the corona is filled with a rood designed by Sir Giles Gilbert Scott (1913). Beyond can be seen the tapering canopies of the choir stalls – a feast to come. Before moving on we can see the Norman arches which form the base of the (never completed) N.W. tower – now the Baptistery – and the 17th-century furnishings of the Consistory Court under the (uncompleted) S.W. tower. The mosaics on the north aisle wall are by J.R. Clayton (of Clayton & Bell), 1883–6.

Reaching the crossing, we shall be struck by the enormous south transept, of four bays with east and west aisles, built to accommodate many altars; owing to the close abutment of the monastic buildings, the north transept could not be enlarged. Indeed it is very small, and screened by Scott's open-arched organ gallery and organ (1876): behind this will be seen the Norman arch leading to the Sacristy, and the Norman arcade above; this is the oldest part of the Cathedral (c. 1100).

It is a great thrill to enter the chancel: here is one of the two or three most spectacular sets of medieval choir stalls in England, comparable with those at Carlisle, Ripon and Lincoln. They date from the late 14th century, and display a gorgeous wealth of carved canopies, elbow rests and misericords (to these the Cathedral publishes a special guidebook, with full details and plans). The Bishop's throne is by Scott, and the mosaic reredos by Salviati (1876); the lectern is early 17th century, the pair of bronze standard candlesticks late 16th century Italian; the sanctuary is paved with marble and mosaic by J. R. Clayton. Beyond the High

Chester Cathedral: the nave with a distant glimpse of the choir and its stalls

A detail from the Chester choir stalls

St Werburgh's Shrine in the Lady Chapel

Altar there is a glimpse of the E.E. Lady Chapel with its lancet windows and rib vault.

We can make our way here through St Werburgh's Chapel in the north choir aisle – a Perp addition, with stained glass by O'Connor (1857) – and admire the Lady Chapel in detail: there is excellent glass by Wailes (1859); and what remains of St Werburgh's Shrine stands at the west end – restored and pieced together in the late 19th century. Returning through the north choir aisle we can note the late-16th-century Spanish iron gates here and at the entrance to the south choir aisle. This is the Chapel of St Erasmus (set apart for private prayer), with its eastern apse by Scott.

The monastic buildings are among the most complete and extensive in England. A door in the north aisle leads into the cloisters – originally of Norman date, but much rebuilt in the 13th century (east side), and again extensively in the early 16th. On the east side, the chapter house vestibule, with its simple shafted 13th-century vaulting, is a building of the greatest charm, and leads into the chapter house itself, with its wonderful rib vaulting and lancets – perhaps the most distinguished part of the whole cathedral. Above the Abbot's Passage

The cloister garden at Chester

(S.W. corner of the cloister) is the Chapel of St Anselm, which was originally the chapel of the Abbot's Lodging. It was refurnished by Bishop Bridgeman in the early 17th century, with handsome screen and altar rails and stucco ceiling: a delightful chapel, easily missed. On the north side stands the Refectory, a building of great splendour (late 13th–early 14th century), with its projecting triangular pulpit in the south wall. The Cloister Garth is charmingly laid out as a garden, with sunken pond and fountain – and seats set out, for us to sit and gaze up at the great church presiding over all this wealth of attendant buildings.

Chester, with its unusually complete monastic parts, its magnificent chancel furnishings, its intimate devotional atmosphere, and its setting in a secluded precinct in a medieval walled city, is at once enchanting and rewarding.

Cranes poised menacingly over the ancient monastic church at Birkenhead

Birkenhead Priory

Birkenhead Priory must now be as odd in its setting as any monastic church in England: it stands right up against the shipyard, with a dry dock just over the fence and giant cranes poised menacingly nearby.

The Priory was founded *c.* 1150 by Hamo de Masci for Benedictine monks: it was then in an isolated position on the south bank of the Mersey, with uninterrupted views across the river; the monks had the right to ferry travellers across, and ran a guesthouse for them. Trade boomed. There was a grand 13th-century cruciform church, and the monastic buildings stood round the Cloister Court on the north side. The foundations or walls of some of these survive, but those of the church are lost for ever in the adjacent dry dock.

A building which stands intact is the Norman chapter house – the oldest part of the Priory – which has been in use as the parish church since the Dissolution. It is a chapel of the very greatest charm, with a quadripartite vault rising from clustered columns in the walls. There is one original Norman window: the east and north windows are Perp insertions, and the former is filled with Comper glass (1921).

The unwary may at first be confused by the ruins of the church standing at the east end of the churchyard. This was in fact built in 1819–21 (and designed by Rickman) to serve the growing population which was now overflowing the small chapel. With the gradual departure of almost all the local population this has been made a 'preserved ruin', the spire surviving as a landmark. The Chapter House Chapel is in full use, as it has been since 1150.

Chichester Cathedral

CHICHESTER IS the only ancient English cathedral which can be seen from the sea – from Selsey Bill, from Chichester Harbour, from Bosham, the spire is visible, a tall slender finger pointing to Heaven. And descending the Downs from the north, along the road from Midhurst, or from Petworth, or from the slopes above Goodwood, there is the spire piercing the sky – the sea itself the horizon.

It is always a pleasure to be in Chichester: few cathedral cities are so intimate, few so well preserved. The centre of the city is the Market Cross, built by Bishop Story in 1501. It is rewarding to walk down East Street or South Street (and explore the little streets behind); North Street is the best of all, and leads to the Ship Hotel (with its wonderful staircase), the Festival Theatre, and the City Walls. And in West Street is the Cathedral.

It stands in the very heart of the town. From the Cross we can stand and absorb the building – the splendid 'build-up' of long low Lady Chapel, chancel, transepts, crossing, with the tower and spire rising as a great tapering climax over all; and then the eye is carried on to the long line of the nave, to one of low western towers, and so to the Bell Tower, standing on its own closer to the street.

The see of Chichester was founded in 1075 – transferred by the Normans from Selsey, where the original cathedral, founded by St Wilfrid, was submerged by the sea: its bells, it is said, are still heard at high tide under the ocean. It is a cathedral of the 'old foundation' (so called), meaning that it was never monastic: a Dean and secular canons presided, as they do now. Building began towards the end of the 11th century under Bishop Ralph de Luffa, and much of the building we see was completed by 1123. A fire in 1187 destroyed the timber roof, and severely damaged the east end:

in the reconstruction, a new clerestory and stone vault were introduced, and the former apsidal east end was replaced by the present retrochoir, which is a particularly distinguished example of the Transitional style. In the 13th century chapels were added to the nave, forming outer aisles, and the central tower built, to be crowned with a spire in the early 15th – although, as we shall see, the present tower and spire were re-built by Sir Gilbert Scott after the great fall of 1861. The Bell Tower was erected in the 15th century, to relieve the central tower of the weight of the bells when the spire was built. From the outside Chichester appears all Gothic: inside, however, it is a Norman church, and a church of such simple primitive beauty as only a Norman church can be. There is the hint of the E.E. in the clerestory and in the vault, there are the triple lancets above the High Altar – but, otherwise, a Norman church it is, all glistening white, relieved only here and there by single shafts of Purbeck marble. And then, through the open arches of the screen, we are hit by the radiant glow of John Piper's tapestry behind the high altar: brilliant reds and blues and greens and gold provide a feast of warmth and colour – ever more compelling as we move into the chancel, wonderfully thrilling as we stand at a distance here.

And there is another thrilling feature of this nave: the Arundel screen. Erected by Bishop Arundel in the 15th century, removed in 1860, when the new passion for 'open vistas' was at its height, and replaced by a wooden screen of little merit, it was mercifully stored in the base of the campanile and re-erected in 1960 as a memorial to Bishop Bell. It is in any case of great beauty: to re-erect it was a stroke of genius. With its open arches it separates nave and chancel, but it does not divide; it gives a sense of awe and mystery to choir and sanctuary, and that sense of awe and

Chichester Cathedral: Sir George Gilbert Scott's spire. The fall of its predecessor in 1861 was perhaps the inspiration of John Meade Falkner's Nebuly Coat

mystery extend into the nave: it unites the church.

As we move into the crossing we can reflect on the disaster of 1861, when after rumbling and shaking for several days, and in accordance with ancient prophecies long quoted by the superstitious, the spire collapsed 'as one tube of a telescope slides into another'. In the Library of Lancing College there is a fascinating photograph of the crossing, filled with the rubble of the entire spire, a gaping hole above. It was speedily and successfully rebuilt, and completed in 1866. It is extraordinary how so much of the 14th-century choir stalls survived; their misericords are worth inspecting. Here it is possible to stand and absorb John Piper's tapestry, with its gorgeous wealth of colour and deeply religious symbolism. The subject is the Trinity, 'represented' – in Mr Piper's own words – 'by an equilateral triangle among flames, and, related to this, symbols of the Father (a white light), the Son (a Tau cross), and the Holy Spirit (a flaming wing)'. On either side are symbols of the Elements and the Evangelists. It was woven at Felletin, near Aubusson, and installed in 1966.

The retrochoir was built at the very end of the 12th century: its Transitional style, with Purbeck marble pillars and clustered shafts, its carved capitals and sculptured spandrels in the triforium, its combination of round and pointed arches, fulfils the earlier, simpler Norman of nave and chancel. Here in front of Bishop Sherborne's screen (early

The Lady Chapel at Chichester

Chichester: Detail of Bishop Sherborne's tomb (1536)

16th century) is the simple but moving altar shrine of St Richard, Bishop of Chichester 1245–1253. And to the east end is the long low Lady Chapel, with its wide Dec windows filling every bay (the glass by Clayton & Bell, 1870), and one bay of the vault decorated by Lambert Barnard, recalling his similar work at Boxgrove (q.v.) (early 16th century). Nearby is St Mary Magdalene's Chapel, refurnished in 1961, with its altar by Robert Potter, candlesticks and altar rail by Geoffrey Clarke, and altarpiece by Graham Sutherland – depicting Mary Magdalene meeting Our Lord after the Resurrection, and mistaking Him for the gardener. In the north aisle is Chagall's window (1978), which with its flaming reds and other brilliant colours represents the glory offered to God by all creation (Psalm 150). Tribute must here be paid to Dean Hussey (Dean 1955–75), himself a great patron of the arts, to whom is due the work of so many distinguished modern artists which is to be seen at Chichester.

In the south aisle are outstanding Romanesque sculptures (*c.* 1125) depicting the Raising of Lazarus, and Christ being greeted at Bethany by Mary and Martha; nearby, in a recess, is the spectacular tomb of Bishop Sherborne (d. 1536), with his vested figure, gilded crozier and mitre, and angels above supporting his arms. And throughout the Cathedral there are many other tombs and monuments: in the nave is the tomb of Richard

FitzAlan, Earl of Arundel (d. 1376), showing his hand extended to hold his wife's; there are many tablets of the 18th century (or later), including one (in the north aisle) to William Huskisson (M.P. for Chichester), who had the sad distinction of being the first person to be killed by a train (1830): all the same, he wears Roman dress. In the north transept are memorials to Thomas Weelkes and Gustav Holst; in the south one to C. E. Kempe: there is glass by him in the Cathedral, notably that in the east window.

The cloisters are a special pleasure – and an unexpected one, as the Cathedral was not monastic; they are also in an unexpected position, embracing the south transept, and arranged like a somewhat deformed square, enclosing a green court called Paradise. They were built *c.* 1400, and are broad and spacious, with wide Perp windows and simple open wooden barrel roof – a covered way leading to St Richard's Walk, which passes between high walls into Canon Lane. In this secluded street stand the canons' houses, and the Deanery (1725), a grand early Georgian house of restrained baroque character. A gatehouse at one end leads into South Street – another at the other is the entrance to the Bishop's Palace. Here the bishops have lived since earliest times, and much of the house is medieval or Tudor, though Georgian sash windows overlook the spreading lawns of the garden front. The garden is private, but the view across the lawns, with the house in the foreground, the Cathedral behind, is often photographed or painted. It is a view which for its splendour and tranquillity is unforgettable, and unmatched.

Boxgrove Priory

Boxgrove – the grove of box trees. Where the South Downs slope gently down to the level lands round Chichester stands Boxgrove Priory, the chancel, crossing and abbreviated nave of one of the most evocative and intimate monastic churches anywhere in England. The village is but a stone's throw from the A27, but it is a world apart. The quiet village street leads off the busy road, to the church, and on to Halnaker (pronounced Hann-acre), the medieval manor house, and to Goodwood, the 18th-century mansion of the Dukes of Richmond.

Boxgrove: the rump of the nave and the central tower

Boxgrove Priory was founded *c.* 1115 by Roger de la Haye of Halnaker, as an offshoot of the Benedictine abbey of Lessay in Normandy, with which he had close family connections. The nave (mostly in ruins), the transepts and the crossing with its low central tower date from these earlier years: the long chancel is a rebuilding of *c.* 1220. The setting is perfect: a churchyard of old tombs and headstones, a medley of trees, mown grass, the Downs in the background. The exterior of the church is perfect, too, with its walls of stone and flint, its roof of warm red tiles, the loftier chancel upheld by flying buttresses. At the west end are the fragmentary ruins of the nave: a low Transitional arch or two, the arcade blocked on the north side where the cloisters abutted, the low Norman arched entrance to the chapter house, still standing attached to the north transept; and, to the north, the tall, gaunt, gabled ruin of the guest house.

The south door leads into the two surviving bays of the nave – to the pulpitum on the left, with its two doorways into the parochial nave now blocked, and the space above walled up to form the west wall of the truncated church. This crossing is spacious: in the north transept there are two or three handsome monuments of the 18th century – to Sir William Morley (1728) with his marble urn on a bold plinth, and his daughter Mary, Countess of Derby (1752) adjacent – later owners of Halnaker; the south transept is the Chapel of St Blaise, with a figure of the saint by Professor Tristram in the niche above the altar. To the east is the monastic choir, now nave and choir of the parish church.

This is a building of singular beauty and charm.

There are eight bays of low E.E. pointed arches, under wide round arches, each pierced with a quatrefoil, a clerestory above with narrow lancets, serving also as triforium, and above that the vault, prettily painted in the early 16th century with tendrils of trees and flowers encircling shields of arms. This design of double bays is to be found elsewhere only in the sanctuary of Portsmouth Cathedral (q.v.) – though imitated by Sir Gilbert Scott in 1880 at his church of St Paul in Spalding – and is of special interest. The first two bays have octagonal piers and Purbeck marble capitals; the next two round Purbeck piers; and, in the sanctuary, clustered Purbeck shafts surrounding the central pier. Slender Purbeck shafts adorn the clerestory, and the triple lancets at the east end; this east window is filled with richly coloured glass by O'Connor, and beneath is a sumptuous reredos by Sir Gilbert Scott, to which the handsome baroque altar ornaments provide a splendid foil.

In the third bay on the south side stands the Chantry of Thomas, 9th Lord de la Warre of Halnaker (d. 1554), whose wife, Elizabeth Bonville, was a descendant of the founder. Built of white stone, it is a gorgeous little oratory, part Gothic, part Renaissance: intricately carved columns support an elaborately vaulted roof, with richly coloured weighty pendants – and a richly decorated canopy where Gothic angels alternate with Renaissance cherubs in displaying shields of arms. There is no tomb within, no altar – only a crucifix to adorn the reredos; the Dissolution had occurred before Lord de la Warre's death, and he is buried elsewhere. But it was he who employed Lambert Barnard to paint the vault with the flowers and foliage and coats of arms.

Boxgrove: E. E. architecture at its purest

The aisles are low and vaulted: around the walls, here and elsewhere, are many early marble tombs; there are Dec traceried windows filled with good Victorian glass, and the chapels at the east end are simply but effectively furnished. Boxgrove is numinous – a church to pray and worship in. Few monastic churches are so redolent of the simple, austere but cheerful atmosphere of the Benedictines.

DIOCESE OF
COVENTRY

Coventry Cathedral

COVENTRY IS an ancient city: Sir William Reid Dick's equestrian statue (1949) of Lady Godiva in Broadgate reminds us of this almost legendary figure, who with her husband Earl Leofric founded the Benedictine Priory here in 1043. From 1102 until 1228 Coventry was a bishopric; from then until the Reformation the see, united to Lichfield, was known as Coventry and Lichfield, and from then until 1846 as Lichfield and Coventry. In 1918 the new see was created, and the parish church of St Michael became the cathedral. Coventry prospered in the Middle Ages on wool and cloth; the Industrial Revolution of the 19th century led to the manufacture of bicycles and motor cars. Medieval buildings still survive in Coventry – St Mary's Hall, Ford's Hospital, Holy Trinity Church, the spire of the Grey Friars (Christ Church), St John's Church – together with a few distinguished 18th-century houses. But much of the city was flattened in the air raid of 14 November 1940, in which St Michael's was completely burnt out. But the spire survived, a symbol of Coventry.

A competition for the rebuilding of the Cathedral was held in 1951, and was won by Sir Basil Spence. It was his idea to preserve the ruins of the old church, and to use the shell as a paved open forecourt leading to the new Cathedral. At one end of this forecourt is the apse, at the other the spire – of ethereal height (300 ft), the perfection of late Gothic architecture: a lofty slim tower, a little octagon, and then the spire, supported by flying buttresses. It was begun *c.* 1371, and completed *c.* 1430: the rebuilding of the 13th-century church followed forthwith, but was not completed till the early 16th century. It is from the N.E. angle of the old N. aisle that steps descend to the W. front (in reality S.) of the new church, to be joined by a flight of steps up from the street. Work began

on the new building in 1956: the Cathedral was consecrated in 1962.

The new Cathedral stands like a great formation of pink rock with jagged sculptured sides – jagged because, rising the full height of the building, the side windows are angled in 'saw-tooth' fashion; nearer the 'W.' end is the enormous bow-fronted window of the Baptistery; and between that and the porch Epstein's bronze figure of St Michael trampling Lucifer. A porch with long slender columns supporting an oddly shaped canopy – for the new Cathedral makes no concessions to the style of the medieval building – leads to the great glass screen, adorned with the engraved figures of angels and saints (by John Hutton), which forms the 'W.' wall and the principal entrance. Through this can be seen the interior of the Cathedral – the gaping Perp windows of the old building perhaps reflected in the glass.

The first sight of the interior is unforgettable: the building is not large (270 ft in length), but the architect has somehow contrived to make it seem so. This great cavernous interior has the 'feel' of a medieval church, a great 'hall church', Gothic in atmosphere if not in detail. The long thin tapering columns upholding a wide shallow vault, the ascent to the altar, the dim religious light shining through the richly coloured glass of the 'eastward'-facing angular windows, the glimpse of organ pipes at the end of the aisle – and Graham Sutherland's vast tapestry at the 'E.' end – all greens and golds and reds and browns – make this interior moving and numinous. Light from the long windows in the Lady Chapel illuminate the dominating figure of Christ in the tapestry: it is His commanding presence that fills the church, His seated figure, with hands raised in blessing, that speaks to the worshipper and stray visitor alike: everything in the church leads to this figure – the font at the 'W.'

Coventry Cathedral: the 15th-century spire and the ruined apsidal east end

Coventry: Epstein's figure of St Michael trampling Lucifer

Coventry: the great glass screen with an angel by John Hutton; in the background is the ruined medieval choir

end, the pulpit, the altar, the biblical texts carved in bold lettering by Ralph Beyer on the splays of the angular windows – 'Come unto Me all ye that are heavy laden . . .', 'Take My yoke upon you . . .'; stirring words from the evangelists whose symbols surround the seated figure in the tapestry. It is only when returning from the altar to his seat that the communicant sees the gorgeously rich stained glass in these 'saw-tooth' side windows – glass by Geoffrey Clarke, Laurence Lee and Keith New. At the 'W.' end the font, an enormous boulder from Bethlehem, stands under the immense bow-fronted window filled with glass by John Piper: here dark reds and purples and blues lead to the centre of things – the burst of light which is Christ.

There are details in this absorbing building which may seem irritating or quirky. The canopies of the choir stalls, for instance, intended to resemble stars, look from a distance like a row of hat-stands; the Chapel of Christ the Servant, and the Chapel of Unity, for all their resourcefulness, may not seem places to pray in: even the Chapel of Gethsemane, with Steven Sykes' figure of the Angel of Gethsemane in mosaic, and Basil Spence's interpretation of the crown of thorns in wrought iron, may seem distracting. It is a pity that a cathedral with so strong a devotional appeal has no really workaday (or more conventional) chapel in which to pray.

Again, opinions may differ about the stark functional exterior: it is the interior which is powerful and timeless. And at night it is thrilling to gaze into the interior through John Hutton's glass screen, to see the candles lit and to hear the choir sing – while the fever of life surges on outside.

Coventry: the choir stalls against the chancel windows

Atherstone Priory

The Watling Street (A5), the River Anker, the Leicestershire border: Atherstone is an ancient town, with many 18th-century houses, somewhat industrialized, somewhat suburbanized. At the N. end of the Market Place stands the parish church, of which the chancel, tower and transepts formed

Atherstone: the narrow arches of the crossing lead into the former monastic choir

part of a priory of Austin Friars, founded here in 1375 by Ralph Lord Basset. The nave is a rebuilding by T. H. Wyatt and David Brandon of 1849 – but the narrow central tower with its octagonal top adorned with small rose windows, embattled and pinnacled, and the spacious chancel, are Perp, and there is a Norman N. doorway which tells of an earlier church built before the arrival of the Friars. Inside, the wide early Victorian nave is spacious but a trifle bleak; the narrow arches of the crossing lead into a chancel with big Perp windows filled with Kempe glass. At the E. end of the church is a handsome Georgian house, and a narrow passage leads through into a new housing estate. But across the suburban gardens, built into the walls of this house, there is a glimpse of blocked-up medieval windows, the solitary surviving relic of the Friars' monastic buildings.

Monks Kirby Priory

It is quite an experience to come upon the enormous Dec red sandstone tower of this former monastic church, suddenly and unexpectedly in the leafy lanes of this small village. The Priory was founded in 1077 for Benedictines of St Nicholas at Angers; there is a grand Dec porch, and the chancel is E.E. – but the dominant feature of the interior is the spacious nave whose soaring Perp

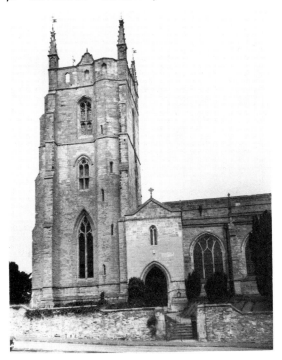

Monks Kirby

arches divide nave from aisle. There is an array of tombs and monuments to the Feildings, Earls of Denbigh, of nearby Newnham Paddox, from Sir William Feilding (d. 1574) in the N.E. Chapel to Victorian and later Denbigh memorials in the nave. The Victorian brass altar rails have fascinating angel heads on the extensions, and there is excellent jewel-like Victorian glass by Hardman – but it is the monastic size and splendour of the church which will impress most, though only the N. windows, placed high in the wall, betray the existence of former cloisters. No monastic buildings survive – and the parapet and pinnacles of the tower are early-18th-century Gothic, built after the fall of the spire in 1701.

Nuneaton Abbey

It was the nuns that gave Nuneaton its name: the Benedictine Abbey here, a daughter house of Fontevrault (see Amesbury), was founded *c.* 1155. After the Dissolution most of the church was destroyed, and the priory buildings, granted to Sir Marmaduke Constable of Flamborough (Yorkshire), were converted into a house. In the 18th century all this decayed, but in the 19th century

rebuilding of the church began – the nave by Clapton Rolfe (1877), the chancel and north transept by Sir Harold Brakspear (1906 and 1930) – to form a new parish church for the growing town. The remarkable crossing piers, the new chancel, screen and High Altar, are powerful and eloquent.

Wroxall Abbey

A long avenue leads to a startling High Victorian mansion, built of flaming red brick for James Dugdale in 1866, by the Liverpool architect Walter Scott. At its feet stands a small medieval church, with a 17th-century brick tower. This is all that remains of Wroxall Abbey, founded *c.* 1141 for Benedictine nuns, and is in fact the N. choir aisle of the nuns' church, built in the early 14th century. At the Suppression this survived as the parish church, and it is filled with a remarkable series of stained glass windows, mostly of the 14th century, but some dating from the 15th. There are also 18th-century monuments to descendants of Sir Christopher Wren, who bought the estate in 1713 (*aet.* 82), in order to establish a country seat for his family. He never lived here himself, though he is reputed to have designed the serpentine wall in the walled garden. There are a few fragments of monastic buildings to the S. of the church. The house is now a girls' school, and the church is used as their chapel.

Wroxall: the surviving fragment of the nuns' church

DIOCESE OF
DERBY

Derby Cathedral

DERBY HAS IN RECENT YEARS been cut wide open by new roads: dual carriageways, underpasses, flyovers have torn apart the entire eastern half of the city; the roads converge, cross the River Derwent by a new bridge, and then drive through the very heart of the town in a deep cutting. It is almost inconceivable that a great and ancient city should be murdered in this way. But across this vast and terrible wasteland one landmark survives from the past: the noble tower of All Saints' Church, now the Cathedral. It stands 178 ft high, 50 ft square at its base, and 40 ft square at its summit, and with Boston Stump in Lincolnshire is the most magnificent medieval parish church tower in England.

In the Middle Ages All Saints' was a collegiate church: secular canons lived here as a college, and the name survives in College Place, which adjoins the Cathedral. At the Dissolution the collegiate foundations, as well as the monastic, were dissolved: the medieval church survived as a parish church until 1723, when the autocratic incumbent, Dr Hutchinson, determined to build a grand classical church in its place. Almost overnight the old church was demolished and James Gibbs was engaged to build its successor, attached to the splendid tower which had been begun in 1511. The Diocese of Derby was founded in 1927, and All Saints' became the Cathedral – to be enlarged in 1972 by the addition of a new east end, designed in strict harmony by Sebastian Comper.

From the Market Place Irongate leads up to the Cathedral – a gentle slope, a gentle curve, with the tower dominating the houses of the street: stand here and absorb its splendour. Or walk down St Mary's Gate, the narrow street opposite the west door, and admire its details – its richly panelled, richly carved lower stages, its enormous traceried windows higher up, its elaborate parapet and tapering pinnacles; then approach the church which James Gibbs attached to this Tudor tower.

The tower of Derby Cathedral seen from St Mary's Gate

It is exceedingly handsome – one of the most distinguished 18th-century town churches in the country. Francis Smith of Warwick was the contractor, and the church was completed and opened for worship in 1725. To walk round the outside is a pleasure: the architect's command of classical details – bold Doric pilasters, grand round-headed windows with rusticated surrounds, the balustraded parapet, the superb masonry – cannot but impress. To enter the church is a thrill. The windows, filled with clear glass, flood the whole inside with light. This wide spacious interior with

Derby Cathedral: Robert Bakewell's screen and Bess of Hardwick's tomb

its Doric arcades and wide plaster vault bears a distinct family resemblance to St Martin-in-the-Fields (completed in 1726). Robert Bakewell's wrought iron screen (which divides nave from chancel) extends across the whole width of the church: its delicate gates, surmounted by the Royal Arms, lead into the choir, to Sebastian Comper's baldacchino, and to his new apsidal sanctuary beyond.

It is to Sebastian Comper that we owe not only the new sanctuary and baldacchino, but the redecoration of the entire building – glistening white, its details picked out in brilliant gold. The wide panels of the vault are painted a subtle greyish purple; above the gilded capitals the architraves are terracotta; Bakewell's lacelike screen is delicately gilded; the baldacchino is brilliant white and gold; stalls line the apse, and the small organ above recalls a baroque church in Bavaria.

And there are many monuments of interest: two take us back to the medieval church – the incised slab to John Lawe, Sub-Dean of the collegiate church (d. *c.* 1430), and the wooden effigy of an unknown priest, no doubt a secular canon of the church (14th century). But pride of place goes to the sumptuous tomb of Bess of Hardwick in the Cavendish Chapel. The daughter of John Hardwick of Hardwick, wife in turn of Robert Barlow, Sir William Cavendish, Sir William St Loe and the 6th Earl of Shrewsbury, she amassed through these marriages an enormous fortune, and built vast houses at Chatsworth and Hardwick, as well as several smaller ones. She died in 1608, and here her effigy lies on a tomb she had erected herself, under a canopy crowned with obelisks and shields of arms, and with a long inscription extolling her achievements. Nearby is Rysbrack's magnificent monument to Caroline, Countess of Bessborough (d. 1760), daughter of the 3rd Duke of Devonshire (who was great great great grandson of Bess) – with her husband, the 2nd Earl of Bessborough (d. 1793) by Nollekens, next to it. Sir William Wheler, 1st Bt., M.P., has a most decorative monument in the N. aisle, with shields of arms strung nonchalantly on ribbons on either side (1666); and there are a number of smaller monuments to the Batemans of Hartington, culminating in Chantrey's to Richard Bateman (1821). And there are many others, to leading citizens and local gentry.

Of touching interest is the tablet in the south aisle, erected in 1945, to commemorate the bicentenary of the arrival in Derby of that tragic figure, Prince Charles Edward, with his Highland army. This was Derby's great historic moment: the Young Pretender reached the town on December 4th, held a council of war all through the 5th, and retreated on the 6th, having (it is said) first heard Mass in All Saints'.

Beauchief Abbey

Beauchief Abbey – pronounced Beechif – is lost in the outer suburbia of Sheffield, and hard to find. But the determined seeker who follows the somewhat inconsequential signposts off the ring road on the southern outskirts (the B6054 which runs between the A625, the A61 and the A616) will discover it all right, surrounded by residential roads on the N. and E. Yet on the S. and W. all is rural: the park of Beauchief Hall and the golf course provide a setting to recall its ancient seclusion when Beauchief was founded as a Premonstratensian abbey *c.* 1175. Little survives of the

Beauchief: the rump of the west tower

monastic church – except the west tower, which stands enormous, square and squat, crowned by a low pyramid roof, all that remains, it seems, of a much taller tower. There is an E.E. doorway (somewhat mutilated), and, above that, a large west window, now filled with 17th-century tracery; and attached to the east side of the tower is a small nave or chancel, built into the original crossing arch, which is clearly visible above the present roof. There are a few monastic foundations on the south side.

The interior is a tremendous pleasure. After the Dissolution, it seems, most of the church was destroyed, and the lands passed into the hands of the Strelley family, whose heiress in the 17th century married Edward Pegge of Ashbourne. It was he who built Beauchief Hall in 1671 (it still stands up the long drive to the west of the church) and rebuilt the church. To enter it is to enter the squire's chapel: it is a lofty little building, its walls washed a deep orange yellow, and it is all filled with its original 17th-century fittings – high box pews, their panels or finials adorned with coats of arms, a somewhat grander squire's pew, a three-decker pulpit, 17th-century altar and font, and a charming little psalm board, complete with hooks on which to hang the numbers. There is one hatchment, and several monuments recall the

Pegges or Pegge-Burnells (as they became on succeeding to the property at Winkburn in Notts). The family remained in possession until 1923.

If the church is locked, the key may be obtained at the cottage by the churchyard gate.

Dale Abbey

Despite the proximity of Ilkeston, Stanton-by-Dale and Derby itself, Dale Abbey is a remote and secluded spot, with the east end of the ruined church standing in a grassy field, and a small museum in what remains of the chapter house nearby. But the Infirmary Chapel is still in regular use as a parish church, and well worth a visit from those who delight in the unexpected and the odd. Half church, half house, half stone, half timber, it is all that remains in use of the Premonstratensian Abbey founded here in 1197, in succession to a small Augustinian priory which had been established here fifty years before. There is a late-12th-century north door, and the windows are either 14th-century Perp or 17th-century domestic. All this is charming: but the interior is the thing. It is

all arranged as it was in 1634, the date of the pulpit which stands with its accompanying reading desk and clerk's pew behind the little altar. The altar itself is a 17th-century table, with cupboards built in below in the 18th century for the storing of the sacred vessels. The whole chapel is a sea of box pews extending into the south aisle and overflowing into the little gallery at the west end. It is all a rare and delightful survival.

After the Dissolution the monastic property came into the hands of the Stanhope family, and there is a tablet on the north wall to 'The Rt. Hon. Philip Henry, Earl Stanhope of Chevening in Kent, Lord of this manor and Lay Bishop of this church, died March 2nd, 1855. Erected by Parishioners.' There are also traces of medieval wall paintings (e.g. the Visitation on the north wall, with the Virgin embracing St Elizabeth), which were restored by Professor Tristram in 1931. And carved out of the cliff in the sandy hillside is the Hermit's Cave, made here, according to the old story, by a pious Derby baker, who in the 12th century, following a vision of the Virgin, gave up all his possessions and retired to this cave. Thus was this holy place first set apart.

Dale Abbey: the interior is the thing

DIOCESE OF
DURHAM

Durham Cathedral

COUNTY DURHAM IS UNIQUE among English counties. From the Conquest until 1832 it was a county palatine, ruled by its Prince Bishops, who enacted their own laws, levied their own taxes, minted their own money and raised their own army. County Durham has thus always been proud and detached – as well as geographically remote from London and the south of England. Its independence explains much of what we see in Durham itself.

The view of Durham from the train is one of the most breathtaking and unforgettable in the world. The railway, raised on its viaduct, commands a prospect of cathedral, castle, city, unequalled anywhere. A few seconds later it is gone – but the impression made is deep and lasting. At Durham, cathedral and castle are indivisible: the cathedral held the throne of the Prince Bishop: the castle was his palace. No cathedral in England, not Canterbury, not York, is so domineering.

For the traveller by road there are wonderful first views too: approaching Durham from the

Durham Cathedral: a grand chevron-ornamented pillar in the nave, the crossing, and later vaulting in the chancel beyond

motorway (A1M), the A690 descends into the city from the N.E.; after passing the roundabout in Gilesgate there is a grand panorama of cathedral and castle above the River Wear. Approaching by the old Great North Road (A167), and forking right at the Cock o' the North, the towers of the Cathedral soon appear above the trees and houses of Church Street. But best of all is to fork left at the traffic lights before entering Church Street, look out carefully for the secret tree-laden approach to Pimlico and South Street on the right (just beyond the gate and lodge that lead to Prebends' Bridge), and enter the city there. After a few hundred yards the Cathedral comes in sight, at first half screened by the trees above the river bank, then revealed in all its glory above the deep ravine of the River Wear. And the traveller by train can find his way here too, on foot from the station.

Here the visitor will wish to stand and stare – at the three tremendous towers, at the Galilee Chapel at the west end, at the monastic buildings and houses of the College to the S., at the castle and attendant buildings to the N., all poised above the precipitous river bank. It was here that the body of St Cuthbert (d. 687) was finally laid to rest in 997: in 999 the first stone church was built here, to be replaced by the present cathedral which was begun in 1093, to serve as both cathedral and abbey church for the Benedictines.

Durham Cathedral is the greatest and grandest Norman church in England: it was completed in 1133, only the Galilee Chapel at the west end (*c.* 1170), the eastern transept, or Chapel of the Nine Altars (*c.* 1240), and the central tower (*c.* 1465, the upper stage *c.* 1490) being later additions. We enter by the north-west door (with the replica of its 12th-century knocker – the original in the Treasury) to receive the first impact of the Norman nave. The great piers of the arcade, alternately round or compound, patterned or plain, the triforium above with its own arcaded openings, the clerestory above that with its windows set in deeply arched recesses, each section of the nave divided from the next by its transverse arch, the whole vaulted with the earliest rib vault in Europe – the impact is tremendous. The eye is carried on and up, past the crossing, through to the chancel, and so to the delicate Gothic of the east end – the enormous rose window, the inspired creation

ABOVE *the nave arcades crowned with the earliest rib vault in England;* BELOW *Bishop Cosin's font cover (1663)*

OPPOSITE *Durham Cathedral: the west front and Galilee Chapel across the tree-hung banks of the River Wear*

The Galilee Chapel at Durham

(somewhat unexpectedly) of James Wyatt at the end of the 18th century.

At the W. end of the nave stands Bishop Cosin's marble font (1663) under its towering canopy: Cosin became bishop at the Restoration, and was the beautifier and restorer of the diocese, introducing in many churches superb woodwork, part medieval, part Renaissance in its detail, unique in England. Against the S. wall of the S. aisle has been re-erected the front of the 1683 organ case, which originally stood on the chancel screen, removed in 1846. Moving east, stand under the tower, and see where the later Perp work meets the earlier, simpler, Norman arches which form the base of the tower. In the S. transept is an exotic and wonderful clock, originally erected in the 16th century, remodelled in the 17th, banished in the 19th, and reinstated in the 20th. Standing on marbled shafts, the great clock face, painted and gilded, is crowned by an open dome, supported by

elaborate pinnacles. Below, the panels are painted with the interiors of a Dutch-like church. It is delightful, theatrical. Gilbert Scott's marble pulpit and screen are more earnest and sober: the screen, in Florentine Gothic, proves a remarkably successful counterfoil to the Norman austerity of its setting, and a dignified entrance to the choir.

This is splendidly, richly furnished: against the pale background of the Norman arcades, Cosin's dark oak stalls stand out in magnificent splendour; further east is the painted and gilded tomb of Bishop Hatfield (d. 1333), the effigy of the bishop under the arch below, the episcopal throne above, surmounted by a pinnacled arcade and canopy, a unique arrangement, providing the prince bishops with the loftiest throne in Christendom. Even the Pope in Rome can do no better. A 17th-century staircase and gallery complete it. The easternmost bay of the sanctuary is E.E. – part of the reconstruction of the east end in the 13th century. The reredos behind the high altar is called the Neville screen, given by John Lord Neville *c.* 1380. Even denuded of its statues, it is of great beauty and elegance. Behind and above hangs Comper's gaily painted tester over St Cuthbert's shrine, which is immediately behind the High Altar. The Chapel of the Nine Altars provides a remarkable Gothic climax to the Norman church, with long narrow lancet windows, tall shafts of Frosterley marble and Gothic arcading replacing rugged columns and small round-headed windows; the floor is almost six feet lower than the chancel, providing extra height. And on the raised feretory, surrounded by an oak screen, is the tomb of St Cuthbert, a simple stone slab on the site of the medieval shrine which was destroyed at the Reformation.

Durham is unique in having no west front as such, no grand west door: there is no room for this, sited as the Cathedral is on the very edge of the river bank. Instead there stands at the west end the Galilee Chapel, built in the very latest Norman style, with slender columns supporting round arches adorned with a wealth of zigzag carving. There is a nave, and on either side double aisles provide a wonderful series of vistas; larger windows, with Dec or Perp tracery, fill the chapel with light, and from the west end there is a dramatic view through the windows of the river below – and across the river to the houses in South Street. Close to the altar is the tomb of the Venerable Bede (see Jarrow).

The cloisters lie on the S. side of the Cathedral: Norman and medieval in origin, they were rebuilt in the 18th century, and the windows have charming Gothick tracery. On the W. side is the Monks' Dormitory (upper floor), which is now the Cathedral Museum, containing notable treasures, including St Cuthbert's pectoral cross, removed from his coffin when it was opened in 1827, and a number of notable illuminated manuscripts. On the S. side is the Refectory, now the Cathedral Library, which, with its 17th-century bookcases, resembles the library of an Oxford or Cambridge college. Durham is fortunate in having preserved so many of its monastic buildings. The Treasury is in the S.W. corner of the cloisters, and contains a very fine collection of plate belonging to the Cathedral and to churches in the diocese. And opposite is the excellent Cathedral restaurant: Durham is the only cathedral to appear in the *Good Food Guide.* On the E. side is the Chapter

House, largely rebuilt in 1895.

The last Prince Bishop, van Mildert, realizing that after his death the Palatinate would be abolished and all its powers and endowments transferred to the Crown, persuaded the Dean and Chapter to found the University, to which a portion of the ecclesiastical funds would be bequeathed; he himself gave Durham Castle (one of the two episcopal palaces belonging to the see – the other, Auckland Castle, remains the episcopal palace today) and £2000 per annum out of his income to the new foundation. The Castle became University College; other colleges were founded later, and two canons of the Cathedral are university professors (on the model of Christ Church, Oxford). Palace Green, on the N. side of the Cathedral, is surrounded by university buildings – library, lecture rooms, and so on. It is a pleasure to walk across this splendid open square towards the Castle, turn and absorb the majestic sight of the full length of the north side of the Cathedral. The Castle is sometimes open to visitors: the Great Hall, the Dining Hall of University College, is as fine as many college halls at Oxford or Cambridge. After Oxford and Cambridge, Durham is the oldest university in England.

A narrow alley, next to the library, leads down to the romantic wooded walks by the river, under the Cathedral; a house here bears a plaque, recording that this was for many years the home of John Meade Falkner (d. 1932), author and antiquary, for many years Hon. Librarian of the Cathedral. Along the river bank there are views up and downstream, to Framwellgate Bridge and Prebends' Bridge – and, climbing up again, there is a mysterious tunnel called the Dark Entry which leads into College Green, the secluded grassy court on the S. side of the Cathedral, where stand the Deanery and the houses of the canons. Leaving College Green by Prior Castell's Gatehouse (*c.* 1510), we can turn right and walk down South Bailey to Prebends' Bridge, a handsome structure of 1778 (by George Nicholson). It is closed to motor traffic, so we can saunter here, and gaze up at the towers of the Cathedral rising above the wooded banks of the river. As we gaze and meditate, we shall see, inscribed on the balustrade, Sir Walter Scott's memorable lines:

> Grey towers of Durham, yet well I love thy mixed
>   and massive piles,
> Half church of God, half castle 'gainst the Scots.

Jarrow Slake is still a marshy swamp as it was in Bede's time; pylons now dwarf the Saxon church and Norman tower

Jarrow Priory

Jarrow is the epitome of County Durham, with ancient English history in strange juxtaposition with modern industry. The 19th-century town lies to the W., with drab streets leading down to the Tyne and its shipyards. Few now recall the events of the 1930s, when the shipyards closed, and the hunger marches followed: a plaque in the Town Hall commemorates those days. Now new industries have been established, great blocks of high-rise flats stand above the wasteland of demolished streets, and new dual carriageways, roundabouts and underpasses connect the new motorway with the Tyne Tunnel; the traffic rushes on its way. A signpost 'TO ST PAUL'S MONASTERY' at a round-about leads to the celebrated church and monastic ruins where Bede lived and wrote his *Ecclesiastical History* (AD 731).

The monastic house of Jarrow, one of the most ancient and famous of all English monasteries, was founded by St Benedict Biscop (see p. 81) in 681. Bede entered the monastery at the age of 12 in 685, and here he remained until his death in 735. Repeatedly sacked by the Danes, and repeatedly refounded, Jarrow became in 1183 a cell of the Benedictine Abbey of Durham, and its importance gradually waned. So no grand medieval church was ever built, and much remains of the place which Bede knew.

Jarrow Slake is still a marshy swamp as it was in Bede's time, but there are new landmarks now: pylons and power lines, cranes by the river, and oil and petrol storage tanks crowning the low hill, timber yards, and the Bede Trading Estate nearby. There are views downstream to South Shields – and across the greensward the neat little late Georgian villa called Jarrow Hall acts as a modern hospitium for today's pilgrims. Here there are refreshment rooms and a small local museum. Important excavations have taken place in recent years, and impressive ruins of the monastic buildings stand to the S. of the church, part Saxon, part 11th century.

The church has a spacious nave and N. aisle built by Sir Gilbert Scott in 1866, to replace the Norman nave which was demolished in 1786. The chancel is the nave of the Saxon church, and between the Victorian nave and the Saxon choir stands the venerable narrow Norman tower (*c.* 1075). The dedication stone, recalling the foundation of the monastery in 681, miraculously survives, as does an ancient chair in the sanctuary, called Bede's chair, but in reality (probably) 14th century. The whole place is redolent of the spirit of early British monasticism, and of Bede himself, who died here, still working on his commentaries and translations, on the Eve of the Ascension, 735.

Monkwearmouth Priory

The very name is monastic – eloquent of one of the most ancient religious sites in England. And the place itself is a magic spot. Here in the heart of modern Sunderland, against a backdrop of the cranes and machinery and sheds of the shipyard, stands the church of the monastery founded by St Benedict Biscop in 674. The tall narrow tower at the west end dates from the 9th or 10th century. There are the crude traces above the little window over the porch of a very early sculptured figure, perhaps of St Peter (to whom the church is dedicated), or of Christ Himself.

Benedict Biscop, founder of Monkwearmouth, was a young Northumbrian of noble birth, who after serving at the court of the Northumbrian king, entered the monastery at Lerins near Cannes, and in 669 returned to England with Theodore of Tarsus who had recently been consecrated Archbishop of Canterbury. In 674 the king granted him land at the mouth of the Wear, and here Benedict founded his monastery, building the church in the following year. In 681 he founded the house of St Paul at Jarrow, and the twin foundations of SS Peter and Paul were run as a single monastery. Like Jarrow, Monkwearmouth became in the 11th century a cell of the Benedictine Abbey of Durham. After the Dissolution St Peter's became a parish church.

Like so many Saxon churches, the nave is exceedingly lofty for its length and width: the west wall is the oldest part of the building, the lower

Monkwearmouth: the tall, narrow tower dates from the 9th or 10th century

part coeval with the base of the tower; here are traces of very early sculpture, badly worn, but still decipherable. The chancel with its arch is 14th century, the N. aisle a rebuilding of 1874, but its doorway 14th century. No traces survive of monastic buildings, but attached to the N.E. corner of the church is the new chapter house (or parish hall), built in 1970, and containing in its museum many important Saxon relics. St Peter's is a church of great romance, eloquent and evocative, its setting a magic blend of antiquity and industry.

DIOCESE OF
ELY

Ely Cathedral

THE FENS ARE DIFFERENT, different from every other part of England: they are strange, desolate, lonely. To drive towards Ely underneath the high bank of the Bedford River – the artificial river made by Vermuyden in the 17th century to drain the fens – is a great experience, for the river is *above* the road. The villages here are built on the old islands – indeed any place name ending in 'y' or 'ey' denotes an island: Thorney, Ramsey, Ely. It is on the biggest island of the fens that Ely stands.

The fens have their landmarks: the churches – their tall towers, their lofty spires – the villages themselves, the farm buildings, the occasional windmill: all these are conspicuous for miles around. And the greatest of all fenland landmarks is Ely. Driving along these lonely roads one is aware of it: that great Cathedral dominating the flat landscape for miles and miles. From the south it is seen lying full length on its long low 'island' – a building of enormous size and extraordinary length, powerful in its unique silhouette of immense western tower and lower central octagon. To approach from the east, down the little hill at Stuntney – another 'island' – is breathtaking too – for the bolder details emerge, of octagon and western tower, pinnacled chancel and detached Lady Chapel. Ely stands supreme in site, sumptuous in scale, unique in silhouette.

The little city has great charm – one of the two or three smallest cathedral towns in England (Wells and Southwell the only rivals). There are streets of Georgian houses, streets of small shops, the quays beside the River Ouse, the romantic precincts of the Cathedral. It is a pleasure to wander all round – and one is never unaware of the stupendous presence of the Cathedral: it is visible round every corner; a pinnacle here, a gable

there, the vast octagon, the colossal west tower, follow one around. We can walk about, absorb the details of the outside – the long Norman nave, the sharp-pointed Dec windows of the octagon, with the forest of pinnacles above, encircling the corona, the long line of the choir – and the simpler E.E. east end with its array of lancet windows, and so round to the vast Lady Chapel on the north side, standing almost detached with its enormous traceried windows; and then, past the octagon once more, back to the west front. From the north, from the south, from the east and from the west, the view is ever changing, the overwhelming scale always the same.

We must stand before the west front – then walk back down Palace Green, past the Palace with its great cliffs of Tudor brickwork, and across the smooth lawns. Now, turning round, we can gaze up at the immense west tower. It stands supreme – with tier upon tier of windows, tier upon tier of arcading, the arches just becoming pointed. The same pattern extends to the S.W. transept with its very grand embattled pinnacles; though here, at the base, the windows, the arcading, are all round-headed still. All this was built at the very end of the 12th century. The octagonal top of the tower was added in the 14th century – with still taller pinnacles, and windows with Dec tracery. And in front of this tower is the Galilee Porch, all pure 13th-century E.E., with narrow lancet windows and double portal below, open to receive us. And now is the great moment, for to stand inside the Galilee, under its vaulted roof, and look into the nave, is an experience of a lifetime.

The first monastery of Ely was founded by St Etheldreda in 673, and life continued uneventfully for two hundred years, for Ely, protected by the fens and swamps, was a remote, secure place.

The nave at Ely, overwhelming in its great height, great length and great simplicity

But in 869 the Danes attacked Ely from the sea, destroying the buildings, killing the inmates – and a cloud descends on the story for a hundred years. Then in 970 the abbey was refounded for Benedictine monks; the present church was begun in 1083; the bishopric was founded in 1109, and the monastic church became the cathedral.

But much building, and rebuilding, went on during the following centuries. In the early 13th century the east end of the choir was rebuilt in the E.E. style, and in the early 14th the new Lady Chapel was begun. But on 12 February 1322 a major disaster occurred: the Norman central tower collapsed, and all attention was diverted to its rebuilding. It is due to the genius of Alan of Walsingham, the Sacrist, that the Octagon was built. After its completion, attention returned to the Lady Chapel, which was completed in 1353.

Little was done in the following century, apart from the erection of two superb chantries – one to Bishop Alcock, one to Bishop West – at the east end. The north-west transept collapsed in the 15th century, and though work on its reconstruction was begun, it was never carried on: somehow, the building impetus, so long sustained, had dried up. After the Dissolution in 1539 Dean and canons replaced the Prior and monks. Sir Gilbert Scott carried out a major restoration in the 19th century:

his work is conspicuous and not unsympathetic.

We are standing, or perhaps sitting, at the west end of the nave, overwhelmed, perhaps, by its great length, its great height, its great simplicity. It must have been begun in the earliest years of the 12th century, and its remarkable rhythm of arcade, triforium only a little less lofty, and clerestory only slightly less lofty again – of the austere Norman pillars, with long shafts between them rising to the full height of the roof, with alternating round or shafted columns in the arcade and triforium, is thrilling. To see it (as so often) bereft of chairs, empty and echoing, is deeply moving; to watch the sunlight and shadows crossing it at midday, the mysteries of octagon and chancel beyond, is unforgettable. The chamfered wooden ceiling, painted by H. L. le Strange and T. Gambier Parry between 1858 and 1865, is extraordinarily effective, and brings to this glistening white interior the warmth of colour. Now we can move on towards the octagon.

To stand here is to experience an almost incredible sense of space – and light, for the octagon is filled with light, not merely from N. S. E. and W., but from the diagonal windows too, and from the windows in the lantern above. All these are filled with Victorian glass of strong colour – deep reds and greens and blues and gold – so one has an astonishing sense of colour pouring in, as well as of light. And then there is another thrill: the amazement that such a building should have been conceived, constructed and completed in the first half of the 14th century. It is the work of a man of genius, Alan of Walsingham. From the eight points of the octagon the narrow shafts ascend to support the vault – and to support the lesser octagon of the lantern above, which in turn is vaulted. The octagon itself is of stone, the vault and the lantern are of wood; giant oak trees came from Chicksands in Bedforshire to provide the huge beams required. It is a marvel of construction.

It seems a pity to fill this marvellous space, this marvellous octagon, with all the clutter of a 'central altar' – a 'kitchen table' of the starkest kind, with choir stalls like packing cases set awkwardly around. However, we can turn our backs on this, to admire Gilbert Scott's chancel screen, a masterpiece, comparable with his screens at Lichfield and Worcester: its delicate lines echo the lines of the octagon and provide a fitting entry to the choir. This was rebuilt at the same time as the octagon,

The octagon at Ely, Alan of Walsingham's inspiration

to replace the Norman nave shattered by the fall of the tower. Here stand the 14th-century stalls and, above, Scott's elaborate organ case: all this is rich furnishing for the richly ornamented Dec work of the building. And moving east we enter the Presbytery, or Sanctuary, built in the middle of the 13th century, the date of the flowering of the E.E. style: here Purbeck shafts and lancet windows, stiff-leaf capitals and spandrels carved with trefoils adorn every wall and each arcade; there is an alabaster reredos by Scott, and jewel-like glass by Wailes.

At the east end, the chantries of Bishop Alcock (N.) and Bishop West (S.) provide an almost exotic display of Perp decoration, of fan vaulting and carved canopies. Bishop Alcock died in 1501 – he was the founder of Jesus College, Cambridge – and Bishop West in 1534: in his chantry Comper's delightful altar (1938) adds wonderful colour to an interior of pale white stone.

The Lady Chapel is approached from the north transept. Begun in the early 14th century, it was not finished until all the rebuilding was completed after the fall of the central tower. Enormous traceried windows fill the interior with light, and the wide spreading lierne vault rises above us in star formation, adorned with a hundred bosses; below the windows there are canopied and recessed seats, and between them niches and stone panelling fill every space. It is an enormous chapel. Every window would have been filled with stained glass, every niche filled with gaily painted figures, every canopied seat adorned with elaborate carving. But now every niche is empty, the carvings round the seats are hacked away, the stained glass is all gone. It is a glorious but somewhat empty interior.

There is little medieval glass in the Cathedral, but much excellent Victorian glass, by all the great 19th-century stained-glass artists, which adds much to the interior. Moreover, in recent years a museum of stained glass has been opened in the north nave triforium, which is well worth a visit.

There is a wealth of monuments, from the medieval to the 19th century: reference may be made to Edmund Esdaile's *Monuments in Ely Cathedral* (published by the Dean and Chapter, and available at the bookstall). There is the tomb of John Tiptoft, Earl of Worcester (1470), under its ornate canopy (south choir aisle); Bishop Gunning (1684) is nearby, with his 17th-century figure propped upon his elbow – he wrote the 'Prayer for All Sorts and Conditions of Men'; there are monuments by the Stantons to Bishop Patrick (1707) and Bishop Fleetwood (1723), and one by Scheemakers to Canon Fleetwood, the bishop's son (1737) – together with many other interesting memorials to dignitaries and local gentry.

Little survives of the cloisters – merely an outer wall which provides a delightful background to the Bishop's beautiful garden on the south side of the Cathedral. But the Prior's doorway, which led from the nave into the north walk, survives, and this is a feature of great importance. Arch, tympanum and side shafts are all carved with foliage, human faces and animals; and in the tympanum is the figure of Christ, seated, with angels with outspread wings on either side. It dates from *c.* 1135. The Monks' door further east is less elabor-

Ely: detail of the Prior's doorway

ate, but of much the same date, and carved with equal feeling. Instead of a tympanum, the arch is trefoiled, and in the spandrels of the trefoil two little kneeling figures hold croziers and guard the doorway. From this door it is a pleasure to walk into the precincts, to enjoy the houses and gardens, and the surviving monastic buildings, many now occupied by the King's School, and, especially, to visit Prior Crauden's Chapel, built for the Prior by Alan of Walsingham (*c.* 1324). Beyond, the Gate or Ely Porta, built at the end of the 14th century, returns us to the outside world. But as we drive away, that remarkable silhouette, so different from the silhouette of every other English cathedral – the silhouette of the octagon and one immense west tower – will accompany us for many flat miles across the empty fens.

Jesus College Chapel (St Radegunda's Priory), Cambridge

It may come as a surprise to many to learn that Jesus College Chapel is in fact the church of St Radegunda's Priory, a priory founded in the 12th century for Benedictine nuns. Numbers were down to two when Bishop Alcock of Ely (q.v.) decided to suppress it (with the King's permission) in 1497, and found his new college, to be called Jesus College. He made use of all the monastic buildings which he could: the refectory became the college hall, the cloisters became the cloisters of the college, the church (or most of it) the chapel. Jesus is, of course, in Jesus Lane: 18th-century gates lead into the Chimney (so called), the narrow paved approach to the Gatetower, with high walls

Jesus College Chapel: E. E. lancets in the sanctuary

protecting the Fellows' Garden on the left, the Master's on the right; Bishop Alcock's statue is above the archway as we enter. Past the porter's lodge, and turning right, we are in the monastic cloisters: the entrance to the Chapel is on the south side.

Bishop Alcock removed the aisles of choir and nave, and the west bays of the nave he cut off to form the Master's Lodge; he also heightened the crossing tower. It makes the perfect college chapel, with short nave and transepts forming as it were the ante-chapel. There is Norman work in the north transept, and the nave is, in its bones, Norman; but entering the choir by the beautiful Pugin

screen we are in the world of E.E., with five narrow lancets on the north side, four on the south, with sedilia and piscina below; at the east end there are five lancets – a reconstruction by Pugin, replacing a Perp window inserted by Alcock, an authentic reconstruction based on irrefutable evidence. Pugin was called in in 1846, when the Chapel was in poor state: his are the altar, the stalls (incorporating some original work), organ and screen. Hardman made the glass and the splendid lectern (based on the lectern in St Mark's, Venice). After Pugin's death, Bodley was appointed architect, and the sympathetic restoration of transepts, nave and tower continued. Morris designed the

Jesus College Chapel: ceiling by William Morris

ceiling of the nave, Philip Webb the ceilings for the transepts, and all were executed by F. R. Leach. Bodley designed the floors in stone and tile by Minton; here all the glass was made by Morris & Co. to designs by Burne-Jones, Ford Madox Brown and Morris himself. It is to these sensitive and scholarly artists that we owe the beauty of the Chapel today: they have bequeathed to us a delightful ensemble of the medieval and the Victorian.

Ramsey Abbey

Monastic countryside – bleak fenland, sought after by monks and holy men. The monasteries follow one another in swift succession: Ramsey, Peterborough, Thorney, Croyland.

Ramsey is a little town of two main streets: at the top of the long High Street Abbey Green and Church Green follow one another, interlock with one another – informal squares of mown grass, lined with cottages ornées, more sober Georgian houses, Tudor Revival cottages. What remains of Ramsey Abbey is mostly buried under the house built by the Cromwell family in the 17th century; the Fellowes succeeded them in the early 18th, and both Soane and Blore added more. This house is now a girls' school: the gatehouse on Abbey Green is 14th century, and of great splendour.

Opposite stands the present abbey church, originally the hospitium or abbey guest house, but used as a church since the 13th century, and certainly as the parish church after the Dissolution in 1539. The west tower is 17th century; there is a long nave of seven bays (c. 1180), with many varied piers and capitals, and a vaulted Norman chancel somewhat earlier in date. Steep steps rise to the High Altar, and round-headed windows with a vesica above fill the east wall. Here and elsewhere there is glass by Morris & Co., some as late as 1920, colourful and decorative.

Standing on the perimeter of the once-powerful Abbey, founded here c. 970 as a Benedictine house, and on the edge of its little town, this church is an important parochial appendage, a *capella ante portas*, still exerting its monastic influence four centuries after its mother church was destroyed.

Ramsey: 17th-century tower and Norman doorway

Thorney Abbey

Thorney, the Isle of Thorns: this is Cambridgeshire fenland at its flattest. It was to this solitary, swampy island that a few monks came from Medehamstead (now Peterborough) in 662, to lead the hermit's life. One of these monks, a man called Tatwin, took St Guthlac to Croyland – only a few miles away – when he was searching for a site for his hermitage in 699. But all this early religious house was swept away by the Danes in 870.

The Abbey was refounded for Benedictine monks in 972: the present church was begun in 1085. 'In November 1089,' records an ancient account, 'we of Thorney entered into our new

The west front at Thorney

church.' It was completed in 1108, and it is a fragment of this church that we see today. The Abbey was dissolved in 1539, and the property granted to the Earl of Bedford; he granted 40 tons of stone to Trinity College, Cambridge, and 146 to Corpus: the church became a ruin.

A century later the then Earl of Bedford and the Dutch engineer Cornelius Vermuyden were engaged in draining the fens: a village sprang up, and the remains of the abbey church were patched up and restored to serve as the parish church. The aisles and what remained of the eastern parts were pulled down, and the nave arcades blocked up. The present transepts and sanctuary were added (by Blore) in Norman style in 1840.

Although no longer an island, Thorney remains an oasis in the bleak countryside: here there are trees, and signs of civilization. The church stands at the crossroads, in the centre of the village, presenting its tall turreted west front to the street – reminiscent of King's Chapel. Up to the level of the original roof these turrets are Norman: it is possible to imagine a west front here as at Tewkesbury, with an enormous Norman arch enclosing a window. In the 15th century octagonal Perp crowns were added to these Norman turrets – connected to each other by a wide horizontal screen, with nine niches still occupied by their original statues: below, a grand Perp window was inserted, then blocked up in the 17th century,

when the nave was rebuilt to form the parish church. 'A.D. 1638' records the date on either side of the west door: much of the tactful work done in rehabilitating the church was 'Gothic Survival' – the smaller west door with ogee arch, and the smaller west window above, with Perp tracery and ogee head, to take the place of the original large window. On the north turret is the clock.

The interior is still impressive. The Norman arches are there, though blocked; the spacious triforium, too, with Perp windows inserted there as in the blocked arches below; the strong Norman shafts lead up to support merely a 17th-century coved plaster ceiling. Blore's east window is filled with excellent Victorian glass, inspired perhaps by 13th-century glass at Canterbury; there are panels of Swiss glass in the nave windows. In the floor are many fascinating ledger stones, some bearing Dutch or Huguenot names: Mark le Pla, 1697, Mary le Hovecq, his wife, 1693, Ann Guern 1721, Abraham Flahau, 1755, and 'the Revd Mr James Ris, A.M. late Minister of the Church, 1758.' Another commemorates George Smith, Steward to the Earl of Bedford, 1651: perhaps it was he who supervised the restoration in 1638.

Thorney: ledger stones in the nave

The grass court to the south of the church is the original Cloister Court: here stand the vicarage and another 17th-century house with projecting gabled wings – delightful companions to the church. And opposite, behind its substantial wall, is Thorney Abbey House, built by the Earl of Bedford in 1660, a particularly handsome small-grand stone house, with hipped roof, big central chimney stack, and splendid gate piers to the street. Thorney remained Bedford property till 1910: the village is full of their Victorian terrace housing – all rather attractive – and there is a mammoth and ornate water tower of 1855 to provide extra entertainment.

DIOCESE OF
EXETER

Exeter Cathedral

THE LONG TRAIN JOURNEY from Paddington, the first glimpses of the Devon countryside with its red soil and undulating tree-hung valleys, its deep lanes fortified by high hedges, its villages of cob and thatch, its red sandstone churches – there is a sense of excitement in the air, a sense of reaching a distant and different part of England. And on arriving at Exeter, the size and splendour of St David's Station denote the capital of the West of England. Much of the medieval city was destroyed by German bombs, but a number of small ancient churches survive, and (outside the medieval city) there are spacious crescents and terraces of Georgian houses. In and around the High Street there has been much commonplace rebuilding since the war, but the 16th-century Guildhall still stands on its granite columns astride the pavement, telling of the wealth and importance of the medieval guilds and merchants.

The Cathedral stands behind the High Street to the S., in no way conspicuous – indeed concealing itself behind the houses of Cathedral Yard. Wide lawns, paved paths, newly planted trees, the seated figure of Richard Hooker (author of *Laws of Ecclesiastical Politie*), houses all around, many ancient, many charming: such is the setting of the Cathedral. The see of Exeter was founded in 1050, when the ancient Bishopric of Crediton and Cornwall was transferred here. A Norman cathedral, on the site of an ancient Saxon church, was built by Bishop Warelwast in the years following the Conquest. Of this only the twin towers, set so unusually to crown the two transepts, survive. The new cathedral, begun *c.* 1275 by Bishop Branscombe, and set between their mighty structures, took nearly a century to build.

It is these two Norman towers that dominate the exterior: there is nothing like them in England, except for the (later) towers at Ottery St Mary,

Exeter's daughter. From every side they dominate, with tier upon tier of blind arcading, tiny narrow windows below, larger windows at the top. In fact they are not identical: the earlier N. tower is plainer, more austere. Then in the 15th century the crenellated tops were added, the square embattled pinnacles with their ogee-shaped lead caps and gilded weather-vanes. Between them rises the Gothic church, lantern-like with its traceried windows, its long rows of pinnacles and flying buttresses. The W. front is the showpiece, the final flourish of the new church, with its long horizontal screen of statues – seated figures of kings below, standing figures of saints and angels above, all occupying elaborate canopied niches; and above and around an almost triangular composition, arcaded, battlemented, pinnacled, enclosing a great geometrical window, and rising to the steep gable of the nave roof, with an almost triangular traceried window at its top.

This unusual exterior is fascinating and impressive. But the interior is thrilling and inspiring. Few cathedrals are so homogeneous. Stand inside the W. door and absorb the amazing rhythm of arches, triforium, clerestory, marching on uninterruptedly from the W. end of the nave to the E. end of the chancel: the traceried Dec windows in clerestory and aisle, the triforium – little more than a shallow arcade – the clustered columns; and, above all, the breathtaking tierceron vault rising over our heads like a forest of palm trees. It is the longest unbroken stretch of Gothic vaulting in the world – uninterrupted by crossing or crossing arches. And the wealth of bosses and richly carved corbels in every spandrel is all part of this overpowering composition, every one of them gilded and painted. Under the second bay from the W. is the elegant marble font of 1687, with its contemporary cover: in the triforium of the fifth, opposite,

The long horizontal 14th-century screen at Exeter Cathedral, with its seated figures of kings and standing figures of saints and angels

is the Minstrels' Gallery, with the figures of fourteen angels playing fourteen different instruments.
And the vista is interrupted in a magical way by
the stone screen, or pulpitum, standing at the
entrance to the chancel, through whose exquisitely
carved open arches there is a glimpse of the glories
of the chancel beyond: above stands the most
splendid of all late-17th-century organs (by John
Loosemoore, c. 1665); 17th-century painted
panels fill the upper arcades of the screen.

Exeter: ABOVE *the nave, with the Minstrels' Gallery adorned
with angels playing instruments;* BELOW *Norman tower and
14th-century west front*

The Norman transepts are narrow – the chancel
is as wide and spacious as the nave. A grand set
of choir stalls (14th century, but much restored
by Gilbert Scott) with original misericords; an
early-16th-century brass eagle lectern; and the
Bishop's Throne, sixty feet high, completed in
1312 and as magnificent as any in England, all
contribute to the exceptional quality of this chancel. And the E. window, a Perp insertion of the
late 14th century, is filled with sumptuous late-
14th-century glass.

The ambulatory leads to the eastern chapels,
and, above all, to the Lady Chapel, begun by
Bishop Branscombe c. 1275. Here on a smaller
scale the same ribbed vaulting encloses a richly
arcaded interior, arched recesses contain tombs,
and traceried Dec windows fill the chapel with
light. On the S. side, at the W. end, is the tomb
of Bishop Branscombe (who initiated the rebuild-

ing of the Cathedral), under an early-15th-century canopy – matching the canopied tomb of Bishop Stafford opposite.

And throughout the Cathedral is a wonderfully lavish array of tombs and monuments – from the tomb of Bishop Leofric (1st Bishop of Exeter) in the Lady Chapel, to Sir John Gilbert (brother-in-law of Sir Walter Raleigh) in the S. transept, and Bishop Carey (d. 1626) in the N. chancel aisle. Sir John Speke's chantry in the N. chancel aisle, Bishop Oldham's in the S., are lavish little late Perp additions to this 14th-century interior; and in the thickness of the W. wall is the tiny chapel of Bishop Grandisson, who was bishop at the time of the completion of the Cathedral. In 1942 a bomb fell in the S. choir aisle, destroying the double chapel of St James and St Thomas; this has been carefully rebuilt.

This wonderfully rich interior is filled with stone screens, sedilia, furnishings of every date. In particular the ancient astronomical clock in the N. transept must be mentioned. It dates from the late 15th century: its gaily painted face is high up on the wall – its works, partly original, partly 16th century, stand on the floor beneath. The earth occupies the centre of the dial, the moon revolves around it – as does the sun (adorned with a fleur-de-lys) pointing to the hours; and the 18th-century dial above tells the minutes. '*Pereunt et imputantur,*' reads the Latin inscription below: 'the hours pass, and are reckoned to our account.'

Pilton Priory

Pilton is Barnstaple, across the River Yeo; yet in reality Pilton is the more ancient borough, and was in medieval times more important. Pilton Street still has an air – with 18th-century (or earlier) houses on either side. H. H. Munro (Saki) – born 1870 – was brought up from the age of two at Broadgate Villa, by a grandmother and two maiden aunts.

At the top of the street, approached through the archway of the pretty early Victorian almshouses (1849 Tudor), stands Pilton Priory, a cell of the Benedictine Abbey of Malmesbury, and traditionally founded by King Athelstan in the 10th century. A tall sturdy Perp tower, of Devonian type, with pinnacles and battlements, stands at the E. end of the N. aisle, and the exterior aisle wall is scarred by the marks of the monastic cloisters and buildings which once stood here

Indeed, inside, this N. aisle – which with the nave and chancel formed the monastic church – is monastic in feeling, and primitive in appearance with its rough-hewn early pointed arches, entirely devoid of columns or mouldings. The S. (parochial) aisle is Perp, with an elegant late-14th-century arcade, as is the chancel, with its S. chapel. Pilton is a church with a distinctive atmosphere, and filled with interesting things. The Perp stone pulpit has, extending from its side, a long outstretched arm (in iron), holding in its hand an hour-glass; there is an interesting late Perp font cover, set under an unusual 16th-century canopy; an ornate 16th-century rood screen, its texture all concealed with thick treacly varnish; an Elizabethan altar rail, and a Royal Arms of Queen Anne (1797). What is more, there are three monuments of some importance: the tomb of Sir John Chichester (1569) stands against the E. wall of the S. chapel; bold lines, bold columns, plenty of heraldry and strapwork, all contribute to a striking composition; Sir Robert Chichester (1627) has a more conventional Jacobean tomb in the sanctuary, with kneeling figures; and the baroque wall monument to Christopher Lethbridge (1713) in the S. aisle is a riot of cherubs, urns, coats of arms and garlands, in every way a remarkable decorative confection.

Pilton Priory

DIOCESE OF
GLOUCESTER

Gloucester Cathedral

GLOUCESTER IS NOT, at first sight, a prepossessing place; there are uninteresting streets with commonplace buildings, providing an unworthy setting for a great cathedral. Much had gone before the war – more has gone since; and the large blocks of modern offices and the jazzy shop fronts of the multiple stores make it difficult to believe that this is a medieval city. A few relics, such as the New Inn, with its courtyard and open galleries, tell of what has gone; and there are a few medieval churches. The big early-19th-century warehouses by the docks, with the Custom House in Quay Street, are an attractive ensemble: the Gloucester and Berkeley Ship Canal was opened in 1827.

Walking down Westgate, and turning into College Green, we are face to face with the Cathedral. It is without question one of the great cathedrals of England. Outwardly it appears all Perp, with its sumptuous central tower, its rows of Perp windows in the nave, a large Perp window in the south transept, and, above all, the grand Perp features of the chancel and the Lady Chapel. But there are a few clues to its Norman origin: the unmistakably Norman turrets and pinnacles of the south transept, and the rounded chapels and ambulatory at the east end, where many windows are clearly Norman, but filled with later tracery.

The first monastic house was founded here at the end of the 7th century, but at the time of the Conquest numbers were down to two. In 1072 William I appointed Serlo, his own chaplain who had been trained at Mont S. Michel, Abbot of the Benedictine Abbey, and the revival was dramatic. At his death there were a hundred monks. He began rebuilding the church in 1089, and much of Serlo's church is what we see today, though the chancel was transformed in the 14th century, and the tower and Lady Chapel were built towards the end of the 15th. Gloucester in the Middle Ages

was a town of great importance: Henry II was crowned here in 1216 (*aet.* 9), and Edward II, who had been murdered at Berkeley Castle, was buried here in 1327. Gloucester at once became a place of pilgrimage: it must have been the offerings of the pilgrims that paid for the tremendous building works in the 14th and 15th centuries. After the Dissolution (1539) Henry VIII created the Diocese of Gloucester (1542), and the abbey church became the cathedral.

We enter by the south porch (*c.* 1420), and the Norman nave is upon us. It is one of the most monumental in England: enormous cylindrical piers, of prodigious height, with the simplest possible capitals, support arches which are only sparingly adorned with zigzag ornament: above, the triforium is low, with small twin openings; above this, the clerestory – but it was much altered when the new vault was added. A fire destroyed the original timber roof in the 12th century, and the present E.E. rib vault was built *c.* 1240. We may feel dwarfed by these huge columns, these severe round arches – but the eye is carried on to the stone screen, on which stands the organ in a noble case of 1665, and on to the chancel with its gorgeous vault, and the east window which fills the entire east wall, looking like an enormous sheet of lace. This chancel is a wonderful contrast, a wonderful foil for the stark simplicity of the nave.

Moving up the nave, we can admire the furnishings which accompany the altar here: the pulpit is 17th century, the choir stalls and Bishop's Throne early 18th. They were originally in the chancel, but banished by Gilbert Scott at the time of his restoration: they are very handsome. And the altar itself, with its embroidered Laudian pall and splendid tall and imposing silver ornaments, is dignified and beautiful.

The chancel is breathtaking: the height, the

Gloucester: the 14th-century transformation of the Norman chancel; the east window is filled with its original glass

enormous east window filled with its original glass given as a memorial of the Battle of Crécy, the lofty windows of the clerestory, the delicate tracery covering the triforium, the stone panelling which fills every other surface of the walls, the lierne vault, 92 ft high, adorned, it seems with a thousand bosses like stars in the sky – it is hard to believe that underneath all this is still the Norman quire. The work of transformation began *c.* 1340. The choir stalls are 14th century, with ogee-arched canopies and a wealth of misericords; the reredos is by Gilbert Scott (1873) and, now that it is coloured and gilded, it is hard to believe that it is not medieval. In front of the High Altar the effigy of Robert Duke of Normandy lies on his tomb. Eldest son of the Conqueror, he died at Cardiff Castle in 1134, but this rare and beautiful wooden figure was not placed here till the 13th century.

Making our way into the north aisle, and round the ambulatory, we find the sumptuous tomb of Edward II. His alabaster effigy, distinguished work of *c.* 1330, and in a remarkable state of preservation, lies on a tomb chest of Purbeck marble, the King's head on a cushion, supported on either side by the figure of an angel, and, above this, an elaborate stone canopy, adorned with finials and pinnacles. The ambulatory with its radiating chapels reminds us that underneath all this glorious Perp work the Norman east end survives: great round piers, the Norman vault, are all apparent. At the east end, the Lady Chapel was completed in 1499; although completed a century later than the chancel there is little change of style: enormous traceried windows fill every bay, and the narrow

Gloucester: ABOVE RIGHT *the alabaster effigy of Edward II;* BELOW *the Norman pillars of the nave*

ABOVE *The cloisters at Gloucester and* BELOW *the Norman crypt*

shafts support a lierne vault. The east window is filled with medieval glass, but it is largely an assemblage of fragments; the altar rails are 17th century, and date from the time when Laud was Dean, restored the altars to the east end, and protected them with handsome rails. And moving round to the south transept we shall see one of the marvels of 14th-century building: the 'flying' arches across the north and south arches of the crossing, built to take the shafts which carry the chancel vault. In the north transept, the 13th-century stone screen – which perhaps formed the entrance to the earlier Lady Chapel – leads to the Treasury, in the former Locutorium, the long narrow room where the monks could talk. Here there is a permanent exhibition of silver and treasures belonging to the Cathedral, and to other churches in the diocese.

The cloisters are another of the great wonders of Gloucester – the most celebrated cloisters in England, begun at the end of the 14th century and completed in the early 15th. Here the Perp style, which has flowered so magnificently in the chancel, develops still further. Here is the first large-scale fan vault in England: through the traceried windows, the full width of each bay, light pours in on the subtle, delicate pattern of the vault, and on the inner walls, elaborately carved and panelled. The four walks differ from each other: in the south are the stone 'carrels' – or recesses, two to each bay – where the monks would sit to read or write or illuminate their manuscripts, each compartment lit by a small traceried window; in the north is the lavatorium, or monks' washing place, with its long stone basin, complete with medieval drains. On the east side a doorway leads into the chapter house: in this historic Norman hall William I had a conference with his barons at Christmas 1085, and gave orders for the making of the Domesday Book, which was completed in 1086. The original east end was apsidal, but this was replaced by the present Perp extension in the 14th century.

Beneath the chancel, and entered by a door in the south transept, is the Norman crypt. Here tremendous squat Norman columns carry a groined roof – but it is interesting to see where the later builders strengthened the crypt and its vault when the choir above was heightened, to bear the greater weight of the new building. In this chilly, mysterious, empty building there are columns with cushion capitals round the ambulatory, where the walls are adorned with arcading, and a piscina recalls that here there once were altars, and that the place echoed with prayer and praise.

There is much good Victorian glass: the west window is by Wailes; and Hardman, Clayton & Bell, and Warrington are all represented in the nave; elsewhere there are windows by Kempe, and in the Lady Chapel much interesting glass by Christopher Whall. And everywhere there is a wealth of good monuments – 17th-century tombs, and (especially in the nave) a number of 18th-century marble tablets to dignitaries and local gentry. In addition, the monument to Sir Hubert Parry, the musician, is of interest (1918), as is the statue to Dr Jenner, the discoverer of vaccination (1825). And particularly notable, as a work of art, is the monument in the north aisle to Canon Tinling (1897), by Henry Wilson.

It is a pleasure to walk round the precincts. Houses of many dates and sizes fill the south side, facing the Cathedral, and the ground slopes gently to the west towards St Mary's Gate. On the north side narrow lanes and passages are a pleasure to explore: here there are grand views of the exterior of the Cathedral, and we can gaze up at the tower, 225 ft high. Built towards the end of the 15th century, it rises with tier upon tier of crocketed canopies to the open traceried parapet and the four immense pinnacles, each one adorned with smaller pinnacles and little spires of open lattice work, made, it would seem, of lace. It is the crowning glory of Gloucester.

Deerhurst Priory

Deerhurst is remote in its watery meadows close to the River Severn, and the priory church is eloquent of the religious life of the remote past as few other monastic churches in England are. It stands in its large churchyard, planted unexpectedly with tall Wellingtonias, with, alongside, an ancient and romantic farmhouse, which incorporates some of the conventual buildings. The tower is tall, narrow, unadorned – in its profile unmistakably Saxon. So is the church, with its herringbone masonry, even though the clerestory windows are Gothic and the aisle windows latest Perp.

A small Saxon door in the tower leads in, to another low Saxon arch, and so into the nave. Here E.E. arcades with stiff-leaf capitals have

pierced the Saxon walls, but the great height of the nave is of Saxon proportions. Above the arcades, on either side, the mysterious small triangular openings are Saxon; there is another in the tower and, above it, a double window into the nave with triangular heads. At the west end of the north aisle is the Saxon font, perhaps the oldest font in England (9th century), its bowl adorned with vine-scroll decoration. The chancel arch is blocked: beyond was the apsidal chancel; but on either side of the present sanctuary the small 'transepts' are Saxon, though now brought into the church by the later aisles.

The Saxon font at Deerhurst, perhaps the oldest font in England

The building history is not easy to unravel, but it is known that a monastery existed here in 804, and the nave, the lower part of the tower, and the little 'transepts' probably date from this time; after being sacked by the Danes in the 10th century the church was restored, the upper stages of the tower added, and the apsidal chancel built. Nor is much known of the earliest religious house; but it is known that Edward the Confessor, not long before the Conquest, gave it to the Abbey of S. Denis in France. As an alien priory it was confiscated during the French wars and, after many vicissitudes, transferred by Edward IV to Tewkesbury; it remained a daughter house of Tewkesbury until the Dissolution. Since then it has been the parish church of this tiny village.

There are things to see in the church, apart from the remarkable architecture. At the east end

Deerhurst: the great height of the nave is of Saxon proportions

of the north aisle is a most interesting brass to Sir John and Lady Cassey (*c.* 1400). He was Chancellor of the Exchequer to Richard II. Her feet lie on her pet dog, whose name 'Tirri' or 'Terri' is given on the brass for our information, the only dog to be so distinguished on any brass or monument. There is good Victorian glass in this aisle, by Wailes, and Clayton & Bell, and the west window of the south aisle contains glass of the 14th and 15th century. The Victorian pulpit is by Slater (of Slater & Carpenter), who restored the church in 1862. The arrangement of the 17th-century stalls and altar in the chancel is a curious and very rare survival. At the west end is the very early sculpture of the Virgin and Child – dating, probably, from the early 9th century; and there are some wonderful corbels of animal heads of much the same date.

In the farmyard at the east end may be seen the foundations of the apsidal east end; in a dark corner adjoining the house an arrow points upwards, marked ANGEL, and above on the wall may be seen a vividly carved angel (10th century). In the farmhouse are a number of features and fragments of the conventual buildings: the long wing to the south, with enclosed garden, forms what was the cloister court.

The Priory was not the only Saxon church in this religious village: a stone's throw away stands Odda's Chapel. It was not monastic, but it must be briefly mentioned. It is attached to a timbered house, and indeed for centuries formed part of it – the nave used as a two-storied kitchen, the chancel divided by a floor to form a room below, a bedroom above. Only by accident was the existence of the chapel discovered at the end of the last century – as happened with two other Saxon churches, at Escomb and Bradford-on-Avon. Now it is restored, and may be visited. Contemporary inscriptions discovered here date the dedication of the chapel: 12 April 1056.

Leonard Stanley Priory

Beneath the steep slopes of the Cotswolds, close to Stroud, lies the village of Leonard Stanley, with the Norman church of the Priory of Augustinian Canons founded *c.* 1121 by Roger Berkeley. It is

Leonard Stanley: behind the Norman church stands the 18th-century Priory House

an austere cruciform building, with an aisleless nave and chancel, and a grand central tower crowned with a pyramid roof, with embattled parapet and taller N.W. staircase turret. The interior is long and lofty, with a spacious crossing with plain Norman arches carrying the tower. In the nave, on the S. side, a narrow arch leads to the stairway to the vanished rood screen – which separated the parochial W. end from the monastic church. Norman doorways in this wall led to the priory cloister. Of special interest are the carved capitals on the vaulting shafts in the chancel – one representing the Nativity, the other Mary Magdalene washing Our Lord's feet. The church is well furnished: the black-and-white marble floor in the chancel is by Bodley; the W. window is a late work by Morris & Co. (1922), and there are 18th-century monuments to the Sandford and Holbrow families.

There are plentiful monastic remains incorporated in the farm buildings to the S. of the church, including a medieval chapel now used as a barn. The Priory is an imposing house, 16th century at the rear with a recessed centre between extending wings – but on the other side a splendid mid-18th-century front, with the Sandford arms in the central pediment.

Tewkesbury Abbey

Tewkesbury stands in its water meadows in that delightful but unsung part of Gloucestershire where the Avon flows into the Severn. It is a small town which prospered in the Middle Ages on wool and cloth, on the trade of its little port, and on the prosperity of its great Abbey. Telford's bridge spans the Severn, the streets are lined with timbered houses – some of them with sailing, sagging, gabled upper storeys, some with later Georgian brick façades – and on the edge of the town to the S. stands majestic the great abbey church.

The descent of the lordship of the manor is interesting and important, because it helps to explain the size of the Abbey, the magnificence of its church, and the presence of the amazing tombs and chantries that are such a feature of its interior. Granted by the Conqueror to Queen Matilda, it descended to Rufus' cousin, Robert Fitzhamon, who founded the Abbey, and so to his daughter who married Robert Fitzroy (illegitimate son of

Henry I), who was created Earl of Gloucester, and continued its building. The de Clares succeeded, held it for two hundred years, and were in turn succeeded by the Despencers and the Beauchamps: all these were great benefactors of the Abbey, and are buried here.

The first monastic church was founded here in the 8th century, but by *c.* 1000 it was so reduced that it became a mere priory of Cranborne in Dorset (q.v.). However in 1102 Robert Fitzhamon, in partnership with the Abbot of Cranborne, decided to reverse the order, found a great new Benedictine abbey here, and reduce Cranborne to a priory. So the great new church was founded, and was consecrated in 1121. It is one of the grandest churches in England, and apart from the great cathedrals only Westminster and Beverley can outshine it.

Enter the churchyard by the splendid wrought iron gates, erected by the 1st Lord Gage in 1734 (he had been M.P. for Tewkesbury, and married a local heiress), and stand and gaze – at the enormous Norman central tower, the greatest Norman tower in England, at the W. front, where the tremendous recessed arch with its six orders of shafts and mouldings now frames a vast Perp window (rebuilt in 1686 after a gale), at the long nave, Norman too, despite its later traceried windows, at the transept with its strong corner buttresses – and so round to the apsidal E. end, rebuilt in the 14th century, with its chevet of radiating chapels, its flying buttresses, its traceried Dec windows enriched with ballflower ornament, and its pierced embattled parapet. The lofty tunnel-vaulted N. porch leads into the nave.

Here there is nothing for it but to stand and stare at this Norman nave completed in 1121 – contemporary with the nave at Gloucester, with which it has so much in common. These gargantuan circular columns are 6′6″ in diameter and 31 ft in height (double the height of those at Hereford, yet of much the same girth); there are eight bays; above is a diminutive triforium, a later (14th-century) low clerestory, and then the sumptuous 14th-century lierne vault, which replaced the original timber roof. It has been criticized for being too low – like a hat worn low over the wearer's eyes – but it is of superb beauty, with gilded bosses the length of the nave depicting the life of Christ. The eye is carried on, to the crossing, and beyond into the 14th-century chancel, where the Norman piers graduate into Dec arches, and (as has been

Tewkesbury Abbey: the greatest Norman tower in England

seen outside) great Dec traceried windows fill the spaces of the apse.

In Benedictine fashion the choir and its stalls, and the 17th-century organ (once at Magdalen) occupy the crossing – leaving for purposes of ceremony and pleasure a spacious chancel and sanctuary beyond. This is crowned with another sumptuous lierne vault, and the seven windows of the clerestory are filled with 14th-century glass, the gift of Eleanor, last of the de Clares, in memory of her husband Hugh le Despencer, who like Edward II had been murdered. And all around stand the chantries: each one seems to exceed the next one in beauty. The first on the N. side is that of Robert Fitzhamon, the founder (d. 1107) – but the chantry was not built till 1395. Within the enclosing stone screens is a tiny fan-vaulted chapel. Next to it on the N. is the chantry built by Isabel le Despencer in memory of her husband Richard Beauchamp (d. 1421). This is of two storeys, the lower fan-vaulted, the upper enclosed with a lierne vault, and canopied niches are filled

with angels carrying heraldic shields. Perhaps the most thrilling of all is that on the S. side, built *c.* 1380 for the purpose of saying masses for the soul of Edward le Despencer (d. 1375). It is fan-vaulted, and again contains a tiny altar; above, occupying a little canopied niche upon the roof is a figure of Lord le Despencer kneeling in prayer, and facing the High Altar. He was described by Froissart as 'the most honourable, gallant and valiant knight in England, much beloved of ladies, for the most noble said that no feast was perfect if Sir Despencer was not present'. There are many other tombs around, or in the ambulatory – such as that of Sir Hugh le Despencer (d. 1348), with the recumbent figures of him and his wife under an open many-pinnacled canopy; on the floor of the ambulatory a grating leads down to the Clarence Vault, where the bones of George Duke of Clarence, brother of Edward IV and Richard III, are preserved in a glass case, together with those of his wife, who was a daughter of Warwick the Kingmaker. And all around the Ambulatory are

Tewkesbury: the Norman nave with its 14th-century lierne vault

beautifully furnished chapels, forming the Chevet; the door of the sacristy (S. choir aisle) is reinforced by armour, flattened out, worn by soldiers killed at the Battle of Tewkesbury on May 4th 1471, when the Yorkists inflicted a shattering defeat on the Lancastrians, who were driven to take refuge in the Abbey. Not far away is a tablet in memory of Mrs Craik (d. 1890), author of *John Halifax, Gentleman*. And opening out of the S. transept is perhaps the most beautiful of all the chapels – the Norman apsidal Lady Chapel, with a late-19th-century mosaic above the altar by Salviati of Venice. But the whole church is most delightfully furnished, decorated in summer with great bowls of flowers, or in winter with autumn leaves and foliage: towards the W. end of the nave, close to the N. porch there stand behind the chairs two magnificent 18th-century gate-legged tables, each one always adorned with a luxuriant vase of flowers.

Tewkesbury: the sanctuary vault; the seven windows of the apse are filled with their original glass

Of the monastic buildings there remain but the Tudor abbey gatehouse which leads to the abbots' house, now the vicarage, which turns its medieval back to the W. front of the Abbey, but on the garden side displays a comfortable brick Georgian façade; and on the S. side of the nave of the church a few battered springers of the cloister vault survive. The church was purchased by the town at the time of the Dissolution to serve as the parish church. Two years or so ago a new Choir School was founded, which occupies the old buildings of the Grammar School. During term time the boys, robed like little Benedictine monks in black habits with white girdles, sing Evensong in the Abbey every day.

DIOCESE OF
GUILDFORD

Guildford Cathedral

THE DIOCESE OF GUILDFORD was founded in 1927, carved out of the ancient see of Winchester, and the Cathedral was consecrated in 1961. So here, for once, there is no long history to rehearse – merely the story of the past fifty years. The first bishop was enthroned in Holy Trinity Church, the 18th-century parish church in the High Street; in 1932 the competition for the new cathedral was won by Mr Edward, later Sir Edward, Maufe; in 1936 the foundation stone was laid, and work began on the building of the chancel. After the interruption of the war, work was resumed in 1952; the Cathedral was consecrated in the presence of the Queen in 1961.

The site is magnificent. Stag Hill, a spine of grassy downland, overlooks the town – the ruins of the Norman Castle, the steep hill of the High Street, the towers of Holy Trinity (which acted for over 30 years as the pro-cathedral) and St Mary's, the medieval church of Guildford. From here, it was felt, the new cathedral would dominate the town, and, visible for miles around, act as a symbol of the new diocese. It has certainly fulfilled this promise.

Liverpool and Guildford are the only cathedrals in England to have been built on a virgin site since the Middle Ages. The Cathedral at Guildford stands in spacious surroundings, accompanied only by a few new houses for the Dean and canons – and, on the N. side, by the buildings of the new University of Surrey. From the bypass (A3), the approach road leads up to the west front.

It was laid down in the conditions of the architects' competition that the building should be 'in the line of the great English cathedral'; so it is. Cruciform, with long nave and shorter chancel, with transepts, and Lady Chapel extending at the E. end, and central tower, it is built of warm-coloured red brick, made from the clay of Stag Hill itself, with dressings of stone from Clipsham

in Rutland, and Doulting stone from Somerset inside. The Cathedral is 365 feet long, and the tower 160 feet high.

The brickwork is attractive and, walking round the outside, the soaring walls are reminiscent of Albi: there is a tremendous sense of power and stability here. But there are disappointing features too: the heavy, bulky tower, supported only by very shallow transepts, appears from many angles top-heavy, and there is a terrible discrepancy between the tall narrow Gothic windows of the aisles and chancel, and the horizintal 'slits' of the clerestory – and the low horizontal windows of the chancel aisles; in many ways, too, the details seem clumsy, and Maufe's squat Gothic arches, which appear again and again throughout the building, are inelegant. But there is an imposing 'build-up' at the E. end, of Lady Chapel and its attendant buildings, chancel, transepts and tower – and at the W. end the lofty frontispiece itself, with its two low cloister wings forming outer porches, is attractive and original.

Inside, Maufe displays his remarkable ability to create a sense of space: the nave, of seven bays, with lofty arches rising from piers without capitals dividing the nave itself from almost equally lofty narrow aisles, is a masterpiece. To stand at the crossing and look W. down the nave, and down the narrow aisles which are processional ways uncluttered by chairs or other furnishings, is breathtaking. Outside, the Cathedral is rose-red in colour: inside, the much greater use of stone, and the plaster rendering of the walls, make it white and cool. As the eye is carried up to the still loftier arches of the crossing, to the wide soaring vault of nave and chancel, and the narrow vault of the aisles, there is no doubt at all that the architect has created an interior of nobility and repose. On either side of the chancel an ambulatory leads to smaller chapels, to vestries and the Lady Chapel.

The nave of Guildford Cathedral. Here Sir Edward Maufe displays his remarkable ability to create a sense of space

Guildford: the narrow nave aisle

Guildford: ABOVE *the occupations of men – low reliefs by Vernon Hill on the bronze doors to the south transept;* OPPOSITE *the west front from the approach road. The foundation stone was laid in 1936 and the cathedral consecrated in 1961*

But there is disappointment inside, too. The furnishings are unworthy of the noble interior: in place of a reredos there is merely a hanging of enormous length below the small round window; sedilia, stalls, and – above all – Bishop's throne are pedestrian in design, neither 'Gothic' nor 'modern'; altar ornaments, font cover, altar rails, iron screens are all equally depressing. An interior of such originality and power calls for fittings of distinction and panache. May they yet be provided.

Guildford: 'O praise God in His holiness' – engraved glass by John Hutton in the south transept

HEREFORD

Hereford Cathedral

THE VIEW FROM the Wye Bridge is justly famous: the river, of course, and the panorama of brick or whitewashed houses, the Bishop's Palace with its cedar trees and lawns descending to the river, and, beyond, the tall Georgian bay window of the Hall of the College of Vicars Choral. Above all this rises the Cathedral: the row of tall clerestory windows in the nave, the pinnacled west and east ends, the plain gable of the south transept, the long lower roof of the Lady Chapel, and the grand four-square central tower with its massed pinnacles.

Hereford is not a large town and, approaching from the south, from Monmouth or from Ross, the city spreads before us – a mass of streets and houses, two tall church spires, and the red sandstone cathedral. The see of Hereford is one of the most ancient in England (*c.* 676), and covers Herefordshire and south Shropshire, some of the most delectable and remote countryside in England; it has been affectionately termed 'the Dead See'.

Crossing the bridge, the main road and its traffic surge forwards up the new ring road to the north, passing relics of the city walls on the right: we can turn right (on foot it is to be hoped) up King Street; and where the street turns left into Broad Street, exposed upon wide lawns, unprotected by walls or railings, stands the Cathedral. It has had its misfortunes. The west tower, pinnacled and Perp, familiar from old engravings, collapsed in 1786, bringing down the west end of the nave; the chapter house, stripped of its lead in the Civil War, was pulled down in 1769; much severe rebuilding and restoration (not all of it unsympathetic) was carried out in the late 18th and 19th centuries – by Wyatt, Cottingham and Gilbert Scott; the pulpitum, crowned with a handsome 18th-century organ, was demolished in the mid 19th century; finally, the chancel screen, designed by Scott, and

executed by Skidmore in 1862 to take the place of the pulpitum, was removed in 1967: a sad loss.

The west front which we see today was erected (1902–8) by Oldrid Scott to replace the much less ornate frontispiece designed by Wyatt after the collapse of the west tower – which by the end of the 19th century was disapproved of. We enter by the north porch, a spectacular piece of Perp building, with three open arches, large traceried windows above, and the polygonal staircase turrets on either side crowned with little oriel windows. The nave arcades are Norman, with cylindrical columns and capitals carved with interlaced strands adorned with animals and foliage; above the arches, Wyatt's triforium and clerestory, and his wooden vaulted roof, discreetly painted, are a most successful pastiche. Turning east, the view is disappointing: the chancel is very short, and, without the Skidmore screen, everything is seen at one glance. The screen, a *tour de force* of brass and iron, and cut and polished stones, was delicate and light: nave and chancel were united, but there was separation, a division, an elegant lace-like curtain (as it were) between choir and nave. Now all is exposed; there is no mystery, no half-hidden world beyond, no holy of holies. There is talk of the restoration of the screen (which, mercifully, has been preserved): may it be replaced quickly; the whole interior will be doubly enhanced.

The small chancel is Norman too, with enormous bulbous columns embracing the triforium arcade – a wonderful effect. The east end is a recreation by Cottingham: a Norman arch, a Norman blind arcade above, and a triple lancet window filled with glass designed by Pugin, made by Wailes. The low reredos is by Cottingham too, gilded and ornate: above, the spandrel of the retrochoir arcade is carved with Cottingham's florid decoration – figures of St Ethelbert and the

Hereford Cathedral: Norman arcade and 14th-century choir stalls in the chancel

Hereford: acute, almost straight-sided arches in the north transept

Virgin; there is a glimpse through to the Lady Chapel beyond. The choir stalls and Bishop's throne are 14th century, and very fine: the misericords are one of the best sets in England. The Willis organ above, with its gaily painted Victorian case, is adorned with a woodpecker, to commemorate the recent rebuilding (by Harrison) largely through the generosity of Bulmers, of Woodpecker cider fame.

The transepts are of great interest: the south displays the earliest Norman work in the building, with its wide blank arcades, its triforium and clere-story; the wide arcades are now filled with three tapestries by John Piper, depicting in soft browns, blues and greys the Tree in Eden, the Tree of the Crucifixion, and the Tree in Paradise. The altarpiece is a German 16th-17th-century triptych. The south window is a Perp insertion (glass by Kempe, 1895). Nearby is the painted alabaster tomb of Alexander Denton of Hillesden, Bucks, with his first wife, a Herefordshire lady from Sugwas, who died *aet.* 17 in childbirth, in 1566; he himself died in 1570, *aet.* 31, and is buried at Hillesden among so many of his family, in the church which Sir Gilbert Scott described as 'an exquisite specimen of the latest phase of Gothic art'.

The N. transept is also special, with its sumptuous arcades and triforium, and its acute, almost straight-sided arches, its geometrical tracery and elaborately carved diapering; here is the shrine of St Thomas Cantilupe (Bishop 1275–82) and, nearby, the elaborate canopied tomb of Bishop Aquablanca (d. 1268), the builder of the transept. The geometrical N. window is filled with important glass by Hardman (1864).

Sumptuous gates by Scott and Skidmore lead into the chancel aisles: walking up the north aisle we can inspect the *Mappa Mundi*, made *c.* 1280 by Richard of Holdingham, Prebendary of Hereford and of Lincoln, depicting on vellum the world, with Jerusalem at its centre. Opposite, a door leads up to the Chained Library; and, just beyond, is the Stanbury Chantry, with its fan vaulting, and tomb of Bishop Stanbury (d. 1473) opposite. He was confessor to Henry VI, and nominated first Provost of Eton (though he never actually took office); Eton appears in the stained glass (by the Bromsgrove Guild, 1923), with the mottoes LAUS DEO and (unexpectedly) FLOREAT ETONA.

The east transepts and retrochoir lead to the Lady Chapel: the retrochoir took the place of an earlier apsidal east end, and dates from *c.* 1200; the Lady Chapel *c.* 1220; the eastern transepts *c.* 1300. Steps lead up to the Lady Chapel, a building of the purest E.E. with lancet windows – many filled with excellent glass of 1852 by Gibbs; but the west window on the south side contains the best glass in the Cathedral (13th century), with much grisaille patterning, and panels depicting the Crucifixion, the Agnus Dei, Christ in Majesty, and so on. The reredos is by Randoll Blacking (1950); and there are striking and colourful medieval monuments – to Joanna Bohun, Countess of Hereford (1327), and Peter de Grandison (1352), with an elaborate open screen above, adorned with

Hereford: little pigs in be-chevroned rugger jerseys adorn the tomb of Precentor Swinefield

figures of saints, Our Lord and the Virgin; at the west end a panelled, painted screen divides the Lady Chapel from the Audley Chantry, a two-storeyed, vaulted chapel which commemorates Bishop Audley (1492–1502; afterwards Bishop of Salisbury); nearby, below the steps, is the tomb of Precentor Swinefield (d. 1311): little pigs in be-chevroned rugger jerseys run around the apex of the arch amid acorns and foliage. Beneath the Lady Chapel, the crypt has recently been formed into a Treasury: among many treasures of plate on exhibition is a 13th-century Limoges reliquary, made to contain a relic of St Thomas Becket.

In the S.E. transept there are various monuments: of special interest are the ledger stones to Bishop Croft and Dean Benson, side by side, hands clasped. Herbert Croft was Dean during the Civil War, and a member of the Croft family of Croft Castle; it was he who, from the nave pulpit in 1645, rebuked the Cromwellian soldiers marauding the Cathedral. After the war, Croft became Bishop, and George Benson Dean; they were great friends, died within a few months of each other, and are buried here side by side, '*In vita conjuncti, in morte non divisi*', reads the inscription.

The south door here leads out into one of the great delights of Hereford – the Vicars' Cloister, an attribute unique among English cathedrals. The College of Vicars Choral was founded in 1396 for priests (or members of minor orders) responsible for singing the daily offices. A cloister walk from the south door leads into a charming quadrangle, built at the end of the 15th century, with small houses set around the courtyard garden. On the south side is College Hall, with its big Georgian bay window; here the gardens descend to the river. On the east side the former chapel is now the Chapter Room, appropriately set up and furnished for this purpose after the destruction of the Chapter House.

Returning into the Cathedral, we can admire the 16th-century nave pulpit from which Dean Croft rebuked the Cromwellian troops, and the larger 17th-century pulpit under the crossing, with its 18th-century Gothick sounding board. And the Norman font must not be missed, with the twelve apostles seated under the arcading, their feet seemingly dangling over the edge; four friendly lions support its base.

Here the south door leads into the Bishop's Cloister, built in the 15th century. There is Perp fenestration and Perp vaulting – except close to the nave where Wyatt, perhaps, replaced it in Gothick plaster after the fall of the west tower. We pass the 14th-century doorway to the former chapter house – Chapter House Court is now a delightful garden – and the gate at the end is the entrance to the Palace, and is PRIVATE. The south walk is used partly as the Song School, partly as a Lower Library. The cloisters are half open on the west side: this happy accident provides a perfect view of the south side of the Cathedral from the lawn outside, and of the great tower, built in the early 14th century, in all its majesty.

The Chained Library is the great glory of Hereford: there are some 1500 chained books, ranging from the Anglo-Saxon Gospels, written in Latin *c.* 800, and including many other early manuscript versions; the Hereford Breviary dates from *c.* 1270, and there are two Caxtons – not to mention important volumes of the 16th, 17th and 18th centuries. The Chained Library, in its early-17th-century bookcases, is housed, as has been said, in the upper north transept, and is open regularly.

Abbey Dore: almost the only Cistercian church in England still in use for worship

Abbey Dore

This is frontier country – the frontier between Herefordshire and Monmouthshire, between England and Wales. From Pontrilas in the south to Hay-on-Wye in the north the Golden Valley runs through countryside of ever increasing beauty and remoteness, watered by the little River Dore; pastoral country to the east, the Black Mountains to the west. Here in deep lanes, surrounded by small farms and orchards, stands Abbey Dore, one of the very few Cistercian churches in England still used for the worship of God. A grassy path leads down to a timbered porch in the south transept: a lofty transept, a lofty chancel, with a simple, narrow, embattled tower set in the angle, lower aisles and eastern ambulatory, tall lancet windows everywhere. We are at the door. 'Visitors please be gratefull [*sic*]' – reads a notice on the door – 'to all who erected and beautified this old Abbey, Do not leave it without a prayer. It is the House of God, therefore it is the house of prayer.' Step inside, and we are in the spacious crossing of a great monastic church, built in purest E.E. style: the transepts, chancel, aisles and ambulatory survive; the arch which led into the nave is blocked, and a 17th-century minstrels' gallery stands against this wall; a gorgeous 17th-century screen, surmounted by carved obelisks and cartouches of arms surrounded by scrollwork, divides crossing from chancel.

The wall of the transept opposite is adorned with the Royal Arms of Charles I painted on the plaster, with faded pictures above of David with his harp and Time with his scythe. Underneath is an inscription which reads: 'A great part of this church being broken down, and all of it together with the tithes of this parish being made a lay fee by Act of Parliament at the dissolution of the Abbey . . . this remainder of the said church was restored to a sacred use, the walls thereof being greatly repaired, the roof and tower entirely rebuilt, the Rectory founded and bountifully endowed with all ye parochial tithes and with glebe and manse by the pious and ever memorable JOHN Lord Viscount Scudamore upon ye 22nd day of March Anno Domini 1634.'

Abbey Dore was founded in 1147 as a Cistercian house by Robert of Ewyas, a grandson of the Conqueror. The present building was begun in

Abbey Dore: Laudian furnishings in the crossing

1180, and in the early 13th century the choir was enlarged and the aisles and ambulatory added. In 1260 Bishop Aquablanca of Hereford granted an indulgence to all who contributed to this work, and it was consecrated by St Thomas Cantilupe, Bishop of Hereford, *c.* 1280. At the Dissolution in 1535 the property was granted to John Scudamore of Holme Lacy. It was his descendant John, 1st Viscount Scudamore (known as 'the good Lord Scudamore'), a devout High Churchman and friend of Archbishop Laud, who restored the building – then little more than a roofless shell. It was reconsecrated on Palm Sunday, 1634, which was Lord Scudamore's birthday.

Lord Scudamore employed the celebrated Hereford 'architector' John Abel: the ruined nave was blocked off, and new roofs of Herefordshire oak from the Holme Lacy estate were provided for transepts, crossing and chancel. The screen, which bears the arms of Charles I, of Archbishop Laud, and of Lord Scudamore, leads into the chancel, all furnished by John Abel with stalls and pews, pulpit and altar rails. Above and around, the arcades and lancet windows are of simple and austere Cistercian beauty; only in the ambulatory, with its four piers, each with eight shafts and stiff-leaf capitals, is there more elaboration. The aisles and ambulatory have retained their vaulting. In the chapel of the south transept is the tomb of John Hoskyns, Serjeant at Law and M.P. for Hereford, friend of Sir Walter Raleigh and Ben Jonson, and famous wit (d. 1623). The chapel has been furnished as a memorial to many generations of the family, baronets of Harewood (nearby); of these not the least distinguished were Sir Edwin, 12th Bt., Bishop of Southwell (d. 1924), and his son, also Sir Edwin, Fellow of Corpus Christi, Cambridge, and eminent New Testament scholar (d. 1937).

Sheep graze in the orchards which accompany the north side of the church, where once stood chapter house and cloisters: a few fragments of the nave survive – all else is grass. Abbey Dore, in its setting and in its surviving building, is perfection.

Bromfield Priory

On a wooded promontory above the River Teme, close to where it is joined by the little River Onny, stands a church with a sturdy N.W. tower. At first sight it might pass for an ordinary village church, but abutting the churchyard wall is an imposing gatehouse, with 14th-century stone base, massive buttresses, and a slightly later timbered upper storey with a gabled bay window over the archway. This was the entrance to Bromfield Priory, the church itself a fragment of the monastic church. On walking round its exterior, it is a great surprise to find adjoining the east end what appears to be a ruined Tudor house, with porch and gaping mullioned windows. At the Dissolution the Priory was granted to Charles Foxe of Ludford, the village on the Teme close to Ludlow, who formed this house out of the monastic chancel and added a wing on the south side – now this curious ruin.

Bromfield Priory: the gatehouse

This small Benedictine priory was founded here in 1155, an offshoot of the Abbey of Gloucester: the nave and aisle were the parish church, the chancel, transepts and east end of the nave were monastic – and it was this which Charles Foxe converted into his house at the Dissolution. Entering the church under the tower, which forms a spacious porch, it will soon be seen what has happened. Blocked-up Norman arches at the east end provide the clue to its original 12th-century plan, with chancel, transepts and aiseless nave. In the early 14th century a north aisle was built, with a simple arcade between nave and aisle, and the N.W. tower was built.

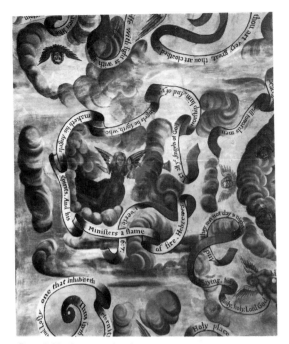

Bromfield: the painted ceiling

his are the handsome choir stalls, screen and reredos. And there are windows by Kempe, aglow with his own rich dark greens and blues, which add much to the atmosphere of the church.

Chirbury Priory

Spectacular Shropshire – Welsh Border countryside, and an imposing church which in reality is the nave of an Augustinian priory founded in the early 13th century; chancel and transepts have disappeared, and the small brick sanctuary was built in 1733. The nave is wide and lofty, with tall E.E. arcades. A small bronze matrix for casting small statues of the Virgin, for sale to medieval pilgrims, was dug up in the churchyard here; it is believed to be unique. Lord Herbert of Chirbury,

Charles Foxe's daughter married Matthew Herbert, grandson of Sir Richard Herbert of Montgomery, and the Herberts came into possession. In 1665 Foxe's house attached to the church was burnt, and the family removed to the Keeper's Lodge in Oakley Park – which adjoins Bromfield – which was subsequently rebuilt and glorified into the present mansion, and is still the home of their descendants. Richard Herbert, Matthew's grandson, restored the east end of the nave to the church to serve as chancel, and in 1672 erected a coved plaster ceiling, which was gloriously painted by Thomas Francis. It is of unique interest, and the glory of the church.

Here angels with outspread wings float amid clouds and ribbons bearing texts: 'And they rest not day and night, saying Holy, Holy, Holy, Lord God Almighty, which was, and is, and is to come . . .' A billowing cloud in the centre surrounds the symbol of the Holy Trinity, with worshipping cherubs all round: 'There are three that bear record in Heaven, the Father, the Word, and the Holy Ghost, and these three are one . . .'; in this rustic but deeply pious picture of Heaven the angels are depicted in devout attendance on God. It is a most moving painting, in soft greys and whites, blues and reds. There is a grand Royal Arms of Charles II in the nave, which was perhaps also painted by Thomas Francis.

Hodgson Fowler restored the church in 1890:

Chirbury: a rustic cherub on an 18th-century monument

Chirbury: the canons' stalls now in Montgomery church

Leominster: the Norman north arcade

elder brother of George Herbert, bequeathed his library to the parish: it is now kept in the County Archives in Shrewsbury. Some of the monastic furnishings from the destroyed chancel are now in the church at Montgomery, three miles away across the Border, and well deserve a visit.

Leominster Priory

Leominster can boast a population of 6000 souls – and as such is the second largest town in Herefordshire (*incredibile dictu*). There are narrow streets, with overhanging timbered houses, still narrower alleys, some stouter Georgian houses – and Church Street leads down to the Priory, standing detached and a little aloof in its enormous churchyard, with open countryside beyond. Built of warm red sandstone, it appears outwardly all Dec or Perp – with grand geometrical windows, studded with ball-flower ornament, in the south aisle, a large Perp window at the west end of the nave, and a pinnacled Perp tower beyond. Only the Norman base of the tower, with a gorgeous Norman doorway below, betrays the presence of

a Norman building behind; but for this we must wait.

The Dec south porch is the main entrance, and leads into an exceedingly spacious south aisle, lit by the enormous Dec windows, and so into the equally spacious nave – of much the same date. And then, surprise of surprises, the north arcade is Norman, and beyond this is an even more impressive second Norman nave; and there is a narrower Norman north aisle beyond that. This is the monastic nave, with squat, solid, solemn Norman arcades, triforium and clerestory.

There was a nunnery here in the 9th century, which was dissolved in 1046. Henry I gave the manor of Leominster to Reading Abbey in 1123, and very soon afterwards the Benedictine Priory was founded here as a cell of Reading. The Norman nave was consecrated in 1130. At the end of the 13th century the new (parochial) south nave was built, and its south aisle was added soon after. The Priory was dissolved in 1539: the apsidal east end, the Lady Chapel beyond, and the transepts (all revealed in plan from 19th-century excavations), cloisters and monastic quarters were all destroyed, leaving only this incredible rump of four stately naves – or aisles – to serve as the parish church.

A fire swept the building in 1699: the arcade between the nave and south aisle was rebuilt with Tuscan pillars; the present elegant arcade is an inspired rebuilding by Sir Gilbert Scott at the time of his restoration (1872–9). There is a handsome organ of 1739, stained glass by Mayer of Munich (west window) and Kempe (south aisle), and in the north aisle an extraordinary ducking stool. 'The ancient and universal punishment for common scolds', reads the notice, 'and for Butchers, Bakers, Brewers, Apothecaries and all else who give short measure or vended adulterated articles of food.' It was last used in 1809, when one Jenny Piper was paraded through the town, then ducked in the river near Kenwater Bridge. A splendid G III R Royal Arms is banished to the east end of this aisle, and a magnificent 15th-century chalice is on view in the south aisle in a glass-fronted safe. From here there is a remarkable view across the whole width of these three parallel naves of the church.

Before departure, the Norman west door – which was noticed so briefly on our arrival – should be examined: it is fascinating work of *c.* 1150. The arches are unadorned, apart from a little zigzag

Leominster: scenes of human and animal life on the Romanesque capitals of the west door

ornament, but the capitals are elaborately and vividly carved, with birds, lions or snakes amid trailing foliage, or with men working in the garden; there is more pretty carving in the frieze above. A few fragments of the monastic buildings are incorporated in the old people's home on the north side of the church, but otherwise nothing survives.

'I, Robert, by the Grace of God Bishop of Hereford, to all Christian men, greeting: I pray you and exhort you by the Lord Jesus Christ, by whose blood we are redeemed, that ye will think favourably of the church of St Peter at Leominster. We know, and have learnt by undoubted proofs that the said church is loved of God . . .' So proclaimed Bishop de Bethan at the Consecration in 1130. We in 1986 cannot do otherwise.

DIOCESE OF
LEICESTER

Leicester Cathedral

LEICESTER IS UNFORTUNATE in its new buildings. The large blocks of modern offices, the high-rise flats, the new dual carriageways of the inner relief roads, the empty derelict sites in the middle of the town, make it difficult to realize that this is one of the most ancient towns in England. As its name suggests, Leicester was a Roman town, and there are interesting Roman remains to be seen here; it was a Norman town, and impressive Norman work is to be seen – in St Mary de Castro, and St Nicholas' Church, and the hall of the Castle; it was a medieval town, and of this there is still much to see – in the Guildhall, the Castle Gateway, and several ancient parish churches. There are still 18th-century streets in the old town, and a number of good houses, especially near the Cathedral. The spire of the Cathedral was the most prominent of Leicester's landmarks – but it is now hemmed in by so many modern blocks that the church is hard to find. Suffice to say that it is close to the Clock Tower, in the very centre of the town.

There was a Saxon diocese of Leicester from 680 to 870, but the site of its cathedral is not known. The present diocese was founded in 1927, and St Martin's Church became the cathedral. The ancient civic church of the town, though much rebuilt in the 19th century, it stands dignified and quite impressive, close to the Guildhall in a very cramped setting. The tall, tapering broach spire between nave and chancel is by Raphael Brandon (1867); there is a S. porch by Pearson (1897) – indeed outwardly the church appears entirely 19th century. The outer south aisle was the medieval chapel of the Corpus Christi Guild: from here there is a vista of the interior – broad, dark, and well furnished with its handsome oak fittings: organ gallery, chancel screen, the Chapel of the Leicestershire Regiment, the Consistory Court, with endless rows of chairs and well-polished parquet floors everywhere. The nave arcades are medieval: most of the rest of the church is a

rebuilding, or at least a thorough restoration, by Brandon (1861–7). The chancel is filled with choir stalls and canons' stalls and Bishop's throne by Sir Charles Nicholson (*c.* 1927), and has the air of a well-furnished college chapel – small but dignified. The N. Chapel contains many memorials to the old Leicester family of Herrick (the earliest is 1589), with many tomb slabs erected round the walls. The father of Robert Herrick, the poet, was born in Leicester; the mother of Dean Swift was a Herrick, and is buried here; the S. Chapel contains many 18th-century monuments. There is decent Victorian glass throughout the church; of greater interest is the (early-20th-century) east window by Christopher Whall – there is also a smaller window by him at the west end of the S. aisle.

But the monuments are the thing. In the floor of the chancel is a slab inscribed:

RICHARD III
King of England
killed at Bosworth Field
in this county
22 August 1485
Buried in the church of the Grey Friars
in this parish

There is a grand monument (N. aisle) to John Whatton (1656), signed by Joshua Marshall, and another, of Rococo design (chancel) to the son and wives of Gabriel Newton, Alderman of Leicester (1746), the great benefactor to education in the city. In the S. Chapel is the tablet by Bacon (1814), erected by John Johnson, Architect, to his parents; it also commemorates the architect himself, 'late of the parish of St Mary-le-Bow, London'. He was architect of the County Rooms here, and of the Shire Hall at Chelmsford, and rebuilder of the nave of Chelmsford Cathedral (q.v.). And there are many more memorials, often with delightful inscriptions, reflecting the civic pride of this ancient city.

Leicester Cathedral: the Newton monument in the chancel

Breedon-on-the-Hill: the priory on its hilltop

The Priory, Breedon-on-the-Hill

Some hill: it stands suddenly erect, 200 feet high, a solid lump of carboniferous limestone, here on the borders of Leicestershire and Derbyshire, with a square, severe-looking church in dramatic isolation on its top, and its village below. The drive to the top amply rewards the effort, as does the search for the key at the vicarage in the village. This is a very ancient site: an iron-age fort (*c.* AD 1); a 7th-century Saxon monastic church; then an early-12th-century priory of Augustinian Canons, founded as a cell of Nostell Priory in Yorkshire. It is the central tower and chancel of this which

survive – used as the parish church since the Dissolution. Traces of the arch into the vanished parochial nave are to be seen in the base of the Norman tower; what now serves as the nave is the 13th-century monastic chancel, with its square E. end and vaulted aisles. And here the most remarkable things are to be seen. Earliest in date are the Saxon sculptures – not merely individual carved stones, but long friezes (there are some 60 ft of them) of sculpture which now adorn the E. end and aisle: friezes of carved foliage, human figures, beasts and birds, figures of saints and of the Virgin, which have been miraculously preserved from the Saxon church which was destroyed by the Danes in the 9th century. And perhaps most moving of all is the figure of an angel, in the first floor of the tower, with one hand holding a cross, the other held up in blessing. This is some of the most important Saxon sculpture in England, and is far too little known.

And this is not all: 18th-century box pews, reading desk, W. gallery, fill the church, and in the N. aisle is the 17th-century family pew of the Shirleys of Staunton Harold – like a great family coach, ornamented with obelisks and carved scrolls; nearby are their 16th-century monuments: John (1570), Francis (1571), and George (1588), with their effigies, and each with his wife, occupying grand alabaster tombs. Breedon was the family's church and burial place before the church at Staunton Harold was built in 1653.

From this precipitous hill-top – made more precipitous on two sides by the quarrying below – are wonderful views over the Trent Valley and Charnwood Forest, and across to the plantations of Staunton Harold and Calke Abbey.

Breedon-on-the-Hill: Saxon sculpture

Launde Abbey

A magnificent, remote, rolling park, in the delectable uplands of N.E. Leicestershire, close to the Rutland frontier, far from main roads in its own little world of lonely lanes and ancient woodlands. From all directions the drives lead to the house, an H-shaped Elizabethan and 17th-century manor house, with gabled wings, gabled dormers. Unsuspected and unexpected, the chancel of the Augustinian priory church stands behind the north wing, still in use for worship.

Launde was founded for Augustinian Canons in 1125: at the Dissolution the property was granted to Thomas Cromwell, Lord Cromwell of Oakham (1525), Earl of Essex (1540), Henry VIII's great minister. At his disgrace and beheading the earldom was forfeited, but his son Gregory was allowed to inherit the barony: it was he who built the house.

The monastic chancel is small and intimate, a Perp rebuilding of the late 14th or early 15th century; at the west end is the original crossing – but nave and transepts were destroyed at the Dissolution. There are two special pleasures in this chancel – one is the distinguished early-15th-century glass in the east window, and the more

Launde Abbey: the tomb of Gregory Cromwell (1551) in the chancel

fragmentary remains in the south windows, tactfully and harmoniously augmented in the early
19th century; the other is the tomb of Gregory
Cromwell in the sanctuary. A rare piece of early
Renaissance sculpture (1551), the centrepiece is a
gorgeous cartouche of arms, held up by two flying
horses as supporters, and surmounted by helmet
and eagle crest. Beneath is the inscription, and
all around the grand framework of pilasters and
pediment, supported by cherubs.

The Cromwells, impoverished, departed: other
owners followed; Launde is now the Retreat
House of the Diocese of Leicester, a most appropriate use for this beautiful monastic fragment,
with its attached mansion occupying the site of the
monastic buildings. There are panelled rooms in
the house, and an elegant 18th-century staircase.
All these are in constant use – not least the Chapel.
Launde Abbey has, in the 20th century, returned
to religious use.

Owston: inexplicably grand for a parish church

Owston Priory

One of the pleasures of Leicestershire, Owston
(pronounced Ooston) is a remote and tiny village
in the steep uplands to be found in the N.E. of
the county, close to the Rutland border and far
from any main road – a countryside of deep valleys,
secluded hamlets and inconsequential lanes. Owston is a village of stone cottages sitting higgledy-
piggledy around every corner; close to the lane
which leads to Maresfield stands the rump of the
ancient priory church, founded here for Augustinian Canons *c.* 1160.

There is a tower of *c.* 1300, with a short spire,
which serves as a porch at the N.W. corner: inside,

we are in the spacious, lofty nave of the monastic
church. Two wide bays (*c.* 1300) divide nave from
aisle – all, otherwise, inexplicably grand for a
village church. The blocked south door led to the
conventual buildings – long since destroyed: the
monastic choir would have extended east into what
is now the orchard of the Priory House (for many
years the rectory), a charming early-19th-century
stone house, with one or two medieval features
from the monastic buildings incorporated in its
walls.

Altogether, an idyllic spot.

DIOCESE OF
LICHFIELD

Lichfield Cathedral

MOST PEOPLE THINK that Staffordshire is all Potteries – or all Black Country. The Potteries are
there all right, in the north; the Black Country is
there all right, in the south. But the heart of the
county is agricultural – indeed agriculture is the
county's greatest industry. It is in this agricultural
heart of Staffordshire that Lichfield lies, a countryside of tall brick farmhouses and trim brick villages,
Lichfield its cathedral city. But Lichfield is the
mother church not just of Staffordshire, but of the
whole Midlands. Ever since the days of St Chad,
who died in 672, Lichfield has been a holy place.
The first cathedral was built in 700 – the cathedral
of all Mercia – and the body of the saint buried
here. Lichfield became a place of pilgrimage and,
for a short time in the 9th century, an archbishop-
ric. Lichfield is also Dr Johnson's city: his birthplace is in the Market Place. Here stands his
statue, and nearby stands Boswell's. It is a city of
Georgian streets and Georgian houses, which give
it its intimate character. The main street – St John
Street, Bird Street, Beacon Street (it changes its
name as it progresses) – brings us to Minster Pool:
here we can pause to admire the view of the
Cathedral with its three spires rising above the
houses in the Close, rising above Minster Pool. It
is worth walking the length of the pool as far as
Dam Street, to enjoy the view of the south side of
the Cathedral – then, crossing Dam Street, to
continue the walk along Stow Pool (if there is time)
to St Chad's Well. The view of the east end of the
Cathedral across Stow Pool is unforgettable. If
time is short, we can merely walk up Dam Street
into the Close, and from there make a circuit of
the Cathedral. If time is shorter still we can continue up Beacon Street from Minster Pool, without
any of these diversions, and turn in by the narrow
entry to the Close, which leads to the west front.
By whichever way we come, we must certainly
stand here.

As has been said, Lichfield owes its importance
to St Chad: nothing is known about the first church

– the Saxon church – nor of what came next; but
it is certain that a Norman cathedral was built soon
after the Conquest, of which nothing remains.
Work began on the present cathedral *c.* 1200, with
the building of the first three bays of the chancel;
the transepts and chapter house followed; then the
nave, *c.* 1260, followed by the west front. The
central tower and spire were begun *c.* 1300, and
the west spires soon after; the Lady Chapel and
eastern part of the chancel were built in the early
14th century. The Cathedral suffered serious
damage during the Civil War, and repairs were
put in hand at the Restoration. But a complete
restoration did not take place till the 19th century.
Sir Gilbert Scott started work here in 1857,
and it is to him and his son Oldrid that so much
of the appearance of the Cathedral today is due.
This very thorough restoration went on until
1901.

The west front is the Cathedral's most spectacular feature. The great façade, built in red sandstone, is adorned with a tremendous display of
statues and arcading, of trefoils, quatrefoils and
cinquefoils; at the centre is a geometrical window;
below, three elaborately carved porches. The west
towers form part of the façade, and carry on the
scheme round the north and south sides, albeit
less sumptuously. The spires rise in a great cluster
of pinnacles and crockets, to be capped by gilded
18th-century weather vanes.

The beauty of the interior consists in its delicate
feminine grace; the nave was built at the time when
the simplicity of the E.E. style blossomed in the
richly cultivated perfection of the Dec. The clustered columns are adorned with foliated capitals,
the spandrels of the arches decorated with cinquefoils divided by the long shaft of the vault; the
triforium is ornamented with stiff-leaf capitals and
dog-tooth, and the clerestory lit by unusual windows in the shape of spherical triangles filled with
geometrical tracery. We can stand at the back and
enjoy the view to the great windows of the apse,

and the even rhythm of the nave and chancel vaulting.

The crossing is adorned with the magnificent pulpit of brass and iron, with its double staircase, and even more by the chancel screen. Both were designed by Gilbert Scott, and executed by Skidmore (1859). The screen is a High Victorian masterpiece, delicate, transparent, ornamental – and now that it has been cleaned it has come into its own. The comparable screens at Salisbury and Hereford have been removed, and that at Salisbury destroyed – an act of vandalism. But this screen here at Lichfield is increasingly admired. In both north and south transept there is a delightful collection of 18th-century marble monuments, all recently cleaned and regilded to great effect. They reflect the taste and elegance of 18th-century Lichfield, when the cathedral dignitaries and local

OPPOSITE *Lichfield Cathedral: the Ladies of the Vale across the Minster Pool;* ABOVE *the Skidmore Screen*

The nave arcade at Lichfield

gentry enjoyed each other's company in the perfect setting of close and city.

As has been said, the three western bays of the chancel represent the oldest part of the present Cathedral (*c.* 1200), but it will be seen how skilfully they were blended into the later bays of the presbytery and retrochoir. The arcade is low, the clerestory lofty, and some of the windows are 17th-century Perp insertions of Bishop Hacket's restoration after the Civil War. There is no tri-

Lichfield: the apse – sumptuous work of the Dec period

forium proper – only a galleried walk with embattled parapet under the windows, and the splays
of the windows are patterned with quatrefoils. The
chancel with its Gilbert Scott reredos, Gilbert
Scott stalls, Gilbert Scott screens, seems comfortable and opulent, the Victorian setting *par
excellence.*

The Lady Chapel is the great glory of Lichfield.
Nine enormous windows of trefoil tracery occupy
the apse and fill the entire upper space above the

panelled and canopied arcading of the lower wall. Seven of these windows are filled with Flemish glass from Herckenrode Abbey near Liège, and were bought at the sale of the dissolved abbey by Sir Brooke Boothby of Ashbourne in 1802. Even on a dull day the warmth and glow of the glass fill the east end of the Cathedral with colour. The glass in the two western windows is also Flemish, but its exact provenance is unknown.

On the north side of the chancel a vestibule leads to the chapter house: this is octagonal, and the vaulted roof springs from a central pillar. On the west wall, over the door, is a 15th-century wall painting of the Assumption. There is a further vaulted chamber over the chapter house, which serves as the library. On the south side of the chancel is the Consistory Court, with the chapel of St Chad's Head above it.

In addition to the monuments already mentioned, there are some of special interest. First, the busts of Dr Johnson and David Garrick in the south transept: both are of 1793, both by Westmacott. In the north chancel aisle are the kneeling figure of Bishop Ryder (1836) by Chantrey, the bronze bust of Bishop Woods (1953) by Epstein, and the recumbent figure of Bishop Lonsdale (1867) by G. F. Watts. In the south chancel aisle is Chantrey's celebrated monument of the sleeping children (1814), the two daughters of Canon Robinson; close to this is the effigy of Bishop Hacket (1670), who was responsible for the restoration of the Cathedral after the Civil War. In the small chantry on the south side of the Lady Chapel is the tomb of Bishop Selwyn (1878), who was first Bishop in New Zealand before becoming Bishop of Lichfield – Selwyn College, Cambridge is named after him; the effigy is by Nicholls, the tiles by de Morgan. In the south aisle of the nave is a tablet to Dean Addison, father of Joseph Addison; close to the N.W. door one to Lady Mary Wortley Montagu, by Scheemakers.

There is more of the Herckenrode glass in the north and south choir aisles – as also, glass by Kempe; the west window is by Clayton & Bell; Burlison & Grylls, and Ward & Hughes, are also represented by glass in the nave aisles.

The close is charming – compact and intimate – with many delightful houses. Vicars' Court is a little quadrangle of timbered houses tucked away in the N.W. corner; the Deanery is a handsome house of 1704, with wide pediment and sash windows; next door the splendid Bishop's Palace (now used as the Choir School) was built in 1687, and designed by Edward Pearce, one of Wren's masons; it is one of those perfect houses which only the late 17th century knew how to build.

With its three spires Lichfield is unique among the ancient cathedrals of England: across the flat lands of the Trent Valley, or when seen from far away, from the high ground of Cannock Chase, their silhouette is unmistakable and unforgettable – the Ladies of the Vale.

Fairwell Priory

A little hamlet lost in deep lanes to the west of Lichfield, and a little fragment of a Benedictine priory founded *c.* 1140 by Roger de Clinton, Bishop of Lichfield: only the early-14th-century chancel survives, with a few old stalls with misericords. The brick nave and low tower are simple Georgian work of *c.* 1745.

Fairwell: the fragment of a Benedictine priory

Lapley Priory

North of Watling Street, in Staffordshire, are a number of unknown, unspoilt villages – among them Lapley. Unexpectedly, the church has an immense central tower: it is the church of a small Benedictine priory, founded here in the 11th century. Albeit shorn of its transepts, it is still an awe-inspiring building. Nave and chancel are oddly aligned, and through the dark space under the central tower the view of the chancel from the nave appears distant and mysterious. It is a Norman building, but there are many later windows and the top of the tower, with its parapet and

Lapley: the central tower

many pinnacles, is Perp. It still has the feel of a monastic church. Nothing remains of the conventual buildings, apart from a few fragments built into farm buildings nearby.

To the west there are beautiful stretches of the Shropshire Union Canal – well-wooded, long, straight and silent.

Shrewsbury Abbey

Shrewsbury is a hill-top town, embraced on three sides by the River Severn, with innumerable narrow streets, alleys and courtyards, innumerable black-and-white houses, and innumerable red brick Georgian ones; the tall spires of St Mary's and St Alkmund's pierce the sky; Shrewsbury School looks down its steep bank upon the river and its boathouses; Lord Hill, Wellington's General, looks down from the largest Doric column in the world; there is the pink sandstone Norman castle, the grey stone Victorian Tudor railway station, the younger Pugin's R.C. Cathedral, George Steuart's St Chad's – and a host of lesser churches. Two bridges of classic beauty, the English Bridge (1774) and the Welsh Bridge (1795), cross the river into the town:

> 'High the vanes of Shrewsbury gleam
> Islanded in Severn stream.'
> (Housman)

And somewhat outside the medieval town, close to the English Bridge, bereft of its monastic buildings, close to railway sidings, and stranded by heavy traffic, stands Shrewsbury Abbey.

The Benedictine Abbey of SS Peter and Paul was founded by Roger de Montgomery, kinsman of the Conqueror, in 1083. In its day it was one of the most important abbeys of England, and its abbot sat in the House of Lords; its monastic buildings occupied most of the ground between the church and the river, and among its great treasures were the relics of St Winifred, which were brought here from Holywell in North Wales in 1137. After the Dissolution the nave became the parish church of the Holy Cross and the chancel was destroyed. Old prints of the 18th century show substantial ruins of the monastic buildings still standing, but all was swept away when Telford constructed the new Holyhead road (A5) close to the S. side of the church in 1836. Pearson restored the building, and rebuilt the chancel and transepts in 1886: such is the church we see today.

The west front is imposing – Norman (*c.* 1100), with Norman doorway, and Perp window above, with elaborate tracery and crocketed ogee gable, and with canopied niches for statues to left and right, and another above, between the two windows of the Perp tower; the interior is imposing, too, with its lofty proportions, Norman arcades, Norman crossing arches, and Pearson's impressive

Shrewsbury: Norman arcades in the nave

east end. The two westernmost bays of the nave
were rebuilt in the 14th century (when the tower
was built), but the rest are sturdiest Norman work,
with plain circular piers and the simplest round
arches – the pattern repeated in the triforium
above. The clerestory is Pearson's restoration. It is
difficult to exaggerate the importance of Pearson's
contribution to this interior. Apart from rebuilding
the clerestory and the high timber ceiling, he
rebuilt the crossing, the transepts and the sanctuary. This sensitive, scholarly east end is the making
of the church, with its three long lancet windows,
its lofty vault, and the many steps leading up to
the High Altar with its gorgeous triptych. Pearson
designed both glass and triptych – indeed Pearson
realized what these churches were for – to bring
the worshipper to his knees, and raise his eyes to
Heaven.

There are a number of interesting monuments
in the aisles, and a small 14th-century seated figure
of the Madonna in the nave. The glass in the W.
window is heraldic (1814), perhaps by Betton of
Shrewsbury.

And opposite the S. door, railed off in a little
garden on the far side of the road, with the railway
yards behind, is a final surprise: the little 14th-
century stone pulpit of the monastic refectory. It
stands like a little lantern, with sculptured figures
below each opening, an unusual fragment of monastic furnishing, an unexpected survival in a very
unexpected setting.

Tutbury: elaborate Norman carving on the west front

Tutbury Priory

The little town stands above the River Dove, which
here forms the frontier between Staffordshire and
Derbyshire. On the heights above stand the jagged
ruins of the Castle, where Mary Queen of Scots
was imprisoned three or four times between 1569
and 1585; and there are Georgian houses and
cottages in High Street and Castle Street, with
the tall timbered Dog and Partridge Inn, with its
overhanging upper floors, to delight us in the High
Street. Between the castle and the town the priory
church is an imposing fragment of the Benedictine
priory, which was founded in the late 11th century
by Henry de Ferrers. There is a sumptuous west
doorway (*c.* 1160), with elaborate carvings and
decoration; the large Norman window above is
also elaborately decorated – but filled with late-
13th-century curvilinear tracery; interlaced arcading adorns the wall on either side, with three tiny
round windows in the gable; in the low south tower
is another Norman doorway, with a boar hunt in
the tympanum. Inside, the grand nave survives,
with Norman arcades and triforium above, now
filled with Perp windows to form a clerestory.
Transepts, central tower and chancel were pulled
down at the Dissolution: G. E. Street built the
present shorter apsidal chancel in 1866. There are
furnishings by Street, and a metal Royal Arms of
Queen Victoria above the west door.

From the churchyard there is a grand view
over the wide Trent Valley, with the breweries of
Burton at our feet, and the enormous power
stations along the river bank beyond.

Lincoln Cathedral

NO CATHEDRAL IS MORE EXCITING to approach than Lincoln. I once met a man who was walking from Edinburgh to work in the Kent hopfields: he crossed the Humber from Hull, and walked down the long straight road, the Ermine Street (A15), towards Lincoln. All the time, he said, there were the three towers of the Cathedral in straight line ahead, and they never seemed to get any nearer. We can approach Lincoln this way. Or we can approach it from the S., along the lonely Brant Road which runs parallel with the Cliff, and after Brant Broughton passes no villages, but provides a wonderful view of the Cathedral from afar. It is rather like approaching Chartres, where in much the same way the spires of that cathedral are visible for miles across the rich cornfields of central France. Or from the E., from Washingborough: there is the view of the Cathedral which de Wint loved. Or come from the S.E. down Canwick Hill: the view of the Cathedral from Canwick is breathtaking. Or from the W.: soon after crossing the Trent, on a clear day even from Markham Moor, the Cathedral comes in sight, and on approaching nearer it is possible to pick out the details of the west front. Indeed, on a clear day, the Cathedral perched on its hill is visible across half the county. It is only on entering the city that disappointment assails us: Lincoln grew enormously in the 19th century, and there are long streets of dreary red houses spreading everywhere. Half the city is 'above hill', half 'below hill': from the top we look down upon factories and drab streets – but from the lower town we catch glimpses of the Cathedral sailing above – and this is one of the great sights of Europe.

Lincoln Cathedral is a giant: when we have at last ascended Lindum Hill, or (better still) walked up Steep Hill, and stand in front of the Exchequer Gate, we shall be aware of its tremendous scale. The houses of Minster Yard, the gateways, everything nearby, is dominated by its stupendous presence. Passing under the gateway, standing before

the west front and walking round the exterior, the visitor will examine towers, pinnacles, transepts, flying buttresses; inside, awestruck, he will observe the arcades, traceried windows, medieval woodwork, vast spaces. 'Probably,' writes Mr Alec Clifton-Taylor, 'all things considered, Lincoln is the finest of our English cathedrals.'

The Cathedral is built of stone quarried from the ground on which it stands, a honey-coloured limestone, contrasting with the dark grey, or brown, or green of the Purbeck marble shafts – a great feature of the interior. Originally all three towers were crowned with spires of lead-sheathed timber. The steeple on the central tower, which crashed in 1542, made the building the highest object made by human hands in Britain. The smaller steeples on the western towers were taken down in 1807.

The see of Lincoln was founded in 1072, and Remigius, the first Norman to be given an English bishopric, became the first bishop – transferring the see from Dorchester-on-Thames. Until the formation of the see of Oxford in 1542, the diocese of Lincoln stretched down as far as the Thames. The Bishop of Lincoln was, and still is, Visitor of Eton College. There had been a Saxon minster on the hill, but this was pulled down to make way for a new cathedral which was twenty years in building; all that remains of it is the façade of the west front and the lower part of the west towers. The original timber roof was destroyed in a fire of 1141, and the stone vault which replaced it was too heavy for the masonry below; in an earthquake of 1155 the greater part of Remigius' cathedral collapsed. St Hugh, who became Bishop of Lincoln in 1192, after being Prior of Witham in Somerset (q.v.), was the founder of the new E.E. cathedral.

St Hugh started his new building with the choir, planning to work down to the west end, and join up with the Norman west front. Following the French practice, the E. end was apsidal, with

ABOVE *Lincoln Cathedral: Lord Tennyson surveys Minster Yard under the shadow of the central tower;* RIGHT *the Norman west front, with the 13th-century screen added above and around it*

radiating chapels. In the middle of the following century this was pulled down, and in its place was built the Angel Choir in the new Decorated style – to enlarge the cathedral eastwards, and to provide a worthy setting for the shrine of St Hugh. This is the cathedral which stands today.

Standing before the west front it is easy to distinguish the Norman façade, with its round arches, from the lofty Gothic screen which was built above and around it. In this Norman façade is the sculptured frieze (*c.* 1145), of which only portions now remain, portraying on the left the tortures inflicted on the wicked in hell, and on the right scenes from the stories of Noah and Daniel.

Lincoln: the Angel Choir – angels above, the Lincoln Imp below

These sculptures have features in common with similar work at St Denis Abbey near Paris, as rebuilt by Abbot Suger, and the frieze on the façade of Modena Cathedral in Italy. The large windows are Perp insertions. From behind the Gothic screen rise the two Norman towers, to which the upper stages were added at the end of the 14th century. This tremendous west front, terminating in two tapering pinnacles, rises sheer above the street in the narrow confines of Minster Yard like a colossal cliff of masonry, reducing its surroundings to pygmy proportions.

The nave belongs to the first half of the 13th century: the bays are wide – typically English – and the triforium has broad low openings. The vault has a complex, palm-like, pattern of ribs. Most of the glass here is Victorian, and very good

– the work of Ward & Hughes, Preedy, Hedgeland, and Canon Sutton of Brant Broughton. The font is of black Tournai marble, one of seven such in England.

The Great Transept was completed at the beginning of the 13th century. Stand here, and absorb its enormous spaciousness: it is as large as the nave and choir of several lesser cathedrals. The original central tower collapsed in 1237: the lower stages were rebuilt soon after, and the elegant Galilee Porch added to the S. transept as a state entrance for the bishop. The upper stages of the tower were built in the early 14th century. And here in the transepts is the finest glass in the Cathedral: the rose window at the N. end, known as the Dean's Eye, contains glass made for it between 1200 and 1220; the Bishop's Eye, at the

S. end, with its flamboyant tracery, contains a medley of ancient glass assembled here in the 18th century; much of the grisaille glass in the lower windows is coeval with the building. Beneath stands the seated figure of Bishop King (d. 1910), his hand raised in blessing, by W. B. Richmond (1913), a striking tribute to the saintly man.

St Hugh's Choir, and the eastern transepts with their small apsidal chapels, were built at the very end of the 12th century: there are curious, almost experimental architectural features here, such as the lop-sided vaulting of the choir. The double arcading in the aisles is of the greatest beauty, and only to be found elsewhere at Beverley and Worcester. The old Medicine Chapel in the N.E. transept is now the Treasury: the show-cases were designed by Louis Osman, the glass by Geoffrey Clarke. In the choir itself the stalls, with their profusion of pinnacles and wealth of misericords, are 14th century; they are one of the finest sets of stalls in the country, and have much in common with those at Chester.

The retrochoir, or Angel Choir, was consecrated in 1280. Built to house St Hugh's Shrine, it is a monument of Decorated Geometrical work. 'It is of supreme beauty,' wrote Sir Nikolaus Pevsner, 'but it no longer possesses the freshness of spring or early summer: the abundance of rich and mellow decoration has the warmth and sweetness of August and September, of harvest and vintage.' The glass in the E. window is by Ward & Hughes (1853), but some of the 18th-century glass made for this window by Peckett of York is now in the N.E. transept. The N.E. spandrel of the Angel Choir contains the Lincoln Imp – a stonemason's joke, which has become as celebrated as the Cathedral itself. Attached to the Angel Choir are three small Perp chantries. One of these, the Chapel of St Blaise, was decorated with murals by Duncan Grant in 1958; in the Longland Chantry is one of the four surviving first editions of Magna Carta.

The chapter house belongs to the middle of the 13th century, and is the earliest of the specifically English octagonal Gothic chapter houses built round a central pillar. Sombre Victorian glass darkens the interior: the exterior is graceful with its array of flying buttresses and steep pyramid roof. Three sides of the cloister are Dec, with wooden vaults; the N. side was rebuilt in 1674, and designed by Wren – a Tuscan colonnade, with Library above. To stand under its almost Italianate loggia, with bay trees grown in tubs under the arcade, and gaze up at the N. side of the Cathedral, its towers, transepts, flying buttresses, is an unforgettable pleasure.

Lincoln is not rich in great monuments. The mutilated shrine of St Hugh stands in the Angel Choir. Part of the remains of Queen Eleanor, wife of Edward I, were buried here before the rest were conveyed in solemn cortege to London; she died at Harby, just across the Nottinghamshire border, in 1291. Bishop Grosseteste, Bishop of Lincoln, and first Chancellor of Oxford University, was buried in the S.E. transept in 1253; his modern tomb is by Randoll Blacking. Close to the High Altar is the tomb of Katherine Swynford, third wife of John of Gaunt, and great great grandmother to Henry VII. There are impressive Victorian tombs in the Angel Choir – including one to Peter de Wint – and throughout the Cathedral are to be found delightful 18th-century tablets, and in the floor many finely engraved ledger stones.

There are houses of many dates all around, all dwarfed by the Cathedral – the most distinguished being the Chancery, at the E. end, with its late-15th-century brick front with stone oriel window; Tennyson's statue (by G. F. Watts, 1905) presides over the lawn to the N.E. Tennyson was born at Somersby in the Lincolnshire Wolds. And it is worth exploring the narrow alleys and streets nearby: a short walk down the Bail leads to the Roman Newport arch, built *c.* AD 200.

'I have always held,' wrote Ruskin, 'and am prepared against all comers to maintain, that the cathedral of Lincoln is out and out the most precious piece of architecture in the British Isles, and, roughly speaking, worth any two other cathedrals we have.'

Bourne Abbey

Bourne is an ancient little town on the edge of the Lincolnshire fens, the reputed birthplace of Hereward the Wake, the birthplace of William Cecil, Lord Burghley. The road from Grantham passes Vanbrugh's Grimsthorpe, passes Edenham Church, where Dukes and Earls of Ancaster are buried, meets the road from Stamford, and descends. The little town with its houses of brick and stone, with the tall tower of the abbey church, lies below the long low wooded escarpment of the Stone Belt. All roads lead into the market place:

Bourne: paired lancet windows in the base of the north-west tower

the early Victorian Gothic Angel Hotel, the 17th-century Burghley Arms, and Bryan Browning's classical town hall (1821) are the landmarks here: a short distance to the south, and Abbey Road leads to the Abbey. The Bourne stream accompanies this quiet cul-de-sac, an elegant little cast iron foot-bridge leads across to a pretty house opposite, with old mullioned windows and some later Gothic ones, set in its riverside garden – and the front of the Abbey is before us.

Bourne Abbey was founded in 1138 by Baldwin FitzGilbert for Arroasian Canons (a branch of the Augustinians). It was neither large nor wealthy, and at the Dissolution in 1536 there were only nine canons. Nothing remains of their monastic buildings, which lay on the north side of the church – the site occupied by a trim bowling green. But this 13th-century west front is one of considerable beauty: paired E.E. lancets adorn the bases of twin towers (the N.W. tower never completed), triple lancets (a 19th-century restoration) form the west window of the nave; blank arcading decorates the whole base of the front; there is a Perp west door,

and the S.W. tower was only completed in the 14th century – a Perp tower with paired bell openings, embattled parapet and tall pinnacles. Entering by the N.W. door into the base of the uncompleted tower, it will be seen that this and its S.W. counterpart are lofty hall-like chambers, with tall E.E. arches. There seems to have been an unfulfilled scheme to rebuild the whole nave, but funds were clearly low: the Norman nave survives, with its sturdy 12th-century round piers, scalloped capitals and round arches. The clerestory is Perp, and must date from the time of the completion of the S.W. tower. At the Dissolution the nave survived as the parish church.

What stood to the east is unknown: there are traces of a demolished crossing, of demolished transepts, but the present chancel was rebuilt in 1807, spacious but plain, with re-used materials and re-used Perp windows. There are a number of minor monuments, some colourful Victorian glass, and a great brass candelabra dated 1742.

Croyland Abbey

Like the hulk of an enormous wrecked ship the remains of Croyland Abbey loom upon the flat landscape of the deepest Lincolnshire fens. This was the spot to which St Guthlac came on St Bartholomew's Day, 699. Guthlac was a member of the Mercian royal house, who, tired of soldiering, entered the monastery of Repton and after two years of study resolved to embrace the life of a hermit. He vowed that he would found his hermitage on whatsoever island among the swamps his boat first became stranded on. Croyland was that place, his anchorage three-quarters of a mile from the present abbey, still called Anchor Church Field. The Benedictine Abbey was founded in his memory by King Ethelbald in 713, a year or so after Guthlac's death. All was destroyed in the Danish raids in the 10th century, and, after rebuilding, much was destroyed again in a fire of 1091. Work was resumed soon after, and went on despite an earthquake in 1114 and another fire in 1146. It was completed *c.* 1195, when the remains of St Guthlac were solemnly translated to the shrine in the newly rebuilt church. There are remains of this Norman church to be seen, but the most spectacular parts are E.E. and Perp.

Croyland is an odd, eerie, withdrawn little town, in that fenland east of Peterborough where holy

Croyland: E. E. west front to the right; Perp tower and porch to the left

men came to withdraw from the world before the Norman Conquest. Ramsey, Peterborough, Thorney, Croyland, are all in close proximity: Croyland seems strange, secluded, even now.

A narrow street leads to the church, past the Abbey Hotel with its Victorian gabled timbered front; and we stand before the great west front.

To the right are fragments of the Norman south aisle; in the centre the enormous empty window above a spectacular E.E. doorway; to the left the tremendous Perp tower crowned by its stumpy short spire, and the two-storeyed porch which leads into the parochial north aisle – now the parish church. Even as a partial ruin this west front is of spectacular beauty. The E.E. doorway has in its tympanum a decorative quatrefoil, containing scenes from St Guthlac's life, including the day of his arrival here on the island swamp of Croyland; on either side of the doorway, and above, on either side of the vast window, are tall blind panels with trefoil heads or canopied niches, each one still containing original statues – all comparable with the west front at Wells. The west window was originally E.E. or Dec with geometrical tracery: it was heightened in the 14th century, and received Perp tracery, and a further row of smaller figures was added above. The nave is empty now, an eloquent ruin: at the east end stands the pulpitum, its twin doorways leading now to nothing; above stands a mammoth Norman chancel arch – and the nave arcades are latest Perp, merging into earlier Norman arches at the east end. Large traceried Perp windows in the clerestory appear in Buck's engraving (1726): all are fallen now.

The porch under the N.W. tower leads into the parochial aisle. It is ten past five on an autumn evening, but the church is still open, *Laus Deo*. The nave with its spreading Perp vault is dark; a wooden screen (in part original) divides nave from chancel, and a sanctuary lamp burns before the High Altar. Along the north side, in the deep bays, are chapels – one occupied by the organ – and in the easternmost bays are windows filled with sombre pink Victorian glass, with bordures of purple – calculated to cast funereal gloom. But it is all part of the dim religious light of Croyland. Looking west from the sanctuary there is a view of the enormous Perp west window: indeed the whole tower is a lantern of light. The clock strikes a quarter to six; under the tower are many carved stones lying around – and on the walls many framed prints of Croyland in the past. From the churchyard, packed with gravestones, there are wide views across the fens, and a chilly breeze blows up from the Wash.

In the middle of the little town children are bicycling around; and at the crossroads stands one of the greatest of all curiosities: Croyland Bridge, the triangular bridge with its three arches meeting one another at the centre, an uneasy ascent once, from the three streets that met here, over the three streams of the River Welland. All are dry now. The bridge is 14th century, but apparently there was an earlier bridge of similar design before the Conquest. At the S.W. approach there is a seated stone figure, perhaps of Christ, and perhaps the

top-most figure of the west front, removed here in the 18th century.

Driving away down the broad street, and heading N.W., the road turns and lurches west – and then follows the long straight canal-like River Welland for mile after straight mile; the sun sets, and twilight descends. Turning back, the tower of the Abbey stands still visible against the darkening sky: in twilight the spirit of St Guthlac seems never far away.

Deeping St James

Deeping St James Priory

The long street which joins Deeping St James to Market Deeping, lined with stone houses and cottages, is accompanied all the way by the River Welland: at Deeping Gate a 17th-century bridge crosses the river, and soon we are at St James. The church lies back, half concealed by houses: a bold early-18th-century tower and spire, an array of large Dec windows – at first sight just another grand village church, one among many in these parts. But entering by the south porch, there is a great surprise – a long Norman-Transitional south arcade of such grandeur that Pevsner has described it as 'astounding'. This is late 12th century; the arches, though round, have an inkling of E.E. about them, and the columns, though massive, are many-clustered. Above is an E.E. triforium and clerestory combined. From the third and fifth pier springers emerge as though to carry transverse arches, but these were never built, and what they were meant to carry is obscure; there is a flat early-19th-century ceiling. This is the nave of the Benedictine Priory, founded by Baldwin FitzGilbert in 1139 as a cell of Thorney, dissolved in 1539. There is no north arcade: the monastic buildings stood here, and they have disappeared; the transepts, too, were pulled down at the Dissolution. There is still a long low chancel, with the same low botched-up flat ceiling: here there are long round-headed windows with clustered shafts, sedilia and piscina, 19th-century furnishings, depressing 20th-century glass. The whole church is over-filled with ordinary Victorian furniture – but, though knocked about, it is a remarkable monastic fragment. There are two 14th-century effigies, a few 19th-century monuments, and a curious sentry box, to be carried to a graveside for the officiating minister in wet weather. The early-18th-century tower, with its tall spire, is interesting and unexpected: what it replaced is unknown. And at the road junction nearby stands the 15th-century market cross, a remarkable and highly decorative little building, sadly mutilated in the 19th century when its shaft was destroyed and its base converted into a lock-up – and now disfigured by an outrageous electric lamp standard.

Freiston: a fragment of a larger Benedictine priory church

Freiston Priory

A grand fragment in a large churchyard filled with old headstones and trimmed by friendly sheep: a tall sturdy Perp tower with embattled parapet, and a big west window to light the nave – with a single figure in a canopied niche above; a long row of lofty Perp windows in the clerestory, with a Norman corbel table above; a north aisle built of 15th-century brick, with Perp windows here; an E.E. porch. It is a wonderful multi-coloured, multi-textured exterior as one approaches from the north; and the Norman corbel table gives a clue to what there is to see inside – a long nave of nine bays, the six easternmost squat Norman, the three to the west somewhat loftier E.E., and over all the tall Perp clerestory. This is but the nave of the priory church; the crossing arch remains, blocked up, with a Victorian window here. Beyond stood transepts and monastic choir.

Freiston Priory was founded in this sea-girt parish, close to the Wash, in 1114 by Alan de Creon for Benedictine monks, and became a cell

of Croyland soon after. A (much restored) Norman south door led into the cloisters and the conventual buildings, of which nothing remains. At the Dissolution the nave survived as the parish church: standing here on the edge of a large fen village it is not easy to imagine the big monastic church as it was, complete with chancel, transepts and Norman central tower.

But what remains is impressive: the Norman nave was extended in the 13th century, and the clerestory and west tower added in the 14th or early 15th. The interior is well furnished: there are old screens to the north and south chapels, and the octagonal Perp font is crowned with its original canopied cover suspended from above; there is the original 15th-century roof, and an ancient north door; the delightful 17th-century house called The Priory was long used as the rectory. A fresh breeze blows in from the sea, and there are the cries of the seagulls overhead.

Kirkstead Abbey

A few miles S.W. of Woodhall Spa – which Sir John Betjeman described as 'that Bournemouth-like settlement in the middle of Lincolnshire' – there stands in lonely, bumpy fields the gaunt fragment of Kirkstead Abbey: a tall craggy rock of masonry, hard to interpret. It is in fact the southeast angle of the south transept. But a little farther south across the fields, and approached by the same farm track, stands St Leonard's Chapel, the

Kirkstead: one of the most evocative monastic churches in England

little monastic *capella ante portas* of the Cistercian abbey founded by Hugh Breton in 1139. Samuel Buck's engraving (1736) shows the whole south wall of the transept standing – with St Leonard's Chapel in the background. The print is dedicated to the Revd John Disney, D.D. 'owner of these ruins': his mother was the daughter of Henry Fynes-Clinton, owner of Kirkstead; his son, another John Disney, was an ardent Presbyterian, and the chapel was used for dissenting services from 1736 to 1812 – illegally, because the chapel had always properly belonged to the parish. After a century of decay the church was beautifully restored, and reopened for worship in 1914. The last days of the Abbey had been terrible: in the Lincolnshire Rising of 1536 the local leaders threatened that they would burn the abbey over the monks' heads if they did not join the rebellion. In the upshot, after supporting the Rising, the Abbot and three monks were put to death, and the monastery and its possessions were forfeited to the Crown (1537).

There can be no two opinions about St Leonard's Chapel: it is one of the most beautiful E.E. buildings anywhere. It is tiny (some 44 × 20 ft), just large enough for a small body of layfolk or pilgrims to meet in and attend the Divine Office. Every detail is perfect: there is a west doorway with narrow shafts and stiff-leaf capitals, a blind arcade of three bays above and a vesica window above that. Inside, there are narrow lancets all around, with elegant shafts and delicate carved capitals, with triple lancets at the east end; dwarf shafts, resting on the corbel table, support the vault; there are foliated bosses in the nave, and the boss in the sanctuary is carved with the Agnus Dei. The original wooden screen, coeval with the chapel, divides nave from sanctuary; there is a stone altar, simply furnished, and a late Norman font. The effigy of an unknown knight of *c.* 1250 is one of the earliest military monuments in England.

This exquisite little chapel is used regularly for worship, adorned with flowers, its churchyard carefully tended. Its setting is perfect, too – remote and silent, but for the bleating of the sheep. It is hard to find (the key is kept at the local farm), and only to be discovered by the most persistent, but the tiny church, reached at last, will amply reward every seeker. It is indeed a holy place – one of the most evocative monastic churches in England.

Knaith Priory

An idyllic setting by the Trent, a fascinating fragment of a nuns' church close to the river – and, across the lawn, Knaith Hall, a long, low, old house, done up early in the 19th century in Regency Gothick. The Cistercian nunnery of Heynings was founded in the early 12th century, and it is not easy to explain what we now see of their church, be it part of the nave, or be it a surviving transept. There is herringbone masonry in the west wall (11th–12th century), 14th-century tracery in the two south windows. Inside, three early-18th-century arches divide the present nave from the chancel; there is a Jacobean pulpit with candle-snuffer canopy, and an array of Jacobean seating; one incised slab is perhaps to a nun (*c.* 1440): another to William, son of Lord D'Arcy de Knaith (1408). There is a notable Dec font, and, on the wall above it, a stone tablet recalls the birth here in 1532 of Thomas Sutton, founder of the Charterhouse.

Kyme: the Umfraville tower and the canons' church

Kyme Priory

An oasis in the fens, a secret, unexpected place, where old trees guard the tall 14th-century keep of the castle of the Kymes and Umfravilles, which stands all by itself in the middle of a meadow, with the beck running by. There is a good-looking 18th-century house on one side, the Priory Church on the other. Kyme Priory was founded *c.* 1150 by Philip de Kyme for Augustinian Canons. What remains is the Dec south aisle, which in 1890 Hodgson Fowler formed into the present dignified church. There is an imposing early-14th-century south porch, containing in a niche the remains of a very fine sculpture of the Coronation of the Virgin, and a grand Norman doorway within. Inside, there are fragments of Anglo-Saxon and Norman carvings built into the north wall, a brass of 1530 to 'Gylbert Taylboys, Lord Taylboys, Lord of Kyme', many later monuments, and stained glass by Kempe. All the conventual buildings have disappeared, and only the solitary tower survives of the once great castle of the founder's family.

Knaith Priory: fragment of a Cistercian nunnery

DIOCESE OF
LIVERPOOL

Liverpool Cathedral

THE RIVER FRONT at Liverpool is impressive: the docks with their grand warehouses, the parish church with its pretty early-19th-century steeple, the Royal Liver Building with its twin 'art nouveau baroque' cupolas, the green-domed Dock Office. The city rises behind – with the enormous 20th-century Cathedral on the hilltop, lying parallel with the river, with its all-commanding tower rising perhaps ethereal through the mist. And from anywhere the Cathedral is impressive: driving in from the N.W. – through Walton-on-the-Hill – suddenly the top of the enormous pinnacled Gothic tower appears above drab roof-tops. And as we approach – from any direction – this tower appears, looming above us. It is the most important building in the city – indeed one of the most important modern buildings in England; its completion has aroused immense interest. It is the largest cathedral in England, larger than York, larger than St Paul's, and in all Christendom second only to St Peter's in Rome. Manchester and Birmingham, when those dioceses were created, made do with a converted parish church; so have Leicester, Wakefield, Sheffield, Bradford. Liverpool has far excelled them all.

The diocese of Liverpool was created in 1880, founded out of the ancient diocese of Chester. To begin with, St Peter's Church did service as the pro-cathedral – but ambitions were high. A fine site on St James' Mount was acquired, and in 1901 a competition was held. Mr Giles Gilbert Scott, then aged 22, was appointed architect – grandson of Sir George Gilbert Scott, and member of a talented architectural family which had already produced three distinguished architects. As he was so young, Bodley was appointed joint-architect, but on Bodley's death in 1907 Scott became sole architect, and so remained until his death in 1960.

Work began in 1904; the Lady Chapel was completed in 1910, chancel and eastern transepts in 1924, the central tower in 1942, and the nave and west front in 1978.

The site chosen was superb, commanding on one side the whole city and riverside, and on the other a deep ravine enclosing an old churchyard. And, all around, streets of late Georgian houses and charming terraces made it an ideal situation. At the far end of Hope Street now stands the Roman Catholic Cathedral, where above Lutyens' crypt Sir Frederick Gibberd's strange concrete 'wigwam' is crowned with its spiky lantern.

Sir Giles Gilbert Scott, as he became, revised and amended his plans several times: the plan of the Cathedral as built is original and interesting. Nave and chancel are of equal length: in between is a long central space, from which double transepts extend, and, between them, rises the central tower. At the foot of the tower, linking the transepts, is a grand portico approached by a flight of many steps. As the site is aligned N.–S., the liturgical east is in fact south, and so on.

The Cathedral is built of local red sandstone, and as we approach the enormous Gothic mass of the building seems overpowering. It seems incredible that such a church should have been embarked upon, and completed, in this pagan age. Walking along the south side, we can examine the towering walls, the traceried Gothic windows, the unusual arrangement of the double transepts with the central tower not over the crossing, but between the transepts. Above the porch a tall window extends right up into the tower. This is undoubtedly original and ingenious. At the east end, almost detached on the south side and on a slightly lower level, stands the Lady Chapel, which is large enough to be an impressive parish church in its

Liverpool Cathedral: begun in 1904, completed in 1978, the largest cathedral in England

Liverpool: the bridge across the nave

own right. At the N.E. corner is the chapter house. The design is repeated on the north side.

Entering by the west door, our first impression will be one of awe – awe at so vast and thrilling an interior, with immense vistas down the side aisles, and an even more overpowering vista down the nave towards the 'crossing', chancel and High Altar. This looks a mile away. The nave itself is empty: three or four steps lead down into it from all sides, and a lofty bridge across its eastern end makes some division here, as a screen or pulpitum might do in a medieval cathedral. Beyond this the central space is long and of tremendous height, with the vault under the central tower soaring to

Liverpool: the Lady Chapel

175 feet, and capable of accommodating a tremendous congregation. At the far end the chancel leads on and up to the High Altar. This great Gothic interior is numinous, mysterious, majestic, and full of atmosphere.

It is a thrill to walk about this immense church, absorbing now this vista, now that – lost, like a dwarf, under the huge vaults, or lost in the long low aisles with their strong contrasts of light and shade; an echoing ambulatory extends round the sanctuary, leading to unexpected features: the chapter house on the north side, the Lady Chapel on the south.

This Lady Chapel is the most beautiful part of the Cathedral. Entering from the ambulatory, we are in its western gallery, and can look down into the interior with its tall traceried windows, its triforium, its narrow aisles divided from the Chapel itself by low arcades – and to its apsidal east end, resplendent with the triptych designed by Bodley and Scott; we can then descend into the Chapel itself. Bodley's hand is in evidence here, in the purer Gothic details, in the elegance of the furnishings. Scott never quite achieved the same again in his furnishings, for chancel, chapels or baptistery. Nevertheless, there is in all his work here an undoubted Spanish quality; increasingly, it seems, this was Scott's inspiration.

Liverpool is a cathedral of great dignity, great originality, great power. To embark on its erection in 1904 was an act of faith: to have completed it in 1978 is a triumph.

Upholland Priory

Near Wigan: this does not sound promising, but open countryside is at hand, and Upholland preserves its character as an old stone-built Lancashire village, with a long street climbing the hill and turning the corner where the priory church stands. There is a bold Perp west tower, and an imposing Victorian chancel: between them stands the nave built in the early 14th century.

Upholland Priory was founded for Benedictine monks by Walter de Langton, Bishop of Lichfield, in 1318: a collegiate church had been founded ten years earlier by Sir Robert Holland, but his scheme had foundered. What is now the grand nave of four spacious Dec bays was built as the chancel of the new Priory, but the transepts, central tower and nave were never built, and in the end the church was completed with the Perp west tower in the early 16th century. After the Dissolution the chancel became the parish church, and served as nave and sanctuary; the new Victorian chancel was added in 1883. The interior is attractive with its flat 18th-century plaster ceiling, comfortable pews – including some old bench ends, and splendid churchwardens' seats at the back – a number of monuments and hatchments of the Bankes family, and handsome candelabra; there is also some very good late-19th-century glass by Henry Holiday.

A few fragments of the monastic buildings survive in the adjacent walls, where the enormous churchyard slopes down the hillside, filled with old tombs and headstones; in the distance can be heard the roar of the new motorway.

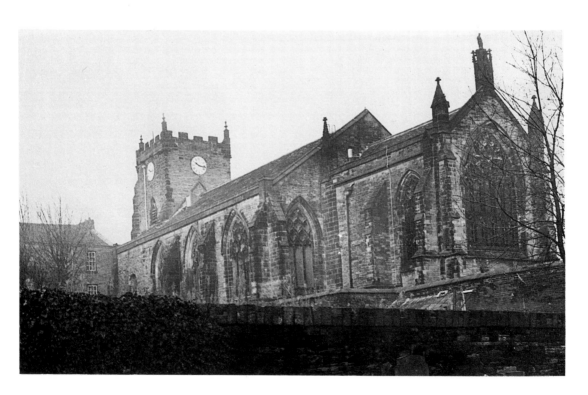

Upholland: the monastic chancel is now the parochial nave, with a new chancel added in 1883

DIOCESE OF
LONDON

St Paul's Cathedral

AMONG ALL THE OLD CATHEDRALS of England, St Paul's stands quite alone. No other cathedral was designed and built by a single architect, no other cathedral was built to a single design. Exeter is built in pure Dec style – but its towers are Norman; Salisbury is pure E.E. – but its spire a Dec afterthought. At St Paul's one man had the chance to build, or rebuild, a great cathedral from scratch, and he completed it in thirty-five years. And alone among the cathedrals of England St Paul's is built in the classical style. Those who prefer a Gothic cathedral have twenty-five to choose from. The lesser company, who have the preference for a classical building, have only one to choose – and that the masterpiece of Sir Christopher Wren, England's greatest architect.

Two pictures of St Paul's come to mind. First, Canaletto's famous painting (at Goodwood House) of the City from the terrace of Richmond House. The river sweeps by in its broad curve, lined with lesser houses and buildings; sailing boats and rowing boats ply their way up and down, and, above the roof-tops of the City, the towers and spires of Wren's churches pierce the sky, St Paul's with its dome and western towers, its stonework glistening in the sunlight, supreme and dominant in the centre. The picture was painted *c.* 1750.

The second is very different – but its symbolism is the same. It is night, and the night sky reflects the flames of the burning city; houses in the foreground are being consumed, and clouds of smoke ascend to surround the dome and western towers of St Paul's, which stand supreme and dominant, unscathed in the general conflagration. It is 29 December, 1940, a terrifying night when a great part of the City went up in smoke in a colossal fire-bomb raid.

The dome of St Paul's is symbolic in our national life as no medieval tower or spire can ever be – not Canterbury, not York, not Salisbury. This is the debt we owe to Wren.

But now the celebrated view has gone, destroyed by our own generation: no longer is the dome dominant in the City's skyline. High-rise buildings pierce the sky to rival its dominance. The rot began in 1932 with the erection of Faraday House in Queen Victoria Street – a building at the time loudly condemned. Recently, far taller, more brutal abominations have been accepted by our present passive generation. What will our grandchildren say?

We make our way up Ludgate Hill: the western towers are upon us, and the dome rises behind. Queen Anne, in whose reign St Paul's was completed, stands on her plinth to welcome us. But commonplace post-war buildings, great lumps of concrete, stand close to the N.W. corner – too tall, too formless: a modern 'piazza' behind, empty, soul-less, out of scale, out of sympathy with the Cathedral. The Victorian buildings on the south side are at least modest and human. But there is not a single building round St Paul's which is worthy of its setting. Even the new Choir School, attached to the surviving tower of St Augustine's Church at the east end, is a disaster. But the Cathedral, though hit twice during the war, and now disgraced by its surroundings, still stands supreme.

We can walk round, admire its details, so many revealed by the recent cleaning of the exterior stonework, Portland stone, glistening white: the rusticated walls, the Corinthian pillars and pilasters, the pedimented windows, the carved festoons, the cherubs' heads, the statues, urns and garlands, the balustraded parapet. The most talented masons were employed: Joshua Marshall, Thomas Strong, Christopher and William Kempster, John Thornton; and, among the carvers, Grinling Gibbons, Caius Gabriel Cibber and Francis Bird. It was Bird who executed the relief of the Conversion of St Paul in the western pediment. We can enter the Cathedral beneath its portico, sit

down in the nave, contemplate this grand baroque interior, contemplate the long history of the see.

Mellitus was consecrated Bishop by St Augustine in 604 – and a short-lived wooden cathedral was built, to be replaced by a stone cathedral at the end of the century. This was destroyed by the Vikings in the 9th century. Another cathedral was built in 962, which was destroyed by fire in 1087. Thereupon work began on a new Norman building – the cathedral which we know as Old St Paul's – which was completed in 1240. To this a new Gothic chancel was soon added, and, in 1315, a colossal spire of wood and lead which rose to a height of 489 feet – the loftiest spire ever built. This was struck by lightning in 1561, and never rebuilt. General deterioration set in: in the early 17th century Inigo Jones carried out certain repairs, and erected a classical portico at the west end; but in 1666 the Great Fire broke out in a baker's shop in Pudding Lane, and largely destroyed the old cathedral. 'Thus lay in ashes that most venerable church, one of the antientest Pieces of early Piety in the Christian world', wrote John Evelyn.

Sir Christopher Wren, Surveyor-General of the King's Works, was appointed architect, and after much disagreement, and the rejection of his first plan, his second design was accepted in 1673. The site was cleared, and work began on the new building in 1675.

In many respects, as built, St Paul's is both conservative and traditional in plan: it is cruciform, with nave, chancel, transepts – and broad aisles to these component parts; the interior is vaulted, and indeed flying buttresses support these vaults – but these are invisible, concealed behind the high screen walls which rise above the aisles, so that from outside the very existence of these aisles is not suspected, and St Paul's presents to the outside world a pure classical façade, which rises majestic and symmetrical to support the dome. As we sit in the nave all this can be comprehended. Corinthian pilasters, enormous round arches, support the clerestory, and below the windows an iron-balustraded balcony, like a triforium gallery, runs round the whole church; the vault above is composed of saucer domes, and the windows in the aisles – which are also vaulted with saucer domes – flood the nave with light. The nave is wide and spacious – and ahead is the vista of the dome and central space, with the chancel and High Altar far beyond.

St Paul's: the south-west tower from the dome

St Paul's: cherubs' heads and garlands in Portland stone

OPPOSITE *St Paul's Cathedral from the South Bank – now hemmed in by recent buildings*

St Paul's: ABOVE *Corinthian pillars and pilasters, festoons and rusticated stonework on the west front;* OPPOSITE *Corinthian pilasters and enormous round arches support the clerestory vault and dome. Beyond is the chancel and the baldacchino of the High Altar.*

As we move east, the immense width and height of this central space become apparent – with the almost unbelievable, ethereal, overwhelming dome suspended far above our heads: the Whispering Gallery, then the dome itself decorated with Sir James Thornhill's murals depicting St Paul's life, and then the lantern. For those who have the

strength, many hundred steps may be ascended to the Whispering Gallery; and, beyond, steep stairs, poised between the inner dome and the outer, will carry the energetic to the very top of the dome, to the lantern. It is an experience worth the trouble.

After the dome, the chancel, resplendent with Grinling Gibbons' stalls, Grinling Gibbons' organ

case, Tijou's iron screens; and at the east end, the High Altar, beneath the towering baldacchino, designed in 1958 by S. E. Dykes Bower and Godfrey Allen – but based on an original design by Wren which was never executed. It is the making of the sanctuary. And above, and all around, the vaults and spandrels are all aglow with the mosaic decoration by Sir William Richmond (1890), which extends to the space beneath the dome, providing an exuberance of gilt and colour, opulently Victorian, triumphantly successful.

Throughout the Cathedral there is a magnificent display of monuments to the nation's heroes – to Lord Kitchener and General Gordon, Admiral Rodney and Sir John Moore, Lord Howe and Lord Collingwood: most conspicuous is the memorial to the Duke of Wellington (1857, by Sir Alfred Stevens), most distinguished the statue of Nelson (1808, by Flaxman). Sir Joshua Reynolds and Dr Johnson are nearby, as is Lord Leighton; most moving is the figure of John Donne in his shroud (1631, by Nicholas Stone).

A staircase in the south transept leads down to the crypt, which extends, white and spacious, under the whole Cathedral. Massive columns support the groin vault, and under the dome more elegant Tuscan pillars carry a shallow dome. Here is the tomb of Nelson, a black marble sarcophagus made by Benedetto da Rovezzano for Cardinal Wolsey, but confiscated by the Crown on Wolsey's fall: now it bears a cushion, and on it a Viscount's coronet, with the simple inscription HORATIO. VISC. NELSON. Nearby is the tomb of the Iron Duke – a sarcophagus of Cornish porphyry, on a pedestal of Peterhead granite. And, in comparison modest, is Wren's own tomb: a simple black marble slab – 'Here lieth Sir Christopher Wren Knt. The builder of this Cathedral Church of St Paul, &c. Who dyed in the year of Our LORD MDCCXXIII, and of his age XCI.' And above is the famous epitaph 'SI MONUMENTUM REQUIRIS, CIRCUMSPICE' – 'If you are looking for his monument, gaze around you'.

St Bartholomew the Great

Smithfield, and St Bartholomew's Hospital: a timbered gatehouse over a 13th-century doorway leads into a little yard, and to a Perp porch of 1893 (by Sir Aston Webb); above stands a 17th-century brick tower crowned with a little white-painted cupola: the W. end of the church, the transepts, are of stone and flint – unexpected here in the City of London, and part of Sir Aston's restoration. Nothing prepares us for the great Norman church which we now enter.

St Bartholomew's Priory was founded by Rahere for Augustinian Canons – an order which he himself later joined; and with the Priory he also founded the Hospital nearby, on land granted to him by Henry I. After the Dissolution the nave was pulled down, together with much of the transept and Lady Chapel, by Sir Richard Rich, to whom the property had been granted. The chancel survived as the parish church. Much restoration took place at the end of the 19th century at the hands of Sir Aston Webb.

St Bartholomew's is precious, not only because it is one of the handful of medieval churches to have survived the Great Fire and the bombing of the Second World War, but also because it is in itself a noble church, of noble proportions. Norman arcades and a Norman triforium lead to an apsidal E. end (partly rebuilt in 1893): vaulted aisles lead to a vaulted ambulatory, and so to an early-14th-century Lady Chapel at the E. end – also a late-19th-century restoration, after centuries of desecration. It is an interior full of mystery, with unexpected vistas opening up from the aisles across the chancel, or across the transepts, with chapels and tombs and monuments appearing everywhere. Rahere's tomb in the sanctuary – a 15th-century canopied effigy encloses his place of burial, and little figures of bedesmen on either side of his figure hold open books to recite their prayers; the tomb of Sir Walter Mildmay (d. 1589), Chancellor of the Exchequer, and founder of Emmanuel College, Cambridge, in the S. aisle; and many smaller pretty monuments everywhere – all these will give pleasure. And from the S. triforium, close to the sanctuary, built out above the arcade is Prior Bolton's Watching Chamber, from which he could watch proceedings below. The chancel is arranged college chapel-wise, and the musical tradition of the church is justly famous.

A final surprise is the surviving walk of the 15th-century cloister, on the S. side: here restoration was not completed till 1928. After the Dissolution different parts of this great church were used for different secular purposes – a blacksmith's forge occupied the N. transept, a printing works the Lady Chapel. Sir Aston Webb's restoration in 1893 was sympathetic and scholarly.

St Bartholomew the Great: a noble church, of noble proportions

St Helen's Priory, Bishopsgate

An incredible oasis – a remarkable tree-shaded courtyard off Bishopsgate, with towering office blocks on all sides. A Benedictine nunnery was founded here *c.* 1110: St Helen's is its church. Outwardly the west front is modest, with twin Perp windows and a 17th-century timber bell tower: the S.W. door leads into an interior enormous and resplendent – two parallel naves, the nuns' choir to the north, the parochial church to the south; steps lead down into a building of unexpected splendour. Night stairs in the north wall, now blocked, led up to the priory buildings; there are squints from here into the church; medieval stalls, the Chapel of the Holy Ghost, and the Lady

St Helen's Priory: the nuns' choir and the parochial nave

St Helen's Priory: a musical cherub adorns the 17th-century organ

Chapel, in what survives of the south transept – these speak of the monastic past; there is a grand array of tombs and monuments of City worthies –

most notably that of Sir Thomas Gresham (1579) – a wealth of 17th-century woodwork, and an array of 19th-century stained glass, by Mayer of Munich, Powell, Gibbs, and Heaton, Butler and Bayne. Outside again, the 17th-century Baroque south doorway is not to be missed.

St John's Priory: the crypt was long used as a wine cellar

St John's Priory, Clerkenwell

'To St John's Priory' reads a surprising notice in the Clerkenwell Road: the church, standing in St John's Square, is in fact scarcely noticeable, surrounded as it is by other buildings – but the magnificent early-16th-century gatehouse, a stone's throw to the south, is a powerful presence, a reminder of the important Priory of the Sovereign Order of St John of Jerusalem, founded here *c.* 1140, a religious order with a particular duty to care for the sick; as Knights Hospitaller they also had a military role in the protection of those taking part in the Crusades. The order in England was dissolved in 1540. After many vicissitudes, the chancel of the church, which in turn had served as a private chapel of the house which was built on the priory site, as a presbyterian chapel, then as a parish church, was in 1931 handed back to the Order of St John, refounded in England in 1888, with Queen Victoria as its head. Bombed in 1941, it was restored after the war, and is used regularly for services of the Order, and for investitures. Beneath, the 13th-century crypt, long used as a wine cellar or charnel house, is once again in use for worship, and contains many recent memorials to dignitaries of the Order, and one

St John's Priory: the tomb of Don Juan Ruys de Vergava

superb tomb, that of Don Juan Ruys de Vergava (1575). After serving as public house, coffee house and printing works, the gatehouse was repurchased in the 19th century, and is now the Headquarters of the Order of St John, and of the St John Ambulance Brigade. It contains Chapter Hall, Council Chamber and Library – and a fascinating Museum, open to the public at certain times.

Westminster Abbey

The sight of the Abbey now, in the heart of modern Westminster, the heart of modern London, with the traffic swirling round Parliament Square and up and down Victoria Street, with pedestrians crowding the pavements and Big Ben booming in the background, makes it hard to realize that this was once Thorney, the isle of thorns in marshy ground close to the river, where a Benedictine monastery was founded on a solitary site, or to visualize the life of this community. The date of its foundation is uncertain. St Dunstan, when Bishop of London, is said to have brought a dozen monks to Westminster *c.* 960; but it was Edward the Confessor who founded or refounded the Abbey, and built the first great church. His shrine stands behind the High Altar today. The Conqueror was crowned here on Christmas Day 1066 – and royal patronage continued. After the Dissolution Henry VIII created a new Diocese of Westminster in 1540, to embrace most of Middlesex, with the Abbey as its cathedral; but this was suppressed in 1550. In 1556 Queen Mary

revived the Benedictine Abbey – but this was again dissolved after her death. Then in 1560 Queen Elizabeth founded the Royal Collegiate Church of St Peter of Westminster, with a Dean and canons, exempt from the jurisdiction of the Bishop of London and of the Archbishop of Canterbury; and so it continues today.

Henry III, who was crowned here in 1220, began the rebuilding of the Confessor's church in 1245. Chancel, transepts, and the first bay of the nave were completed within ten years; then four more bays were added, and in 1269 the body of St Edward was translated to its new shrine. Chapter house and cloisters were also built, but the rest of the Norman nave remained – until in the 1370s the last six bays were built, under the master mason Henry Yevele. It was he who was in charge of the rebuilding of the nave at Canterbury (q.v.), in the latest Perp style – yet, here at Westminster, he carried on the building almost exactly as it had been begun a century before. This is fascinating. Minor differences may be noticed, but the new work is according to the early Gothic design of the

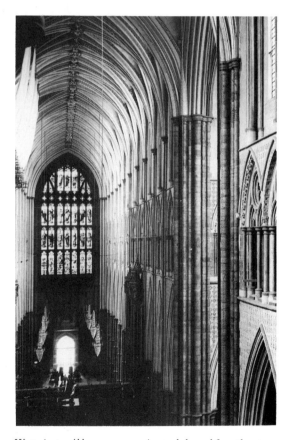

Westminster Abbey: nave, crossing and chancel from the apse

chancel and crossing. An inborn conservatism? Or a case of architectural good manners? Whichever it was, it is laudable, and the completion of the church a triumph. At the west end there are Perp features: the west window, the west porch (reminiscent indeed of Canterbury) and the base of the towers. These were never completed – till in the 18th century Nicholas Hawksmoor added the present half Gothic, half classical towers. These are such a familiar part of the London scene – yet how many people realize their date? Until then, the only addition to the Abbey was Henry VII's Chapel, which was begun in 1503.

Walking round the exterior, the north front will impress most: here the north transept appears the principal entrance, with its triple porch and grand rose window: on either side rise apsidal chancel and longer nave, both of exceptional height, both supported by immense flying buttresses. At the east end of the apse are radiating chapels, and, beyond, the fantastic and ornate façade of Henry VII's Chapel – 'nice embroidered work' as Christopher Wren called it. The west front, by comparison, seems a modest afterthought. But we must enter here.

And here the first impression is overwhelming – the first impression of immense height. No other medieval church in England can compare with it. The height from floor to vault is 103 ft – at least 30 ft higher than any comparable interior of this date. Here, at the west end, we are, of course, in Henry Yevele's nave (c. 1375): yet how many visitors realize that it is a century later than the rest of the nave? Westminster Abbey is the most French of all medieval English churches, both in plan and proportions, and the King's mason responsible for the design is known to have been Henry of Reyns. It is tempting to assume that 'Reyns' is Rheims, and to associate his work here with that cathedral – so similar in plan and inspiration – or with Amiens or Beauvais. The chevet – the radiating eastern chapels – is to be found in all three French cathedrals: the triple portal of the north transept here seems inspired by the west front at Amiens.

Near the west door is the tomb of the Unknown Warrior – interred here on 11 November, 1920 – and nearby another stone in the floor is inscribed 'Remember Winston Churchill'. The walls and floors are crowded with memorials to the illustri-

Victorian angel in Dean's Yard, Westminster

ous: Lord Salisbury, Prime Minister, is nearby, as is the 7th Earl of Shaftesbury; there is a monument by Westmacott to William Pitt the Younger, Prime Minister, and a plaque to Franklin Roosevelt, 'A faithful friend of freedom and of Britain, four times President of the United States'. And as we move up the nave we shall see in the floor stones commemorating such names as Thomas Tompion, David Livingstone, Thomas Telford, George Stephenson, Sir Charles Barry, Sir George Gilbert Scott, G. E. Street and J. L. Pearson. South of the nave altar are buried the ashes of two more Prime Ministers, Andrew Bonar Law and Neville Chamberlain. By the entrance to the choir in an unmarked vault lies the body of Edward Hyde, Earl of Clarendon (1674).

In Benedictine fashion the choir occupies the four eastern bays of the nave, and is separated by Blore's stone pulpitum, with two large monuments occupying its arcaded front – Sir Isaac Newton and the 1st Earl Stanhope, both by Rysbrack. And so we pass into the choir, with its gilded stalls, also by Blore (1848). The crossing, of course, is the

OPPOSITE *Westminster Abbey: the 'nice embroidered work' – as Sir Christopher Wren called it – of Henry VII's Chapel, with the Palace of Westminster beyond*

setting for the coronation: every sovereign from the Conqueror to Elizabeth II has been crowned here, with the exception of Edward V and Edward VIII. The reredos was designed by Gilbert Scott, with mosaics by Salviati (1867).

It is the north transept which some wag has likened to a gallery at Madame Tussaud's: here are the standing figures of 19th-century Prime Ministers: Peel, Palmerston, Disraeli, Gladstone – as well as grand monuments to William Pitt, George Canning, Castlereagh and other distinguished statesmen. The south transept is celebrated as Poets' Corner. There is the 16th-century tomb to Chaucer (d. 1400) – and everybody else, it seems, is commemorated if not buried here, from Shakespeare to Tennyson, and, from our own day, T. S. Eliot, Masefield, Auden and Dylan Thomas.

Behind the High Altar is the Confessor's Chapel. The original shrine was set up by Henry III, but destroyed at the Reformation. Queen Mary restored it in 1557, and this is what we see today. At the west end of the chapel stands the Coronation Chair, made *c.* 1300 to contain the Stone of Scone; and all around there are royal tombs: Henry III himself, and Edward I, on the north side, Richard II and Edward III on the south; at the east end is the chantry of Henry V, placed on a bridge across the ambulatory, with two spiral staircases to lead up to it. On either side at the east end are the tombs of Eleanor of Castile, wife of Edward I, and of Philippa of Hainault, wife of Edward III. And all around the ambulatory are the radiating chapels of the chevet, each one filled with fascinating monuments, chiefly of ecclesiastics or courtiers.

Henry VII's Chapel was begun in 1503, taking the place of the 13th-century Lady Chapel; it is the most sumptuous example of Perp architecture in the country, almost certainly designed by the King's masons, Robert and William Vertue. It comprises nave and sanctuary, with north and south aisles, and small radiating chapels at the east end; enormous traceried windows occupy the clerestory, rows of canopied figures occupy the space between the arcade and these windows, and the most lavish fan vault with elaborate pendants crowns the main chapel and the aisles. On either side of the nave are the stalls (*c.* 1520) of the Knights of the Bath, with their banners suspended above; the altar is a reconstruction by Sir Walter Tapper (1934), which incorporates portions of the original altar, and the altarpiece is a 15th-century

Madonna and Child by Bartolommeo Vivarini. Behind this, surrounded by a brazen screen, is the tomb of Henry himself and his Queen by the Florentine artist Pietro Torrigiani. The tomb of Elizabeth I, by Maximilian Colt, stands in the north aisle, and the grander one to Mary Queen of Scots, by Cornelius Cure, in the south – erected by James I, when he transferred her body here from the cathedral at Peterborough. There are many other splendid tombs, such as those to Lady Margaret Beaufort, mother of Henry VII, and to Margaret Countess of Lennox; in some cases only brief inscriptions mark the burial of a king or queen, or of royal children, in a vault below. In his will Henry VII made provision for 10,000 masses to be said for his soul: how many were said before Henry VIII swept all this away?

A door in the south aisle leads into the cloisters (13th–14th centuries): it is a pleasure to walk round, keeping one eye on the host of small tablets on the walls – another on the magnificent view of the south side of the nave, with its tier upon tier of flying buttresses; and then to visit the chapter house, built by Henry III *c.* 1250, one of those elegant octagonal chapter houses like those at Salisbury and Wells which are an English speciality. A little farther on a dark passage leads into the Little Cloister, with its 17th-century arcades, round which the canons' houses are built; this is one of the most charming corners of the Abbey. Beyond lies Little Dean's Yard, surrounded by the houses and buildings of Westminster School, refounded by Queen Elizabeth in 1560, and occupying some of the former monastic buildings. A gateway leads into Dean's Yard, and so back to the west front of the church. Standing here in Dean's Yard, with the Victoria Tower in the background, it is possible to absorb something of the atmosphere of this remarkable royal monastic church, which enshrines so much of the history of the nation.

Westminster Abbey: more angels in the triforium of the south transept

DIOCESE OF
MANCHESTER

Manchester Cathedral

THE DIOCESE OF MANCHESTER was created in 1848, founded out of the ancient diocese of Chester: it was the first new diocese to be founded since Henry VIII's foundations in 1542, and the old collegiate church of St Mary, St Denys and St George became the cathedral. It stands in an unpromising position, with the inevitable blocks of high-rise offices on one side, and the inevitable enormous car park on the other; beyond run the railway lines into Victoria Station. This is a splendid building, the terminus of the Lancashire and Yorkshire Railway: it is amusing to walk under its canopy and read the names of distant places which could be visited by the L & Y R. There is only one other building of note here: Chetham's Hospital, which stands with its medieval gatehouse and open quadrangle facing the north side of the Cathedral. By some incredible stroke of good fortune this survives: we should stand here and survey the Cathedral: the two buildings are intimately linked.

In 1421 Thomas de la Warre, Lord of the Manor of Manchester, obtained licence from Henry V to found here a collegiate church, dedicated to Our Lady, St Denys and St George. The foundation was to comprise a warden, eight priests, lay clerks and choristers, and he gave his own manor house to be the collegiate building: this is now Chetham's Hospital. The church itself was rebuilt in two stages: the chancel first (*c.* 1422), and then the nave (*c.* 1465). The chapter house and outer aisles (for chantries) were added a little later on, but the whole building is entirely homogeneous. This is what we see today. The college was dissolved in 1547: the buildings were bought by the Earl of Derby to be a town residence; the church became merely a parish church. In 1653 Humphrey Chetham, merchant of the town, purchased the buildings to found his school: this survives as Chetham's School of Music, and supplies the Cathedral with its choristers. Its Great Hall, kitchen, small Cloister Court, Library and wide

open quadrangle facing south stand opposite the Cathedral – which stands embattled and many-pinnacled, with bolder staircase pinnacles at the junction of nave and chancel, richly carved parapets everywhere, and a western tower. There was much restoration in the 19th century, and the tower was rebuilt (1862) by J. P. Holden, who added 6 feet to the top. At the turn of the century Basil Champneys added the west porch and cluster of vestries there, and the annexes to form the Library and other appendages on the south side; Sir Hubert Worthington added the choir rooms next to these in 1934, and restored the whole building after the bomb damage during the war.

On entering the building, it will be seen that this is a particularly fine parish church: the spacious nave with its Perp arcades and clerestory, the double aisles with vistas across the whole width of the church, cannot fail to impress. It is unfortunate that the nave itself should be cluttered with an undignified nave altar and all the usual litter of choir seats and chairs set at odd angles. Behind stands the remarkable wooden Perp pulpitum – it is more than a mere 'screen' – which gives access to the chancel, the glory of the church.

Here stand the magnificent early-16th-century stalls, complete with canopies and misericords, which rank with those at Carlisle and Ripon as the finest in the north of England. There are twelve on either side, with three more 'return' stalls on either side of the screen. The chancel is not large, but it is spacious, and with its other excellent furnishings – 18th-century candelabra, wrought iron altar rails and side screens with Gothick features, and, above these, open wooden screens with wide ogee arches – it is extraordinarily attractive and dignified. Before the altar there is a large brass to John Huntington, the first warden and builder of the chancel (d. 1458). It is a pity that Sir Gilbert Scott's organ with its beautiful case, which adorned the screen, has been removed: it provided

Manchester Cathedral: embattled and pinnacled

Manchester: the early-16th-century canons' stalls

that extra quality of mystery and grandeur to the whole church, and gave it something of a cathedral air. At the east end, the small Lady Chapel was rebuilt after bomb damage, but its medieval screen survives, and forms, as it were, a reredos for the High Altar. From the aisles here there are splendid vistas across the chancel and sanctuary.

Walking round, there are chapels in the outer aisles, and, on the south side, the small octagonal chapter house (*c.* 1500). Nearby is the recumbent effigy of Bishop Fraser, second Bishop of Manchester (d. 1885), by Forsyth. And at the west end of the north aisle is Theed's seated figure of Humphrey Chetham.

And close to the choir screen (north side) is a very early stone, an Anglo-Saxon carving of an angel carrying a scroll – a tiny fragment from the earliest church which once stood on this site.

OPPOSITE *Newcastle Cathedral: the 15th-century lantern and the Library, which resembles a Palladian town house*

DIOCESE OF
NEWCASTLE

Newcastle Cathedral

FROM THE CHURCHYARD at Gateshead there is a fascinating view of Newcastle across the river. Ships are tied up along the quayside; there are good-looking Georgian and Victorian buildings along the river front itself; there is the elegant 18th-century spire of All Saints' Church behind – and the enormous steel span of the Tyne Bridge in the foreground on the left. Behind this there is a glimpse of the Norman keep of the Castle, hemmed in by railway lines – and then the steeple

of the Cathedral. Steep streets and narrow alleys lead up into the city from the river. Newcastle is a place of antiquity, and strong character.

The Cathedral stands in a dignified setting near the centre of the city, where there are grand streets, such as Grey Street, laid out in the early 19th century by Richard Grainger and John Dobson, with good classical buildings: in Grey Street itself Lord Grey surveys the city from his monument, a column 135 feet high, designed by Benjamin Green (1838); the inscription pays tribute to the 'Champion of Civil and Religious Liberty'. Close to the Cathedral is the Castle; there are only a few modern blots to disfigure the scene.

The great thrill of the Cathedral is the magnificent steeple: the tall, square, buttressed tower rises to a crown of four lofty pinnacles capped with little crocketed spires, and from these pinnacles flying buttresses rise to support the corona, an open lantern which, poised in mid air, rises to another crocketed, pinnacled spire above. On the tower there are also smaller pinnacles – and on all these pinnacles, and on the topmost spire itself, there are gilded weather-vanes. It is a wonderful sight. The steeple rises to a height of some 193 feet, and dates from *c.* 1470. Walking round the exterior, the Cathedral will seem a large, impressive, town church, with wide transepts and wide aisles, and many traceried Perp windows. It is a surprise, turning into the narrow street on the south side, to find, built onto the choir aisle, what appears to be a Palladian town house, with Ionic pilasters and pedimented windows, rising to three floors. It is extraordinarily handsome, and intriguing. It was, in fact, built as a library in 1736, but the rooms are now used as choir rooms and vestries.

The diocese of Newcastle was created in 1882, formed out of the ancient diocese of Durham, and the venerable parish church became the cathedral. The interior is full of charm. Nave and chancel are spacious and there are wide aisles; the transepts, also, are aisled and spacious; the crossing is lofty, and through the rood screen there is a vista towards the High Altar with its towering reredos, with a grand east window rising beyond. The nave arcades are low, and the octagonal piers rise direct into the arches without capitals – a feature to be noted throughout the church. All this dates from *c.* 1340 – although high up in the N.W. crossing

pier there is a fragment of a 12th-century window, and there are a few other relics of the earlier church. The rood screen (*c.* 1880) leads into a beautifully furnished chancel, with canopied stalls and Bishop's throne, all designed by the Newcastle architect, R. J. Johnson, who also designed the elaborate reredos, with its three rows of figures in canopied niches, its side screens of stone, and the sedilia. The canopied tomb of Bishop Lloyd (1907) is by F. W. Pomeroy. Behind the High Altar is a spacious ambulatory with three eastern chapels; indeed this exceptionally well furnished chancel, with its ambulatory and eastern chapels, has the air of a cathedral in miniature. There is an organ of 1676 in the north transept, with a distinguished contemporary case; at its side a doorway leads down into an intimate, vaulted, crypt chapel. There is a brass lectern of *c.* 1500, and the font is crowned with a pinnacled, canopied cover of much the same date.

Apart from all this, there is an impressive display of monuments. Close to the N.W. door is one of considerable magnificence to Lord Collingwood, by Rossi (1810), with the Admiral's bust on a pedestal set against a background of drapery, his sword and coat of arms above, and a portrayal of waves below; another, by the S.W. door, is to Sir Matthew White Ridley of Blagdon, by Flaxman (1813), showing him as a Roman senator; Matthew Ridley (1787) is by Bacon; Hugo Moises (1806) is, again, by Flaxman – and there is a whole host of others from the 18th or early 19th century throughout the church. Of an earlier date is the ornate and colourful Maddison monument of 1634 – to Henry Maddison and his wife, resplendent with their figures and their children's, and plenty of heraldry. And there is a well-preserved brass of 1441 to Roger Thornton and his wife: he was three times Mayor of Newcastle. All these form a notable feature of the interior, and add no little to its atmosphere of dignity and civic pride.

Blanchland Abbey

Blanchland is a small secluded village in a remote valley of the upper Derwent. Wild, wooded countryside on all sides embosoms it: roads from Hexham to the north, Durham to the south and

---

OPPOSITE *Newcastle Cathedral: rood screen, reredos and chancel stalls, designed by R. J. Johnson*

Blanchland: the abbey church and the village seen across Beldon Brook

Hunstanworth to the west lead into it. An ancient bridge crosses the Beldon Brook: low stone cottages with stone roofs face each other across a wide gravelled L-shaped double square, and at the top stands a medieval gatehouse, with, at right angles, the Lord Crewe Arms, a grand medieval building delightfully enlivened with Georgian Gothick windows and a large heraldic inn sign, displaying the arms of Lord Crewe, Bishop of Durham. Beyond this, shady lime trees shield the small but stately fragment of the monastic church.

Blanchland Abbey was founded in 1165 for Premonstratensian Canons. The gatehouse, now one of the entrances to the square, is the late-15th-century Abbey gatehouse, the Lord Crewe Arms the former guesthouse. In the early 18th century the property was acquired by that great Bishop of Durham, Nathaniel Lord Crewe, who restored the church, then in a ruined condition.

Later in the century the Crewe Trustees laid out the village among the former monastic buildings to house the workers in the local lead mines: it is the perfect planned village, undisturbed since that date, and still the property of the Crewe Trustees.

The abbey church is L-shaped, too, and comprises a long north transept and the chancel. There never was a south transept, and the nave has disappeared. There is a tower attached to the transept: through this we enter. The interior is lofty and impressive, for all its modest size: there is an eastern aisle to the transept, now enclosed as a Lady Chapel; throughout the church there are handsome modern furnishings, and what remains of the building dates chiefly from the 13th and early 14th century. The cloisters have disappeared, but the garden of the Lord Crewe Arms, which adjoins the south side of the church, still has the air of the enclosed cloister court: indeed cloisters and chapter house stood here. It is to Lord Crewe that we owe what survives: his portrait and that of his wife dominate the dining-room upstairs in the hotel: from its windows there is a delightful view across this garden to the countryside beyond.

Brinkburn Priory

The countryside between Rothbury and Long-framlington is well wooded and remote. Driving along the B6344 there is an unexpected D. o. E. signpost to BRINKBURN PRIORY: ANCIENT MONU-MENT. A field gate leads along the drive to a car park, and another gate bears a notice TO THE PRIORY. No cars are permitted beyond this point, and the drive leads on through scenery of ever increasing loveliness, where the valley is hung with beechwoods of brightest green in spring, golden bronze in autumn. After descending some way, we find at the foot of the hill a great monastic church standing in miraculous isolation in its dene, with the River Coquet bubbling by.

Brinkburn was founded *c.* 1130 for Augustinian Canons by William Bertram, baron of Mitford. At the Dissolution in 1536 an ecclesiastical district was attached to the church, and services continued to be held – somewhat surprisingly in view of the remoteness of the spot. Decay set in: no wonder, in view of the size of the church and the scattered population far from any village. During the course of the 17th century the roof fell in and services ceased. So things continued, until in the middle of the 19th century Cadogan Hodgson-Cadogan, the owner of the estate, decided to restore the church, and appointed Thomas Austin of New-castle architect. A most sensitive restoration took place: work began in 1858, and by 1868 the church was furnished and the stained glass inserted. In 1965 Mr H. A. Cadogan Fenwick, great-great-grandson of the restorer, placed the Priory in the care of the Ministry of Public Buildings and Works (now D. o. E.): the church is open to the public daily, and services are held occasionally.

Brinkburn is not only miraculous in its setting: it is also a building of great distinction and interest. It is cruciform, with a long nave, a short chancel, transepts with eastern aisles and a low central tower. There is no south aisle to the nave: here the cloisters would have stood. We enter by the S.E. nave door (which originally led into the cloister) and are at once overwhelmed by the size,

Brinkburn: the unusual synthesis of E. E. lancets and Norman windows in the east end

the splendour and the simplicity of the interior. Standing under the crossing, the nave is on our left, empty but for a few rows of chairs, with an arcade of octagonal piers bearing pointed arches; above is a triforium with paired round-headed openings; above that, round-headed clerestory windows. The aisle windows are lancets, and there are triple lancets at the west end. The aisles are all vaulted. The transepts and chancel are short and soaring, and here the unusual synthesis of Gothic lancets and Norman round-headed win-dows continues – at the east end there are round-headed windows above, and longer lancets in the two stages below. There is a Victorian marble reredos, an altar with six candlesticks and crucifix: it is solemn and numinous. Above and around is jewel-like Victorian glass: Austin designed the glass on the south side of the sanctuary, which includes some ancient grisaille found during the restoration; the nine east windows are by Clayton & Bell, and there are others by Wailes. The organ by William Hill (1868) was the gift of Sir William Armstrong of Cragside.

To the south of the church stands the house called Brinkburn Priory, which incorporates some of the conventual buildings. The older part is late Georgian Gothick with a wide bow window facing east; Dobson added the castellated extensions to the west between 1830 and 1837. It is hoped to open the house to the public in due course; the estate still belongs to the Cadogan Fenwick family, who live nearby.

The beechwoods provide a wonderful back-ground on the north, and all around smooth lawns surround the church – with seats along the terraces inviting us to sit down and absorb the idyllic set-ting, and listen to the Coquet bubbling by.

Hexham Abbey

Hexham is a border town, with a wonderful air of independence and remoteness: the wild moors which accompany the road from Blanchland, the Tyne Valley, the proximity of the Roman wall, the rich farming country which goes on for mile after mile towards the Tweed, the border castles and pele towers, and defensive-looking villages with squat churches, all contribute to this indefinable atmosphere. There is a good view of the town gathered on its hill above the river, where Robert Mylne's bridge (1785) crosses the Tyne. The Abbey presides.

The first church here was founded by St Wilfrid *c.* 675, and the Bishopric of Hexham was established soon after. Of this earliest church the Saxon crypt (built of Roman stones) survives: all else was destroyed in the Danish raids towards the end of the 9th century. The church was refounded as a priory of Augustinian Canons in 1113. The nave was destroyed in the Scottish raids in the 14th century – and only rebuilt by Temple Moore in 1909. This is the church that today stands prominent at the end of Beaumont Street, in the Market Place, the E. end (rebuilt by Dobson in 1858) facing the 14th-century Moot Hall: the immensely long transepts immediately catch the eye. The principal entry is through the Slype, into the S. transept.

These monumental transepts are the great feature of Hexham, and will make the visitor gasp. In the S. transept the Night Stair is often photographed – with its well-worn steps leading up to the door to the Dormitory, from which the monks hastened down to the night offices. It is of monumental scale, and one of the most important relics of medieval monasticism in England. The transept itself (*c.* 1200) is austerely beautiful, with its simple group of lancets and wall passages, and large areas of plain wall around the staircase. The N. transept is a little later in date, and without question one of the most beautiful examples of E.E. architecture anywhere. Immensely long lancet windows in the N. wall, and an arcade of four bays with clustered columns, with triforium and clerestory above, opening into an E. aisle, and more long lancets in the W. wall, and trefoil arcading all around below – it is a superlative composition.

The nave which Temple Moore rebuilt in a chaste Dec style is curiously disappointing for the

Hexham Abbey from the market place: Dobson's remarkable east end

Hexham: the north transept from the Night Stair

work of so sensitive and scholarly an architect: the white stone and somewhat mechanical workmanship seem strangely cold. What is disastrous is the oversize modern organ set so assertively and incongruously upon the exquisite wooden pulpitum. This most delicate creation of *c.* 1500, adorned with medieval paintings and carvings, called for something smaller and in keeping.

The chancel (*c.* 1180) is a little earlier than the transepts, and is intimate and moving – with its ancient stalls (with misericords), its medieval chantries and pulpit, the superb fragment of a 15th-century painted reredos adorned with saints and bishops (N. side of sanctuary), and its rare Saxon episcopal stone throne. Prior Leschman's Chantry (*c.* 1491), part stone, part wood, contains the stone effigy of the prior, his cowl drawn over his eyes in death; Prior Ogle's (*c.* 1410) is all of timber, with a painted reredos; it so closely resembles W. B. Woodard's Chantry in Lancing Chapel (by Temple Moore) that the architect must have gained his inspiration here.

The crypt is approached by a narrow staircase in the nave, and is tiny and thrilling – comparable with Wilfrid's other crypt at Ripon. And throughout the church there are many other features of great interest – painted panels, Roman stones with inscriptions, St Acca's Cross (8th century), a Roman soldier's headstone. Little remains of the monastic buildings, though there is a fragment of the Lavatorium built into the back of a house on the S. side of what were the cloisters. The church became the parish church after the Dissolution of 1539.

DIOCESE OF
NORWICH

Norwich Cathedral

NORFOLK IS a proud, independent, individual county, a county of ancient houses, remote villages, noble churches, grand country houses, wide horizons, wide skies. And Norwich is a proud, independent, individual city, a city of narrow streets, winding alleys, ancient houses, noble churches – dominated by its Cathedral, whose spire, the second highest in England, floats over all.

Norwich is a medieval city, and the cathedral close is like a medieval village, enclosed, gated, within that city. The Bishop's Gate (from Palace Street), the Erpingham Gate and St Ethelbert's Gate (from Tombland) admit us to this private world: there is the Upper Close and the Lower Close, there is Green Yard and Almery Green; there are the buildings of Norwich School, larger, grander houses in the Upper Close, smaller houses and cottages in Hook's Walk – but everywhere there are gardens and gables, sash windows and mullions, and always more unexpected corners and alleyways to discover and explore. We can walk round and absorb the outside of the Cathedral – the immensely long nave, the shorter chancel, the tremendous build-up at the east end, of apse, chevet, flying buttresses, traceried windows, eastern chapels, the long arms of the transepts, the Norman central tower crowned by the 15th-century spire. We can walk round to the west front, and enter the Cathedral there.

The original seat of the bishop was at Thetford, but was transferred to Norwich in 1094. The present Cathedral was begun in 1096 by Bishop Herbert de Losinga, who also founded the Benedictine priory here, and before his death work had proceeded to the eastern bays of the nave. The main church was completed in the middle of the 12th century – but in 1362 the spire fell, damaging the chancel clerestory, and the oppor-

tunity was taken to rebuild the east end in its present dramatic form. The cloisters were begun at the very end of the 13th century, but were not completed till c. 1430, no doubt because the rebuilding of the east end had to be completed first, and the spire rebuilt. There was a disastrous fire in 1463, which destroyed the original timber roof. The 15th-century vault was then constructed – Norwich's crowning glory. At the Dissolution in 1539 the 'new foundation' of Dean and canons was established.

The interior of the nave will make an immediate, powerful impression: the wonderful rhythm of the Norman arcades, with their round or clustered columns, the spacious triforium above, the lofty clerestory above that; all this was completed in the first half of the 12th century. And then, a remarkable foil for this austere Norman work, the 15th-century vault, with its intricate ribs and gorgeous wealth of bosses, its liernes spreading like the branches of a forest above us, rises from this 12th-century arcade. The stone pulpitum, with organ above, stands in the tenth bay of the nave – but the vista of the vault goes on, to the crossing, and so to the apse beyond.

We have caught a glimpse of the traceried Perp windows at the east end: there are indeed later Perp windows all around, set into the Norman aisles, or the triforium or clerestory; there is a Perp west window, too (filled with glass of 1854 by Hedgeland, which recalls the pictorial windows of the 18th century); and here and there there are other Perp modifications to the Norman church – two bays on the south side of the nave have been so adapted, with Perp vaulting inserted in the Norman aisle. All this prepares us for the transformation made in the sanctuary in the 14th century.

Norwich Cathedral: Norman nave and 15th-century vault – the cathedral's crowning glory

Norwich Cathedral from the east: the immense flying buttresses hold the vault in place

The choir is splendidly furnished with 15th-century canopied stalls (with notable misericords) – and we are face to face with the sanctuary and apse. Here on either side the Norman arches have been recast in Perp, and all around the apse lofty traceried Perp windows fill the clerestory. It is a remarkable synthesis of Norman and Perp, with Norman arches surviving round the altar, and all around the triforium; here the Norman shafts terminate, and delicate Perp shafts take over to surround the clerestory windows, and bear the vault above. The excellent glass in the clerestory is by Warrington (1847).

There is more to come. The ambulatory leads

Norwich: the north-east doorway in the cloisters, one of the most perfect Gothic portals anywhere

round the apse to the chapels in the chevet – apsidal Norman chapels, with simple stone arcading and barrel-vaulted roofs – and these are some of the most beautiful features of the Cathedral. St Andrew's Chapel, the Jesus Chapel, St Luke's Chapel, the Chapel of Our Lady of Pity – these surround the apse, delightfully furnished, intimate and devout. Here there is a wonderful display of medieval painted panels, the work of the 14th- (or 15th-) century Norwich school of painters: the reredos in the Lady Chapel, the Despencer reredos in St Luke's, are outstanding work, rare surviv-

ing examples of English medieval painting.

As for monuments, the tomb of Bishop Goldwell (d. 1499), to whom we owe the rebuilding of the apse, is on the south side of the sanctuary, where his alabaster effigy lies on a painted tomb under a vaulted canopy; nearly 350 years later, the seated figure of Bishop Bathurst is the last work of Sir Francis Chantrey (1841). Nearby, the recumbent figure of Bishop Pelham is by James Forsyth (1896). Curiously, Norwich is not well off for great episcopal tombs, but the walls of the Cathedral are everywhere adorned with an interesting and varied collection of 18th-century monuments by Norwich sculptors. And in the S. arcade of the nave, under one of the Perp-remodelled arches, is a distinguished tablet by William Stanton to Dean Fairfax (d. 1702), showing his books in great piles alongside the marble columns of the monument. Nearby is the entrance to the cloisters.

These cloisters are among the most splendid in England; though they were built over a long period they display a remarkable harmony of style. The tracery of the windows moves from the early Geo-metrical, through the Curvilinear, to the late Per-pendicular, and the spreading tierceron vaulting displays everywhere an amazing wealth of bosses. And the N.E. doorway, leading into the nave, must be regarded as one of the most perfect Gothic portals anywhere. On either side of the doorway there are four detached shafts with simple capitals: above the doorway radiating figures under crocketed canopies adorn the arch itself – Our Lord in the centre, with an angel on either side, and four other saints. It dates from *c.* 1310. On the E. side remains the doorway to the chapter house, pulled down after the Dissolution; from the S. side is one of the most spectacular views of the Cathedral – the two-storeyed cloister, and, above that, the full height of the south aisle, with the windows of the triforium and clerestory rising to the steep pitched lead roof, with Norman arcading everywhere, buttresses, battlements: this south side of the Cathedral rises like a great cliff of stone before our eyes, crowned by the spire.

A final pleasure must be to walk through the Close to Pull's Ferry, and there see the Cathedral from the river.

Binham Priory

Binham stands on the north Norfolk coast, not far from the sea, not far from Blakeney with its marshes and little harbour and grand church. 'The spring is always cold and late on the Norfolk coast,' wrote Wyndham Ketton-Cremer in his enchanting book *Felbrigg*: 'for weeks at a time the cold wind blows in from the sea, a chill drying wind, northerly or easterly. The trees ... come slowly into leaf under a reluctant sun. There will be days, and even whole weeks, when the weathercock swings round to the south – days of continuous sunshine and birdsong, of leaves almost visibly unfolding ... But it will not be long before the wind goes

Binham Priory

back to the north or east, and the fog creeps in from the sea.' Such is the setting of Binham.

On such a day we may find ourselves there. The gatehouse on the lane leads down to the west front: there are stone walls which once protected outbuildings of the Priory but now enclose green meadows; it is a horse grazing that welcomes us, not a Benedictine monk. We are face to face with the superb fragment of the E.E. west front. This is the view that Cotman painted in 1838: there is a little bell turret and, beneath, a geometrical west window, blocked up with brick. It would be sad indeed, were it not so beautiful, this rare combination of silvery stone and warm red brick. On either side is E.E. arcading: below, the central doorway, with shafted columns and stiff-leaf capitals, is set between twin pairs of tall blind arches, the outer pair forming the lower stages of the buttresses; the spandrels are adorned with sexfoil, the upper spaces with trefoil or cinquefoil ornament; on either side the long aisle windows open into nothing. It is all a work of great beauty, an echo of the west front at Wells or Newstead.

Inside, all is different: it is a grand Norman nave, shorn of its aisles. Round arches are blocked up, with Perp windows inserted; there is a spacious triforium, a clerestory above with little lancet windows. The east end is blocked, too, above the pulpitum, with a dull little straight-headed 16th-century window above the altar, the blocked-up doorways of the screen on either side. There is an impressive Seven Sacrament font; nearby are the remains of the lower sections of the rood screen, with Gothic lettering – texts from the Tyndale version of the New Testament barely concealing earlier paintings behind – and many oak benches with poppyheads, and two stalls with misericords. There is a Royal Arms (1815) in a pretty Gothic frame.

Outside again, it is possible to study the remains of the crossing, the transepts and choir, and the foundations of chapter house, refectory, cloisters and many domestic buildings. All is tended by the D. o. E., the walls preserved, the lawns mown.

Binham was founded for Benedictine monks in 1091 by Peter de Valoines, nephew of the Conqueror; Matthew Paris, historian of St Albans (the mother church), records that the west front was built by Richard de Parco, Prior between 1226 and 1244; if so, this is earlier than comparable work at Westminster – a fascinating speculation. The Priory was dissolved in 1540, the nave becoming the parish church.

There is little to the village – merely a handful of cottages and farms. Otherwise is it only remote and beautiful Norfolk countryside, with – from the higher ground to the north – a view of the sea.

branch of the Augustinians: they had but four houses in England, and Ingham was their mother house, founded in 1360 by Sir Miles Stapleton. The tower stands 100 ft high, there is a three-storeyed porch (a great rarity), a spacious nave and a grand chancel – the monastic choir – lit by enormous traceried Dec windows. Between nave and chancel stand the remains of the stone pulpitum, and close to the sanctuary is the tomb of Sir Oliver de Ingham (1343), whose daughter married Sir Miles Stapleton. In the nave is the tomb of Sir Roger de Bois and his wife, also of the mid 14th century. The church was tactfully restored in 1876 by Ewan Christian and J. P. Seddon. Walking round the outside, it is fascinating to discover there the fragments of the arches of the cloisters, and high up against the chancel wall remains of rooms built on to this north side of the church. The survival of the complete church is unusual: these fragments of the domestic quarters are unexpected and specially interesting.

Weybourne Priory

The north Norfolk coast at Weybourne is dramatic, and it is but a short walk from the Priory to the beach. The first sight of the Priory is dramatic

Ingham with its 14th-century tower and three-storeyed porch

Ingham Priory

The church stands magnificent, close to the Norfolk coast, not far from the lighthouse at Happisburgh. It was a priory of Trinitarian Canons, a

Weybourne: brick and flint in the south porch

too: the chancel is all in ruins and rising cliff-like on the north side of the present (parochial) chancel is the tall fragment – in fact the entire south side – of the 11th-century central tower. This was the central tower of the original parish church, which was taken over by the Augustinian Canons when the Priory was founded here *c.* 1200 by Sir Ralph de Meyngaren. To this the canons added the long monastic chancel, chapels, transepts – all now in ruins – and a new parochial nave and west tower (*c.* 1420). This survives as the parish church, but its north aisle is in fact the original nave of the earlier church. The two-storeyed porch is a delightful example of brick and flint chequerwork. The cloisters and conventual buildings which stood on the north side have vanished.

Wymondham Abbey

The Benedictine Abbey with its incredible towers stands on the edge of the little town: the towers are amazing landmarks across the countryside – the west tower, tall, blunt and square, the east, of equal height, but octagonal and now completely hollow. They stand like the towers of some enormous lightship, one at the stern, one at the prow – a lightship strangely marooned here in the depths of the Norfolk countryside. Wymondham is an ancient market town: in the market place there is a timbered octagonal Market Cross, built in 1615, and streets, wide and narrow, lead off, with larger Georgian houses and many smaller timbered ones. From the town green, Vicar Street leads to the church.

Wymondham with its two towers

Wymondham Abbey was founded in 1107 by
William de Albini. Outside it appears all Perp,
with these vast Perp towers and big Perp windows.
Inside, all is different. We enter by the north
porch into a sumptuous Norman nave, nine bays in
length, with a spacious triforium after the pattern
of Norwich. Above is a lofty Perp clerestory, and
above that a high-pitched hammerbeam roof, with
angels, wings outstretched, surveying the nave. It
is a long, lofty, narrow interior. But the climax is
the east end, where a glorious reredos, ablaze with
gilt and colour, fills the blocked-up wall – the work
of Sir Ninian Comper (1935). It is as high as the
triforium, and the screen itself has Our Lord in
glory as its dazzling centrepiece: two rows of saints
under ornate canopies surround this, a wide tester
extends above, crowned with the figures of angels
blowing trumpets, and in the blank apex of the
wall, on a gilded rood beam, there is a tremendous
gilded crucifix, with the figures of Our Lady and
St John on either side, and angels with outspread
wings to left and right. Six immense candlesticks
and a tapering crucifix adorn the altar; it is one
of Comper's greatest masterpieces, and pulls the
whole church together. In the sanctuary the tomb
of Abbot Ferrers, of white-washed terracotta and
reminiscent of the Bedingfeld tombs at Oxburgh
(*c.* 1525), serves as sedilia. The north aisle is wide
and Perp, with another hammerbeam roof; in a
gallery under the west tower is a handsome 18th-
century organ.

Town and Abbey were constantly at loggerheads
– hence the two rival towers, the monastic at the
crossing, the parochial, defiant, at the west. After
the Dissolution chancel and transepts were pulled
down; the parish kept its nave. Of the conventual
buildings only the eastern gable of the chapter
house survives. The monastic tower, hollow and
open to the sky, on its high crossing arch open to
the winds, stands as a reminder of the departed
monks.

Wymondham: Sir Ninian Comper's reredos

Christ Church Cathedral is the smallest in England; it is arranged as a college chapel

DIOCESE OF
OXFORD

Christ Church Cathedral

CHRIST CHURCH has been described as 'the smallest, shyest and squarest of English cathedrals' (Harry Batsford and Charles Fry, *The Cathedrals of England*, 1934). It is the smallest because the 12th-century priory church, never very large, lost four of its nave bays in 1525, when Cardinal Wolsey began to build the great quadrangle of his new college, to be known as Cardinal College (indeed he planned to demolish the whole church when he had completed the grand college chapel which was to have occupied the N. side of the quad). It is the squarest because the chapels added to the N. side of the chancel during the 13th century, together with the broad transepts and the short stump of the nave, the rectangular chapter house and the three surviving walks of the cloister, make the whole building as wide as it is long. It is the shyest because the Cathedral conceals itself modestly behind the college buildings, and the spire rises diffidently above the E. side of Tom Quad.

According to tradition the priory here was founded by St Frideswide in the 8th century: what is certain is that a priory of Augustinian Canons was established, or re-established, in the early 12th century by Henry I. This was suppressed by Wolsey in order to make way for his college. Wolsey began to build his quadrangle – designed to be the largest in Oxford – built his Dining Hall, but then fell from grace in 1529. Henry VIII refounded the college as Christ Church (*Aedes Christi* – hence its name 'The House'), and made the priory church the cathedral of the new diocese of Oxford, which he had founded in 1542. It was also to serve as the college chapel, the Dean of the Cathedral was to be Head of the College, the Canons Professors, the College and the Chapter being one indivisible foundation. So it has continued – and Christ Church, being both college and cathedral, is of course unique.

So we approach the Cathedral, entering Tom Quad under Tom Tower – the lower part of the gate being Wolsey's Tudor gateway, the upper the wonderful fantasia designed by Wren in 1682. On the S. side of the quad is the Dining Hall, with the big square bell tower (by Bodley) in the corner; nearby, in the E. side of the quad, two inconspicuous doorways lead into the Cathedral. There is a short ante-chapel, dominated by the organ screen and the organ with its splendid 17th-century case, and we are in the nave.

The nave is of three bays, the chancel of four, and it is arranged as a college chapel, with the seats and stalls facing inwards and occupying choir, crossing and nave. There is a Jacobean pulpit at the crossing, but nearly all the furnishings are by Scott (1872), with iron screens behind the stalls by Skidmore. The eye is led to the E. end, with its wheel window and round-headed 'Norman' windows beneath (a re-creation by Scott), and Bodley's brightly gilded reredos. But it is the Norman arcades of nave and chancel which catch the eye next, with their curious double arches rising from enormous piers – one above, rising from the boldly carved capitals and enclosing the blind triforium, and the other below, the true arch of the arcade rising from half-capitals in the aisle to bear the aisle vault. It is an ingenious, attractive device, designed to produce an effect of greater height. And then the vault: an elaborate early-16th-century lierne vault spans the chancel, with lantern-like pendants suspended in mid-air. This vault is the glory of the church.

The N. transept is double-aisled, and here three chapels, added in the 13th and early 14th centuries to the N. choir aisle, form a delicate Gothic annexe to the Norman church. In the Lady Chapel stands a reconstructed fragment of St Frideswide's Shrine: facing this the 15th-century Watching Chamber, with its pinnacled, canopied, wooden upper chamber, has miraculously survived, standing between this and the Latin Chapel. Medieval stalls

Christ Church: Tom Quad and bell tower; cathedral and college are indivisible

and medieval glass (N. side), with one of the best of all Burne-Jones' windows at the E. end, make this a moving, numinous interior. In St Lucy's Chapel (S. transept) is the best medieval glass in the Cathedral: the Becket window (*c.* 1320), made to commemorate the martyrdom of St Thomas. And nearby is a fascinating group of late-17th-century monuments – to members of Charles I's household who died in Oxford when the city was the Royalist headquarters during the Civil War, and the King himself lodged in Christ Church.

Throughout the Cathedral there is a most interesting collection of tombs and monuments – to Bishop King, last Abbot of Osney and first Bishop of Oxford (1557), to Richard Burton, author of *The Anatomy of Melancholy* (1639), to Dean Aldrich, amateur architect, to whom Oxford owes so much (1710), to Bishop Berkeley, the philosopher (1752), to Dr Pusey, Professor of Hebrew and saintly leader of the Oxford Movement (1882), and to Dean Liddell, of Liddell and Scott fame, and father of Alice-in-Wonderland (1898); Lewis Carroll (the Revd. C. L. Dodgson) was a don at Christ Church. And there is interesting glass everywhere: in addition to the windows already mentioned, there are others by Burne-Jones, and by Clayton & Bell (E. windows, and N. transept); and of special note is the superb Jonah window at the W. end of the N. aisle by Abraham van Linge (1631).

Three sides of the small Perp cloister survive on the S. side; the fourth was pulled down by Wolsey to build the Hall. On the E. side a Norman doorway leads into a spacious E.E. chapter house, which houses the Cathedral and Diocesan Treasury. From the Cloister Court there is a rare view of the exterior of this shy cathedral – nave, S. transept, and E.E. spire, one of the earliest spires in England. And through a narrow alley it is possible to go out into the Meadow, walk down to the river by the Broad Walk – or round towards Corpus and Merton to see the E. end of the Cathedral from there. And here the towers of Merton and Magdalen are visible across the Meadow.

Christ Church is the grandest of the Oxford colleges: Wolsey's Dining Hall, approached by the dramatic staircase with its 17th-century fan vault, is filled with portraits of its illustrious alumni. The House has produced no less than thirteen Prime Ministers, and eleven Viceroys of India. Tom Quad, Peckwater Quad, Canterbury Quad, the monumental Library, the Picture Gallery – these may be visited at appropriate times.

As we walk about the House it may be observed that when the Cathedral clock is striking the hour, the clock in Tom Tower is pointing to five past the hour. This is no accident: the Cathedral keeps Oxford time, five minutes behind Greenwich time. Oxford is indeed the home of lost causes – and charming anachronisms.

Chetwode Priory

Romantic and unexpected in this remote, gently undulating, hunting country between Bicester and Buckingham – the spacious chancel and the abbreviated parochial nave of an Augustinian priory founded in 1245. Sir Gilbert Scott tells us in his *Recollections* how he visited the place as a boy – his father was Rector of the adjoining parish of Gawcott – found the church locked, and peered through the keyhole in amazement at the five long lancets of the E. window; in amazement because he had never seen lancet windows before. And even to us they are amazing and supremely beautiful, delicate work of the 13th century, with groups of three-stepped lancets on either side of the sanctuary. The S. window is filled with 13th-century glass, the E. with remarkable glass of 1842 by Holland of Warwick. There are later traceried windows in the nave, and through an arch in the N. wall steps lead up to the family pew of the Chetwode family, complete with fireplace and monuments to the Chetwodes; of special interest is that to Field Marshal Lord Chetwode (who was Sir John Betjeman's father-in-law). In the nave there are hatchments, a Royal Arms in a carved frame, a little Gothick organ, and a Chetwode banner. A 17th-century painted reredos is suspended on the S. wall. 'The law was given by Moses,' it proclaims, 'but Grace and Truth came by Jesus Christ'; and, it adds, 'This church was repaired A° 1696. W. Lawley Churchwarden.' Outside, the little tower 'has accidentally arrived at the N.W. corner', wrote John Nash in the original *Shell Guide to Buckinghamshire*; next door a handsome early-19th-century stone farmhouse occupies the site of the priory buildings. And half a mile away to the N.E. is the gabled Jacobean manor house, ancient seat of the Chetwodes.

Chetwode (see previous page): the five long lancets of the east window, admired by the youthful Gilbert Scott through the keyhole

Dorchester Abbey

Dorchester Abbey stands in watery meadows close to where the River Thame flows into the Thames. A long balustraded stone bridge crosses the Thame, commanding a view of the whole length of the church – while on the other side the charming little R.C. church of St Birinus (by W. Wardell, 1849) nestles below. The Thames pursues its stately course to the south, and Wittenham Clumps stand sentinel over the landscape. The village street twists and turns, lined with a delightful medley of houses and cottages of many dates: opposite the 16th-century George Hotel a lychgate designed by William Butterfield leads to the Abbey. Dorchester, as its name implies, was once a Roman town – then a Saxon bishopric. In 624 St Birinus, a Benedictine monk, was sent by the Pope

Dorchester Abbey: the parochial nave and altar, with a 14th-century mural of the Crucifixion above

to convert the West Saxons, and he built the first church here. The bishopric of Dorchester stretched from the Thames to the Humber: in 1072 the see was moved to Lincoln, and Remigius, the last Bishop of Dorchester, became first Bishop of Lincoln. In 1140 Bishop Alexander of Lincoln refounded Dorchester as a house of Augustinian Canons; they took over the old Saxon cathedral, and began to build the Norman abbey. The building history of this great church is hard to unravel, but some of this 12th-century building survives, added to, altered, mutilated, restored over the centuries.

Approaching it through the lychgate, we pass on the left the monastic guest house (now the Museum) – all that remains of the conventual buildings; the west tower is squat and a rebuilding of 1602, with chequer-patterned turrets of flint and stone; a 15th-century porch leads into the south aisle. The first impression is thrilling. This was the parochial nave, and it is wide, lofty, spacious – terminating in a blank wall adorned with fragments of medieval paintings. Here up a flight of steps stands an altar, a 14th-century mural of the Crucifixion, all in buff and terracotta, as its reredos; an arcade of three tall 14th-century arches leads into the nave proper, and surrounding one of the pillars a wonderful extruding carved corbel – at shoulder level – depicts a group of sleeping monks; there is a rare and most interesting 12th-century lead font, with figures of the twelve apostles round – one of only thirty or so such fonts in England; and so into the nave itself. This is empty and awe-inspiring: there is no arcade on the north side – the cloisters stood on this side – just the sheer wall, with a window or two high up. This is the Norman nave, what was the nave of an aisleless cruciform church. Beyond is the crossing with its arches, but the south transept is now absorbed by the wide south aisle, and the north transept collapsed in the early 17th century – or perhaps was pulled down – after the destruction of the cloisters.

Moving up into the crossing is a revelation: not only does the majestic chancel open up before us, but beyond that blind wall which terminated the parochial south aisle is revealed the monastic choir aisle, the Lady Chapel, with its two altars standing side by side under vaulted sanctuaries (Gilbert Scott built or rebuilt the vaulting in 1872); this is of particular beauty. On the north side is the narrow chapel of St Birinus, with its geometrical tracery. Magnificent arcades of three towering early-14th-century arches separate these chapels from the chancel itself, of which the climax is a sanctuary of great splendour. The east window fills the entire wall; it is traceried all over and divided in the centre by a plain stone buttress (the site being marshy), which adds to its special quality: it is resplendent with 14th-century glass – and 19th-century glass by O'Connor at the top, which was reconstructed by Butterfield (*c.* 1850) when he restored the chancel and raised the roof to its original height. To the left is the Jesse window, for which Dorchester is justly celebrated: here Dec tracery and sculpture combine with medieval glass to portray the descendants of Jesse, culminating in the Virgin and Christ Himself; it is remarkable that so many figures remain intact. The south window has tracery which is almost Perp; here there is medieval heraldic glass; there are small quatrefoil windows below, within the

canopies of the sedilia.

In the Lady Chapel is the Shrine of St Birinus, an inspired reconstruction by Mr Russell Cox (1964) of the original, and incorporating medieval fragments; nearby is the remarkable cross-legged effigy of Sir John Holcomb, grasping his sword (*c.* 1280), and the tomb of Judge Stonor (*c.* 1350), ancestor of the Stonor family of Stonor, that romantic house not many miles away where the Reformation never took place, where the medieval chapel has never ceased to be in communion with the Holy See, and where the Stonor family still live. There is also good Victorian glass to be seen, by O'Connor, Hardman and Mayer of Munich.

It is due to Richard Beauforest – whom Leland described as 'a great rich man of Dorchester' – that almost complete monastic church survives. He bought the church at the time of the Dissolution (1536), and subsequently presented it to the parish, to serve as the parish church. The churchyard is full of atmosphere, too: on the north side the grass is neatly mown, and it is possible to imagine the line of the cloister court. But on the south side there are old tombs and headstones, and grass is allowed to grow: here is the genuine character of an Oxfordshire village churchyard. Walking round the building it is possible to appreciate the details of the church – the red tile roof, the long line of Dec traceried windows, the squat tower – which gave so little clue, when seen from the bridge, of the glories to be revealed within.

Hurley Priory

This is Thames-side commuter country. A pretty village street leads off the busy Henley–Oxford road, and reaches the church, surrounded by venerable buildings and old walls which were once part of the Benedictine Priory founded here in 1087 by Geoffrey de Mandeville as a cell of Westminster Abbey. A timber bell turret crowns the modest buttressed W. front, with its Norman doorway and Norman window above (the details much restored in the 19th century); to the left an archway leads into the former cloister court, now the private garden of the romantic-looking house which was formed out of the Refectory and its adjacent buildings after the Dissolution. On the

Hurley: LEFT *archway into the cloister court;* RIGHT *old headstones in the churchyard*

far side of the lane stand the 14th-century dovecote and barn of the monastery. The church itself is like a long narrow barn, dark and mysterious inside with its small Norman windows. Henry Hakewill restored the church in 1852: to him is due the odd neo-Norman stone reredos, which stands like a pulpitum across the E. end, separating the sanctuary from the vestry behind. There are Elizabethan monuments to the Lovelace family, who acquired the monastic property soon after the Dissolution, and built a grand house called Ladye Place to the E. of the church (demolished in 1837); and many smaller tablets of the 18th and early 19th century – one by Flaxman. And the churchyard on the S. side of the church, secluded behind its long high wall, is filled with old tombs and headstones.

DIOCESE OF
PETERBOROUGH

Peterborough Cathedral

TRAVELLING FROM KING'S CROSS on a high-speed train, Peterborough is probably the first stop. The train slows down after passing those endless brick fields, where the earth has been dug up to uncover the clay and unnumbered chimneys raise their heads to the sky. As we approach the station and cross the river the Cathedral appears, lying long and low above the houses and warehouses and factory buildings; it is an unpromising town in an unpromising setting, but, for all that, the Cathedral is majestic. Travelling from the north, the situation is no better: endless railway tracks, endless railway buildings, endless factories and endless rows of railway cottages line the route: above all this the Cathedral is just visible, with its low square central tower, the mass of pinnacles and little spires and lofty gables at the west end.

Until the middle of the 19th century Peterborough was still a quiet cathedral city: in the 1840s, it is said, sedan chairs were still to be seen in the Precincts, where the dignitaries and local gentry pursued their scholarly secluded lives: *otium cum dignitate.* The coming of the railway, the opening of the brickworks, changed all that; now the air is heavy with the smell of bricks, and traffic pours in along the main roads which all lead to Peterborough. What is more, and what is worse, Peterborough has in recent years become a 'New Town', strangled by the new dual carriageways that encircle the place, strangled by the 'inner relief roads' that engulf the town itself. It has become a nightmare town of multi-storey car parks, shopping precincts, 'walkways' and 'through-ways'; blocks of vast new buildings rear their ugly heads near the Cathedral; St John the Baptist, the ancient parish church, is overshadowed by an office block, standing within a few feet of its noble 15th-century tower. How could

this have been countenanced? There are few buildings of any age or any note: the charming 17th-century Guildhall stands sad and solitary in the pedestrianized Market Place. To pass through the gateway from the Market Place into the Precincts is like reaching an island of civilization from an ocean of despair.

The Benedictine Abbey of Peterborough (or Medehamstead, as it was originally called) was founded *c.* 650 by King Peada of Mercia. After the usual sacking by the Danes in the 9th century it was refounded, and then burnt in the usual great fire, *c.* 1116. Rebuilding began soon afterwards, and the Norman church, much as we see it today, was built during the ensuing century, culminating in the west front, which was completed in the early 13th century. The New Building – the Perp retrochoir – was added in the earliest years of the 16th century. After the Dissolution (1539), Henry VIII founded the new Diocese of Peterborough in 1542, and the abbey church became the cathedral.

We are standing before the west front: it is familiar, of course, from photographs, because it is one of the two or three greatest west fronts in England – but perhaps nothing has prepared us for its immense size, its immense height. At either end there is a slim tower, culminating in a small tapering spire, with a wealth of pinnacles around its base; three lofty gables, punctuated by tall pinnacles, stand between, and beneath these three tremendous arches rise to the full height of the building, half concealing, half revealing under a quadripartite vault the west wall behind, strongly patterned with tall blind arcading and friezes of smaller trefoil arches: the patterning continues on the narrow towers at either end. There is wonderful profusion of carving in the gables, where little wheel-windows are surrounded by statuary, and

Peterborough Cathedral: exterior from the south

Peterborough: one of the two or three greatest west fronts in England

there is more statuary in the spandrels of the arches. From behind the gables small square towers rise above the western transepts – the south tower never completed above its base, but the north tower rising to full height, crowned with tall pinnacles. The effect is curious, asymmetrical, but not unpleasing – it adds to the profusion of spikes and spires. In addition to all this, the next century thought nothing of adding a Perp porch within the central arch, and Perp windows in every arch. It

Peterborough: Norman apse, Perp tracery

is an amazing composition, its silhouette changing and varying with every step taken.

We enter by the Perp porch, and the full length of this grand Norman church bursts upon us. There are no secrets at Peterborough: all is revealed at once – nave, choir, crossing, sanctuary. But it is an interior so tremendous, so rich, so complete, that it never disappoints. The wonderful rhythm of Norman arch after Norman arch, of the spacious triforium above, and the clerestory above that, of the profusion of shafts, the perfection of proportions, the abundance of daylight pouring through windows in aisle, clerestory and triforium

– all these combine to create an interior of severe, serene simplicity. Far above our heads the rare painted early-13th-century wooden ceiling glows with colour, the lozenge-shaped compartments filled with the figures of saints or kings, queens or monsters. It is one of the most important works of medieval art anywhere.

Moving up the nave it is possible to admire the aisles vaulted in stone, their walls adorned with interlaced arcading, the large Perp windows, here and above, which are later insertions, the choir stalls (by Pearson, 1894) occupying the two eastern bays of the nave, and the new hanging rood, its golden figure on a crimson cross, at the entrance to the choir, presented to the Cathedral as the result of a dream, designed by G. G. Pace (1975): STAT CRUX DUM VOLVITUR ORBIS. The nave, indeed the whole Cathedral, is wonderfully spacious, wonderfully clear, wonderfully free from clutter: there is no 'nave sanctuary', no nave altar – an altar being erected here only when required.

The central tower was rebuilt by Pearson in 1884; through its lantern windows the crossing is bathed in light. The transepts are wide and spacious, with eastern aisles and original wooden ceilings, all in the same strong, solemn, Norman idiom. And, facing east into the chancel, it is the same rhythm there: of four more bays leading to the apsidal sanctuary; but here the windows above the altar are filled with Perp tracery and fragments of medieval glass. Below stands the High Altar, under Pearson's sumptuous baldacchino. This makes the sanctuary – indeed it makes the whole interior: it must have been a bold innovation in 1894. And the marble floor, the mosaics, the metal screens, the altar rails, are Pearson's too.

Nearby, in the north aisle, is the burial place of Queen Catherine of Aragon, first wife of Henry VIII. She died at Kimbolton (1536), and Henry promised her burial 'in one of the goodliest monuments in Christendom'. Here her body lies, though her tomb was destroyed by Parliamentary soldiers in 1643. The plain black marble slab was set here in 1895: above hang the banners of England and Spain in her honour. And so to the New Building or retrochoir.

This is the great surprise of Peterborough, a masterpiece of latest Gothic architecture – a staggering leap in time and style from the rest of the church. Built between 1496 and 1508 by Abbot Kirton, whose long reign began in the former year, it forms a new and marvellous ambulatory behind the eastern apse. It is two bays deep, and as wide as the Cathedral, and is spanned by one of the most splendid fan vaults in England. Perp windows fill every bay, and there is stone panelling beneath. It is possible that John Wastell, who built the vault of King's Chapel, and was a native of East Anglia, may have designed the building.

Mary Queen of Scots, who was beheaded at Fotheringhay in 1587, was buried in the south choir aisle – before being removed by her son James I to Westminster: a stone tablet here marks the spot. At the west end of the nave is the portrait of Robert Scarlett, gravedigger, who died in 1594

Peterborough: the New Building, a masterpiece of late Gothic architecture

aged 98 – and who had buried these two queens.

Nothing remains of the Lady Chapel, which stood, as at Ely, on the south side of the chancel; nor of the Chapter House. And of the cloisters only the outer walls stand, with a few vestiges of the vaulting shafts and doorways. But it forms a secluded grass court from which to survey the south side of the Cathedral. And the Precincts provide many delightful surprises. To the S.W. the Abbot's Lodging is the Bishop's Palace, while to the S.E. houses for the canons have been formed out of the remains of the monastic buildings. It is a pleasure to walk here, under the arcades of the Infirmary Hall, now open to the skies, and discover that houses have been built on either side in the aisles. Patched-up medieval buildings, high walls, secret gardens are perhaps an unexpected feature of the Precincts here, but they give some idea of the extent of the former monastic foundation. From here it is a pleasure to walk back to the west front through the slype, the narrow passage which leads past Laurel Court into the cloister, and from this confined space gaze up at the monumental mass of the great church towering above.

Canons Ashby Priory

Down long inconsequential lanes in the heart of Northamptonshire stands a church with a grand square pinnacled tower, and a large lofty truncated nave alongside it, hard upon the road: the church of a house of Augustinian Canons, founded here *c.* 1250. A short distance away, hard upon the road on the farther side, is the long back of the ancient house of the Dryden family, romantic with Tudor gables and Queen Anne sash windows – recently rescued by the National Trust from a state of dereliction and near collapse. A small park, walled gardens with gates and obelisks and urns, surround the house; wonderful interiors, with panelling and ornate plasterwork, tapestries and family portraits (including one of John Dryden), with much original furniture restored to the house, complete a rare and remarkable ensemble.

And the church is part of this ensemble: after the Dissolution it became the property of, first, the Cope family, then (by marriage) the Drydens. Both families were fervent Puritans, and they ran the church as their own private Puritan place of worship, which served the estate and tiny village: they maintained the services, and appointed and paid the incumbent. So it continued. Like the house, the church now belongs to the National Trust: a great restoration has taken place, and it is hoped that it will be used for occasional services and concerts: it is open to the public at the same time as the house.

There is an imposing west front, with 13th-century arcading, and a grand doorway with a later, Perp, window above to light the nave; the 14th-century tower stands on the left. Inside, the truncated nave is of great height, with two lofty bays separating nave from north aisle. Round the east window, wall paintings have been discovered, of cherubs holding crimson curtains – perhaps part of the decorative schemes of Miss Elizabeth Creed (a cousin of the Drydens), of which there is much more in the house. There are brasses to John Dryden (d. 1584), the first of the family to come to Canons Ashby, and of his son the first Baronet (d. 1632). There are many more Dryden

Canons Ashby: eloquent of a remote age

monuments, no less than eleven hatchments, and, of special interest, the helmet, banner, tabard, sword, shield, gauntlets and spurs for the funeral of Sir Robert, the third baronet (d. 1708) – an amazing example of a medieval practice surviving into the 18th century. Pulpit and altar rails are 18th century too. Buried here in remote Northamptonshire, untouched by the heavy hand of the Victorians, both church and house are wonderfully eloquent of a remote age and a vanished world.

Portsmouth Cathedral

OLD PORTSMOUTH is one of the pleasant surprises of England: after the long wide drab streets of the Victorian city, it is a delight to find oneself in the Old Town. Here there are streets lined with 18th-century houses, with shops and old public houses. The High Street leads down to Grand Parade, and to the bastions and fortifications which face the harbour. These are in origin medieval, but were greatly augmented and strengthened by Charles II. At the lower end of the High Street, surrounded by smooth lawns, stands Portsmouth Cathedral.

Architecturally it is a hotch-potch, and an unfinished hotch-potch at that. But it is a building of great charm and character, with some important architectural features. The sanctuary and eastern transepts are 13th century; the chancel and central tower are late 17th; the nave and main transepts 20th; a temporary wall at the west end awaits the completion of the church. The plain square tower is crowned with an octagonal domed cupola, with a gilded weather-vane of a sailing ship on its lantern top (1710). St Thomas' Church, as it originally was, was founded *c.* 1180, in honour of St Thomas of Canterbury, and belonged to the Augustinian Canons of Portchester and Southwick. It became the cathedral of the new diocese of Portsmouth in 1927; Sir Charles Nicholson was responsible for the enlargements, which are as yet incomplete.

The south porch leads into Nicholson's nave; imposing stone arcades in a free Romanesque style, with round pillars, square capitals and round arches lead up to low clerestory windows with Perp tracery; nave and aisles are groin-vaulted, and, beyond, are lower outer aisles; large Perp windows flood the nave with light. What was the west tower of the old church has become the central tower of the Cathedral, with lofty arches leading into the choir; a low round arch at the base forms, as it were, the pulpitum, with an ornamental 18th-century organ on top. The round arches in the nave, and their circular piers, are a happy compliment to the 17th-century arches in the choir: it is a pleasing synthesis of styles, and, even in its incomplete state, a spacious interior. Only three bays of the nave were built between 1935 and 1939, when war brought building to a halt. One longs for its completion – to Sir Charles Nicholson's design.

Entering the chancel under the pulpitum, we are in what was the nave of the parish church. There are slender Tuscan piers with round arches: dormer windows light the shallow plaster ceiling; there are appropriate modern stalls, a west gallery to accommodate the organ, and a magnificent pulpit of 1693: from its sounding board an angel is blowing a trumpet across the whole church.

The sanctuary is only two bays in length, but of rare interest and beauty. There are low arcades, with two paired pointed arches under a wider round arch, as at Boxgrove (q.v.). There are lancets above, lancets at the east end, and both sanctuary and aisles are vaulted. The chancel at Boxgrove is a little later in date, and more elaborate: both must have been designed by the same masons; they are of special beauty, and unique in England. The eastern transepts are narrow (*c.* 1190), and contain the Lady Chapel (N.) and the Martyrs' Chapel (S.). There are many monuments in the chancel aisles: of greatest interest is that to George Villiers, Duke of Buckingham, murdered in a house in the High Street in 1628 – a splendid piece by Nicholas Stone, with a marble urn set against a black back-

Portsmouth Cathedral: 17th-century tower, 18th-century cupola and 20th-century transept – a hotch-potch of great charm

Portsmouth: 13th-century sanctuary and 17th-century chancel

and a still taller pinnacled staircase turret crowned with a gilded weathercock stands sentinel. The nave is Norman, with a late-12th-century S. arcade, with circular piers and pointed arches: above this are two early Norman windows, half blocked by the later arches below. The chancel arch is blocked, as are the little windows on either side. But this imposing interior has the air of a monastic church. A doorway in the N. wall led into the cloisters – but this and all the conventual buildings have disappeared. Carisbrooke was a Benedictine priory, a cell of the abbey of Lyre in France; it was dissolved, like so many alien priories, by Henry V – but the nave survived as the parish church.

Carisbrooke: the late-12th-century arcade

ground, and cherubs with trumpets supporting his coat of arms and ducal coronet. There is a majolica plaque by Andrea della Robbia of the Madonna and Child (*c.* 1500), given to the Cathedral in 1945 by Sir Charles Nicholson.

A fragment of the White Ensign worn by HMS *Victory* at Trafalgar, and carried in Nelson's funeral procession, many other naval flags and regimental colours, memorials to admirals and other officers of the Royal Navy and Royal Marines, and a host of other service souvenirs, bring the Navy and the sea constantly to mind. St Thomas' is, and always has been, the great church of a great naval garrison.

Carisbrooke Priory

Carisbrooke is romantic because of its associations with Charles I, who was imprisoned in the Castle here from 1647 to 1648 – and made two abortive efforts to escape. Below the Castle to the N., and standing high above the village street, stands the Priory, the only medieval monastic church surviving in the Isle of Wight. It has lost its chancel, but its broad S. aisle and spacious nave survive, and at the W. end the Perp tower with its tall pinnacles

There are interesting monuments: of special note is the early-16th-century tomb of Lady Wadham (d. 1520), with its row of little saints surrounding her kneeling figure. Nearby is a painted wooden plaque inscribed: 'Here lyeth the body of the Rt. Worthy William Keeling, Esq., Groome of the Chamber to our Sovereigne King James, General for the East Indies Adventurers, who dying in this Isle at the age of 42, A° 1619 Sept 19, hath this remembrance here fixed by his loveing and sorrowful wife.' A stone tablet of 1697 commemorates Sir William Stephens, 'some years Lieut. Governor of this Island'. There is a Cromwellian pulpit, a Royal Arms of 1689, with the date and inscription altered to 'A.R. 1704', and a number of hatchments. A beautifully furnished church.

Portchester Priory

Down the long village street – with its Georgian or earlier houses – on and on to the wide greensward where, on its low promontory, surrounded on three sides by the sea and commanding Portsmouth Harbour, stands Portchester Castle. The outer walls are Roman, the keep is Norman; four gates on the four sides lead into the enormous grass courtyard, and round bastions guard the corners and outer walls: it is a wonderful amalgam of Roman, Norman and medieval. And in the S.E. corner stands the Norman Priory, with its low central tower crowned with a squat pyramid roof. The Priory was founded here within the castle walls by Henry I in 1133, but later in the century the monastery was transferred to a more spacious – and more tranquil – site at Southwick, N. of Portsdown Hill, leaving the church as the parish and castle church. It is an austere, aisleless building, the W. front with its richly carved doorway, and round-headed window above, set between blank arches on either side, forming an imposing frontispiece. Inside, a long lofty nave, a spacious crossing with noble tower arches, a N. transept – the S. transept gone – and a mutilated, abbreviated chancel, make an imposing interior, with round-headed windows high up, scalloped capitals at the crossing, and fragmentary arcading in choir and transept. There are 18th-century altar rails, and within the sanctuary a monument by Nicholas Stone to Sir Thomas Cornwallis, Governor of the Castle, and in the floor his ledger stone: 'Under this stone lyes buried the body of Sir Tho.

Portchester: the west front

Cornwallis, Knt. whose monument you may see placed here above. A° Dom. 1620'. On the N. wall of the nave is a large painted board with the Royal Arms and attendant cherubs: 'By the Bounty of Queen Anne this church was Repaired and Beautified 1710'.

An ancient yew tree stands in the churchyard. Through the Water Gate there is a wonderful prospect of the harbour, with the water lapping the foreshore, a pair of frigates or a cruiser at anchor in the distance, and the cries of the gulls circling all around.

DIOCESE OF
RIPON

Ripon Cathedral

RIPON IS AMONG the little-known pleasures of England – a small, remote cathedral town, in remote Yorkshire countryside. Harrogate, Fountains Abbey, Studley Royal, Wensleydale: these are known and visited; Ripon remains little visited and unsung.

A small monastery was founded here *c.* 660. St Wilfrid, its second abbot, built a church, of which

the tiny crypt under the east end of the nave survives. The monastery was destroyed by the Danes in the 9th century, but in the 10th a college of secular canons was established here, with the Minster its collegiate church. So it remained throughout the Middle Ages. Like Beverley in the East Riding, and Southwell in distant Nottinghamshire – in the extreme south of the vast archdiocese

Ripon Cathedral sitting above the lowly roofs of its little town

– Ripon was an auxiliary cathedral, an 'episcopal stool' for the Archbishop. The college was dissolved by Edward VI, but restored by James I, with a Dean and six Prebendaries (or Canons). In 1836 it became the cathedral of the new Diocese of Ripon.

From a distance, sitting above the lowly roofs of its little town, the Cathedral appears squat. And Ripon is a squat little town, with one modest square – the Market Place – with an obelisk in the centre erected in 1781 to celebrate sixty years as M.P. for Ripon by William Aislabie of Studley Royal, and, on the south side, the Town Hall by James Wyatt (1801), with its pedimented front and Ionic pilasters. 'Except ye Lord Keep ye Cittie ye Wakeman Waketh in Vain', proclaims the text in the frieze; here, in the Market Place, every night at 9 p.m. the Wakeman's horn is blown, and curfew rung at the Cathedral, as it has been for the past 1000 years. In the 19th century Victorian terraces and public gardens were laid out to provide accommodation for visitors to the Spa, always, alas, overshadowed by Harrogate. An odd, mysterious, little town it is, with winding narrow streets. And one of these leads us to the Cathedral.

The west front is austere, even forbidding: three doorways occupy the centre, with clustered columns and much dog-tooth in the arches; above there is a row of five lancets, and above that five more, stepped to emphasize the gable; finally a triple lancet in the gable itself. On either side the twin west towers are similarly treated, with trefoil arcading at the base and stepped lancets in three stages above, blank or containing windows as may be. Built in the first half of the 13th century, this is a composition unique in England, an example of E.E. architecture at its simplest and its purest. And walking round outside, we can note the Perp windows in the nave, Norman fenestration in the north transept, and – great surprise – the vast Dec window at the east end. On the south side there appears a Perp addition to the chancel, built, it would seem on a Norman undercroft; there are Perp and earlier windows in the south transept. With its three low towers, short nave and chancel, the church seems squat and square, with a rough-hewn North Country character about it.

Inside, the tall Perp arcades of the nave, with large clerestory windows above, and a stone gallery in place of a triforium, lead the eye up to the crossing and stone pulpitum. But the nave is not all Perp. At the west end are the remains of the earlier, Transitional, aisleless nave – the fragment of a triforium, of a clerestory above; something similar appears at the east end, too. The original nave was indeed aisleless: in the 14th century the walls were pierced, the arcades inserted, and the aisles built. And walking up the nave, another oddity appears: on the south side of the Norman crossing a taller, clustered Perp column rises, only to stop abruptly at the arch: its companion on the other side was never built, and the loftier Gothic arch was never built to match the others of the crossing. As we may have noticed outside, the north and west faces of this tower are Norman: the east and south are Perp. In the 15th century the south side of the tower collapsed; piecemeal reconstruction followed, but with the Dissolution was never completed.

The charm of Ripon is its patchwork quality: the north transept is Transitional – the south largely rebuilt in Perp. Under the central tower is the Saxon crypt, approached by stairs behind the nave stalls. It is tiny, originally used for the veneration of sacred relics. It now houses the Treasury, where silver from the Cathedral and other churches in the diocese is on view. Another staircase at the east end leads up under the screen. This is 15th century, and impressive with its ogee arch and canopied niches, filled with recent statuary.

The chancel is a patchwork, too: the first three bays on the north are Trans – on the south they were rebuilt in Perp, after the fall of the tower. But the eastern bays are all distinguished Dec work of the earliest 14th century, and culminate in the tremendous Geometrical east window, filled with glass by Wailes (1854). Beneath stands the High Altar, with its reredos by Sir Ninian Comper, lavishly adorned with statues, lavishly gilded. And apart from all this the choir stalls are of great magnificence – with Carlisle, Chester and Lincoln the most splendid in the country. Dating from the late 15th century, they are grandly canopied and pinnacled, and there is a good set of misericords. The organ case is by Gilbert Scott, and the ancient gallery above the doorway is furnished with an entertaining accessory: a wooden hand, which can be moved up and down for beating time.

On the south side of the chancel is the Norman chapter house, with crypt beneath; the chapter house is low and vaulted, and has an apsidal east end; the crypt below is furnished as a chapel. Stone stairs in the south transept lead up to what

was the Lady Chapel, above the chapter house – the Perp building noticed outside. It is now the Cathedral Library, and contains many treasures, ranging from a 12th-century MS Bible to medieval printed books.

The Cathedral is not rich in monuments. There are 14th- and 15th-century tombs of the Markenfields of Markenfield Hall in the north transept and, throughout the church, some 18th-century tablets. At the east end of the nave, close to Henry Wilson's pulpit (a delightful Arts and Crafts affair of 1913), is the monument to Hugh Ripley, last Wakeman and first Mayor of Ripon. And in the south transept is the bust of William Weddell of Newby (1793) by Nollekens. Set on an elegant pedestal in a rotunda of Corinthian columns, he faces the transept as though surveying his famous garden at Newby from one of his garden temples.

Marrick Priory

Lonely and romantic, close to the River Swale, stands Marrick Priory, a church with a ruined chancel and a tall 15th-century tower; on its south side is a farmhouse with ample farm buildings. The sight of this from the Richmond road, across the water meadows, with the steep hills of Swaledale erect behind, is unforgettable. But the approach is by a dead-end lane, on the other side of the river, across the bridge at Grinton.

Marrick was founded in this solitary, holy valley in the middle of the 12th century for Benedictine nuns: two miles to the east along the river bank a Cistercian nunnery was founded at much the same time at Ellerton – also visible from the Richmond road – but there all is ruined, with only a Perp tower standing and two stately cedar trees occupying the walls of nave and chancel. Whoever was the genius who planted those trees?

But at Marrick part of the church survived as the parish church, and in the bones of the farm are the bones of the conventual buildings. In 1811 the church was reduced in size: across the sanctuary a 13th-century arch, its piers and two half arches were re-erected, and old windows, old materials, were skilfully re-used. There are many

Ripon: William Weddell surveys the south transept

ancient ledger stones, fragments of medieval glass and 17th-century furnishings, and a William and Mary Royal Arms, which, on the reverse side, turns out to be a hatchment of the 1st Duke of Bolton. After a long period of decay and disuse Marrick was rededicated in 1970 as a Ripon Diocesan 'Youth Centre': the sanctuary remains as the chapel; the nave is the refectory, and in an upper floor here, and in an adjacent building, dormitories and bathrooms provide for the young, who come here in their thousands every year to walk and engage in 'outward bound' activities. Canoes are stored within the walls of the ruined

OPPOSITE *The choir stalls at Ripon are some of the finest in England*

Marrick: a lofty 15th-century tower surrounded by farm buildings, against the steep hills of Swaledale

chancel: everywhere are signs of energetic activity. There is a resident warden in Holy Orders. So today Marrick is used again, in what is perhaps an unfamiliar 20th-century idiom, for religious purposes.

H. F. M. Prescott's historical novel, *The Man on a Donkey*, tells a tale of life at Marrick on the eve of the Dissolution.

ROCHESTER

Rochester Cathedral

THE ROAD FROM LONDON, the A2, passes through Strood, and then descends towards the river. As it does so, the panorama suddenly opens up – the panorama of Rochester, with Castle and Cathedral set in the midst of the riverside city, with small craft tied up in the Medway, cranes and larger boats, warehouses and factories along the estuary, a sprawl of housing everywhere. In the background are the low hills and green fields of Kent.

Next to Canterbury, Rochester and London are the most ancient English sees, founded by St Augustine in 604. A tremendous Norman Castle, a Cathedral of unmistakable antiquity, a city of narrow streets and old houses, speak of this ancient foundation. But it is the Castle that dominates the scene: the Cathedral, almost dwarfed, seems to shelter in its shadow. There is no great tower, no lofty spire, no mass of Gothic pinnacles. Its silhouette is modest, unassuming. So Rochester is little visited, little appreciated, among English cathedrals: a grave injustice.

The High Street is 'pedestrianized' now: it is narrow, and it is a pleasure to walk down its length. There are no buildings of special note, but plenty to provide passing pleasure – like the Bull and Royal Victoria Hotel, a late Georgian hostelry in stock brick, with an old yard and many Dickensian associations; and the Corn Exchange, built in 1701 by Sir Clowdisley Shovell, Admiral and M.P. for Rochester, with its delightful projecting clock. And a narrow opening leads up to the Cathedral, through College Gate.

The Precinct is informal, homely, charming, of the same scale as the Cathedral itself, the town, the High Street. St Nicholas' Church is on the left, the former parish church for the Close (now an SPCK bookshop). We can walk round the Cathedral outside, admire the Norman west front, and turn into Minor Canon Row, a tall red-brick terrace of 1736, with orderly rows of sash windows, and steps up to each front door. From here we

can take in the full length of the church: the nave with its low pitched roof, the tower (a rebuilding of 1904 by Hodgson Fowler), squat, with a stocky lead spire, the higher-pitched transepts, and, beyond, the chancel longer than the nave, with eastern transepts and steeply gabled east end. The cloisters became ruined at the Dissolution, but we can walk round the grass court, noting the Norman blind arcading and the doorway to the chapter house – now, also, a ruin. Close to Minor Canon Row is Prior's Gate, another medieval gateway.

On the north side we can walk through the churchyard under the very shadow of the Cathedral, and through another gate past the venerable mass of Gundulph's Tower, which is set oddly and awkwardly between the transepts, built by Bishop Gundulph at the very end of the 11th century. It does not really form part of the church, and was probably built for defence. Gundulph became Bishop in 1077: it is to him we owe the building of the Norman Cathedral.

But the west front is the showpiece of the exterior, with its bold outer pinnacles, its narrower, taller, inner ones framing a big Perp window, its blind Norman arcading everywhere. And the doorway is remarkable – with elaborately carved shafts and capitals, richly decorated voussoirs and deeply cut tympanum. Here is the figure of Our Lord in glory, surrounded by angels and the symbols of the evangelists, and, on the lintel, the tiny figures of the twelve apostles. On either side, the second shaft is a figure – Henry I on one side, Queen Matilda on the other. These are reminiscent of the sculptures at Chartres; indeed this whole doorway is the most French-inspired piece of Romanesque sculpture in England.

Inside, Gundulph's nave is light and airy, broad and horizontal in its emphasis. The arcades are low, the triforium spacious, the Perp clerestory windows large – and these, and the windows of the aisles (which incorporate the triforium), flood

Rochester Cathedral: OPPOSITE *the crossing and the north transept;* ABOVE *Gundulph's west front*

the nave with light. The flat Perp timber ceiling is a disappointment, overemphasizing the horizontal quality of the nave: imagine a lofty vault to crown this nave! But the eye is carried on to the screen, set up many steps, with the dignified nave altar on its broad plinth half-way up: through the central doorway there is a glimpse of the High Altar, raised again up many steps; the organ divided into two parts reveals the east window far beyond, and the chancel vault.

Moving up the nave, it will be noted that the two eastern bays are E.E. – part of the rebuilding of crossing, transepts and choir which began in the late 13th century, and was intended no doubt to include the entire nave, but funds or enthusiasm evidently failed. Here we can turn and absorb the E.E. transepts: elegant marble shafts, elegant lancet windows, blank arcading below, a sexpartite vault above. The north transept is especially beautiful. The south choir aisle leads up to the eastern transepts; here an elaborate 14th-century doorway (S.E. transept) leads into the Chapter Room; and, turning left, we are in the choir – so curiously, unusually, entirely enclosed. Solid walls separate it from its aisles, and these walls are decorated below the string course with painted patterns, the lion of England and the fleur de lys of France (a restoration of 1876). The effect is austere, and as most of the stalls and other furnishings are Victorian, the whole choir is somewhat cold and cheerless. The Presbytery and Sanctuary are very different: here there is a wealth of Purbeck marble shafts, lancet windows, deep recesses, richly coloured glass by Clayton & Bell, an ornate reredos by Gilbert Scott, Victorian brass altar rails, strongly coloured encaustic tiles, mosaics on the east wall. The effect is numinous, warm and solemn.

The crypt is one of the best things at Rochester: under the chancel is Gundulph's Norman crypt, of two bays, with slender columns and square

The 13th-century crypt at Rochester

capitals, and a groin vault – all simple and solid: beyond is the spacious 13th-century crypt, built beneath the later eastern transepts and sanctuary, with round and octagonal columns and a quadripartite vault – a wonderful forest of columns and vaults. The entrance to the crypt is in the south choir aisle. And returning to the south transept we shall find the last structural addition to the building: the Lady Chapel, built at the very end of the 15th century in the angle of the transept and the nave, with tall Perp arches opening into the nave, and tall Perp windows: a happy afterthought.

The Cathedral is rich in monuments: in the sanctuary are many early bishops – Bishop de St Martin (1274) and Bishop John de Sheppey (1360), and, of special interest, Bishop Walter de Merton, founder of Merton College, Oxford, in the N.E. transept (1277). In the south transept is the recumbent effigy (by F. W. Pomeroy) of Dean Hole (1905), the great horticulturalist and rose grower, who was Dean of Rochester for seventeen years, and carried through the Victorian restoration of the Cathedral. Nearby is a tablet to Charles Dickens, who lived for many years at Gadshill, nearby; also a monument by Grinling Gibbons to Sir Richard Head (1689). In the south aisle Lady Anne Henniker is commemorated by grand figures in Coade stone – Truth and Time – the monument itself designed by Banks (1792); Lord Henniker by an imposing monument by Bacon (1806). And there are many memorials to distinguished members of the armed services, reminding us of the proximity of the garrisons at Chatham and Sheerness.

Rochester, Cathedral of England's second oldest diocese, little known, little appreciated, little visited, is also delightfully uncommercialized, delightfully uncluttered, delightfully unspoiled by the 20th century. Long may it so remain; yet it is a place which deserves to be loved and honoured more.

West Malling Abbey

MALLING ABBEY WAS founded in 1090 for Benedictine nuns by Gundulph, the first Norman Bishop of Rochester (q.v.) The 14th-century gatehouse still leads off the village street, and brings us face to face with the vast rump of the Norman west front of the church, comparable with Gundulph's west front at Rochester, crowned with

West Malling Abbey: comparable with the west front of Rochester

the remnant of its octagonal tower. After the Dissolution the property passed through various hands, and most of the church was pulled down. In the 18th century what remained was acquired by Frazer Honywood, London banker and member of an old Kentish family, who proceeded to build on the south side a subdued Gothick gabled mansion, which incorporated part of the cloisters. At the end of the 19th century this was acquired by Miss Charlotte Boyd, and presented to the Church: in 1916 a community of Anglican Benedictine nuns, originally founded at Baltonsborough in Somerset, returned to Malling, and for the past seventy years restoration of the Benedictine house has proceeded. A new church (by Maguire and Murray) was consecrated in 1966, the original guesthouse has been restored, and a new cloister court formed, incorporating the supremely beautiful surviving range of the 13th-century cloister (this is part of the nuns' enclosure, and not open to the public). Entering the gatehouse, into the garden court watered by the cascading Ewell stream, it will be found that the 14th-century chapel attached to the gatehouse still survives, and is in regular use as the Pilgrims' Chapel, a little oratory of the greatest charm, with Dec traceried windows and a sparkling white interior. On the far side of the grounds the magnificent tithe barn, which long served the nuns as their chapel, is now used as their church by the monks of the new Anglican Cistercian Order, recently established here.

DIOCESE OF
ST ALBANS

St Albans Cathedral

ST ALBANS is only twenty miles from London, but it preserves its character and its atmosphere as a Hertfordshire country town, and as a place of great antiquity. There are medieval churches and many streets of 18th-century (and earlier) houses. It is close to the Roman city of Verulamium, where Alban, the first British martyr, was put to death as a Christian in 209. Alban sheltered a Christian priest in his house, was so impressed by his goodness and his character that he himself became a Christian, and gave himself up in the place of the priest at the time of Diocletian's persecution – allowing his guest to escape. Alban was beheaded on the hill above the Roman city where the Cathedral stands today.

The great church dominates the city from this hill: it is not a matter of tall towers or a lofty spire – but of the immense length of the building, and its enormous bulk. Indeed the exterior is exceedingly plain – hardly a pinnacle, not a single flying buttress is to be seen, only the long nave roof, the long line of lancet windows in the clerestory. At the crossing is the Norman tower, built of Roman bricks from Verulamium: indeed it is the use of these bricks, and of local flint, which gives the Cathedral its ruddy colour.

The Benedictine Abbey of St Alban was founded by King Offa in the 8th century, but the bulk of the church which we see today was built by the first Norman Abbot, Paul of Caen. Part of the nave, the crossing and the transepts are his building. The nave was extended in the 13th century – and, following the collapse of the S. side of the Norman nave, this E. end of the S. arcade was rebuilt in the early 14th century. The church was extended eastwards at this time – with a retrochoir to replace the apsidal E. end, to form a fitting shrine for St Alban's relics, and with a long eastern

Lady Chapel. After the Dissolution all the monastic buildings – apart from the gatehouse – were pulled down, and the church was purchased by the town to serve as the parish church. The upkeep of so vast a building was too much for the parish, and decay set in. A rescuer appeared in 1877 in the person of Sir Edmund Beckett, 5th Bt., 1st Lord Grimthorpe, banker, lawyer, amateur architect, millionaire, who at his own expense and to his own designs rebuilt the W. front, the façades of the transepts, and much else. He has been much criticized for his heavy-handed work – but without him the church would have collapsed. He was anxious to make the ancient abbey a fitting cathedral for the new diocese of St Albans, which was founded in 1877, and which covers the counties of Hertfordshire and Bedfordshire.

It is Lord Grimthorpe's W. front which greets the visitor – pretentious maybe, but an earnest essay in English 14th-century architecture; it took the place of a much plainer W. front, with a large Perp window. Inside, steps lead up into the tremendous nave, with its bay after bay of E.E. arcading on the S. side – and, on the N., the E.E. arcading giving way to the primitive Norman arcading towards the pulpitum. This is of great solid beauty, with simple, almost archaic arches, triforium, clerestory piercing the immensely thick wall. Here on the W. side of several pillars 13th- and 14th-century murals of the Crucifixion adorn the stonework, to provide an altarpiece for a series of tiny altars which once filled each bay. The 14th-century pulpitum divides nave from choir – a remarkable piece of almost homespun charm, erected, it would seem, with curious disregard of symmetry, where the central niche above the altar is not in the centre, and the canopied niches on one side do not balance those on the other.

St Albans Cathedral: crossing and chancel

The crossing is imposing with its austere Norman arches, enlivened like those in the nave with original diapering; and in the gaunt Norman transepts there is a triforium composed of pillars reusing Saxon monoliths from the earlier church, with Roman bricks forming the arches. In Benedictine fashion the choir occupies the easternmost bays of the nave, E. of the pulpitum: here the organ case, choir stalls and episcopal throne are by Oldrid Scott. But the climax of the whole chancel is the elaborate reredos screen, with its sumptuous carvings and wealth of canopied niches, erected by Abbot William of Wallingford in 1484, now filled with a grand array of late Victorian figures, and a long panel of the Resurrection over the altar itself by Sir Alfred Gilbert. On either side of the sanctuary are the Perp chantries of Abbot Wallingford and Abbot Ramryge. The latter (N. side) is the last work completed before the Dissolution, and dates from 1521: an exquisite fan-vaulted interior encloses a tiny altar, and above this elaborately carved niches stand empty.

The ambulatory leads into the retrochoir, and to the Lady Chapel. For three hundred years blocked off from the rest of the church, this served as the Grammar School; a public passageway led through this eastern arm, and the three lofty arches which now once again lead into St Alban's Shrine were also sealed off: the martyr's shrine was used

St Albans: 14th-century mural in the Norman nave arcade

as a vestry. In the event, in the thickness of the walls which filled these arches were found mutilated and broken the hundred and one fragments of the Shrine itself, which had been knocked to pieces at the Reformation. With infinite pains these were pieced together, and the Shrine now stands once more where it always stood: a miracle of restoration. Here once again lamps and candles flicker, and the chapel, soaked in the prayers of the centuries, is once again the focus of the prayers and devotions of the faithful of today. On the N. side stands the galleried early-15th-century Watching Chamber, on the S. the Chantry of Humphrey Duke of Gloucester (brother of Henry V), who died in 1447, a friend of Abbot John of Wheathampstead – so contrived that through the iron lattice of the lower arches the shrine of the saint is visible.

Apart from the magnificent 14th-century brass to Abbot de la Mare, very few monuments survived Lord Grimthorpe's sweeping restoration, and there is no glass of special note. But the fragments of wall paintings, uncovered from layers of whitewash, and the medieval painted wooden vault of the chancel, are precious reminders of what once must have been an interior glowing with colour. And the air of Benedictine solemnity which pervades the building cannot be destroyed.

St Albans: Humphrey Duke of Gloucester's Chantry

A new chapter house, designed by William Whitfield, was completed in 1982, connected by the slype to the S. transept. Built of bricks specially made at Bovingdon to blend with the Roman bricks of the tower, this new building lies like a great galleon tied up alongside the Cathedral, and contains a refectory and library, vestries and Song School, approached by a suspended staircase connecting its three storeys. Below, and all around, the grass slopes of the low hill where the monastic buildings once stood provide a perfect setting for a cathedral which in its day was pre-eminent among all English abbeys, and whose Abbot ranked above all other English abbots.

The west front of Dunstable Priory, lopsided but magnificent (see overleaf)

Dunstable Priory

Dunstable has always been a place of importance, standing as it does where Watling Street and the Icknield Way cross. Henry I had a palace here, and it was he who founded the priory for Augustinian Canons in 1131. But now the long tentacles of industrial Luton have crept out: subtopia and suburbia are triumphant, and impersonal modern buildings envelop the ancient place. The priory church stands grand and austere, marooned in the middle of the town while the traffic rushes by.

The visitor will stand spellbound before the west front, so odd, so lopsided, but so magnificent. There is a grand Norman doorway; there is Norman arcading on its left – then another, smaller but remarkable E.E. doorway; above this there is E.E. arcading, which leads across to two tall lancet windows above the Norman door – with another row of taller blank arcading above, all finely cusped and carved – and yet more arcading on a row above. And then, on the right, there is nothing but blank walling, and a heavily buttressed corner turret. To add to this confusion, there is a square embattled Perp tower, heavily buttressed also, above the E.E. arcading on the left. It is a spectacular frontispiece – but what has happened?

The church was consecrated in 1213: at that time there were two Norman western towers – and the Norman door, and the Norman arcading beside it, are survivors of that original·west front. In 1222 both towers collapsed in a terrible storm; the E.E. work is either the beginning of the rebuilding of this front – which was never completed – or perhaps all that survives of a frontispiece of which the right-hand part was later rebuilt.

The S.W. door leads into a nave of unexpected width. It is a remarkable interior, with grand Norman arcades, the triforium with its outer arches slightly overhanging the arches below. Perp windows now fill the triforium on either side, and the clerestory has gone: a later lower timber roof spans the nave. The screen – the original rood screen – divides the nave from the choir; the High Altar is set against the original pulpitum, its two doorways now blocked, but its niches, now restored with new statuary (1962), forming a striking reredos. The blocked doorways led into the crossing with its central tower, and into the monastic choir beyond, all demolished in 1540 after the Dissolution.

The nave had been made parochial in 1392, so

it was the parishioners who removed the clerestory – and at the same time built the N.W. tower, which in design is very much a Bedfordshire parish church tower. Even now it is a nave of some splendour: standing by the rood screen and looking back, the west wall, with its gallery of seven E.E. lancets, is a special pleasure. The south aisle is a remarkable rebuilding of the Norman aisle, complete with vaulting, by Somers Clarke (1882); there are small brasses here (16th and 17th century) and in the north aisle there is a whole gallery of splendid 18th-century monuments, including one by Thomas Green of Camberwell (1712), which give some clue to the fashionable importance of Dunstable at that time.

Little remains of the monastic buildings, except for the gateway to the S.W. of the church; further to the west, a Georgian-fronted house in the High Street contains a vaulted room, which may have been the hospitium. And travelling still further west, suburbia is finally left behind, and there is a grand drive along the spine of the Dunstable Downs towards the Vale of Aylesbury. The Canons of Dunstable were great sheep farmers: here the flocks of monastic sheep can still be imagined, feeding across this wide downland landscape.

Elstow Abbey and the ruined Hillersdon Hall

Elstow Abbey

Elstow was the birthplace of John Bunyan, whose statue by Boehm (1874) adorns St Peter's Green in Bedford. He was born here in 1628, and there is much in this attractive village that he would recognize today – the long row of timbered cottages in the main street, the Moot Hall (*c.* 1500) of timber and brick, with its overhanging upper floor, and, of course, the abbey church.

The Benedictine nunnery of Elstow was founded *c.* 1075. The church stands in a field, guarded by stone walls, behind the Moot Hall and the timbered cottages, and, with its free-standing N.W. tower with its little flêche, makes a delightful composition. What we see is most of the nave; crossing, transepts, chancel and Lady Chapel were destroyed after the Dissolution, in 1580. The west front is a fine early-13th-century frontispiece, in a somewhat fragmentary state, with an E.E. doorway with clustered columns; above is a four-light window, perhaps an early-17th-century insertion; and at the south end the one remaining monastic building, called the Chapter House, a remarkable vaulted 13th-century chamber. Outside, it adds no little to the impact of this west front, with its buttresses, E.E. shafts and lancets. It is now used as the vestry.

Inside, there are two E.E. bays at the west end, with stout octagonal piers, capitals with stiff-leaf carving and lofty arches. Beyond is the severest of severe Norman arcades, with almost square pillars, and the plainest of plain arches. There is no triforium, only a clerestory of small Norman windows; yet with its narrow proportions it seems a lofty interior. At the east end there are late Perp windows, no doubt inserted when this wall was built and the transepts and eastern parts demolished; there are Perp windows in the aisles, and a Norman north doorway (outside), very much restored. The furnishings are mostly Victorian, but there are a few 17th- and 18th-century monuments; of greatest interest are those to Thomas Hillersdon (1656) and his son John (1684); there is a magnificent brass to Margery Argentine (1427) and another to Elizabeth Herwy, Abbess (1527). The interior was cruelly scraped in the 19th century, but its gaunt, almost grim arcades breathe the air of early monasticism and call to mind the tough Benedictine women who worked and worshipped here.

The great surprise of Elstow is to walk round to the south side of the church – and discover there a ruined early-17th-century mansion, Hillersdon Hall, adjoining the Chapter House. Thomas Hillersdon bought the monastic remains in 1616, and built this E-shaped house from the stone of the nunnery. It has long been a ruin, but it is still possible to appreciate the pillared doorway and the gaping mullioned windows.

Royston Priory

Royston grew up at the crossroads where the Icknield Way and the old Great North Road cross – a village of little importance and a priory founded *c.* 1180 by Eustace de Merk, Lord of Newsells, for Augustinian Canons. The canons established a market, and the town grew. But the priory was not the parish church; Royston lay in several neighbouring parishes, and after the Dissolution the people were forced to use their distant parish churches until they could buy what remained of the priory church for their use.

The church still stands at the crossroads, the surviving choir of the priory, much patched up in the 17th century, partially rebuilt in the 19th. The tower is a Victorian recasing of the tower built in the 17th century; the chancel is of 1891. Inside, the nave arcades are part medieval, part Gothic survival of *c.* 1600; at the east end of the nave, on either side, are fragments of the original E.E. lancet windows which lit the canons' sanctuary. The most interesting thing in the church is the headless statue of the Virgin, a fragment of 15th-century alabaster of great beauty. The late Victorian chancel is dignified and harmonious.

Royston Priory: stone, flint and ogee-headed windows in the north aisle

St Edmundsbury Cathedral: the mammoth Norman gate-tower of the vanished abbey

DIOCESE OF
ST EDMUNDSBURY

St Edmundsbury Cathedral

BURY ST EDMUNDS IS a delightful town, spacious, orderly, with streets of Georgian houses, churches, the remains of one of the greatest of all medieval abbeys, and the wide Suffolk sky above, shedding its clear light on all around. There is Robert Adam's Town Hall (1780), the late-17th-century house in Butter Market called Cupola House, with seats inside the cupola from which to enjoy the view, and the early-18th-century Presbyterian Chapel in Churchgate Street – a distinguished building of rich red brick. Angel Hill is a long open square, dominated by the Angel Hotel on the W. side, the Athenaeum (Assembly Rooms) on the S., and the superb early-14th-century Abbey Gateway on the E., broad and embattled, with its tiers of empty canopied niches, and its great gate open to receive us. The site of the Abbey is a public garden. 'There is still an indefinable atmosphere,' wrote Norman Scarfe in the *Shell Guide to Suffolk*, 'a remoteness from the outer world, a silence that survives the click of the bowls and the slow exchange of commonplaces by old men on rustic seats: through it one hears the last evaporating notes of choir and precentor; and he is very earth-bound who does not try to restore in his mind the lofty, murmuring monastery. The tangible remains of the Abbey are slight. Truncated piers mark the position of the nave, and one can see the graves of six abbots.'

There were three churches in the abbey church-yard – of which St James' has since 1914 been the cathedral of the new Diocese of St Edmundsbury and Ipswich. It stands a few hundred yards to the S., with its imposing Perp W. front, and, just beyond it, the mammoth early-12th-century Norman tower of the vanished Abbey – with its enormous gabled gateway below, and tier upon tier above of small Norman windows and carved arcading adorning the plain stone façades of each side. No parish church cathedral can compete with such a majestic campanile.

St James' is a very grand church, built in the early 16th century, perhaps by John Wastell who designed the vaults and upper parts of King's Chapel, and perhaps the New Building at Peterborough. He lived at Bury, and died in 1515. The spacious nave with its wide aisles is nine bays long: the aisle windows and clerestory flood the church with light. The original chancel disappeared, was replaced by a small Georgian sanctuary, then by a new choir by Scott (1869). This in turn has been swept away, and the grand new chancel, transepts, chapels, central tower, cloisters have been (or are being) built since 1961.

Here at last is a parish church cathedral where there is a determination to build something worthy of its new status. The architect is Mr Stephen Dykes Bower – perhaps the one person in England today who could be relied upon to build a grand new Gothic church in the spirit of the Middle Ages. His lofty crossing, lofty chancel, spacious transepts and chapels have already transformed St James' into a church worthy to rank as a cathedral of recent foundation. The Lady Chapel (on the outer N. side of the chancel) – which is to be large enough to accommodate the E. window of Scott's choir (with its Hardman glass), its roof and its stalls – is not yet built, nor is the upper part of the central tower. Meantime, half the cloisters on the N. side have been completed, to connect the church with its attendant buildings: chapter house, library, choir school and so on. Dykes Bower's furnishings – the dignified altars and ornaments – are an additional attraction.

There are good 18th-century monuments in the nave, such as that to James Reynolds, Chief Justice of the Exchequer, who faces us with his robed and bewigged figure (1738), and a whole set of Clayton & Bell windows in the nave aisles. There is also one 16th-century Flemish window (first window from the W. in S. aisle).

The spacious gardens to the S. which now form

St Edmundsbury: the early-16th-century nave

the Cathedral Close, the setting with the monastic ruins, and the Georgian streets opposite, all contribute to make Bury St Edmunds outstanding, indeed unique, among the latter-day cathedral foundations of England.

Bungay Priory

Bungay is just in Suffolk, but the Norfolk frontier is very close: there are two medieval churches, the impressive remains of a 12th-century castle, and streets of Georgian houses radiating from the octagonal Butter Cross, which was erected after the great fire that swept through the town in 1688. St Mary's with its immensely grand Perp tower (*c.* 1470) is in origin the priory church, founded *c.* 1160 for Benedictine nuns by Gundreda, wife of Roger de Glanville: what survives is the nave, grand and spacious Perp work of the 14th century,

Bungay Priory

Great Bricett: a blocked archway at the east end

St Edmundsbury: a cherub from the 18th-century organ above the Royal Arms

preserved after the Dissolution as the parish church of the town. The ruins of the nuns' choir to the east tell their tale. Inside, there is a delightful array of 18th-century monuments in the north aisle, a plain 18th-century pulpit, and a font of *c.* 1700 carved with cherubs' heads and flowers; a ledger stone near the chancel step marks the burial place of Dr John Davies, Master of Sidney Sussex College, Cambridge, who died in 1813 aged 36. But it is the tower which is the glory of the church: it is 90 ft high, with tall tapering pinnacles and flushwork decoration in the lower stages: the upper part seems to have been rebuilt after the fire.

St Mary's is now in the care of the Redundant Churches Fund, and its neighbour Holy Trinity, a stone's throw away across the churchyard, has become the principal church; but St Mary's is still used for occasional services, and is open every day.

Great Bricett Priory

Great Bricett lies just off the road from Sudbury to Needham Market: the church was an alien priory of Augustinian Canons, founded in the early 12th century and belonging to the Abbey of St Leonard near Limoges. It was once a large cruciform building, with apsidal chapels to the transepts and a long chancel, as excavations have revealed. Now only the long aisleless nave survives, with Norman doorways and one or two Norman windows; there is a late Norman font, and a window in the south wall contains good 14th-century glass depicting the four evangelists. It is a simple, spacious, lovable interior: blocked-up doors and windows speak of its monastic past. At the west end the Hall Farmhouse is joined onto the church, and originally formed part of the conventual buildings: beneath its stucco it is a timber-framed building of the late 13th century. Its north wing overlooks a square lawn; here there seems a hint of the vanished cloister court.

Leiston Abbey

(Pronounced Laceton.) THE ruined east end of the church stands tall, gaunt and beautiful, surveying cornfields, close to the Suffolk coast: vast empty windows bereft of their tracery, flint walls. and buttresses, elaborate flushwork decoration against the Suffolk sky. The abbey was founded in 1180 by Sir Ranulf Glanville for Premonstratensian Canons. It was then closer to the sea, and transferred to its present site in the mid-14th century: fragments of the earlier church were reused in the grand Perp rebuilding. After the

Leiston: gaunt ruins across a cornfield

Dissolution a hotch-potch house was formed within the monastic buildings, and the property passed through various hands – until in 1918 it was opened as an Anglican Retreat House, and the Lady Chapel (N. chancel aisle) was reroofed for worship. The house is now used as a music school, but the chapel remains in regular use.

Letheringham Priory

A wonderfully remote and inaccessible spot, approached by back lanes between Wickham Market and Framlingham: a church in a spacious setting of old walls, meadows and copses, with a farmyard close at hand; moss-covered steps over the farmyard wall, or a path by the farm buildings, lead to the church. A 15th-century brick gatehouse in the S.W. corner of the churchyard is all that survives of the monastic buildings.

Letheringham Priory was founded *c.* 1194 by William de Bovile for Augustinian Canons, as a cell of the larger Augustinian Priory at Ipswich: there is a 14th-century west tower of flint, with

flushwork decoration, and a short rectangular nave; the monastic choir has vanished, and the nave is the result of 18th-century patching and restoration, with Norman fragments and Dec traceried windows. The brick south porch is dated 1685.

The interior is one of great charm, with an 18th-century pulpit and box pews, 18th-century altar rails, an 18th-century font with a pretty cover, two glorious brasses – one to Sir John Wingfield (1389), one to another Sir John Wingfield (1481) – and fragments of later tombs which were tragically destroyed at the time of the demolition of the chancel in 1789. The manor descended from the Wingfields (themselves descended from the de Boviles) to the Nauntons: 'Here lies Sir Robert Naunton Knight, Sometime principal Secretaire and after Maister of the Wards & Councellor of State to our late King James of happy memories & to our now Souverain Lord King Charles &c and' reads the fragment of an inscription. Sir Robert built a grand house to the south of the church, which has also vanished.

Over the south door there is a Royal Arms of

George III, with an enchanting lion; the list of those serving in the Great War still hangs in the porch, and below is a photograph of the local Home Guard in the Second World War.

Letheringham: flint tower and brick porch

The font at Redlingfield

Redlingfield Priory

The quiet Suffolk countryside: a Benedictine nunnery was founded here *c.* 1120, and the little early-14th-century church is petite and endearing – of brick and flint, stone and plaster, with the stump of a tower, saddle-backed and gabled. There is a Perp front adorned with lions and emblems of the Evangelists, and the two-storeyed barn to the south incorporates part of the monastic buildings.

Rumburgh Priory

Remote back lanes between Halesworth and Bungay: here a Benedictine priory was founded in 1064 as a cell of St Benet's Abbey in Norfolk; in the 12th century, after various vicissitudes, it was transferred to St Mary's Abbey, York. The church stands back across the fields, and by the churchyard gate the pond is alive with the quacking of ducks. It is a romantic, unusual-looking building, with its wide, flat, 13th-century west tower with three tall lancet windows and timber belfry above; the walls of the church are all wonderfully textured – with stone, flint, brick and stucco. The rustic stuccoed porch, with wooden ogee arch and painted sundial above, leads into an imposing aisleless hall-like interior, with wide ancient roof and Perp traceried windows. There are poppy-headed pews, a Jacobean pulpit, many well-lettered ledger stones in nave and sanctuary, and a superb Perp screen with perfectly preserved tracery, albeit coated in brown paint and varnish. Nothing survives of the monastic buildings which stood round the cloister on the north side, but Abbey Farmhouse is said to stand on the site of the refectory.

Rumburgh: traceried screen and poppy-headed pews

DIOCESE OF
SALISBURY

Salisbury Cathedral

IT IS THE SPIRE that calls: it appears suddenly, like a finger pointing to heaven, or a sentinel rising unexpectedly in a fold of the hills or across the water meadows, slender, ethereal, irresistible, magical. Like a magnet it draws the traveller driving over Salisbury Plain, or approaching the city from Old Sarum or along the Wylye Valley. Salisbury spire casts its spell across the countryside and over the city. There is no escaping.

Three gates lead into the close – the High Street Gate from the N., St Anne's Gate from the E., the Harnham Gate from the S. All lead to the spire, now standing right over us, and – on a sunny day – casting its long shadow across the smooth lawns. The High Street Gate brings us to Choristers' Green, to Mompesson House, the College of Matrons, the Hungerford Chantry, the Wren Hall; through Harnham Gate we reach that secluded corner of the close where some of the grandest houses – the Walton Canonry, Myles Place – face the west front; from St Anne's Gate it is but a short step to that incomparable view of the Cathedral from the N.E., where the gables of the Lady Chapel, the chancel, the transepts, the nave, and the long line of roof of these component parts, all build up to the climax of tremendous tower and tapering spire. And wherever we wander in the close, admiring now this house, now that – there is the spire above us, an all-commanding presence.

The Cathedral, of course, is all of one date – unique, more or less, among the medieval cathedrals of England. The earlier, Norman cathedral was on the wind-swept, bleak low hill of Old Sarum. In the early 13th century Bishop Poore decided to move the cathedral to New Sarum, and it was he who laid the foundation stone of the new church in 1220, here in the water meadows by the River Avon. The main building

was consecrated in 1258, the cloisters and chapter house were completed about 1300, and work on the building of the spire began some thirty years later.

Outside, the symmetry of the design is amazing: the long rows of lancet windows, the orderly rows of buttresses and flying buttresses, the parapet of trefoil-headed panels, the trefoil-headed frieze: everywhere there is the greatest simplicity, the most dazzling purity. Only on the west front is there any elaboration: here blind arcades and rows of quatrefoils, the triple porch and the triple lancet window, the rows of statues and the sculptured buttresses, combine to form a frontispiece which seems crowded, less inspired. But nothing can detract from the overpowering presence of the spire.

And here we move into the world of Decorated architecture, of long traceried windows, ornate friezes, ball-flower ornament: the tower itself is a masterpiece of 14th-century craftsmanship – and then, from a cluster of lavish pinnacles, the spire soars upwards, 404 ft to the cross. How does the spire stand up? The crossing arches below were never built to hold this colossal weight of masonry; indeed the spire was an afterthought. Look at its base here outside, at the flimsy flying buttresses, the bands of iron braces to hold and support it, the whole composition of tower and spire seems a miracle. Over the centuries anxiety for its safety has never abated. In the 15th century 'strainer' arches were built under the crossing at the entry to the transepts, like girders of panelled stone. Architects have been called in – Wren, Wyatt, Scott – yet the spire still stands, a tribute to the men who designed and built it.

The interior matches the exterior. There is the same symmetry, the same simplicity, the same

Salisbury Cathedral and its spire: ethereal, irresistible, magical

Salisbury: the nave

purity of style and form, the same majesty: indeed this is one of the most majestic of all cathedral interiors. The arcades, the triforium, the clerestory, the long shafts of Purbeck marble, the lancet windows – the interior is very light, very spacious. Yet there is a certain coldness, a lack of mystery, a lack of colour, which is disappointing. But this is not the fault of the building: it is due to the poverty of the furnishings. Wyatt, at the end of the 18th century, swept clean: out went medieval glass, down came Perpendicular chantries. Scott, in the 19th century, swept cleaner still: out went chancel screen, out went organ, out went Wyatt's stalls. In their place came Skidmore's delicate iron screens, new stalls, reredos, tiles, Victorian fittings. These were all excellent of their kind: they brought the warmth of polished oak and marble, of Victorian colour and comfort. But now even these have gone: the 20th century has swept cleaner still, and wreaked a terrible vengeance on the Victorian age. Scott's reredos has gone, the Skidmore screen has been broken up, colourless tiles have replaced

Scott's colourful ones, and the sanctuary now has the air of a modern bathroom – chilly and hygienic. Now there is an unimpeded vista from the west end of the nave to the east end of the Lady Chapel: everything can be seen and absorbed at once. These great churches were not built to be so treated: chancel and nave were designed to be two churches. Salisbury cries out for the replacement of its stone screen: much of this survives, built against the wall of the N.E. transept – the original 14th-century pulpitum. It could be replaced – as has happened (with such success) at Chichester. It would be an incalculable enhancement to this interior.

There is much pleasure to be found in the grandeur of the transepts – in the monuments, the grisaille glass; much pleasure, too, in the choir aisles, eastern transepts and retrochoir. Here there is some good Victorian glass, the wonderful Audley Chantry, a number of grandiloquent tombs of the 17th century: the Earl of Hertford (1621), Sir Richard Mompesson (1627), and Sir Thomas Gorges (1635) – this last a special delight with its 'barley-sugar' columns. And there are medieval tombs, too, like that of Bishop Giles de Bridport, with his effigy lying under a canopy of stone and Purbeck marble (1260). And in the N.E. transept is the brass to Bishop Wyville (1375), showing the bishop fully vested standing under a Gothic fortress tower.

Salisbury: two ancient cedars in the cloister court

Salisbury: the full length of chancel, crossing and nave, seen from behind the High Altar

The cloisters are of great size and special beauty: through the open Geometrical windows there are views into the grass courtyard, where stand two ancient cedar trees – and up to the spire sailing above. And here stands the chapter house, one of the earliest and grandest of late-13th-century chapter houses, with its central pier with detached Purbeck shafts, and its spirited carved scenes in the spandrels above the arcading. There is admirable Victorian grisaille glass (by Ward), which very nearly fell a victim to the 20th-century sweepers. Mercifully, wiser counsels prevailed.

And so to the outside once more. Salisbury spire and Salisbury close are inseparable. Both are perfection. To leave them is always a wrench – to return soon always an obligation.

Amesbury Abbey

The special interest of Amesbury, originally founded as a Benedictine nunnery in the 10th century, is that it was refounded in 1177 as a priory of the Benedictine order of Fontevrault, an aristocratic order much favoured by the Angevin kings: Henry II and Richard I, the Lionheart, were buried at Fontevrault. Only four such houses were established in England. John Webb built one of the first Palladian houses in England on its site in 1661, for the Duke of Somerset; here sixty years later John Gay wrote the *Beggar's Opera*, while staying with the Duke of Queensberry; in the early 19th century the house was largely rebuilt for Sir Edmund Antrobus. The monastic church stands on the edge of the town, built of flint, and glistening against the backdrop of the trees in the park – a

Amesbury: long lancet windows in the nuns' choir

considerable cruciform church with a central tower, largely built in the 12th and 13th centuries, tactfully restored by Butterfield in 1853. The nave was parochial, the grand chancel the nuns' choir. Daylight pours in through long lancet windows into this beautiful white interior; of special note are the vaulted chapel of the N. transept, the Norman font, the 15th-century screen, the ancient timber roofs and fragments of medieval glass.

Cranborne Priory

Cranborne is an engaging little town, once the market town for Cranborne Chase – dominated by the manor house of the Salisburys, with its celebrated, romantic, ancient garden, and its grand parish church, once the church of a Benedictine priory attached to Tewkesbury Abbey. Founded in the 10th century, Tewkesbury was once subordinate to it – but the latter grew in importance, Cranborne declined, and from the 11th century

Cranborne: the west tower from the garden of the manor

became merely a cell of Tewkesbury, and, after the Dissolution, merely the parish church. There is a tall square Perp west tower of stone and flint, a late Norman north doorway, and a spacious nave with 13th-century arcades of stone and Purbeck marble; the imposing chancel is of 1875, by David Brandon. There are fragments of 14th-century wall paintings above the nave arcade (St Christopher clearly visible), a 15th-century oak pulpit bearing the initials T.P. (for Thomas Parker, Abbot of Tewkesbury and Cranborne), and two or three 17th-century monuments. No traces survive of monastic buildings – which lay on the S. side of the church; but through an iron gate in the W. wall of the churchyard there is an enchanting glimpse into the garden of the great house – with a long grass path leading up to the towers and gables and tall chimneys of Robert Cecil's hunting lodge.

Edington Priory, founded by William of Edington, Bishop of Winchester, in 1352 (see overleaf)

Edington Priory

The long line of the Wiltshire Downs, the White Horse of Westbury, the Great Western main line, a small village, and a grand cruciform church: approaching Edington from the N. the view is unforgettable. There is very little to the village: the church is all. It stands beside the lane, long and embattled, with a low square tower at the crossing, clerestoried nave and lofty aisleless chancel; there is a three-storeyed S. porch, like the porch tower of a medieval manor house. Edington Priory was founded, here in his birthplace, in 1352, by William of Edington, Bishop of Winchester, Chancellor of England, first Prelate of the Order of the Garter, for the Augustinian order of Bonhommes. The nave was to serve as the parish church, the chancel as the monastic choir. Providentially, the whole church has survived, and has indeed been enhanced within by discreet work of the 17th and 18th centuries, thanks to the taste and beneficent role of the Lords of the Manor who came into the monastic property after the Dissolution in 1539: the lordship passed through several families, to whom there are monuments inside. The church was consecrated in 1361, and is of great architectural interest, displaying as it does the transition from Dec to Perp: the windows in the chancel, transepts and nave aisles are Dec: the E. and W. windows, and the clerestory windows in the nave, are Perp.

The interior is moving, many-vistaed and beautifully furnished: a traceried, galleried, Perp screen divides nave from chancel, and a richly ordered nave altar provides for the parochial congregation, as it always must have done; a handsome 17th-century pulpit stands nearby. But what gives this interior its special character and charm is the remarkable 17th- (and in the chancel 18th-) century plaster ceiling. The fan vault under the crossing, the panelled, patterned ceiling in transepts and nave (dated 1663), gaily painted brown and white or pink and cream, bring wonderful warmth and colour to the whole interior. Spacious transepts, spacious crossing – there are delightfully furnished chapels (a 17th-century reredos in the N. transept) – and through the screen we enter the chancel. Austerely grand and sparkling, with tapering canopied niches on either side of the E. window, and between the windows on the N. and

Edington: the tomb of Sir Edward Lewys (1664)

S. walls, the whole choir is vaulted with a delicate late-18th-century Gothick plaster ceiling, white and crisp like icing sugar; there is an unusual early-17th-century altar rail, alarmingly spiked, and a dignified reredos and High Altar by Randoll Blacking (1926).

And this is not all. There is interesting medieval glass: an important and complete window in the N. transept (the Crucifixion with Our Lady and St John), a number of canopied figures in the N. clerestory, and an assemblage of fragments elsewhere, all more or less coeval with the church. And there are monuments: under the nave arcade the chantry of Sir Ralph Cheney (c. 1400), and in the S. transept the elaborate late-15th-century canopied tomb to a canon (identity uncertain); in the choir is the sumptuous alabaster tomb of Sir Edward Lewys and his wife Lady Ann Beauchamp (1664), with a winged angel suspended above, proffering a celestial crown; and in the sanctuary Chantrey's white marble monument to Sir Simon Taylor (1815).

Nothing remains of the monastic buildings: the cloister must have abutted the N. aisle – but the 16th-century house called the Priory, N. of this, is a charming fragment of the Prior's house; N. of this is the brethren's fishpond.

Edington has in recent years become celebrated for its Music Festival, held for a week every August, when cathedral and collegiate choirs assemble here to sing the daily services and provide concerts and recitals. But at all times of the year the church is well used, open, filled with flowers, loved and prayed in. William of Edington died in 1366: his chantry stands in Winchester Cathedral, in the nave whose rebuilding he so gloriously initiated.

Milton Abbey

The setting is superb: a long valley between the chalk downs, now wider, now narrower, hung with beechwoods, landscaped by Capability Brown in the second half of the 18th century for Lord Dorchester, who erased the little market town of Milton Abbas, replaced it with the long curving street of the present village – out of sight of the great house and lined with thatched cottages – preserved the Abbey as the grandest of grand private chapels, and employed Sir William Chambers and James Wyatt in the erection of his 18th-century quadrangular mansion, Gothick without, classical within, which sits so comfortably and melodiously alongside the monastic church.

Milton Abbey was founded *c.* 932 by King Athelstan as a college of secular canons, and refounded by King Edgar for the Benedictines thirty years later. The Norman church was destroyed by fire in 1309, and rebuilding began forthwith. The long chancel, the crossing, and S. transept – then the central tower and N. transept were all completed. The nave was never built: the Dissolution inter-

vened. Outside, flying buttresses and large Dec windows in the chancel and S. transept give way to Perp windows in the N. transept; the grand central tower with its twelve delicate pinnacles closely resembles the tower of Sherborne (q.v.). The extending chapels at the E. end have been shorn off: springers for the cloister vault on the N. side of the choir betray the existence of former cloisters. A modest W. porch against the blocked-up crossing arch is by Sir Gilbert Scott (1865).

Inside, the crossing and transepts are spacious and impressive: lierne vaults in the transepts, a fan vault under the tower – and a stone pulpitum leads into the chancel. Cool, white and bare, the eye is carried on at once to the Perp reredos, with its rows of empty canopied niches, repaired in plaster by Wyatt, a seven-light Dec window above; a simple rib vault encloses all. There is a Dec sedilia, open to the S. aisle, and a number of original oak stalls, with a few surviving misericords. Of particular interest is the towering canopied Perp pyx (to house the Blessed Sacrament), now affixed to the N. wall, a rare and precious relic. In the S. aisle is an unusual alabaster altar by Wyatt with a carved super-frontal resembling drapery; in the S. transept the great window is filled with Pugin glass (1847).

There are monuments of interest – in the N. aisle to the Tregonwell family, who acquired the Abbey after the Dissolution, and to the family of Sir Jacob Bancks who succeeded them. Most touching is the important monument in the N. transept by Robert Adam to the wife of Lord Dorchester who built the house (d. 1775). In the sanctuary is the canopied tomb of Baron Hambro (d. 1877) by Gilbert Scott: the Hambros were the last private family to occupy the house, which incorporates the Abbot's Hall, built *c.* 1495, resplendent with its hammer-beam roof. Round this Sir William Chambers designed the quadrangular mansion for Joseph Damer, 1st Earl of Dorchester, in 1771; James Wyatt was employed to decorate some of the interiors in chaste late-18th-century taste. It is now Milton Abbey School, the new public school founded in 1953.

Aligned on the E. end of the church, more than a hundred grass steps lead up to the tiny medieval St Catherine's Chapel set in the wooded hillside, built as a chapel for pilgrims to the Abbey. From these slopes there is a wonderful view across the Abbey and mansion to the smiling countryside beyond.

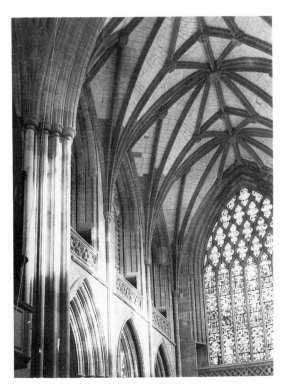

Milton Abbey: the south transept with its great window filled with Pugin glass

Sherborne Abbey: the nave – rebuilding was completed at the end of the 15th century

Sherborne Abbey

Romantic Dorset–Somerset border country: where else could we find village names like Queen Camel or Ryme Intrinseca? And Sherborne is an ancient little town of charm, famous for its market,

famous for its schools. Sir Walter Raleigh's fantastic high-towered Castle stands to the E., and along the old L & S W R line the trains chug quietly by on their way from Waterloo to Exeter.

The great Abbey dominates the town: it is outwardly all Perp, with traceried windows, flying buttresses and a pinnacled central tower much resembling that at Milton Abbey. But there is a much older, Norman or even Saxon, building partly hidden under this 15th-century exterior. Sherborne became the see of the Bishops of Wessex in 705, but in 1075 the bishopric was transferred to Old Sarum. Originally the church of secular canons, in 978 this early church was made over to the Benedictines, and a Benedictine house it remained until the Dissolution. A parish church, dedicated to All Hallows and attached to the W. end of the nave, was built in the 14th century: the town purchased the Abbey at the Dissolution to serve as the parish church, and All Hallows was pulled down. But in the rough-hewn walls of the W. front there are relics of the E. end of this

Sherborne: the exterior of the chapel of St Mary-le-Bow resembles a 16th-century Dorset manor house

church; and a Norman doorway here, and the Norman S.W. porch (the upper part rebuilt by R. C. Carpenter *c.* 1850) betray the true antiquity of the building.

Inside, at first, all appears Perp – but on reflection it will be seen that three of the crossing arches are Norman: at the E. end of the S. aisle a Norman arch leads into the transept, and at the W. end of the N. aisle there is a Saxon doorway. These are precious relics. But the glory of the church is the later, Perp work. Rebuilding of the chancel began *c.* 1420, and the nave was completed at the end of the century. But certain irregularities in the nave arcade prove that this is in fact a recasing of the Norman nave.

This interior is extremely satisfying: the lofty Perp windows in the clerestory with their panelled, carved surrounds, the late Perp arches, with no capitals, but all richly carved and panelled, exuberant yet restrained – and, above all, the ethereal fan vault which encloses the whole church: chancel, crossing, nave. The proportions are perfect, and the eye is carried on and up to the large E. window of many lights above Carpenter's elaborate reredos. Here and there in the aisles there are relics of Norman work, but Perp windows and Perp vaulting have obliterated nearly all. There are chapels on the way, and the ambulatory leads on and round to the Lady Chapel at the E. end. Here there is E.E. work – rib vaulting, Purbeck marble

Sherborne: the tomb of John Leweston (1584)

shafts, stiff-leaf capitals, but the E. end, which had been destroyed at the Dissolution, was rebuilt as a Great War Memorial by W. D. Caroe in Perp style, to marry with the adjacent chapel of St Mary-le-Bow. A remarkable engraved glass reredos, illustrating the attributes of the Virgin, by Laurence Whistler (1968), and a splendid brass candelabrum (1657) contribute much to the chapel.

There are early monuments to abbots and priests; but it is the post-Reformation tombs which are spectacular. Sir John Horsey (d. 1546) and his son, also Sir John (d. 1564), of Clifton Maybank lie together on a canopied white stone tomb in the Wykeham Chapel, a tomb distinguished for its early Renaissance decoration; there is the still more remarkable tomb of John Leweston and his wife (1584) in St Katherine's Chapel – where they lie on a great canopied six-poster; the work is attributed to Allen Maynard, who worked at Longleat. And in the S. transept is the grand standing monument to John Digby, 3rd Earl of Bristol (d. 1695), signed by John Nost. The Earl stands between the figures of his two wives, and the inscription tells us that he 'scorned the hurry of a public life'. The Digbys, and later the Wingfield-Digbys, succeeded Sir Walter Raleigh at Sherborne Castle, and have ever since been patrons and benefactors of the church.

Sherborne School occupies the site and such conventual buildings as remain of the Benedictine monastery. The origins of this ancient monastic school are lost in the mists of time: King Alfred is said to be an Old Boy. The school was refounded by Edward VI, and for a time even occupied the eastern chapels of the church. Indeed St Mary-le-Bow Chapel formed for a long time part of the headmaster's house – which explains the unexpected domestic appearance of its exterior. Indeed it could pass for the wing of a Tudor or early Elizabethan manor house – the kind of house in which this Dorset countryside so delightfully abounds.

Wimborne Minster

Wimborne Minster is not, strictly speaking, a monastic church – but like Beverley, Ripon and Southwell, a former collegiate church of secular canons. Ripon and Southwell in the 19th century became cathedrals: Beverley and Wimborne,

The towers of Wimborne Minster dominate the small houses and narrow streets of the town

shorn of their canons at the Dissolution, became mere parish churches – but as former major collegiate churches, as minsters of great importance, they are included in this book.

Wimborne is an attractive little market town, just out of reach of the silver birch and pine tree dormitory suburbs of Bournemouth and Poole, and it retains its rural soul. Driving into the town, the two sturdy towers of the Minster stand above the small houses of the narrow street – and, turning into the Market Place, the N. side of the church stands full length along the S. side of the square, almost unique in England in the possession of a central tower and a single tower at its W. end. The central tower is Norman, with a 17th-century parapet with big obelisk pinnacles added at the top after the fall of the spire. The W. tower is Perp (*c.* 1450), and of much the same height as its sister: it was built to house the bells. The curious mottled appearance of this exterior is attractive too, built as it is of golden brown and silver stone, which gives it an unusual, pleasing, speckled texture.

The Minster is dedicated to St Cuthburga, sister of King Ina of the West Saxons, who founded a monastery here *c.* 713. The nunnery was destroyed by the Danes in 1013, and refounded as a college of secular canons by Edward the Confessor in 1043. After the Dissolution in 1537 it became the parish church.

Inside, the Norman work predominates, with the grand Norman arches of the crossing upholding the Norman lantern tower, built *c.* 1140; the nave is a little later, with its round Norman pillars and its pointed Transitional arches all enlivened with dog-tooth – and the first bays of the chancel are of similar character. But the E. end is E.E. (*c.* 1250), with triple lancets with Purbeck marble shafts, terminating in quatrefoil or cinquefoil roundels at the top; and the two W. bays of the nave are Dec (14th century). Four steps lead up into the chancel, and seven more to the sanctuary, thus raised dramatically above the level of the church. Beneath this sanctuary is the crypt (mid 14th century), approached from the eastern chapels, and a place of special beauty – three bays wide, three bays deep, and vaulted, with cusped arches leading from the 'nave' into the E. chapel.

There is much to see in the church: above the vaulted sacristy (adjoining the S. choir aisle) is the Chained Library, founded in 1686, containing over 200 handsomely bound ancient books, theological and historical; there are many monuments: the little brass (*c.* 1440) in the sanctuary to King Ethelred, brother of Alfred the Great, who died in 871; the alabaster tombs of John Beaufort, Duke of Somerset, and his wife (*c.* 1440), and the Marchioness of Exeter (1557) nearby; and 17th-century monuments to Sir John Uvedale (1606) in St George's Chapel, and to Thomas Hanham (1650) and his wife at the W. end of the N. aisle. And there are many others throughout the church. There is early-16th-century glass in the E. window, and good 19th-century glass elsewhere by Willement & Gibbs; the choir stalls are 17th century, and there is an early-13th-century Purbeck marble font. On the wall nearby a Victorian brass plaque commemorates Matthew Prior,

'Poet and Scholar, born at Eastbrook in this town 1664, died 1721. Perennis et fragrans.' And of special interest is the 14th-century clock under the W. tower, with its 24-hour dial, the sun in the outer circle representing the hour hand, the moon in the middle circle marking the phases of the moon in the lunar month, and the earth in the centre. And outside, in the N. window of the tower, a quarter jack dressed as a grenadier of the Napoleonic Wars strikes the passing quarters on the small bells at his side.

Nothing remains of the collegiate buildings, but in remarkable rural seclusion in its park, only a stone's throw from the Minster, stands Dean's Court, occupying the site of the former Deanery. Still the seat of the Hanham family, the present distinguished early Georgian house, of red brick with stone dressings, was built for Sir William Hanham, 3rd Bt., in 1725. The house and garden are open to the public on certain days in spring and summer.

DIOCESE OF
SHEFFIELD

Sheffield Cathedral

SHEFFIELD IS ENORMOUS – enormous and intimidating, with its vast blocks of high-rise flats which seem to occupy acres of the city like gigantic human broiler houses. What kind of civilization is this? Yet in the heart of the old city there are still signs of civilization: small streets of Georgian houses, a few fine Victorian buildings, an occasional church spire. And the presiding spire is the spire of the Cathedral, which stands on its hill in the heart of a city which is indeed ringed with hills. Here there is still some dignity, with the Cutlers' Hall (1832), imposing with its grand Corinthian columns, and the awe-inspiring bank buildings of Williams and Glyns and the Midland; all these are in Church Street, where stands the Cathedral.

The see of Sheffield was founded in 1914, and the parish church was made the cathedral, an imposing big town church, cruciform with central tower and spire, pinnacled, embattled, outwardly all Perp. All this survives – with various (at first sight) seemingly inexplicable extensions and additions. Every possible misfortune seems to have assailed the plans to enlarge the church, and plans have been again and again made and unmade. Immediately after the First World War Sir Charles Nicholson prepared plans, which came to naught. Then fresh and ambitious plans were produced (again by Sir Charles) in the 1930s: a new cathedral (virtually) was to be built, N.–S. across the existing nave (largely an early-19th-century rebuilding); spire and chancel were to remain – and be repeated on the W. side, with a second spire and balancing transepts. These plans were not only accepted, but work began. The old chancel was to become a transept; a new Lady Chapel was completed, the new chancel built, and work on the new nave was scheduled to begin on Monday 4 September 1939. All was, of course, abandoned. After the war, although hopes were expressed for work to be resumed, Sir Charles Nicholson died,

and Dr Jarvis, the Provost who had been behind these grand schemes, retired. In the end Mr G. G. Pace was asked to prepare plans for the completion of the Nicholson building – but these came to naught. Finally Messrs Ansell and Bailey were commissioned to complete the building to a more limited plan. Nave and chancel surviving were to remain; Sir Charles Nicholson's Lady Chapel and chancel were to remain, but to be used as detached chapels; and a new west end and entrance tower built. This is what we see today.

The new S.W. tower is in outline attractive – but the details, neither 'Gothic' nor 'modern', are not. Inside, the idea of the new west end with lantern is brilliant – but the details of the lantern are not. Below the lantern, below the crossing, there appear to be a whole lot of feet dangling

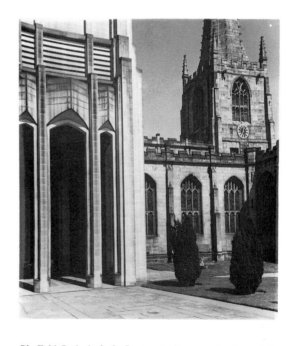

Sheffield Cathedral: the Perp central tower and spire and the new south-west tower

down. What they represent is uncertain: the effect is curious and unattractive.

As for the rest of the church, the nave, rebuilt in the early 19th century by William Flockton, is dignified; it is sad to visit the Nicholson Lady Chapel and chancel, with the crypt chapel beneath, which so nearly became the ritual E. end of the new cathedral. Of great interest, however, is the Shrewsbury Chapel, on the S. side of the chancel. Here are the alabaster effigies of the 4th Earl (1538) and his wife on their table tomb – and, opposite, the magnificent tomb of the 6th Earl (1590), with no wife, of course, because he was estranged from his second wife, who was no less a person than Bess of Hardwick, to whom he had been fourth husband. The chapel had long been screened off as the burial place of the Shrewsburys (in the 16th century Lords of the Manor), and out

of use. It was Dr Jarvis who restored it and cleaned the tombs. To its rededication he invited the then Earl of Shrewsbury (the 21st). He pointed out to the Earl how his ancestor's little finger had been carved with three knuckles – and upbraided the sculptor. 'But,' said the 21st Earl, 'we all have three knuckles on our little finger' – and he displayed his for the Provost to see.

There are other things to look at: a 15th-century oak sedilia in the N. Chapel, and the screen to this chapel by Randoll Blacking; many windows by Christopher Webb, and a number of other monuments, not least one to Sir William Sterndale Bennett, Professor of Music at Cambridge (d. 1875). His father was organist here (d. 1819). And in the churchyard, at the E. end of the Cathedral, is a monument to James Montgomery, the hymn writer.

Sheffield: the Shrewsbury Chapel, with the tomb of the 6th Earl of Shrewsbury

DIOCESE OF
SOUTHWARK

Southwark Cathedral

ELECTRIC TRAINS clanging along the line from Waterloo to London Bridge, ceaseless traffic swirling past the east end, boats plying their way along the river, H.M.S. *Belfast* at anchor in the Pool – Southwark Cathedral is hemmed in on every side. Standing in the middle of London Bridge, the visitor will see the tower on the far side, close to the river, with warehouses almost concealing it from view – and then, standing before the east end, he will see the Cathedral lying half a level below the street: the four-aisled, four-gabled retrochoir, the triple lancets at the east end, the later traceried windows in the south transept, the tall Perp tower at the crossing, with lofty pinnacles and chequer-patterned parapet, the flying buttresses – a grand medieval church, hugged by a big London terminus and a phalanx of warehouses.

The priory church of St Mary Overie, alias St Saviour's, was founded in 1106 as a priory of Augustinian Canons, in the diocese of Winchester – for London south of the Thames was in that vast diocese until 1877, when it was transferred to Rochester; Winchester House, the London palace of its bishops, was nearby. St Mary 'Overie' meant St Mary 'over the ferry', an allusion to the earlier church here, founded in the 9th century when St Swithin was Bishop of Winchester – before London Bridge (on the site we know it) was built. With the building of the bridge (at the end of the 12th century), Southwark became the heart of London. It was from here that Chaucer's pilgrims set out for Canterbury; Southwark became 'theatreland' – it was to the Globe that Shakespeare came in 1599. After the Dissolution the Priory became a parish church, and as Southwark decayed, it decayed too. The nave became dangerous in the early 19th century, and was pulled down

– to be replaced by a temporary building, 'a mean structure'. It was not rebuilt till the end of the 19th century. But that is to anticipate. Southwark became the Cathedral of the new diocese in 1905.

A flight of steps leads down from the street to the door in the south transept. Enter here, and stand under the crossing. To the east the chancel is purest 13th-century E.E., the east end closed by Bishop Fox's reredos screen (1520); to the west is the nave rebuilt by Sir Arthur Blomfield in 1890. It is worth walking to the west end to survey the whole church from there. Blomfield, using old pictures and following the old foundations, rebuilt as far as possible the 13th-century original which so closely resembled the choir: the arcades are supported on strong round (or octagonal) pillars, sparingly adorned with narrow shafts; the arcaded triforium is composed of four narrow lancets, and there are lancets in the clerestory; long shafts from floor to clerestory support a quadripartite vault. The eye is carried up to the east end and to the high altar beneath Bishop Fox's screen, gorgeously gilded by Sir Ninian Comper in 1933; Comper's deep red damask hangings and his glass in the east window bring warmth and colour to the sanctuary: indeed this glow of gold and crimson radiates the church.

As has been said, in 1877 South London was transferred to Rochester, and Anthony Thorold was appointed to the see. Not long after becoming bishop, Thorold set on foot a scheme for the restoration of St Saviour's, realizing the need for the creation of a new diocese to embrace South London – of which Southwark would be the cathedral church. Blomfield was appointed architect, and the rebuilding of the nave began. Though he was translated to Winchester in 1891, and died

Southwark Cathedral: a grand medieval church hemmed in by a big London railway station and a phalanx of warehouses

Southwark: the retrochoir is of supreme beauty

in 1895, Bishop Thorold is usually termed the founder of the see: the rebuilding of the nave on so grand a scale is entirely due to him.

Returning east, and entering the chancel, it is possible to absorb the reredos, restored by Blomfield and filled with new figures. Anthony Thorold is there, as is his successor Randall Davidson (afterwards Archbishop of Canterbury), and Edward Talbot, first Bishop of Southwark. On the south side of the sanctuary is the tomb, brilliantly regilded, of Lancelot Andrewes, Bishop of Winchester (d. 1626), author of *Preces Privatae*, and the last bishop to reside at Winchester House.

The retrochoir is of supreme beauty – and all the more thrilling for being, until the last minute, hidden from view. There are four equal chapels, divided from each other by slender E.E. piers, supporting an elegant quadripartite vault; triple lancets at the east end, wider, traceried Dec windows at the sides, the building was beautifully refurnished by Comper in the 1930s. It was he who designed the screens which separate one chapel from the next, and the four altars. Hangings of rich damasks, embroidered dorsals, or riddel posts, furnish these altars: Comper had an unerring eye for colour, which here stands out fresh and brilliant against the limewashed walls and vaults.

The Harvard Chapel (north transept) was restored by members of Harvard University in memory of John Harvard, who was baptized in St Saviour's in 1607; and there is a wealth of monuments everywhere, many of them recently regilded. From a 13th-century oak effigy of a knight to the 17th-century figure of Dr Lockyer – 'Here Lockyer lies . . .', and the lines go on to praise his famous pills; from the tomb of John Gower (1408), poet and friend of Chaucer, to the alabaster figure of Shakespeare, reclining against a background portraying the Southwark of his day (by H. V. McCarthy, 1912) – 'In memory of William Shakespeare, for many years an inhabitant of this parish, born 1569, died 1616' – the sequence is continuous, with many smaller tablets brilliant with newly painted coats of arms. At the crossing there is a magnificent brass candelabrum of 1680.

Trains rattle by along the viaduct only a few yards from the Cathedral, to disturb our contemplation. And we emerge once more from this remarkable oasis to the cries and sounds and glare of London Bridge and the damp squalor of South London.

Southwark: 'Here Lockyer lies' – the tomb of Dr Lockyer in the north transept

DIOCESE OF
SOUTHWELL

Southwell Minster

SOUTHWELL IS ONE OF the great surprises of England, undoubtedly the least known of all our ancient cathedrals. 'Where is Southwell?' people will ask. And to the reply 'In the heart of Nottinghamshire,' they will look little the wiser.

Drive from Newark – leaving a fair-sized town and the Great North Road behind. Before long, just beyond the village of Upton, the Minster comes in sight. Or approach from Nottingham: after passing Halloughton the road descends the hill, and there is the full length of the Minster below, presiding over the little town. Cathedral and town are completely unexpected, and the sense of surprise is one of Southwell's special charms. Coming from any direction, the two lead spires and the square central Norman tower suddenly appear – a great church in what appears to be little more than a large village. Southwell is indeed much the smallest cathedral town in England.

Driving into this little town from the E., Easthorpe is an informal villagey street of Georgian houses and cottages: the Bramley Apple inn recalls that this excellent cooker was first grown, and is still much cultivated, here. And ahead the E. end of the Minster and the tall pyramid roof of the chapter house loom high above the houses – and Church Street is lined with grand 18th-century houses, standing in their gardens, facing the great church.

The manor of Southwell was given by King Eadwig to Oakytel, Archbishop of York, in 956. A century later a college of prebendaries (or canons) had been established here, and as a collegiate church the Minster served as a kind of sub-cathedral, an 'episcopal stool' in the great archdiocese of York, just as Ripon did in the West Riding, and Beverley in the East. The collegiate status of Southwell survived the Reformation, and in 1884 the Minster became the cathedral of the new

Diocese of Southwell; but it had always been the mother church of Nottinghamshire. The prebendaries had their prebendal houses in Southwell, named after the village where their estate and parish lay: there were Prebendaries of Rampton and Oxton, Muskham and Normanton, three Prebendaries of Norwell, and so on; they took turns to come 'into residence' at Southwell, though a few would always be there. It is these handsome prebendal houses which stand around the Minster today, and which give the place such dignity and such atmosphere – though none, alas, are now occupied by their prebendaries. In the interest of 'progress' the collegiate foundation was abolished in 1841 – but the last prebendary of the old foundation only died a few years before the establishment of the new foundation of the cathedral, and the last surviving Vicar Choral actually lived long enough to continue to serve the church in its new cathedral status.

Approach the W. front: Southwell is not only unexpected, it is also unusual. The lead spires, the 'Rhenish caps', are unique in England, and give this austere W. front the character of a church in the Rhineland. The Perp W. window is, of course, a 15th-century insertion, but otherwise this W. front is the finest surviving Norman W. front in England, and dates from *c.* 1140. The Norman nave, built in these first decades of the 12th century, is equally austere. With its plain drum pillars and round arches, the wide round arches of the triforium above, and the smaller arches of the clerestory, the arcades are somehow reminiscent of a great Roman aqueduct – like the Pont du Gard in Southern France. There are grand Norman arches at the crossing and, beyond the screen, a glimpse of the vault of the E.E. chancel beyond. Walking up the nave, and standing under this crossing, the same austerity and simple splendour

Southwell Minster, one of the great surprises of England

of the Norman transepts matches the nave. Thus far Southwell is a Norman church.

The chancel screen, or pulpitum, is a triumph of the Dec style, with three richly carved canopied arches opening into a vaulted vestibule: through the tall narrow central arch there is a superb view into the chancel – with a magnificent 18th-century brass candelabrum, an early 16th-century brass lectern and, at the E. end, the four lancet windows filled with 16th-century Flemish glass above the High Altar. This E.E. chancel (completed *c.* 1250) is a wonderful foil for the Norman nave and transepts: here clustered columns, rib vaulting, lancet windows, strike an entirely different note. The nave is dark and solemn, the chancel light and joyous. And the E. side of the pulpitum is even more exuberantly carved and decorated than the side facing the nave. The Flemish glass in the lower lancets above the altar was rescued from the

Temple Church in Paris, and given to the Minster in 1818 by Henry Gally Knight, M.P. for the county, distinguished antiquary and author of books on Gothic architecture. The upper windows are filled with glass by Clayton & Bell (1876); in the aisles there is interesting glass by Kempe of the same date. And on the S. side of the sanctuary is the moving figure of Bishop Ridding, '43rd Headmaster of Winchester, 1st Bishop of Southwell. Ruler, Scholar, Divine' (d. 1904). The figure is by F. W. Pomeroy, the base by W. D. Caroe (1907), the cathedral architect, who also designed the organ case for the screen thirty years later. Two low E. transepts lead out of the chancel, and on the N. side a short enclosed cloister leads to the chapter house.

This is the great climax of a visit to Southwell, its greatest and most glorious surprise. Built at the very end of the 13th century, it is perhaps the

The chapter house doorway at Southwell: 'the leaves of Southwell'

Southwell: the Norman west front with its 'Rhenish caps'

supreme achievement of the Dec style in England – 'among chapter houses as the rose among flowers'. An elegant doorway with one slender central column and marble shafts in the columns at the side, a wealth of carvings in the capitals and in the arch itself, leads into the chapter house. It is the only chapter house in England with a stone vault unsupported by a central pillar; great traceried geometrical windows filled with clear glass, with only fragments of medieval stained glass set in them, flood the building with light. Below the windows, the arcades, which provide shallow canopied recesses for the canons' seats, are decorated with an incredible display of carved foliage – *the Leaves of Southwell.* Thirty years ago Sir Nikolaus Pevsner produced a King Penguin volume so entitled, entirely devoted to these carvings, and extracts from it were read at his Memorial Service in 1983.

In the N. transept is the 11th-century tympanum

over the small N.W. doorway, which came from the earlier, Saxon church. Nearby is the alabaster tomb of Archbishop Sandys (d. 1588), showing him wearing the eucharistic vestments of a medieval prelate – but with his children's figures below. And nearby is the charming bust of Sir Edwyn Hoskyns, 12th Baronet and 2nd Bishop of Southwell (d. 1925), by Reynolds Stephens. In the nave is an interesting font of 1661, the work of a local school of Post-Restoration font carvers. Opposite is the Norman N. porch, with its tunnel vault: there is a room above, and it will be seen that one of the pinnacles is in fact a circular chimney. All around the outside of the nave and transepts a wavy corbel course runs the length of the building under the roof; the gables of the transepts are richly patterned, and many of the windows are surrounded by a heavy 'rope' moulding – a feature which appears on the crossing arches inside.

And the setting of the Minster is divine: on the S. side stands the Palace – once a palace of the Archbishops of York. A charming garden has been made in the ruined E. parts: W. D. Caroe built the new house within the ruins on the W. and S. sides, attached to the medieval Great Hall. To the E. stands Vicars' Court, a little open quadrangle of Georgian houses, built about 1780 to house the Vicars Choral, the Residence at the far end for the canon-in-residence – in the 18th century the canons came and went – and this is now the Residence of the Provost. The four smaller houses are now occupied by other dignitaries of the Cathedral. On the farther side of Church Street stand the former prebendal houses – South Muskham Prebend, Normanton Prebend, Woodborough Prebend; the most distinguished is the early-18th-century Cranfield House (or Oxton Prebend), built by Prebendary Mompesson, with a touch of Mompesson House in Salisbury Close about it – built at much the same time for another member of the family. On the W. side are the Sacrista Prebend, and the Rampton Prebend, its delightful stuccoed gables and sash windows concealing a much older, Jacobean house. But everywhere there are good houses to enjoy – along the Burgage, where Byron lived as a boy with his mother, too impoverished to live at Newstead; and along the little narrow streets of shops. Southwell, unexpected, unknown, unusual, is also unspoiled. Long may the Philistine – and the outside world – be kept at bay.

Blyth Priory: the Norman nave

Blyth Priory

Blyth is one of the best villages in Nottinghamshire: there is a long green, lined on either side with houses and cottages of varying dates and varying sizes, of brick or stucco, terraces with Gothick windows, and old hostelries – for Blyth was for centuries a coaching village on the Great North Road. It is a peaceful village now, with the traffic of the A1 rushing past along the new by-pass.

The tall Perp tower of the priory church dominates the village, dominates the landscape – a tower of great beauty, with a lace-like traceried parapet connecting its many pinnacles. Walking up the churchyard path, the building at first glance appears all Gothic, with its Dec porch, embattled south aisle, and many Dec traceried windows: only at a second glance do the small Norman windows in the clerestory give a clue of what is to come. The door opens: at first the attention is caught by the broad south aisle, all furnished and set out as though this were the church itself, with altar, organ, pulpit, screen, pews. Suddenly there is a glimpse of the Norman nave beyond – which bursts upon one miraculously. There is a colossal arcade of the utmost severity, a triforium of stark simplicity, a clerestory of small Norman windows, and a very early quadripartite vault above. It is breathtaking.

Blyth Priory was founded in 1088 as a cell of the Benedictine Abbey of St Cuthbert at Rouen. The nave must have been begun at the very end of the 11th century. It is French in character, primitive, solemn, almost grim – but of rocklike beauty. At the end of the 13th century the south aisle was rebuilt to serve as a parochial nave, as indeed it still does. In the nave itself there are seats, but no altar: only the blank east wall which divided the parochial church from the monastic choir beyond. At the Dissolution central tower, transepts and choir were all destroyed: what survives was claimed by the parishioners as their church. The Norman north aisle is narrow and mysterious, dark with richly coloured Victorian glass.

There is much to see in the church: medieval screens with painted panels of saints, early sepulchral slabs, an early Purbeck marble effigy of a knight, a 17th-century font with contemporary cover, a Jacobean pulpit, and many hatchments of the Mellish family, all recently cleaned and restored. In the Lady Chapel is the imposing monument, by John Hancock, to Edward Mellish, whose bewigged figure reclines between Corinthian pillars (1703). 'It was extremely difficult,' wrote Rupert Gunnis in his *Dictionary of British Sculptors*, 'to find Hancock's signature . . . indeed I was only able to discover it by climbing a ladder, for it was tucked away at the top of the right hand pilaster supporting the carved pediment.' It was Edward Mellish who built Blyth Hall, which stood to the west of the church (and was demolished in 1972); it was an interesting late-17th-century mansion – 'a very sweet house and gardens and grounds', wrote Celia Fiennes; 'it stands high and commands the sight of the country about.' Its gardens surrounded the church to north and east – indeed the eastern bays of the nave, still standing beyond the dividing wall, which were the western bays of the monastic choir, were used by Edward Mellish as his aviary: here he kept his exotic birds. This east end of the church is crowned with his odd early-18th-century pediment. The view from the west end of the churchyard is still much as Celia Fiennes saw it – with the church standing high, and commanding the sight of the country about.

Lenton Priory

The old village of Lenton became completely submerged by Nottingham in the early 19th century: a few old houses survive in the street, a few fragments of the once great Cluniac Priory founded by William Peverel in the early 12th century. A small church called Lenton Priory, partly medieval, partly Victorian, stands in the old priory churchyard at the crossroads – the chapel of the priory hospital. The nave with its little bell turret was largely rebuilt in 1883: the chancel is 12th century; there is a rare Royal Arms of Charles I. But in the big parish church, built nearby in 1842 (by Stevens of Derby) stands the magnificent 12th-century font of the original priory church: rectangular, with its sides carved with representations of Our Lord's Baptism, Crucifixion and Resurrection, it is one of the most notable fonts in England, and for this alone Lenton merits a visit.

Lenton Priory: the 12th-century font, now in the parish church

Newstead Abbey

TO MOST PEOPLE Newstead means Byron, and indeed from the Dissolution until 1817 Newstead belonged to the Byrons. The Augustinian Priory was founded here by Henry II *c.* 1170 (it was never in fact an abbey), and the E.E. west front of the church still stands, open to the sky, open to everything – one of the most perfect 13th-century west fronts in England, like a smaller version of Wells. Round the cloisters, Sir John Byron formed a commodious country house: the church, apart from the west front, he pulled down. George Gordon, 6th Lord Byron, the poet, succeeded in 1798, and it is his spirit that pervades the place. On the east side of the cloisters stands the chapter house, which since the Dissolution has been used as a chapel – a rectangular chamber, where elegant clustered E.E. columns uphold delicate ribbed vaults. It makes a chapel of great beauty, enhanced by delightful Victorian decoration. Newstead now belongs to the City of Nottingham, and is beautifully maintained as a Byron museum: the chapel is used for worship every Sunday.

Newstead Abbey: from the cloisters into the chapel

Thurgarton Priory

The village of Thurgarton is prettily set in a tumble of low hills on the west side of the Trent valley in Nottinghamshire, on the main road (A612) from Nottingham to Southwell. At first sight there is not even a glimpse of the priory church, but near the Red Lion a quiet inconsequential lane, which hugs the wall of the kitchen garden of the big house, leads on and up – and soon a noble E.E. tower appears, with long lancet windows and blind E.E. arcading adorning its sides.

Thurgarton Priory was founded for Augustinian Canons in 1187 by Ralph d'Eyncourt. The mutilated fragment of their church stands against the 18th-century house called Thurgarton Priory, which faces west across a small undulating park. The church originally had a grand west front with two towers: at the Dissolution the nave became the parish church and the monastic site and buildings were granted to William Cooper, cup-bearer to Henry VIII. The Coopers remained here for 300 years, and in 1777 John Gilbert Cooper built the present red-brick house with its orderly pedimented façade – but he did not think twice about demolishing the S.W. tower, which stood in the way of the left-hand wing of his mansion. Even in its truncated state the west front of the church, with its E.E. doorway and surviving N.W. tower, cannot fail to impress and delight. Three bays of the E.E. nave survive, imposing work of the late 12th century; and in 1852 T. C. Hine of Nottingham added a harmonious chancel. The interior is dark with rich Victorian glass; there are three 15th-century stalls with misericords, and a number of 18th- and early-19th-century monuments to the Coopers.

John Gilbert Cooper was a scholar and minor poet, who receives an occasional mention in Boswell. In a long poem he is enraptured by the

Thurgarton with its noble E. E. tower

arcadian pleasures of Thurgarton, and speaks of Horace and Catullus drinking Falernian wine after wandering in his company in his groves. In 1884 the first Bishop of Southwell (Dr Ridding) came to live here – before the archiepiscopal palace next to the Minster was rebuilt – and delighted in the church, which he described as the finest episcopal chapel in England. The house is now occupied by Boots, who use it as the headquarters of their research department. Gardens and surroundings are immaculately kept, and the church remains a grand parish church for the village.

Worksop Priory: the E. E. Lady Chapel, which remained roofless till 1922

Worksop Priory

'Worksop, Gateway to the Dukeries' proclaims a signboard welcoming us to the town: driving into Worksop from the E. or W., past the collieries of Manton or Shireoaks, or from the N., past factories and industrial estates and rows of raw red semis, it is perhaps not easy to appreciate this. But entering the town from the S., between the vast ducal estates of Welbeck and Clumber, along the B6005, is a different matter. Park Street, narrow and lined with 18th- or early-19th-century houses is attractive, and leads into the market place. From here, on the right, Potter Street still contains a few 18th-century houses – though many have been successfully torn down of late to make way for the dreary, ugly and enormous new extensions to the Victorian Town Hall: this is the way to Worksop Priory.

The Priory was founded *c.* 1120 by William de Lovetot for Augustinian Canons. The 14th-century gatehouse faces the street: it is tall, gabled and buttressed, with figures of St Augustine and St Cuthbert on either side of the large traceried window on the first floor, another, of the Trinity, in the gable. On one side of the archway, the porch with its delicately traceried parapet led to a small oratory; there was a large guest hall above, in which to entertain visitors. And behind lies the full length of the south side of the church.

The west front with its twin towers is Norman architecture at its most simple and severe. The pinnacles and parapets of the towers are, of course, Perp additions: otherwise it is only a matter of a few small windows, two grand doorways and a big Norman window over the central door; all else is bare and unadorned. Inside, the nave is long and imposing: the arcades are Transitional, with nail-head decoration in the alternate round and octagonal piers, a triforium composed of large round arches and narrow pointed ones, with the round arches breaking into the clerestory, and a clerestory of round-headed windows set above the narrow openings below. It is an unusual, somewhat restless, design. At the Dissolution the monastic parts of the church were pulled down, with the exception of the Lady Chapel, which, opening out of the south transept, remained detached and roofless until 1922, when Sir Harold Brakspear restored it and rebuilt the south transept (1929) and the north transept (1935) on the model of the old work – a sympathetic and harmonious reconstruction. The nave had survived as the parish church.

In the late 1960s, a new east end was built, designed by Mr Laurence King – a low central tower with a tapering fleche and a gabled choir. It is difficult to comprehend how an addition so out of sympathy with the noble church could have been conceived: the design is aggressively 'modern', the details – such as plate glass windows, stalls and organ case – crude. Sir Gilbert Scott's reredos has been banished to the north transept, the Rood to the south, and the organ and choir stalls occupy the east end as in a Protestant chapel. A 'central' altar stands under the new tower. It is a relief to turn into the Lady Chapel, with its exquisite tall lancet windows and slender shafts – E.E. architecture at its simplest and most serene. The chapel is beautifully and devoutly furnished.

There are few monuments or fittings of special note, and, alas, much Victorian glass was in the 'reordering' – fateful word – stripped of its borders or background, and reset in clear glass. It is sad to have to conclude an account of a noble church on so critical a note.

DIOCESE OF
TRURO

Truro Cathedral

TWENTY-EIGHT GRANITE ARCHES carry the Great Western line into Truro – and from this viaduct (built in 1905) there is a breathtaking view of the Cathedral as the train, crossing the valleys of the Kenwyn and the Allen, and bisecting the little city, draws into the station. Nothing can exceed this view. But, approaching Truro by road, the Cathedral can be seen from every side rising noble and erect above the low roof-tops of the town. This is how Pearson conceived it: a great church with three spires pointing to Heaven – but standing in the French manner, tightly packed and girded about in the heart of a city of narrow streets. Not that all the streets are narrow: Lemon Street,

which descends the short hill from the S., is wide and lined with elegant Georgian houses. And at the top is the Lander Monument, a granite Doric column erected in 1835 to commemorate Richard Lander the explorer. And at the W. end of the Cathedral there is a modest market place: here we can stand back and absorb the west front, which with its rose window and twin spires wears the mien of a cathedral in Northern France. This is early Gothic at its purest and most elegant, and undoubtedly owes much (as several of Pearson's churches do) to Coutances.

The diocese of Truro was founded in 1877, and Edward White Benson, later Archbishop of

ABOVE *Truro Cathedral, Pearson's masterpiece;* OPPOSITE *the Baptistery*

Canterbury, was enthroned first Bishop in the parish church of St Mary, whose S. aisle survives as the outer S. aisle of the Cathedral. John Lough-borough Pearson was appointed architect, and the foundation stone was laid in 1880. Chancel and transepts were consecrated in 1887, the nave and central spire in 1903, and the western spires in 1910. Pearson died in 1897, but his son, F. L. Pearson, carried on and completed the work to his father's design. Pearson was a genius among Victorian church architects: his creative spirit, which had so absorbed the atmosphere of Early English or Early French churches, breathed a life and originality into his creations. St Peter's Vauxhall (1863), St Augustine's Kilburn (1870) and St Michael's Croydon (1871) rose like miracu-lous reincarnations of this pure early Gothic style. Truro is the same.

Stand at the W. end of the nave: the appeal is instantaneous – a soaring vault, narrow lancets everywhere, lofty crossing arches, arcades with high pointed arches, a lower triforium, moulded capitals, shafted columns. Stand in the S. transept, by the door, and absorb the cross-vista to N. transept, across aisles and across nave and chancel – and into the Baptistery, which stands in the angle of nave and S. transept, supremely elegant with its clustered columns supporting a narrow pointed vault. Here is the same soaring height, the same emphasis on purity of line and simplicity of style, the same use of lancets and rose windows. Stand in St Mary's aisle, with its 18th-century pulpit, 18th-century organ, wagon roof – a remarkable contrast to the rest of the building – and see how Pearson has here created a still wider vista across the 16th-century arcade to his own chancel and its aisles. The chancel is furnished with Pearson's canopied stalls and bishop's throne: behind the High Altar is a richly sculptured reredos, depicting the Crucifixion and scenes from Our Lord's life. Here the narrow E. transepts provide yet more vistas, yet more changes of light and shade. Throughout the Cathedral the building glows with the warmth of the honey-coloured stone. Except in St Mary's aisle (where there is earlier 19th-century glass by Warrington) the glass everywhere is by Clayton & Bell, colourful and brightly jewelled. In the N. transept is a collection of monuments from St Mary's church, pride of place going to the elaborate tomb of Richard Robartes and his wife (1614), with their stiffly reclining effigies.

If we leave by the S. transept, we can admire the exterior of St Mary's aisle, with its ornate Perp decoration, and the small, slender spire between it and the transept, which with its green copper roof adds an extra unexpected feature to the Cathedral's silhouette.

St Germans Priory

St Germans is an ancient borough, which until 1832 returned two Members of Parliament to Westminster, and the ancient see town of the Bishopric of Cornwall – until 1032, when Devon and Cornwall were united in the new diocese of Exeter. Until the founding of the cathedral at Truro in 1887, St Germans was regarded as the mother church of Cornwall. So the place has a wonderful air of vanished importance. The little town, or big village, stands on its own peninsula at the end of a long creek. With its ancient priory church, and the demesne of Port Eliot adjoining it, St Germans has the air of grand detachment.

The church, ruggedly magnificent, lies below the street, down its sloping churchyard, a vener-able, enormous fragment. A century after the sup-pression of the old bishopric, St Germans was reconstituted as a priory of Augustinian Canons, and the west front, and a portion of the nave, date from the late 12th century. The west front is remarkable with its two towers: both are Norman in their lower storeys, but whereas the S. was completed with a plain embattled Perp top, the N. is surmounted by an unusual 13th-century octagon. Between these stands a splendid Norman doorway under a gable; above and around small Norman windows form the only feature in this massive cliff of rough masonry. Beside the S. tower a narrow vaulted Perp porch, with open arches to the S. and W., leads into the church.

Six steps lead down into the S. aisle: the first impression is one of great size, with what appear to be two parallel naves, divided by a late Norman arcade; in fact the three eastern bays of this arcade are late-16th-century Norman revival: after the Dissolution the long chancel fell into disuse, and in 1592 collapsed, bringing down the eastern bays of the arcade. Carew, writing in 1602 in his *Survey of Cornwall*, describes how 'the devout charges of the well-disposed parishioners quickly repaired this ruin'. The arcade was repaired in granite, and a new E. wall built. In 1802 the dilapidated N. aisle was pulled down, and an extension built on

St Germans Priory: the Norman west front

this side, re-using some Norman features, to form the Port Eliot pew. The S. aisle, once the parochial nave, had been grandly built in the 14th century, and extended towards the W. in the 15th.

Over-zealous restoration in the later 19th century has resulted in scraped walls, new roofs and floors, and a somewhat hard Victorian interior.

But there is much to see – notable glass by Burne-Jones, an early-13th-century Purbeck marble font, a Royal Arms of Charles II, and a number of memorials to the Eliots of Port Eliot in the S. aisle. Most spectacular is the magnificent monument in an unexpected dark position under the N. tower, lit by a dramatic slant of light from a little Norman window nearby, to Edward Eliot (1722) by Rysbrack. His reclining figure lies on the tomb, watched over by a mourning figure, and weeping cherubs stand above.

Nothing remains of the monastic buildings: the property was acquired in 1564 by the Eliots – an old Cornish family who rose to fame with Sir John Eliot 'the Patriot' in the 17th century, and became in time Earls of St Germans. The mansion of Port Eliot incorporates part of the conventual buildings, and received its present delightful form at the hands of Sir John Soane in the early 19th century; the castellated gatehouse near the church is by Henry Harrison (1848). Repton landscaped the park, and it is this and the great beechwoods which give the ancient Priory its incomparable setting.

St Michael's Mount

An island priory, a military stronghold, a country house: St Michael's Mount has fulfilled all these roles. In the 5th century St Michael appeared to fishermen on the western side of the rock, and the island became a place of pilgrimage. In the 11th century Edward the Confessor granted it to Mont S. Michel in Normandy, and a Benedictine priory was established here – to be suppressed in 1425 as an alien foundation. Henry VI granted it to his favourite Brigittine nuns at Syon, and in their hands it remained until the Dissolution – but all the time there was an odd relationship between the religious and the military. After one or two changes of ownership at the time of the Reformation St Michael's Mount passed to the St Aubyn family in 1657 and, although now the property of the National Trust, it still remains their home.

The sight of St Michael's Mount from the land or from the sea is not to be forgotten, and the tower of the church is like a coronet crowning the medieval buildings. Rough-built of local granite, the church was much restored by the architect Piers St Aubyn in the 19th century, but is in origin the 14th-century monastic church. A 15th-century brass candelabra, a late-17th-century Father Smith organ, Flemish and English alabasters in the reredos, Victorian glass and furnishings, family memorials – the building is still in use for worship, and the service every Sunday morning may be attended by the public.

St Michael's Mount

DIOCESE OF
WAKEFIELD

Wakefield Cathedral

WAKEFIELD IS AN ANCIENT TOWN, which grew rich in the Middle Ages on the clothing industry. The large and ancient parish church of All Saints – now the Cathedral – is witness to its importance and its prosperity; the medieval bridge still stands, complete with its medieval Bridge Chapel – one of only three or four such chapels left in England. The clothing industry declined, and collieries were opened all around during the 19th century, bringing a new prosperity; but Wakefield has never become a mammoth city like Leeds, Bradford and Sheffield. It is altogether smaller, and until recently had some of the character of a county town – the county town of the West Riding. Little remains of its medieval past, little of its 18th-century dignity; T. E. Colcutt's Town Hall of 1877, with its tall tower and Jacobethan windows, rises as a splendid witness to Victorian prosperity. But in recent years Wakefield has done its best to obliterate its past: horrifying blocks of high-rise flats, grim office buildings, multi-storey car parks, shopping 'precincts', dual carriageways – all the litter of the 1960s and 1970s – have submerged its old character. The so-called 'Cathedral Precinct' (S. side of the Cathedral) has been given the usual treatment: it has been 'pedestrianized', and the rows of new shops with their jazzy fronts confront the old church with their cold impersonal stare.

All Saints' is an impressive town church – outwardly all Perp – with a tall tapering spire at the west end, 247 ft high, the loftiest in Yorkshire. The see of Wakefield was founded in 1888, and formed out of the diocese of Ripon; the grand eastern extension, comprising transepts and retrochoir, built in 1904, and designed by F. L. Pearson, is of considerable magnificence. Its long Perp windows, its multiplicity of pinnacles, its ornate cresting, marry happily with the more modest features of the rest of the building, and add scale and dignity to the medieval church.

Inside, the long nave arcades betray a much earlier building: round 12th-century piers, 13th-century octagonal piers, quatrefoil piers of the early 14th century, stand alongside each other to support the 14th-century arches: excavations have proved the existence of an earlier cruciform church with a central tower, which collapsed in the early 14th century. It is round these earlier bones that the Perp church was built, with wider aisles and a longer chancel. It is a dignified, spacious interior: the font of 1661 is of interest, and the wide aisle windows are filled with Kempe glass; beyond the screen the chancel carries on the same theme. But it is the screen which makes the interior. This is of 1635, and a rare piece of 17th-century church furnishing, with elaborate Renaissance features. The canopy with gilded rood and attendant figures and angels is a happy addition of 1950 by Sir Ninian Comper. There is an 18th-century pulpit, and the chancel is well furnished with 15th-century stalls with some ancient misericords; there is newer furnishing, too, for the most part in harmony with the old, and a High Altar with painted reredos by F. L. Pearson.

Here the vista through to the retrochoir and Lady Chapel is a pleasure: triple arches divide the sanctuary from the eastern chapels, where tall slender columns support a stone lierne vault. It is an echo of the Lady Chapel at St Michael's Croydon, designed by J. L. Pearson, F. L. Pearson's father. In the S. transept is the tomb of Bishop Walsham How, 1st Bishop of Wakefield (1897) – author of *For All the Saints* – by J. N. Forsyth. In the S. chapel is a grand baroque monument to Sir Lyon Pilkington, with angels sitting on the pediment blowing trumpets before the cartouche of the Pilkington arms, and the bewigged figure of the baronet reclining on a cushion. The sculptor is unrecorded. In the N. aisle is the handsome organ of 1743.

Wakefield is fortunate in having secured the

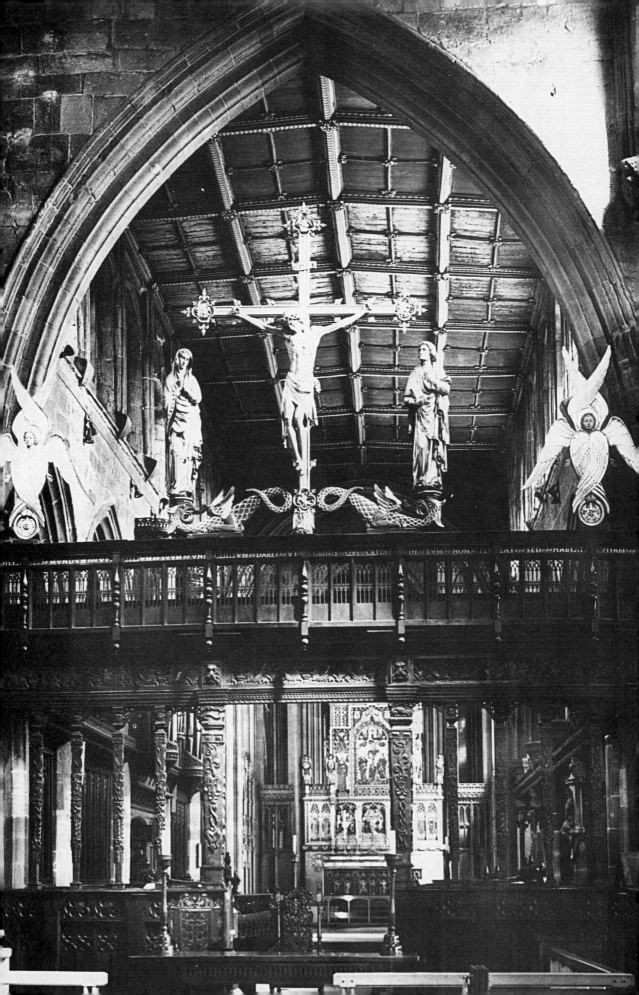

services of a gifted architect to build the extensions to its cathedral: F. L. Pearson's retrochoir and transepts add much to the dignity and interest of the building.

Woodkirk Priory

Scarred West Riding countryside. Woodkirk was a cell of the wealthy Augustinian priory of Nostell, founded *c.* 1110. The medieval tower survives, but the body of the church is largely an early-19th-century rebuilding; there are a few old bench ends, and a 17th-century pulpit.

Woodkirk Priory

OPPOSITE *Wakefield Cathedral: the screen (1635) with gallery and rood by Sir Ninian Comper (1950)*

DIOCESE OF
WINCHESTER

Winchester Cathedral

WINCHESTER IS the ancient capital of England. The West Saxon kings had their capital here, and, according to Camden's *Britannia*, 'adorned it with magnificent churches and an episcopsee'; Egbert, when he became King of All Britain, made his capital here; Alfred the Great is buried here; Edward the Confessor was crowned here; the Conqueror was crowned here as well as in London; the tomb of William Rufus stands here; Henry III was born here; and Mary Tudor and Philip II of Spain were married here. The Cathedral, long, low, solemn, lies in the heart of the city – the exterior often dubbed 'disappointing' or 'uninspiring'. Indeed Canterbury and York may have their three towers, Durham and Lincoln their incomparable hill-top sites, Salisbury its superb spire; Winchester has none of these – only its squat Norman tower and its great length; yet, venerable, ancient, self-assured, it has need of none of them. The appeal of Winchester is quite different.

The original Saxon minster, the church of a Benedictine monastery, lay on the N. side of the present Cathedral, closely abutting the nave; its remains, excavated between 1957 and 1968, may be seen close to the W. door. The present Cathedral was begun in 1079; the transepts, central tower, and indeed the nave – though this was entirely remodelled in the late 14th century – date from this time; the retrochoir was built in the 13th century; the Lady Chapel in the 15th, and the chancel rebuilt in the first years of the 16th. At the Dissolution the last Prior became the first Dean. Walking round the exterior, we can appreciate the tremendous size of the Cathedral, the great length not only of the nave, but of the chancel, retrochoir and Lady Chapel. Winchester is the longest cathedral, not only in England, but in Europe.

Even so, nothing prepares us for the splendour of the interior. The view of the long lofty nave is unforgettable. The arcade is lofty in itself, but it is the tall shafts which accompany each arch, rising to carry the long arms of the vault, rising slender into the clerestory, the long carved Perp panels in every spandrel, the pierced parapet of the balcony-like triforium above these, and the large traceried clerestory windows, which accentuate the height still more. Above, the lierne vault with its elaborate patterning and wealth of carved bosses is the crowning glory. The eye is carried on, beyond the screen and beyond the choir, to the great reredos which is seen white and dazzling through the pinnacled fretwork of the massive oak screen: jewel-like glass in the E. window, high above the reredos, adds a splash of colour to this sparkling white interior.

It is hard to believe that beneath this Perp nave the core of the much older Norman nave lies buried. The scheme of transformation was begun by Bishop William de Edington, builder of Edington Priory (q.v.), *c.* 1350, and continued and completed by William of Wykeham after 1366. The low Norman arches were removed, the tall Perp arches filled the place of these and the triforium above, and a new high clerestory carrying the lofty vault was built. Only at the E. end of the nave do a few Norman 'bones' survive, where, close to the nave altar, a Norman capital juts oddly out. On the S. side of the nave is the Chantry of William of Wykeham (Bishop 1367–1404, founder of Winchester College and of New College, Oxford): on the same side, close to the altar, is the Chantry of William de Edington (Bishop 1345–1366); on the N. side stands the 12th-century black Tournai marble font, one of seven such Norman fonts in England.

Steps lead up to the nave altar, and through the

Winchester: in the retrochoir stand the chantries of Cardinal Beaufort, William of Waynflete, Bishop Fox and Bishop Gardiner

screen (by Sir Gilbert Scott, 1875) more steps lead into the choir, which in Benedictine fashion occupies the crossing and is furnished with early-14th-century canopied stalls, black with age. Prior Silkstede's pulpit is early 16th century, the front carved with skeins of silk; and in the centre of the choir stands the tomb of William Rufus, killed by an arrow in the New Forest (1100). Soon after his burial here the first Norman tower collapsed – the judgement of Heaven? It was thought so at the time. The wooden vault in the crossing is dated 1635, and one of the bosses bears the head and monogram of Charles I. More steps lead up to the sanctuary, enclosed by late-17th-century altar rails, and to the reredos. This gorgeous early-16th-century screen, filled with statues great and

Winchester Cathedral from the Close; in the foreground is the Deanery with its medieval open porch

small, the Crucifixion the centrepiece, is abundantly decorated with carved canopies and friezes: the original figures were smashed after the Reformation, but much of the lacelike ornament survived. On either side of the sanctuary, on the top of the lower stone screens, stand 17th-century painted caskets, containing the bones of early kings and queens.

The nave is majestic, overwhelming – the retrochoir perhaps the most beautiful part of the Cathedral. Purbeck marble piers with stiff-leaf capitals, lancet windows and E.E. rib vaulting all contribute to an interior of great beauty and spaciousness. And here stand yet more Chantry chapels: that of Cardinal Beaufort, Bishop of Winchester (d. 1447), on the S. side, of William of Waynflete, Bishop of Winchester (d. 1486), on the N. Waynflete, first Headmaster of Winchester, was later first Provost of Eton and founder of Magdalen College, Oxford. To the W. stand the Chantries of Bishop Fox (d. 1528), founder of Corpus Christi College, Oxford, and of Bishop Gardiner (d. 1555) – the former on the S. side, the latter on the N. In the centre is the shrine of St Swithin himself, Saint of Winchester – a recent and delicate work by Brian Thomas and Wilfrid

Carpenter Turner, erected in 1962 to commemorate the 1100th anniversary of the saint's death; and, all around, the floor is lined with medieval tiles.

At the E. end stand three chapels: the Lady Chapel, furnished with screens and stalls, dark with Kempe glass, and decorated with early-16th-century wall paintings, is a Perp remodelling of the earlier Lady Chapel; on the N. side the Chapel of the Guardian Angels is E.E. – with its vaulting painted and patterned with innumerable heads of the Holy Angels; there is ancient glass in the E. window, and a bronze effigy by Le Sueur of Richard Weston, Lord Portland (d. 1634); on the S. is the Chantry of Bishop Langton (d. 1500), with E.E. arcading and Perp fan vaulting – gloriously adorned with screens and galleried panelling; close to the entrance is the small bronze figure of William Walker, the diver, who between 1906 and 1912 underpinned this E. end of the Cathedral, which was on the point of collapse owing to its lack of proper foundations.

And no mention has been made of the transepts, which survive, eloquent and severe in their pristine Norman state. In the N. transept, under the crossing, is the vaulted Chapel of the Holy Sepulchre, its walls and low vault decorated with important mural paintings of the early 13th century. In the S. transept a staircase leads up to the Library, where under a 17th-century plaster vaulted ceiling contemporary bookcases hold a notable collection of beautifully bound volumes and manuscripts.

There are many monuments and memorials of interest, in addition to those already mentioned: the plain slab marking the grave of Jane Austen (d. 1817) is in the N. aisle of the nave; nearby on the wall a tablet commemorates Lord Wavell, Field Marshal, Viceroy, poet, Scholar of Winchester, and member of an ancient Hampshire family. In the S. aisle of the nave is Flaxman's monument to Joseph Warton, Headmaster of Winchester (d. 1801); in the S. transept Gilbert Scott's elaborate canopied effigy of Bishop Samuel Wilberforce (d. 1873), prototype of the modern diocesan bishop. The reredos in the Lady Chapel commemorates Charlotte M. Yonge, the Victorian novelist; in Prior Silkstede's Chapel a flat stone is inscribed 'Here resteth the body of Mr Izaak Walton, who died on the 15th of December 1683'; a window above (1914), presented by the fishermen of England and America, is dedicated to his honour, and recalls the subjects of the portraits in his *Lives*.

The Close is varied and delightful, with numerous houses of every date and size – gabled, timbered houses like Cheyney Court, 17th-century houses like the Judge's Lodgings, and others of the 18th century. The Deanery is the most beautiful deanery in England, with its three-bayed open medieval porch and, upstairs, its late-17th-century Long Gallery. It is still the home of the Dean. Wolvesey Palace, the bishop's residence, is just outside the Close, and is a distinguished house, partly medieval, partly late 17th century.

Winchester College, St Cross and the Castle lie within walking distance: St Swithin's Gate will enable us to leave the secluded, magical, world of the Close to explore these delights. 'Winchester,' remarks Sir Nikolaus Pevsner, 'is the richest architecturally of all the English Bishops' sees.'

Beaulieu Abbey: the narrow staircase leading to the pulpit

Beaulieu Abbey

Beaulieu lies on the edge of the New Forest, close to the wide tidal estuary of the Beaulieu River, perfect in its setting today, perfect in its remoteness in the Middle Ages for the founding of a Cistercian abbey. Beaulieu is a forest village, loose-knit, but with one main street: the Montagu Arms is a reminder of its dependence since the 17th century on the Montagu family. It was the 2nd Duke of Montagu who attempted to establish a port at Buckler's Hard – three miles downstream – and certainly this flourished as a ship-building yard in the 18th century; several ships of Nelson's fleet were built here. Buckler's Hard, with its 18th-century brick cottages, is full of charm.

The Cistercian abbey was founded in 1204 by King John. The gatehouse, converted into a house after the Dissolution, greatly enlarged in 1872 by Sir Arthur Blomfield, and known as Palace House, is the home of Lord Montagu of Beaulieu: his celebrated Motor Museum stands discreetly concealed in nearby woods. For the rest, Beaulieu Abbey is a matter of romantic remains. There is one exception: the refectory, converted into the parish church after the Dissolution. It makes a perfect church.

Built *c.* 1230, it is a long lofty hall, with narrow E.E. lancet windows – E.E. architecture at its simple best. A tremendous 18th-century buttress supports the gabled south end (ritually the east end of the church): a little wooden bellcote crowns the north end. And here the doorway leads out into the Cloister Court: the green lawn, the enclosing walls, the doorway to the (destroyed) chapter house – all clearly indicate the monastic pattern; beyond, the foundations of the monastic church, carefully preserved in the sprucely mown grass, tell us a great deal of the size and splendour of the original church. To the north, the lay brothers' quarters are largely preserved, and contain an interesting museum.

Inside, in the thickness of the wall on the right, a doorway leads into a narrow staircase separated from the nave by an arcade of slender Purbeck marble shafts, lit by tiny lancets in the outside wall, and so up to the pulpit, from which originally the brethren were read to during meals. The pulpit (a harmonious 19th-century rebuilding) stands on its original protruding base, its stonework adorned with sumptuous foliage carving. It is altogether a beautifully furnished interior, with a Martin Travers plaque of the Virgin and Child above the Altar, a 17th-century recumbent monument to the oddly-named Margaret Do, and a number of memorials of more recent date to members of the Montagu family.

Christchurch Priory

Christchurch Priory stands superb on a spur of rising ground overlooking the little harbour where the Avon and the Stour meet. At the S. end of the wide High Street a narrow street of ancient houses leads up to the great church lying full length in its churchyard – and what a length! The great scale of the building is overpowering: Lady Chapel, chancel, transept, nave, porch, west tower. And two things stand out: the transept and the porch. Lady Chapel and chancel are Perp – but this transept (despite its Perp window) is Norman, and the stair turret at the N.E. corner with its tiers of intersecting arcading, blind arcading and trellis patterning, is one of the most spectacular examples

Christchurch Priory: the Norman staircase turret of the north transept

of Norman decoration anywhere. The nave is Norman too (despite its E.E. clerestory), and the tower is latest Perp. But the monumental porch, loftier than the aisle, is E.E. Long, tunnel-like and vaulted, it leads into the nave.

Christchurch was originally a collegiate church of secular canons, first established by Ralph Flambard under William Rufus – though a Saxon church of some importance existed here before that. The Norman work must date from Flambard's time. In 1150 it became an Augustinian priory, and so continued until the Dissolution, when it became the parish church; indeed the nave had always been parochial. The view of the interior from the W. end of this nave tells us of its building history – first the Norman nave, plain and austere with its round arches, spacious triforium, E.E. clerestory; then the Norman crossing. And beyond that, and above the stone screen, as though seen through a picture frame, is the Perp chancel, with its lierne vault, terminating in a magnificent early-14th-century stone reredos. This chancel was rebuilt towards the end of the 15th century, after the fall of the central tower and spire.

The crossing is disappointingly cluttered with the choir stalls and other trappings of the nave altar, which impinge upon the screen itself. But steps lead up through the screen into the chancel

Christchurch: the Norman crossing and the Perp screen, with the Perp chancel beyond

– into another world. Light streams in through the Perp windows upon a glorious array of early-16th-century stalls of black oak (with a sumptuous set of misericords), and more steps lead up to the High Altar and the 14th-century stone Jesse reredos, which survives from the earlier chancel. Here Jesse lies above the altar, supported on either side by Solomon and Daniel; the central panel above represents the Adoration of the Magi; above and around elaborate canopied niches stand empty. And above the reredos a recent mural of the Ascension, an effective and characteristic work by Hans Feibusch, brings colour to this E. end. From the lierne vault decorative pendants, close to the wall, recall those at the cathedral at Oxford, and on the N. side of the sanctuary the towering Salisbury

Chantry adds a further festive note.

But this is not all: steep steps lead down to the aisles, and round to the eastern chapels and Lady Chapel. Here there is more Perp work, a little earlier than the chancel: the stone reredos, bereft of its statues, the large E. window, filled with colourful glass by O'Connor, 16th-century tombs, crocketed arcading to adorn the walls, all combine to make this chapel, concealed from view until the last moment, both a surprise and a delight.

And all around, wonderful chantries and tombs – the Draper Chantry, the Berkeley Chantry, the Harys Chantry, in addition to the supreme Salisbury Chantry – make this eastern end of the church a remarkable foil for the austere Norman nave. And there are interesting monuments everywhere: Flaxman's touching group of Viscountess Fitzharris (1815), with the young mother teaching her small sons, stands in the chancel; under the tower is the grand sculpture to Shelley by Weekes (1854): 'To the memory of Percy Bysshe Shelley, POET, born at Field Place in the County of Sussex August 1792, drowned by the upsetting of his boat in the gulf of Spezzia 1822.'

Nothing remains of cloisters or monastic buildings, but there are pleasant walks all round the church – with an unforgettable view of it from the Town Bridge, standing above the gaunt remains of the Norman castle, or rising above the assembly of small boats tied up in the harbour.

Pamber Priory: authentic Benedictine simplicity

Pamber Priory

Remote, and close to deep woodlands, with only a farm for company, Pamber was founded *c.* 1130, as a cell of the Benedictine Abbey of Cerisy-à-Foret, and dissolved as an alien house in 1414. A square, stumpy, Norman tower, crowned with a low pyramid, stands above the crossing; transepts have gone, and only a fragment of the nave wall stands beside the churchyard path. Within, this crossing is spacious and awe-inspiring, with tall Norman arches, blocked up to S. W. and N. – but opening to the E. into a grand, austere, but extremely beautiful E.E. chancel, with long narrow lancets all around and, above the low arches which originally led into transept chapels, small circular windows. The great size of this chancel is, at first sight, a surprise: it has survived to serve as the parish church of a small scattered community. Daylight pours in through clear glass windows on

distinguished E.E. features: there is a trefoil-headed piscina, a 15th-century screen, a 12th-century coffin lid with floriated cross, and the impressive 14th-century wooden effigy of a knight, wonderfully preserved, incarcerated now and padlocked against marauders. Dignified and imposing, the whole building breathes the air of authentic Benedictine simplicity and detachment.

Romsey Abbey

Entering Romsey from the E. or from the S., there is a great moment as the road crosses the River Test, when there is a sudden and unexpected glimpse of Broadlands, of Henry Holland's Ionic portico framed in trees, and the river running by. It is an idyllic picture, as suddenly removed as it was suddenly vouchsafed, and we must continue battling with the traffic as we enter the town. But it is a glimpse which should not be missed: Broadlands, home of Palmerston, and more recently of Mountbatten, and still the home of his family (his grandson is Lord Romsey), presides over Romsey as the Abbey did in the Middle Ages. The centre of the town is the Market Place, triangular in shape, with Matthew Noble's statue of

Romsey Abbey: the Norman nave arcade

Palmerston (1867): streets lead off in all directions. There are few buildings of special note, but Romsey has its charms. And the Abbey stands to the N., just behind the Market Place, but invisible from it. A street called The Abbey leads through the arch of the Victorian-Tudor gatehouse attached (rather oddly) to the Congregational Church, into the Precinct. Here delightful but modest 18th-century houses, occupying the site of the monastic buildings, accompany the church. It is the greatest nuns' church to have survived in England.

Romsey Abbey was founded for Benedictine nuns by Edward the Elder in 907, and refounded sixty years later by King Edgar. As we shall see,

there are still relics of this Saxon church preserved; but the church which we see today was begun *c.* 1120, and completed *c.* 1230. At the Dissolution it was purchased by the town for £100, to serve as the parish church, and so survives today.

We must walk round the church, which stands square, squat and compact: a longer nave, a shorter chancel, transepts with small apsidal chapels, Norman windows everywhere – except for long lancets at the west end, Geometrical windows at the E., and occasional Perp insertions elsewhere. The Lady Chapel, which extended beyond the choir, has disappeared; there is a squat central tower, with a low wooden bellchamber added in the 17th century.

Inside, Romsey is one of the most splendid Norman churches in England: nave and chancel are broad, lofty, spacious, and all of a piece. The rhythm of the grand Norman arcades is solemn and majestic, with lofty triforium and lofty clerestory above lofty arcade: there is variety in the rhythm – in the nave, between the first two bays, a giant circular pier extends right up into the triforium; elsewhere shafted piers extend into the triforium. There are scalloped capitals and zigzag ornament everywhere; the aisles are vaulted: a timber roof encloses choir, transepts, nave. As we stand at the W. end we can absorb it all – and note that the three western bays of the nave are E.E. (*c.* 1230): by the time the nave was completed, the style had changed; but the change is harmonious, the general rhythm the same. And at the E. end, above the High Altar, the Norman windows and Norman triforium have been replaced by two large Geometrical windows of the early 14th century.

Moving E., there is in the N. transept a rare early-16th-century painted reredos above the altar of St Lawrence: in the lower half Our Lord is seen rising from the tomb, angels swinging censers in His honour, Roman soldiers standing behind aghast. And in the left-hand corner is the donor, an Abbess, no doubt the Abbess of the day; and above a row of saints stand against an early Renaissance painted background. The N. choir aisle becomes the ambulatory, and here there are chapels: two arches originally led into the Lady Chapel which was destroyed at the Dissolution – both now contain altars. In the left-hand chapel there are fragments of 12th-century wall painting, and it was here that during restoration work in 1976 there was discovered, walled up, a fossilized rose, the oldest botanical specimen in Europe. In the S.E. chapel there is, above the altar, the Saxon carved stone Crucifixion, originally in an outside wall, but brought inside during the 19th century, and framed in a fragment of a Perp screen to serve as a reredos. It is a beautiful and moving piece of sculpture – of Christ on the cross, with Our Lady and St John at his side, with two Roman soldiers, and two attendant angels above. Nearby, above the High Altar, is a sensitively coloured bas relief of the Madonna and Child, by Martin Travers.

In the S. transept, and at the W. end of the nave, are the most interesting monuments: an early-13th-century Purbeck marble effigy of a lady wearing a wimple lies under a 14th-century crocketed recess – her identity unknown; nearby

The Romsey Rood

is the big wall monument of John St Barbe (*c.* 1650), with his and his wife's busts above, his children grouped below: the St Barbes were the original owners of Broadlands. In the floor beneath, under a restrained and simple slab, lie the remains of Lord Mountbatten.

There are three notable Palmerston monuments at the W. end: the widow of the 1st Viscount (1769) by Carter; the 2nd Viscount (1802) by Flaxman, and Sir William Temple (1856) by Thomas; the 3rd Viscount, the Prime Minister, is buried in Westminster Abbey. And above hang the flags given by Lord Mountbatten: one, his personal standard as Supreme Allied Commander in South-East Asia, and the other flown in Delhi when he was Viceroy of India.

The two doors in the S. aisle led into the cloisters, of which no trace remains – except for one most important relic. In the corner of the transept wall, close to the E. doorway, is the Romsey Rood, a Saxon sculpture (early 11th century?) showing Our Lord on the cross, with the hand of God Almighty pointing to Him from a cloud. It stands here, under a later wooden canopy, where nuns passed daily on their way – a poignant reminder of those distant times.

DIOCESE OF
WORCESTER

Worcester Cathedral

THAT VIEW OF WORCESTER: the Cathedral with
its bold central tower, its west front, across the
River Severn – and a cricket match in progress on
the smooth newly-mown meadows in the foreground. It is the first match of the season: Worcestershire versus the Australians. The view is familiar, a harbinger of summer. Worcester Cathedral
is superb in its position, serene and self-assured.
On either side are the houses of the city, the public
buildings, the warehouses by the river, the Severn
Bridge, the railway bridge. There are the towers
and spires of the city churches, and, invisible from
here, of course, the narrow streets and thorough-
fares of the town.

The see of Worcester was founded in 680.
St Oswald, Bishop of Worcester, founded the
Benedictine monastery in 983, and St Wulstan,
Bishop at the time of the Conquest, rebuilt the
cathedral in the late 11th century. Of this there
are some remains. Wulstan was canonized in 1203,
and King John was buried here in 1216. In 1224
Bishop William de Blois began its rebuilding, and
this continued until the end of the 14th century.
This is the Cathedral which we see today.

We were surveying the Cathedral across the
river. The long nave roof is plain and austere – no
pinnacles, no flying buttresses; there are transepts,
with the same plain roofline, and eastern transepts
beyond; there is the long high roof of the refectory
(College Hall) on the south side, again austere and
unadorned. All the decoration is reserved for the
tower. Completed in 1374, it is one of the great
triumphs of the 14th century, when the Dec style
merged with the Perp: in the lower stages there
are long narrow arcades; but, above, the bell openings are richly traceried, and surrounded by a
wealth of carved panelling and niches for saints;
then an open traceried parapet leads up to the tall

crocketed pinnacles at the four corners. The west
front is ornamented too, with an elaborate traceried window, and an imposing doorway; but this is
all Victorian (1865). We must cross the bridge and
enter the city.

'Worcester,' writes James Lees-Milne, in his
Shell Guide to Worcestershire (1964), 'was repeatedly
sacked by Romans, Danes, Saxons, Welsh and
Roundheads. Though it escaped German bombing in the last War, so much of the old city has
been cleared away to make way for car parks and
commercial development of the sort to be found
in all post-war industrial towns, that the visitor
may have the impression that there has been yet
another invasion . . .' This is only too true: a new
road rushes through the heart of the city; there is
a roundabout close to the east end of the Cathedral, and hideous new buildings, out of scale
and out of sympathy with their surroundings, have
gone up. The heart of Worcester has been destroyed by the city planners. But if we can make
our way through all this, we can reach College
Green, on the south side of the Cathedral, and
entering by the medieval Edgar Tower find some
peace. Here, perhaps, a slight disappointment may
assail us. The Cathedral was extensively restored
in the 19th century, and the hard, somewhat mechanical finish of the exterior, the rows of triple
lancet windows, and many other details, may seem
somewhat forbidding. But come inside.

The Norman door under College Hall (the
monastic refectory) leads into the cloisters – a
distinguished rebuilding of the late 14th and early
15th century of the Norman cloisters (of which
traces remain) – and so into the Cathedral itself.
The first impression is of the great width and
spaciousness of the aisles, then of the remarkable
unity of the whole building. Though the rebuilding

Worcester Cathedral across the River Severn

began with the east end in 1224, and the nave a century later (and the south side, in fact, is later than the north), there is a wonderful unity of design throughout: we can watch the E.E. work in the chancel merging almost imperceptibly with the Dec work in the nave. There is one exception: the two western bays of the nave survive from the earlier church, and are Transitional work of c. 1180, with round and pointed arches. But turning east there is the continuous rhythm of Dec arcades with many-shafted piers, carrying on the whole length of the church to the east end.

We make our way up the nave: unfortunately our progress is impeded by the 'nave sanctuary'. A nave altar is understandable and permissible – but this is an enormous erection: cheap wooden steps lead onto the platform which extends from one side of the nave to the other; cheap wooden furniture of poor design, the usual 'kitchen table' altar, a semi-circle of choir stalls behind, an organ – it is an extraordinary affair. It seems incredible that this glorious nave, never intended for such an arrangement, should be filled with such miserable clutter. The Victorian marble pulpit, designed by Scott and carved by James Forsyth, is magnificent:

Worcester Cathedral: ABOVE *the Norman crypt;* OPPOSITE *the chancel seen from the crossing*

passing this we can make our way to the crossing through the south aisle. Although the transepts were rebuilt in the 14th century, it is interesting to note here more relics of the Norman cathedral. And in the south transept we can descend into the crypt.

The crypt is one of the great thrills of Worcester, and dates from Wulstan's time. The rows of slender Norman pillars with cushion capitals extend like a plantation of trees, the low groined vault spreading above us. The crypt is seven bays long, and four bays wide, and apsidal at the east end: the Norman cathedral was evidently apsidal.

Steps lead up into the chancel. Scott, with his passion for open vistas, removed the stone pulpitum at his restoration (1864–74), and replaced it with his open iron screen – made, like the screens in the chancel, by Skidmore. Mercifully, it has survived – unlike those at Salisbury and Hereford – and with its delicate tracery and foliage, its canopied figures, its marble base, is a work of great originality. The chancel is richer than the nave, with Purbeck marble shafts, a more elaborate triforium, more lavish decoration everywhere; but it is of the same general design. Here there are splendid Victorian furnishings: choir stalls by Scott, with canopies at the west end, iron screens otherwise, an elaborate organ on either side, and a bishop's throne: only the misericords are ancient. The stone pulpit is interesting Gothic survival work of 1642. And here we reach the most moving object in the Cathedral: the tomb of King John. John had a special affection for Worcester: he died at Newark (1216), and by a special codicil to his will directed that he was to be buried here, between Worcester's two saints, Oswald and Wulstan. Here his tomb stands, with the earliest royal effigy in England, the king lying with the heads of the two saints close to his. The tomb chest is 15th century, adorned with the leopards of England. The High Altar, with Scott's sumptuous reredos, makes an effective Victorian climax to the east end; and on the right of the sanctuary is the Chantry of Prince Arthur, elder brother of Henry VIII, who died at Ludlow in 1502. It is gloriously Perp, with traceried windows, pinnacled parapet and a vaulted interior with elaborate reredos and tomb.

The Victorian restoration of the Cathedral began in 1857, at the hands of a little-known local architect, A. E. Perkins. To him is due the entire reconstruction of the east wall: here he removed a large Perp window, and replaced it with the five

lancets which are now such a familiar feature of the Cathedral. They are so convincing and so successful that it is hard to believe that they are not original. The whole retrochoir, with its eastern transepts, is extremely beautiful: the long lancets (many renewed by Perkins), the E.E. arcading, Perkins' rich sculpture, are undoubtedly satisfying, and Hardman's excellent glass adds colour to the pale stone of the walls and the dark grey of the marble shafts.

The Cathedral abounds in monuments – to Bishops, Deans and dignitaries, and to the nobility and gentry of the county. In the retrochoir, the seated figure of Mrs Digby (1825) is by Chantrey, the recumbent tombs of the 4th Lord Lyttelton (1878) and the 1st Earl of Dudley (1888) are by Forsyth: they were both much associated with the Victorian restoration of the Cathedral. In the north transept is a grand monument to Bishop Hough (1743) by Roubiliac; he was ejected from the Presidency of Magdalen College by James II – the scene portrayed on the sarcophagus; in the nave are many more. Of special charm is the Beauchamp tomb, near the north door, showing Sir John and Lady Beauchamp (*c.* 1400), their heads resting on the Beauchamp swan; the tomb is wonderfully preserved and coloured. Nearby, in the north aisle, a window and a tablet commemorate Sir Edward Elgar (d. 1934), who was born at Broadheath; and just inside the west door an inscription in the floor honours the memory of the 1st Earl Baldwin, native of Worcestershire, three times Prime Minister (d. 1947).

The chapter house, approached from the east walk of the cloisters, is of interest as the earliest round chapter house in England. Built between 1120 and 1125, it was re-cased externally in the 14th century, when the Perp windows were inserted, but inside there is Norman wall arcading and a plain Norman central column to support the simple vault. It is the precursor of the celebrated Gothic chapter houses at Wells, Salisbury, Southwell and elsewhere – a style of chapter house found only in England.

In the Epilogue to *John Inglesant*, J. H. Shorthouse describes how Valentine Lee met Inglesant after the Civil War at Worcester. Deep in conversation, they walked down the steps below the west front of the Cathedral, took the ferry across the river and walked for some time in the Chapter Meadows, discussing the religious passions of the times and watching the evening sun descending towards the Malvern Hills. As they spoke, 'the sun, which was just setting behind the distant hills, shone with dazzling splendour for a moment on the towers and spires of the city across the placid water. Behind this fair vision were dark rain clouds, before which gloomy background it stood in fairy radiance and light. For a moment it seemed a glorious city, bathed in life and hope, full of happy people who thronged its streets and bridge, and the margin of its gentle stream. But it was "breve gaudium". Then the sunset faded, and the ethereal vision vanished, and the landscape lay dark and chill.

' "The sun is set," Mr Inglesant said cheerfully, "but it will rise again. Let us go home." '

Leaving the Cathedral by the north porch and descending the steps towards the river, we can visualize the scene. The Malvern Hills are there all right. But in the foreground stand blocks of high-rise flats.

Great Malvern Priory

'The wild country of the Beacons,' wrote James Lees-Milne, 'seems to command England and Wales, and makes Malvern a principality, rather like San Marino in Italy.' The Malvern Hills are indeed a world apart: to see them from afar never fails to arouse a sense of excitement and of awe; to reach Malvern itself is always a thrill. Great Malvern was a mere village until the 18th century, grouped around the priory church: the spa waters were discovered in the 17th century, but the spa town did not begin to develop for another hundred years. The railway arrived in 1858, and prosperity set in. There are earlier stuccoed villas, and roads and roads of large Victorian houses set in gardens lugubrious with cedar trees and pines; there is Malvern College and Malvern Girls' School, there are prep schools and nursing homes, boarding houses and hotels. And in the midst of all this stands Malvern Priory.

The date of its foundation is uncertain: it was a Benedictine house, and Aldwin was the first Prior, and received a charter from William I. Building began soon after 1085. The church, standing in its churchyard planted with evergreens on the slope of the hill, is outwardly all Perp – with lofty clerestory windows in nave and chancel, embattled parapets and pinnacles, a north transept and embattled aisles, a two-storeyed porch (rebuilt in

Great Malvern Priory: the Norman nave arcade with a Perp clerestory, the Perp chancel beyond

1894) and the sumptuous central tower, inspired by Gloucester. This is 15th century, with carved and panelled sides, bell openings under ogee gables – all crowned as at Gloucester with open-work battlements and tall square pinnacles.

The interior is wide and spacious – and here in the nave are the Norman arcades of the original building, with low round arches on plain circular columns. Above and all around the grand 15th-century church has been grafted on – the great

Perp crossing arches to carry the tower, and the Perp chancel beyond. The medieval glass makes an immediate impression: next to York and King's Chapel no great church is so resplendent. The east window is of *c.* 1440, with rows of figures of apostles and benefactors, the Crucifixion, and the Annunciation and Coronation of the Virgin. The west window is a little later, and although partly fragmentary is glorious with its rows of saints and martyrs. The great window in the north transept was given by Henry VII *c.* 1501, and is devoted to the life of the Virgin: with its vivid blues and golds, this is perhaps the most striking of all. The figures of King and Queen and Prince Arthur of Wales are to be seen in the base. But the aisle and clerestory windows in the chancel are nearly all filled with glorious glass. The clerestory windows in the nave are quite different: they are by Francis Eginton, and late 18th century, brilliant in colour and all heraldic.

But the glass is not all: Malvern is very rich in medieval tiles. Indeed they are a rare Malvern speciality; made nearby (the kiln was discovered in 1830), they adorn the sanctuary and the screen walls of the chancel. There are a hundred designs – biblical, heraldic, symbolic, and with their soft colouring they are a special pleasure. They date from the mid 15th century. There is also a very fine set of stalls in the chancel, with two tiers on either side, with well preserved misericords. And all around the church there are handsome monuments, mostly of the 18th and 19th centuries – to members of neighbouring families, or persons who retired to Malvern or came to take the waters. The Victorian mosaic reredos to the High Altar was designed by Blomfield, and made by Powell & Co. (1884).

At the Dissolution the church was bought by the parish: it has lost its Lady Chapel and its south transept, but is otherwise one of the small handful of monastic churches to have survived more or less intact. No monastic buildings, however, survive, other than the (much restored) gatehouse to the S.W. of the church, which divides the early-19th-century Gothick stucco butcher's shop from the mid-Victorian Tudor Abbey Hotel beyond. And from here, and from the heights above, there is the wonderful panoramic view across the flat lands bordering the Severn – to the Cotswolds beyond.

Little Malvern Priory

The approach from Upton-on-Severn is wonderful: first the long line of the Malvern Hills; then, past Welland, as the main road (A4104) begins to climb, Little Malvern comes in sight, set as it were on a shelf of the hills – here well wooded, with the upper heights behind bare and rugged: an old church with a pyramid-crowned tower, lofty chan-

cel with ruined aisles – and an ancient house beside it. Unlike Great Malvern, Little Malvern is sequestered, rural, little known, little visited. Motorists on the main road change gear, and pass on, to Malvern Wells or Ledbury. But for those who stop there are great rewards.

The Benedictine Priory was founded here *c.* 1150, an offshoot of Worcester. The first church was Norman, but little Norman work survives. The lower part of the tower is Dec, the upper is Perp, with elaborate panel work surrounding the windows; the tile-hung cap is post-Dissolution. In 1480 Bishop Alcock (then of Worcester) in a celebrated visitation found 'the great ruin of the church and place', and discharged the Prior and monks 'by reason of their demerits'. He proceeded to rebuild the church and 'the place of their lodging': after two years under correction at Gloucester the monks returned to their rebuilt church and house. It is the chancel, shorn of its aisles, transepts, chapels and nave, which we see today.

The chancel is narrow and lofty: there is a six-light east window, long three-light windows to north and south. Blocked-up arches led into the chancel aisles; a Perp screen, with remains of the rood beam, separates the present nave from the choir; there are stalls with badly damaged misericords, fragments of a 14th-century tomb, 15th-century tiles and a simply furnished altar in the sanctuary. In the east window there are important fragments of 15th-century glass, depicting members of the then Royal family: Elizabeth Woodville, wife of Edward IV is recognizable, but the King's figure is headless. There are other fragments in a north window, and on the walls there are highly decorative hatchments of the Russell and Berington families who came into possession of the monastic buildings at the Dissolution, and whose descendants still live at Little Malvern Court. Here the Prior's Hall, embodied in this enchanting 16th-century (and later) house, is open to the public on certain afternoons in summer. The Russells, and their descendants the Beringtons, have always been Recusant, and Mass has been said in their chapel in the house continually since before the Reformation.

And not the least reward is the view from the churchyard – the sweeping prospect across the Vale of Severn, across villages and orchards and lush pastureland, towards Bredon and the distant Cotswolds.

Little Malvern Priory: the church surveys the wide prospect of the Vale of Severn

Pershore Abbey

Orchards galore, and Pershore plums: the River Avon winds its way among lush meadows, and the little town is one of Georgian elegance. Brick houses, stucco houses, sash windows, Venetian windows, pillared porches, fanlights, balconies and verandahs line the streets, and at the south end a 14th-century bridge crosses the river and leads into open countryside. To the west the abbey church stands amid spreading lawns, its grand tower with dunce-capped pinnacles presiding over all.

It is indeed a grand and noble rump: the nave was destroyed at the Dissolution, and the north transept collapsed in the 17th century; enormous buttresses to shore up tower and crossing were built in 1913. Miraculously it survives. Approaching from the S.E., from the town, none of this is apparent. There is the great mass of the south transept, the longer arm of the chancel – elegant, embattled, apsidal, with flying buttresses to support clerestory and roof, with lancet windows here, later traceried windows in the aisle – the whole Gothic glory crowned with the 14th-century tower.

Inside, enormous Norman pillars uphold the crossing (*c.* 1100); the south transept is Norman too – as is what remains of the north. Above the crossing arches the early-14th-century arcading of the lowest stage of the tower appears, with galleries and small windows; and the eastern arch leads into the choir. This is the great glory of Pershore, built (or rebuilt) in the early 13th century. The arches rise from clustered columns with capitals of stiff-leaf foliage; above, slender shafts enclose a gallery, part triforium walk, part clerestory composed of narrow lancet windows. The east end is apsidal: above the slightly loftier eastern arch there is a

The 13th-century lierne vault of Pershore Abbey

blind triple lancet; and, rising from the corbels, the most elegant lierne vault, a little later than the choir itself, but blending with it in perfect harmony (*c.* 1290).

The original Lady Chapel beyond was demolished at the Dissolution (1539); a small apsidal chapel was added in 1847. There is an imposing Norman font, and there are two Elizabethan or Jacobean monuments to the Haselwood family; most of the furnishings are Victorian and harmonious. Pershore is the magnificent fragment of an important Benedictine abbey, originally founded by King Oswald *c.* 689.

DIOCESE OF
YORK

York Minster

THE EAST COAST RAILWAY LINE to Scotland is most obliging, architecturally most rewarding – with Peterborough, York and Durham, three of our greatest cathedrals, all visible from the train. Approaching York from the south, the train slows down to arrive at the Northern capital: the towers of the Minster now appear, now disappear, among the houses and buildings and roof-tops of the city; but then, as it pursues its way north, it seems to circumnavigate both city and minster in a great sweep, and west front, north side, chapter house and all three towers can be seen to advantage from the carriage window. But for us today it is to alight here. And York Station is the first thrill of our visit – almost a cathedral in itself, of long nave and aisles built on a curve, with rows of iron pillars, and all vaulted in iron and glass. Emerging from the station, the Minster appears before us, and, accompanied by the grassy banks of the city walls, we can make our way towards it, cross the Ouse by Lendal Bridge, and stand spellbound before the west front. Then we can walk along under the very shadow of the south side, absorbing the enormous mass of the church – or explore the maze of narrow streets which come right up to the south transept, gazing up all the time at the

York Minster from the north: the Seven Sisters window, the chapter house and the central tower

pinnacles and flying buttresses which dominate all the little houses round.

York, or Eboracum, was a Roman station of great importance: here in 306 Constantine was proclaimed Emperor. After the departure of the Romans at the end of the 4th century darkness descended; but in 625 Paulinus was consecrated Bishop, and in 627 King Edwin was baptized by Paulinus, and the first church built. Nothing is known of this church, nor of the Saxon minster which took its place. But in 1070 the Norman cathedral was begun by the first Norman archbishop, Thomas of Bayeux, and of this the crypt survives. The Minster which we see today was begun in the early 13th century under Archbishop Walter de Gray, and took 250 years to complete.

The streets of the medieval city press so hard upon the Minster that it is difficult to stand back and grasp its great size: the thing to do is to walk round the east end, pausing on the way to admire the Perp retrochoir with its skyline of pinnacles, the unusual open trellis screens which mask the recessed clerestory windows, and the enormous traceried east window itself, whose ogee frame soars to a tapering finial set in a gable bristling with crocketed pinnacles – then follow the street round to Monk Bar and ascend the city walls. From the wall between Monk Bar and Bootham Bar is the finest view obtainable – of the full length of the north side of the Minster. From here we can appreciate the changing styles of Gothic architecture: the 13th-century transepts, the nave begun soon after and completed c. 1350, the chapter house built in the first years of the 14th century, the chancel and retrochoir completed c. 1400, the central tower of the early 15th century, the west towers completed c. 1475. We can descend at Bootham Bar, and make our way back to the west front.

This frontispiece is spectacular: the two towers completed what had been begun a century before – a 'screen' front, of three doorways, heavy sculptured buttresses, and windows filled with Dec tracery, geometrical in the lower windows, curvilinear elsewhere, the central window vast and surrounded with a wealth of arcading rising to the centre gable. The two towers, so elaborate and crowned with a lavish array of pinnacles and ornament, are a remarkable contrast to the severity of the crossing tower. And so we enter the nave.

York is the largest of all the medieval English cathedrals, and the nave is of prodigious size – lofty and wide, its arcades and aisles vast. Three features will at once impress the visitor: first, this vast scale; then the marvellous whiteness, the incredible lightness of the whole interior. Purists criticize it because the vault is made of wood, not stone. But who would know? This white wooden vault glows with hundreds of gilded bosses – and the eye is carried on to the chancel beyond the screen, beyond the organ, right on to the east window far away – the same amazing vault glowing with gilded bosses. And, above all, the glass will impress: every window is filled with the most sumptuous display of medieval glass; the daylight pours into this glistening interior through windows of the most brilliant golds and reds and blues. York is pre-eminent for its medieval glass.

We stand at the crossing, under the lantern tower. The nave is Dec – these transepts E.E., the work of Archbishop de Gray, whose tomb stands in the eastern aisle of the south transept. Once again, the scale is tremendous – and in the north transept is the celebrated Five Sisters window, five lancets of equal height and austere simplicity, filled with grisaille glass of sombre beauty (c. 1250) which casts its solemn spell upon this immense Gothic space. In the N.E. corner double doors lead into a lofty vestibule, and so into the chapter house.

Like everything else at York, this chapter house is of overwhelming size: begun at the very end of the 13th century, it belongs to the family of octagonal chapter houses which are so peculiar an English invention; but here there is no central pillar, and the soaring vault is of wood, delicately painted by Willement in 1845. The windows are filled with grisaille glass of c. 1300, and beneath the windows stone canopied seats for the chapter adorn every wall.

The chancel is like a great Gothic casket, with light pouring in through traceried windows in clerestory and aisles, bright with medieval glass, on a grandly furnished sanctuary and choir. The stalls are of c. 1830, by Sir Robert Smirke, to replace the ones destroyed in the fire of 1829; the sanctuary furnishings are more recent, by Walter Tapper, Sir Charles Peers and Sir Albert Richardson, decorative and delightful. And everywhere in the aisles and retrochoir there is a wealth of monuments, ranging from medieval tombs to figures of bewigged or mitred 18th-century archbishops, and smaller marble wall monuments to other dignitaries or local gentry. Grinling Gibbons,

York Minster: the high vault of the south-east transept

York Minster: the chancel and the east window

Nicholas Stone, Bird, Rysbrack, Cheere, Westmacott: the list of notable sculptors is impressive. On the south side of the south aisle is the early-14th-century Zouche Chapel, a relic of the earlier chancel; opposite, a stairway leads down to the Norman crypt – all that survives of the Norman Minster – with Romanesque pillars with charmingly carved capitals. And both here and elsewhere – at the east end, and in the transepts – there are beautifully furnished chapels.

But it is the medieval glass which is the supreme pleasure of the interior. The grisaille glass in the Five Sisters, and in the windows of the chapter house, has already been mentioned, and reference has been made to the brilliant windows in the nave and chancel. The great expanses of glass in the east and west windows, and in the long narrow traceried windows in the chancel transepts, constitute some of the largest medieval windows in the world. At York there was in the Middle Ages a flourishing school of glass painters, and these vast windows must have been designed to display their glass. The preservation of this glass, indeed the preservation of the whole Minster, in the Civil War, was due to one man, the Parliamentary General, Lord Fairfax: it is to him that we owe our

York: 13th-century head of Christ high up in the south transept

pleasure today; no other cathedral interior in England can dazzle us so completely as York.

But York has had its disasters and its misfortunes. In 1829 a madman called Jonathan Martin, an artist of striking originality, deliberately set fire to the choir: ten years later a workman's candle accidentally set fire to the nave; in 1984 the roof of the south transept caught fire in a thunderstorm and was completely destroyed. The work of restoration is now proceeding. Indeed, it seems, York's wooden vaults have three times been its undoing. In 1966 it was discovered that the crossing piers were sinking under the colossal weight of the central tower: a great engineering work was begun, and the foundations were renewed in steel and concrete. All this may be seen in the undercroft. So York remains, the last medieval cathedral to be completed in England before the Reformation, and amazingly preserved.

St John the Evangelist in the west window: the medieval glass is the supreme pleasure of the interior

Beverley Minster

Until 1980 a visit to Beverley from the S. was a matter of great excitement – a short sea trip, as it were, by the car ferry across the Humber: from New Holland to Hull Pier the ferries plied. The sea breezes, the spray, and then the landing – the green telephone kiosks (for the City of Hull alone in England maintains its own telephone system, cheaper, more efficient than British Telecom) – all convinced the visitor that he had landed on foreign soil. Now a journey across that magnificent white elephant, the Humber Bridge, is almost equally exciting – with the tremendous views up and downstream, Lincolnshire on one side of the estuary, Yorkshire on the other. And a short drive leads to Beverley, with the twin towers of the Minster sailing above the red pantiles of the little town.

Strictly speaking, Beverley Minster is not a monastic church. Like Wimborne, Ripon and Southwell, it was founded as a collegiate church for secular canons. Like Ripon (in the W. Riding) and Southwell (in distant Nottinghamshire), Beverley acted as a kind of subsidiary cathedral here in the E. Riding, an extra 'bishopstool' in the great archdiocese of York. As a former major collegiate church, as a minster of great importance, it is included in this book. Indeed, as one of the greatest and grandest medieval churches in England – grander than many cathedrals – it must have a place here.

For centuries Beverley has led its own forgotten life, cut off from the outside world by the Humber and the North Sea, far removed from the main traffic routes to the W. Yet this was not always so:

Beverley: the Minster from the south-west

Beverley Minster: The vista from the nave to the crossing and chancel

the great Minster, the splendid parish church of St Mary's, the medieval gateway called the North Bar, all speak of a medieval importance which has long waned. Beverley grew rich on wool, and on the trade of its then important port on the River Hull. But from the 16th century Hull (or Kingston-upon-Hull), standing in its all-important position on the Humber itself, eclipsed

Beverley. As the county town of the E. Riding, where the local gentry had their elegant town houses, Beverley pursued its own secluded life under the shadow of the Minster. It is a delightful town.

St John of Beverley, 4th Bishop of York, founded a church or a monastery here *c.* 690. But all was swept away in the Danish raids. King Athelstan founded the college of secular canons on its site *c.* 935. The present Minster was begun *c.* 1230, and took a century to build – a century which saw E.E. develop into Dec, and Dec into Perp. Stripped of its collegiate status at the Dissolution, Beverley became merely a parish church; yet, miraculously, it has survived. The Saturday Market is the centre of the town: here stands the Market Cross, a delectable little building of 1711, with Roman Doric columns, and elegant urns surrounding an ogee-shaped dome crowned with a lantern. In all directions streets, wide or narrow, lined with Georgian houses, lead to more architectural pleasures beyond. It is a narrow street, called Highgate, that leads to the Minster, which stands in strange detachment on the southern edge of the town, with fields and trees and little terrace houses to keep it company. Here at the end of Highgate, framed by the little houses of this modest street, stands the N. porch.

Beverley Minster is a giant. This lofty, pin-nacled, Perp porch betokens no ordinary important church: the soaring height, the flying buttresses, the large traceried Dec windows, the twin W. towers to the right, the crossing with low central tower and wide extending transept to the left – all this is taken in. Turning to the right, the W. front itself, the twin towers, the enormous Perp frontispiece with 15th-century traceried window, richly carved buttresses, panelled and arcaded walls and canopied niches, stands supreme. On the S. side the pattern is repeated: Dec windows in the nave, lancets in the transept and chancel, a second, narrower, E. transept, and then the E. end. The impact is tremendous. Beverley is of cathedral size – but larger, grander, more magn-ificent than many a cathedral.

Inside, the impression is the same: there is nothing for it but to retire to the W. end, sit down, and absorb this superb nave – ten bays long, with towering arches, intricate triforium, lofty clere-story, and above all this the even rhythm of the long, long, vault. The eye is carried on to Gilbert Scott's organ screen, and to the same rhythm of

vaults and bays beyond. The whole church appears very much of one piece – yet we know that this western half is much later in date than the choir and transepts. Yet that strong conservative English instinct completed the nave here according to the design of the architect of the chancel; only minor modifications may be noted. But it is the homogen-eity which will impress and, with its purity, will overwhelm. Moving to the crossing, the double-aisled transepts will overwhelm too – with their exquisite E.E. details, of lancets and, as in the nave aisles, of wall arcading. The remarkable Victorian glass – Hardman's dark blues and purples in the S. transept – will also impress.

Entering the chancel it is the same rhythm again – but here there are lancets in the clerestory, instead of the traceried windows in the nave; and there is greater use of Purbeck marble. There is a wonderful array of early-15th-century canopied stalls (with a magnificent set of misericords), and in the E. window – a 15th-century Perp insertion – a gathering together of fragments of medieval glass. On the right of the High Altar stands the pre-Conquest stone chair – the Fridstool – a relic of the earliest church; on the S. side of the sanctuary the oak sedilia is 14th century; on the N. side is the Percy Tomb. This, probably the most distinguished example of a Dec tomb in the country, commemorates an unknown member of the Northumberland family, of nearby Leconfield: above the tomb chest, which bears no effigy, no inscription, an ornate lofty canopy, richly carved with angels, saints, heraldic shields and foliage, rises to the figure of Our Lord. The retrochoir is almost a mausoleum of the Warton family, with a number of notable 18th-century monuments – one, to Sir Michael Warton, is by Sheemakers (1725). In the N. choir aisle, in the thickness of the wall, the arcade suddenly breaks into a staircase, which rises behind the Purbeck shafts of the wall arcade – to nothing. It was the entrance to the chapter house, demolished after the Dissolution.

In the 18th century the Minster, bereft not only of its canons, but also of most of its endowments, was in a parlous state. Nicholas Hawksmoor was called in, and carried out a remarkable restoration. Alas that so many of his furnishings were swept away by the Victorians – a grand 18th-century reredos, a baroque pulpit, a Gothick chancel screen. His ogee-shaped dome on the squat cen-tral tower was also removed. But some things have survived – his wonderful west doors, with spirited

Beverley: the Percy tomb

carvings of the evangelists, his lead statues near the S. door of St John of Beverley and King Athelstan, the 18th-century font cover, elaborately carved with cherubs and scrolls, and some outstanding wrought iron gates. Gilbert Scott's replacements, though adequate, are correct and cold. But the glories of the church make up for all – this marvellous church, which so mysteriously, so miraculously, stands in this forgotten town, in this remote part of England.

Bridlington Priory

Approaching Bridlington from the south, from Beverley or Hull (along the A165), there is a grand view of the town set against the grand sweep of Bridlington Bay, with Flamborough Head beyond, and the two towers of the Priory prominent in the middle. Bridlington, alias Burlington (hence Lord Burlington, Burlington House and the Burlington Arcade), is an ancient port, and in the old town

there are delightful streets and many Georgian houses. Bridlington the seaside resort is Victorian, with rows of hotels and boarding-houses facing the sea.

Bridlington Priory was founded *c.* 1113 by Walter de Gaunt for Augustinian Canons. The house produced a number of canons distinguished for their learning and piety, and one saint. St John of Bridlington, John de Tweng (Thwing in the East Riding), became Prior in 1362, and after his death was canonized in 1401, his shrine here becoming the scene of many miracles. The last Prior, William Woode, was executed for his part in the Pilgrimage of Grace (1536).

The Priory gatehouse, known as the Bayle (the only monastic building to survive), makes an imposing approach to the west front – the west front so French in its appearance, with its two dissimilar towers. In fact both are in their upper stages the work of Sir Gilbert Scott, but their origins are very different. The N.W. tower is the oldest part of the church, with its Norman doorway and E.E. work above; the S.W. tower is Perp. Both were incomplete at the Dissolution: for centuries the N.W. did not rise above the level of the clerestory, and the S.W. was merely crowned with an 18th-century cupola. Their completion is one of Scott's triumphs: the N.W. tower has a hint of the old Anselm tower at Canterbury, the S.W. is quite Beverleian. On the south side it is possible to see where the monastic buildings adjoined, with the cloisters and chapter house further east. All has gone; gone, too, is the whole eastern part of the church, aisled transepts, long chancel. Only the nave survived to serve as the parish church. On the north side the porch has a doorway of clustered columns and capitals displaying heads – a king or a queen – among the carved foliage. The west doorway has a crocketed ogee head and ornately carved arch and capitals.

Inside, the first impression is of great magnificence – indeed of cathedral-like proportions. This is a tremendous nave of ten E.E. bays (*c.* 1250), with triforium and lofty clerestory – windows with geometrical tracery on the north side: on the south the arrangement is different, with a Perp traceried screen above the arcade to serve as triforium, enclosing the lower half of the clerestory. Indeed the three western bays have panelled Perp pillars, and the clerestory windows here are Perp also, a later alteration coinciding with the building of the S.W. tower. The south aisle windows are Dec:

Bridlington Priory: the south arcade

those on the north side are E.E. lancets. These various differences help us date the building of the nave in its various stages. The present east window with its geometrical tracery is Scott's, and perhaps too small. Looking back from the sanctuary down the nave the view is magnificent, and gives us an idea of the splendour of the monastic church.

There is a 14th-century font of Frosterley marble, and colourful glass in east and west windows by Wailes. There are many 18th- and 19th-century monuments to Bridlington worthies in the aisles, and at the west end of the north aisle fragments of the 12th-century cloisters have been assembled and re-erected. They display notable stone carving, and give us a clue to the appearance of the first Norman priory church.

Holy Trinity Priory, Micklegate, York

Micklegate is one of the most distinguished streets in York, curving up its gentle slope from the river to Micklegate Bar, and lined with Georgian houses. Opposite John Carr's handsome façade of Micklegate House (1753), set back from the street across its raised churchyard, stands Holy Trinity, founded in 1089 by Ralph Pagnell, and given by him to the Benedictine Abbey of Marmoutier near Tours. The west front, in Priory Street, is imposing, but largely a rebuilding by Hodgson Fowler (1902), and the N.W. tower was the tower of the parish church of St Nicholas, which adjoined the priory church. Only the nave of the Priory survives, with its sturdy late-12th-century octagonal piers and the west piers of the original Norman crossing: central tower, transepts, chancel and north aisle are all gone; the present smaller chancel and narrow south aisle are of 1886 and 1849 respectively; a fragment of the triforium survives above the west bay of the nave, abutting the

York: Holy Trinity Priory

tower; in St Nicholas' Chapel here is a notable 15th-century sculpture of the Holy Trinity. There is a delightful early-18th-century font cover and a number of small monuments, of which the most interesting is that to Dr John Burton (1771), who was Dr Slop of *Tristram Shandy*.

Across the lawn of Brierley's charming Rectory is a small timbered house called Jacob's Well, now used as the parish hall; this and the tall timbered cottages overlooking Micklegate may originally have been built by the Priory.

Lastingham: the crypt

Lastingham Priory

The drive from Pickering is glorious: the main road (A170) to Kirby Moorside passes through stone-built villages – then there is a signpost to Appleton-le-Moors and Lastingham, and the countryside becomes ever more remote and magnificent. Past Appleton, the road descends to Lastingham, and there is the first glimpse of the little village in its deep valley, and of the church, one of the oldest and most romantic monastic churches anywhere. The first monastery was founded here in 654 by St Cedd and St Chad: all was destroyed by the Danes in the 9th century, but in 1078 it was refounded by Stephen of Whitby. The church we see was built by him. Ten years later the monks left Lastingham for York, and St Mary's Abbey there was its offshoot (founded in 1088). The uncompleted monastic church here became the parish church: for the next 140 years a priest from York maintained the church; it became a vicarage in 1230.

Built into the side of the hill, the church with its apsidal east end rises above us – a Norman apsidal crypt, Norman apsidal chancel above. At the west end is a small Perp tower: on either side Norman pillars built into the outside wall of the nave show where the monastic church should have continued, but the work was abandoned when the monks moved away. Inside, it is a wide vaulted interior, with a short chancel and an apsidal sanctuary, and a nave with very early E.E. arches, and over all a groin vault. It is a very French interior, and deeply moving. What we see is in fact the monastic chancel; the crossing, where north and south transepts should have been, became the nave of the parochial church, with the E.E. arches leading into north and south aisles. The west end was built up, and the tower added in the 14th century. The church was splendidly restored by Pearson in 1879, and the vaulting of the nave is his – so convincing that it is hard to believe that it is not original.

In the middle of the nave stone stairs lead down to the crypt, one of the very rare apsidal crypts in England, complete with aisled nave and sanctuary as above. Squat pillars with enormous carved capitals divide nave and aisles. Around the aisles are many relics: the cross-head of a 9th-century cross, fragments of a cross-shaft, and other carved stones from the earlier church. St Cedd is buried here: Stephen of Whitby built this crypt to contain his shrine.

Sheep graze the churchyard: there is the sound of running water from the stream below, and stone cottages, a public house, a shop, comprise the village. It is a holy place.

Nun Monkton Priory

A perfect village, secluded, secret – with a wide green lined with red-brick cottages, and an avenue at the end leading to the priory church, with the 17th-century Priory House to its right, stables and other buildings to its left. Nun Monkton is a cul-de-sac: just beyond, the Wharfe and the Ouse join; there is no bridge, no ferry now. So the place is a little world apart. And it was here, at this solitary meeting place of the two rivers, that Wil-

Nun Monkton Priory: a world apart

liam de Arches founded a priory for Benedictine nuns *c.* 1153. What remains is the nave of their church.

The west front is small, simple and austere. The doorway is late Norman, adorned with much zigzag ornament and, above, in the gable, a small trefoil-headed niche, recalling the N.W. door at Brinkburn. On either side are round-headed niches: in one stands the single battered statue of a female saint. Three narrow lancets occupy the rest of this narrow front, and there is a squat little tower at the top with a pyramid roof. It is a distinguished front, in miniature. Inside, there are lancets and an arcaded gallery around three sides – and, between the windows, twelve trefoil-headed niches. The chancel was pulled down at the Dissolution (1538), and the present east wall is a sympathetic rebuilding by J. W. Walton (1873), with three lancet windows filled with superb Morris glass. There are early coffin lids, perhaps of prioresses or nuns, and a monument to Nathaniel Paylor (1748), of the family who acquired the monastic property here in 1650. It was either his father or grandfather who built the present distinguished Priory House, with its unusual giant pilasters and hipped roof. Its delectable gardens descend to the Ouse, and a little gazebo surveys the place where the two rivers meet.

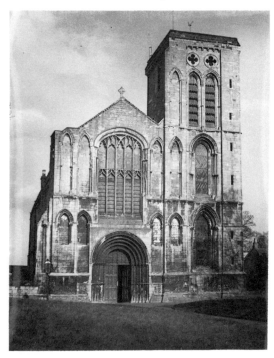

Old Malton Priory is the only Gilbertine church still in use

Old Malton Priory

Malton now is by-passed, but the road from Malton itself passes through Old Malton to join the new road a little farther east. Old Malton is a village of stone houses and cottages, and suddenly there is a glimpse of an ancient church on the right, a church of unusual grandeur, more than an ordinary village church, presiding over a capacious churchyard. This is Malton Priory.

The west front is arresting – a façade of S.W. tower adorned with lancet windows and quatrefoil openings above, a Norman west door with blank lancet arcading on either side, and, above, a big Perp window, whose upper stages are apparently blocked. On the left there is the base of another, N.W., tower which has long since vanished; there is the blocked arcade on the north side, and, at the east end of what was obviously the north aisle, another Norman arch, leading to nothing now, but once the entry to the crossing. Transepts and chancel were destroyed after the Dissolution, leaving the nave to serve as the parish church. The same pattern is repeated on the south side; here, beyond a stone wall, stands a 17th-century house (Abbey House), which incorporates fragments of the monastic buildings.

Malton Priory was founded *c.* 1147 by Eustace FitzJohn for Gilbertine Canons. The Gilbertine order, founded by St Gilbert of Sempringham (Lincolnshire), was the only English monastic order, and had been established in 1131 for canons following the Augustinian Rule, and nuns following the Cistercian. There were twenty-six houses in all, some for canons only, some for nuns, some double foundations where monks and nuns lived their own separate lives: even their church would be divided down the middle by an impenetrable wall – but nevertheless a united house, male and female, offering its life under strict rule to God. The first Prior of Malton was Roger, who succeeded St Gilbert as head of the order: the last, John Crawshaw, surrendered the house at the Dissolution in 1539. Malton is the only Gilbertine church still in use for worship today.

Inside, the nave is shorn of its aisles, shorn of its clerestory. But the blocked-up 12th-century arcades survive, and, above, the E.E. triforium. The roof is set above this, necessitating the blocking of the upper part of the west window. It is beautifully furnished – by Temple Moore, who was in charge of the restoration in 1877. At the east end is his High Altar with tester, on the north side his handsome organ; there is a splendid set of stalls, incorporating original seats and misericords; the low choir screen is in memory of Viscount Ossington, Speaker of the House of Commons, who was three times M.P. for Malton (d. 1873). There is oak panelling throughout, and there are good altar ornaments and brass candelabra.

The east end overlooks open country, and there are views across the stream to the Wolds beyond. A romantic spot.

Selby Abbey

Selby looks magnificent from the train. 'Is it a cathedral?' said a woman opposite me to her neighbour. 'I didn't know there was a cathedral at Selby,' said the other. Selby is little known, unexpected; its three towers, its long line of high-pitched lead roof, its many pinnacles, its immense east window, all give the impression of a church of cathedral status: indeed, it is as grand as several English cathedrals.

The Abbey is only a short walk from the railway station: the white stone gleams through the trees

Selby Abbey: the Norman west doorway

in the public gardens. There are ample Dec windows in the chancel and transepts; narrow lancets in the clerestory of the nave; the central tower appears all Dec, though the small Norman windows in its base betray its older history; the west front with its low twin towers surveys the Market Place.

Apart from Westminster Abbey, only a handful of monastic churches survive intact: Selby is one of them. Good fortune has been on Selby's side here: it has had its fill of misfortunes otherwise. It is hard to credit that the central tower is a rebuilding of 1908, that the original fell in 1690, destroying the south transept and ruining part of the choir, and that the west towers were only completed in 1935. But look at an old photograph of 1900: the church bears a very different mien. No west towers, no south transept, and, above the Norman

Selby Abbey: Norman nave, Dec chancel

base, an 18th-century tower with a balustraded top and vase-like pinnacles: only the long roof-line of nave and chancel declares that it is the same building, and (as we shall see) even this is a rebuilding after a terrible fire in 1906.

Selby Abbey was founded *c.* 1069 for Benedictine monks, an offshoot of the abbey of Auxerre, and the building of the church began *c.* 1100 under Abbot Hugh. Standing before the west front, the Norman door and Norman windows under the

towers will be observed; above and around, lancet windows and E.E. arcading appear; on the north side the impressive porch has another Norman doorway, but the arcading on either side and above is E.E., and the parapet and pinnacles are Perp.

On entering we find ourselves in one of the most splendid Norman naves in England: there are giant round columns, and (as the nave progresses westwards) compound piers. One column is decorated with trellis work – an echo of Durham, indeed the whole nave is an echo of Durham: both were Benedictine churches. The triforium at the east end is plain Norman; as the work progressed west there is greater variety, and on the south side the triforium becomes E.E., and the clerestory is E.E. throughout, with small lancet windows. Some of the flat timber roof survived the fire, as did many of the bosses, which were reinstated and have recently been regilded.

The crossing, like the base of the tower, is Norman too; the north transept received a large Perp window in the early 15th century; the south transept is largely Oldrid Scott's rebuilding (1912). He also rebuilt the wooden vaulting of the chancel, which was destroyed in the fire. The chancel itself is sumptuous Dec work of *c.* 1280–1340: there are clustered columns with carved foliage capitals, and between the bays canopied niches for figures of saints – some empty, some filled with Victorian reproductions. Above the arcades are large traceried windows, and the triforium walk runs along below the windows. At the east end is the tremendous curvilinear window – comparable with windows at Carlisle, York or Heckington – filled with glass of *c.* 1330, depicting the descent of Our Lord from Jesse. There has been a certain amount of restoration (by Ward and Hughes in the 1870s), but very skilfully done. The aisles are vaulted in stone, and on the south side is the two-storeyed sacrarium with scriptorium above: the beautiful lower chamber, with rib vaulting, is now used as a chapel, and contains a 15th-century panel of Nottingham alabaster.

Most of the furnishings perished in the fire: screen, pulpit, stalls, organ case, reredos are all excellent work by Oldrid Scott. But the 15th-century font cover miraculously survived the fire.

The greatest credit must be accorded to Scott: the 18th-century tower was removed in 1902, before the fire – regarded as 'debased' – leaving only the Norman stump. To this Scott added a most inspired tower in the Dec style, so convincing in itself, and now so well weathered, that it deceives all comers. The west towers were raised in 1935, after his death but according to his design: a bold and successful completion of what the Middle Ages had left incomplete.

Selby is an odd, withdrawn little town on the Ouse, in somewhat featureless, flat countryside. There are few buildings of note. Modest Georgian terrace houses line the streets near the Abbey. There are quays along the river front, and flour

mills, and there is a curious 18th-century wooden toll-bridge over the river, reminiscent of the old Toll Bridge at Shoreham. The Abbey dominates the town, and the landscape for miles around.

Swine Priory: the Hilton tombs

Swine Priory

Across the flat fields of Holderness stands the important church of Swine, dominating the little village – the imposing chancel and spacious aisles of what was once a cruciform priory of Cistercian nuns founded here *c.* 1150 – to which a tower of subdued Gothic was added in the late 18th century. Four bays of squat round piers with square capitals and pointed arches, of the late 12th century, divide chancel from aisles; this has been the parish church since the Dissolution. There is a grand Perp E. window, a 15th-century parclose screen encloses the N.E. chapel, there are old stalls with misericords, an early-17th-century pulpit, and a charming little 18th-century font of Coade stone. But the tombs in the N.E. Chapel are pre-eminent – a wonderful display of 14th- and 15th-century altar tombs, with alabaster effigies of knights and ladies of the once-powerful Hilton family, the chests adorned with shields or kneeling angels.

WALES

Penmon Priory: Norman arcading and a Celtic cross in the south transept

DIOCESE OF
BANGOR

Bangor Cathedral

IT IS THE GREAT BOAST of Bangor that it was founded seventy years before Canterbury – in 525. The Cathedral is modest, unassuming, set in the middle of its small seaside and university town, in dramatic countryside close to Snowdonia, separated from Anglesey by the Menai Strait. From the end of the pier the view stretches from Telford's suspension bridge (completed in 1826) to the west – to the solid solemn pseudo-Norman keep of Penrhyn Castle, built by Thomas Hopper for the 1st Lord Penrhyn between 1827 and 1840, to the east. Some pretty Regency cottages and early Victorian terraces line the sea front; above, on the hill, the imposing building of University College holds sway, with Henry Hare's square tower crowning its impressive quadrangle (1906). Indeed from a distance this is often taken for the Cathedral.

Not so; almost undetected amid the crowded narrow streets the Cathedral stands scarcely visible. It appears suddenly round a corner, across a narrow sward of grass, opposite the Castle Hotel, with its low Perp western tower, a long low embattled nave, a dwarf central tower with pyramid roof, and altogether loftier transepts and short chancel; it looks curiously deformed, but in its Welsh way authentic and lovable. From the N.E. where the ground falls away, the view of the east end with crossing tower and north transept is more impressive; Gilbert Scott indeed designed a grander central tower and spire which were never built: the present pyramid roof to the little low tower was only added in 1967.

And so inside, by the south door – into the long low nave, built in the early 16th century by Bishop Skevington: on either side there is an arcade of six bays, with arches of almost Tudor squatness, with a low clerestory and low timbered roof. The west tower was completed in 1532, and a Latin inscription over the west door relates that Thomas Skevington 'built this bell tower and church in the year of the Virgin's giving birth, 1532'. In fact, the crossing, transepts and chancel are earlier (14th century), but much rebuilt by Scott in his extensive restoration (1870–1880). A wooden screen by Oldrid Scott (1908) and hanging rood by Alban Caroe (1950) divide the nave from crossing and chancel: here stand Gilbert Scott's canopied stalls and bishop's throne; the elaborate wooden vault, gaily painted, is also by him. The east window is by Clayton & Bell, the marble reredos by Oldrid Scott: indeed the chancel is redolent of Victorian decoration and recreation.

At the west end the three windows by David Evans of Shrewsbury (1838) are the best glass in the Cathedral, and with their rich colouring most effective. Evans was one of the first pre-Victorian stained glass artists to break away from 18th century pictorialism, and consciously emulate medieval designs. Nearby stands the Cathedral's greatest treasure, the Mostyn Christ. After the Reformation, this life-sized carved oak figure of Christ of the Passion, of the late 15th or early 16th century, came into the hands of a recusant branch of the Mostyn family, by whom it was carefully preserved; it is now loaned to the Cathedral by Lord Mostyn. Elsewhere there are several early-16th-century carved figures of Flemish origin, and at the west end of the north aisle are fragments of early tombs or crosses – but although there are a number of modest later monuments, none is of special interest, which is disappointing for a foundation of such antiquity.

The Library contains several treasures, of which the most distinguished is the Pontifical of Bishop Anian II – a manuscript volume of the episcopal offices, beautifully illuminated (*c.* 1310).

Bangor Cathedral: Gilbert Scott's vault and furnishings in the chancel

Penmon Priory overlooking the Menai Straits

Penmon Priory

Anglesey is enchanting: on a hot summer's day the views across the Menai Strait from Bangor are almost Italian, with gaily painted houses and terraces basking in the sun; at any time of year the views back to the mainland from Anglesey are dramatic, with the little cathedral and university dwarfed under the majestic mountains of Snowdonia. To cross Telford's suspension bridge for the first time is a great experience, and however oft repeated, the excitement never palls.

Penmon Priory stands close to the shore at the easternmost tip of Anglesey, close to Puffin Island: a sweet scene of tranquillity. It is approached along the wooded coast road, through Beaumaris, with its castle built by Edward I and its seaside terraces – Victoria Terrace is grand enough to be in Bath. Then civilization is left behind, and narrow country lanes with high hedges lead on to this scene of monastic seclusion. The refectory with its high walls is roofless now – close to the lane; the little cruciform church with pyramid-crowned central tower stands above, all built of local stone, so that it appears almost like an outcrop of the surrounding rocks.

The first monastic house was established here in the 6th century by Cynlas, who placed it in the care of his brother Seiriol (it is St Seiriol's Church); in the 13th century Llewellyn the Great granted it to the Prior and Canons of Priestholm (Puffin Island), who belonged to an ancient Celtic order; in 1414 it was given to the Augustinians. Since the Dissolution the little church has served as the parish church; the monastic buildings were granted to the Bulkeley family of nearby Baron Hill.

Past the refectory, steep steps lead up into what was the cloister court, now the garden of the Priory House – which once formed the west side of the cloister. Here the south door leads into the church. The chancel, over-restored by Weightman and Hadfield in the 19th century, is used for worship – light and airy, all pitch-pine pews. But the narrow Norman arch under the tower leads into the crossing with its sturdy Norman pillars – into the transepts and the nave. This nave is marvellous – cool, dark, lofty and mysterious, with dim light entering through the tiny Norman windows. There is the grand Norman arch of the crossing, a square, richly carved font – originally the base of a cross (*c.* 1000) – a pillar piscina of the 12th century, the 10th-century Penmon Cross. In the south transept the walls are adorned with 12th-century arcading; another early cross stands here, and there are fragments of medieval glass in the window – and further fragments in the north transept. It is a holy place. Outside, the south-west door has a carved dragon in its tympanum, and nearby is St Seiriol's Well and the fragment of a hermit's cell.

Re-emerging into the outside world, we are face to face with the stupendous view – to the straits, the blue sea, Llanfairfechan and Penmaenmawr on the mainland, the mountains of Snowdonia towering over all.

And a little beyond the church, on the far side of the lane, is the square stone dovecote, with a domed beehive roof crowned with a little open cupola through which the birds flew. Inside, there is a central pillar, with steps to carry a ladder and give access to a thousand nests. It was built *c.* 1600 by Sir Richard Bulkeley of Baron Hill, Constable of Beaumaris, M.P. for Anglesey, favourite courtier of Queen Elizabeth. He formed the deer park here. Dovecote and Refectory are in the care of the D. o. E., and are accessible at all times; if the church is locked, the key may be obtained at the house.

DIOCESE OF
BRECON

Brecon Cathedral

ITS SETTING is wonderful, remote. The Brecon Beacons guard it to the south: the Black Mountains· separate it from England on the east. Dramatic landscapes extend for miles to north and west, with quieter pastoral scenery in the valleys, with villages and small secluded churches, lost in the foothills or clinging to nearby farms – some of them retaining amazing medieval screens. Signposts stand at crossroads, pointing the way to places with unpronounceable names. But wherever you go, you are never far from the Beacons, which rise to near 3000 feet – an awesome presence, sometimes forbidding, always majestic.

And Brecon is delightful, a country town, a

Brecon Cathedral: in quiet, sequestered seclusion

local capital. Here the Honddu joins the Usk, and charmingly named streets – the Bulwark, High Street Superior, High Street Inferior, the Captains' Walk – are filled with Georgian houses, small or great. There is the grand Grecian Shire Hall (now the Brecknock Museum), built by T. H. Wyatt and David Brandon; in the Bulwark the statue of the Duke of Wellington stands before St Mary's Church; nearby is the birthplace of Mrs Siddons. Ship Street leads to the Castle, a ruin since the Civil War. Nearby, on its hill, in quiet sequestered seclusion, surrounded by protective walls, stands the Cathedral.

'The church of St John the Evangelist without the walls' was given by the Norman conqueror, Bernard de Neufmarche, to his confessor, Roger, a monk of the Benedictine Abbey of Battle in Sussex, and in 1093 a Benedictine priory was founded here, and a new Norman church begun. After the Dissolution the church became a parish church, and the monastic buildings were granted to Sir John Price. In 1923 the priory church became the cathedral of the new diocese of Swansea and Brecon, and the monastic buildings, so long alienated, were repurchased, to form Deanery, Canonry and Chapter House – all enclosed within the curtain wall.

The Cathedral stands within its pretty churchyard of old tombs, old headstones and ancient trees – strong, sturdy and simple with its nave, transepts and central tower: it looks at first sight like an enormous country church. Only at the east end is there any architectural distinction. Here the narrow lancets of the chancel, the chapels extending from the transepts, the line of buttresses, the steeply-pitched rooflines, build up to form a distinguished composition. Walking round the east end – and making the full circuit of the church – the visitor will find that long range of the monastic buildings, like a long and ancient manor house, standing tall with a four-storeyed tower in the middle and rows of mullioned windows, all attached to the south side of the nave. Looking south, there is a spectacular view of the Brecon Beacons.

Entering the Cathedral, the nave is early 14th century, spacious, austere, with plain octagonal piers and wide tall arches with small clerestory windows above. And the eye is led on, through the lofty E.E. arches of the crossing, to the chancel. This is the glory of Brecon: it is wide and spacious, and the rebuilding here began in 1201. It is E.E.

architecture at its best: a group of five lancets in the east wall, three more to north and south, narrow and elegant with simple shafts and capitals, triple piscina and sedilia, all of the finest workmanship – and, above, a quadripartite vault.

This vault is one of the great triumphs of Sir Gilbert Scott: it is the making of the Cathedral. At his restoration (1861 ff) he found here only a flat timber ceiling – but the springers were there to carry a vault, a vault which was never built. Scott built it. There is a sumptuous stone reredos by W. D. Caroe, decent glass by Clayton & Bell, and low E.E. arches lead into the transept chapels: the Havard Chapel to the north (Chapel of the South Wales Borderers), and the Sacristy and St Lawrence Chapel to the south – the latter restored and revaulted by Caroe in 1930.

Throughout the Cathedral there are monuments of interest, from medieval effigies to the recumbent figure of Bishop Edward Bevan, first Bishop of Swansea and Brecon (d. 1934), by W. Goscombe John. Of special charm are the many tablets of the 18th or early 19th century – including work by John Bacon senior, Flaxman, and Thomas Paty of Bristol – reflecting the taste and prosperity of the local gentry. And the floors of the transepts are gay with many splendid ledger stones, often with shields of arms, always with beautiful lettering. These are a special pleasure. At the west end of the nave is the 12th-century font, a relic of the Norman church, carved with the grotesque reliefs of masks and birds and beasts; above hangs a noble brass candelabrum of 1722.

Christ College, Brecon

The Cathedral is not the only monastic building in Brecon: in the water meadows on the far side of the Usk stands Christ College, whose chapel was once the chancel of the Dominican Priory of St Nicholas, founded here *c.* 1240. After the Dissolution, Bishop Barlow of St David's transferred to the old monastic buildings the college of Abergwili, partly as a school, partly to serve as a kind of university college for men aspiring to ordination in the Welsh dioceses. As such it continued until the opening of St David's College at Lampeter in 1827. Christ College was then re-established as a public school. New school

Christ College: Stanton's monument in the ante-chapel

Llangenith Priory

The little priory church of St Cennydd stands close to the sea at the far western end of the Gower Peninsula; a primitive 12th-century tower with saddleback top on the north side, a line of farm buildings at the west end marking the site of the priory buildings, and a simple interior containing the 7th-century burial stone of the saint, with its carved interlacing pattern. As an alien Benedictine priory, a cell of Evreux in Normandy, it was dissolved in 1441, and its endowments given to All Souls' College, Oxford. Now Llangenith is but a sloping village green, a handful of cottages, a view of the rocky headlands – and the little church.

buildings were designed by John Prichard of Llandaff and his partner J. P. Seddon, but incorporating the refectory as the dining hall, and the chancel of the church as the school chapel. This is a building of some distinction, with its long line of narrow lancets – eleven on the north side, four on the south (*c.* 1240) – and a rather later traceried east window, which contains striking glass, designed by Seddon, of the Crucifixion. The furnishings are all Victorian, but there are some notable monuments. In the ante-chapel is the grand tomb of Bishop Lucy (son of Sir Thomas of Charlecote), who as Bishop of St David's refounded the college after the Restoration, often resided there, and died there in 1677. There is also a handsome monument to his son, the Revd Richard Lucy, by William Stanton (1697). To the west the walls of the roofless nave serve as the walls of a grassy court – which lead through to the school buildings.

Llangenith with its 12th-century saddleback tower

DIOCESE OF
LLANDAFF

Llandaff Cathedral

A SHORT DISTANCE from the centre of Cardiff – and we are in the village city of Llandaff. The large Victorian houses of Cathedral Road give no clue as to what is to come, but Llandaff High Street with its modest shops brings us to the ruins of the Bishop's Castle, and so to Cathedral Green. A long stretch of grass, some smaller Georgian houses, some larger Victorian Gothic ones, the Preaching Cross, the ruins of the Bell Tower – and there is the Cathedral in its deep hollow beneath us. The figure of Archdeacon Buckley (d. 1924) in his shovel hat and gaiters surveys N.W. tower and S.W. spire, the high gable of the W. front, and the long line of the nave. Descending, the W. front rises before us through the trees that clothe the dell: it is a magical setting. The N.W. tower – the Jasper Tower, so named after Jasper Tudor, brother of Henry VII who built it – is crowned with an ornate lattice parapet and lofty pinnacles like a West Country Perp tower: the S.W. spire is entirely a rebuilding by John Prichard, the local architect who restored – indeed practically rebuilt – the Cathedral between 1850 and 1869. French in its inspiration, French in its details, this gives the W. front a remarkable continental character. It is a triumph of Victorian architecture.

The history of the see has been extremely chequered. There are disjointed records of Celtic bishops going back to the 6th century: with the consecration of Bishop Urban in 1107 we are on firmer ground. It was he who built the first Norman cathedral, of which the arch above the High Altar survives. The long nave and shorter chancel are E.E., and date from the end of the 12th century; the W. front is *c.* 1220, and in the 13th century Lady Chapel and chapter house were built: there was a great dedication service in 1266.

After the Reformation the Cathedral fell into decay: gross mismanagement of the endowments diminished the never wealthy foundation. Bishop followed bishop, but little was done, and the body of the church became largely ruined. In the 18th century John Wood, eminent architect of Georgian Bath, was called in; within the ruined nave he built a small Grecian temple, leaving the W. end in a ruined state; the Jasper Tower lost its crown in a storm in 1703: the S.W. tower collapsed completely in 1723. Such was the cathedral in which Bishop Ollivant was enthroned in 1850: there was no Dean, there were no canons – only a single minor canon presided over its services, and the choir had been disbanded in 1691. Prichard's restoration began almost at once. John Wood's Grecian temple was pulled down, the Georgian plasterwork was removed from the medieval arcades, the entire church reroofed, the W. towers rebuilt. It was a remarkable resurrection. The Chapter was reformed, a new Choir School established, new houses were built for Dean and Canons. But another disaster was to follow: in January 1941 a landmine fell close to the Cathedral, and the whole church was shattered. Restoration under Mr G. G. Pace began in 1949: it is a cathedral resurrected by Prichard, restored by Pace, that we see today.

In the N.W. corner of the churchyard the Old Prebendal House (1691) is now used as a song school for the choir, and for meetings: in front stand two classical urns, which originally crowned John Wood's Grecian Temple: George Pace's curved cloister now forms the principal entrance to the Cathedral, and leads through the Memorial Chapel for the Welch Regiment, which was built by him in 1956, and forms a kind of Galilee. A late Norman doorway leads into the nave.

Llandaff Cathedral: the pinnacles and parapet of the north-west tower and the entire south-west spire are the work of John Prichard, the Victorian architect who restored the cathedral

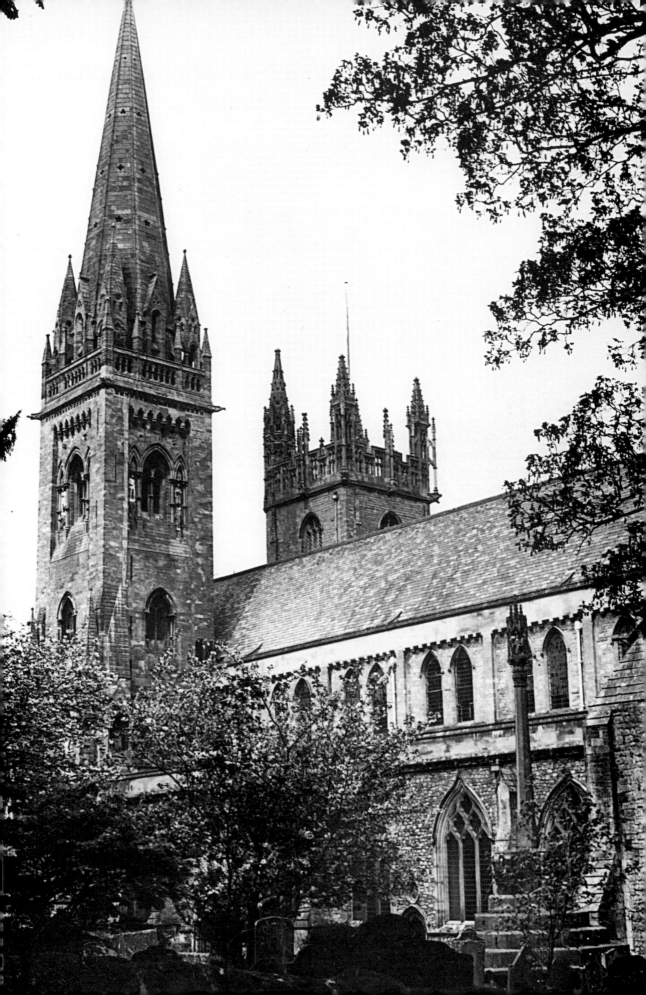

ABOVE *Llandaff Cathedral in decay. An 18th-century watercolour at Croft Castle, Herefordshire.*
BELOW *Bishop Urban's Norman arch, the High Altar and the Lady Chapel beyond*

The first impression is one of spaciousness: the nave is wide, and despite the absence of triforium it seems lofty. The arcades with their delicate clustered columns and stiff-leaf capitals, the tall clerestory above with long lancets, two to a bay with elegant foliated shafts, the flat panelled timber roof, the vista of short but lofty chancel beyond, and, through the Norman arch above the High Altar, to the Lady Chapel beyond that with its geometrical E. window – all this is undoubtedly impressive. But what arrests the attention most is George Pace's 'parabolic' arch which spans the nave and, with Epstein's 'Christus' masking the organ, dominates the interior.

Mr Pace's idea – and that of the cathedral authorities – was to create a division in the church between nave and choir, as the pulpitum did in medieval cathedrals (and as indeed it did here until the ruin of the nave); to ensure that it appeared as a cathedral and not just 'a big parish church' (Llandaff is much more than that, anyway); to provide some mystery, some sense of anticipation

in the worshipper's approach to the holiest places. And in this he brilliantly succeeds. There will be some who do not care for the stocky, oddly shaped, concrete arch – clumsy, perhaps, and hunch-backed in the midst of Gothic elegance. There will be those who do not care for Epstein's 'Christus'. But it cannot be denied, even by its critics, that this modern open pulpitum is both bold and original. The figure of Christ with His hands outstretched in pleading speaks to hosts of worshippers; the drum against which the figure stands contains the organ – and countless little figures of pre-Raphaelite angels, rescued from the damaged choir stalls and brilliantly gilded, seem to fly around its back and sides.

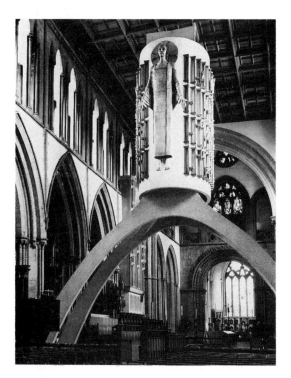

Llandaff: Epstein's 'Christus' and the E. E. nave

And the idea works: passing under the arch (and sparing a glance for the magnificent Victorian lectern) we are in a different church. Mr Pace has repaired Prichard's damaged stalls and bishop's throne; the High Altar stands before Urban's Nor-man arch, decked with six glorious baroque candlesticks and crucifix; the bronze figure – un-expectedly baroque – of Bishop Lewis (d. 1905)

stands aloft on the S. wall, his hand raised in blessing; there is a view through into the vaulted Lady Chapel beyond; and John Piper's glass in the window above Urban's arch portrays in brilliant colours Our Lord at Emmaus. It is a deeply mov-ing, numinous sanctuary – one that brings us to our knees.

A door in the S. aisle leads into the little chapter house (*c.* 1250), with its interior of solemn charm; the aisle leads on to the Lady Chapel (*c.* 1270) – vaulted, lime washed, sparkling, with glass by Geoffrey Webb, and a medieval reredos, its niches gaily painted and adorned with bronze panels de-picting wild flowers of Wales named after Our Lady. The eastern chapels on either side are also richly and devoutly furnished.

The resurrection of Llandaff in the 19th cen-tury, its second resurrection in the 20th, must seem near miracles. All the chapels have been refurnished: in St Utydd's is the Rossetti triptych, depicting the Seed of David – in which the artist made use of Swinburne, Burne-Jones and William Morris and his wife as models. There are tombs of interest, too, ranging from early bishops in the sanctuary to Victorian leaders elsewhere. Of special interest is that of Dean Vaughan, Head-master of Harrow, Master of the Temple, Llan-daff's most distinguished Dean and the refounder of the Choir School.

It is a pleasure to walk round the churchyard, its sloping sides hung with fine trees. Here Cardiff seems a thousand miles away. A lofty cross on the S. side commemorates Dean Conybeare, Dean at the time of the Victorian restoration, and nearby is the tomb of John Prichard, architect (d. 1886), 'restorer of this cathedral, son of Richard Prichard, B.D., for thirty-five years Vicar Choral'; it was he who had held the Cathedral together spiritually during the dark days before Bishop Ollivant.

Returning to Cathedral Green, we can walk back through the ruins of the Bishop's Castle with its enclosed garden: a garden door leads into the orchard which surrounds the Choir School, and so to the School itself. Once the Bishop's Palace, it is a decidedly mid-18th-century house with hipped roof and rows of sash windows, and a Victorian chapel by Ewan Christian. The School, now part of the Woodard Corporation, flourishes – the only choir school in the Principality. Even-song is sung daily: once again the praises of God resound through the Cathedral's twice-shattered walls.

Margam Abbey

A single photograph in Harry Batsford's and Charles Fry's *Greater English Church* (1940) shows a view of the south aisle of Margam Abbey, with its rectangular piers and groin-vaulted roof: nothing in the photograph prepares us for what we shall find here at Margam.

Margam is famous now for its steel works close to the sea, and for Port Talbot, named after the Talbots of Margam. It is an extraordinary landscape of chimneys, blast furnaces and cooling towers – but the old village lying behind is entirely and astonishingly rural, and the main road to Swansea skirts the vast park, now a 'country park' belonging to Glamorgan County Council; on rising ground to the north stands the 19th-century mansion, once the seat of the Talbots. Those who wish to explore the park must enter by the appropriate entrance (clearly signposted on the main road); but those who wish to see the church must turn off at a side lane further west, which winds its way behind the park and delivers us at the west front of the church, in the old village.

The Cistercian Abbey of Margam was founded by Robert Earl of Gloucester in 1147. It became the richest monastery in Wales, and at the Dissolution was granted to the Mansel family, whose descendants the Talbots remained here till the death of its last member, Miss Emily Charlotte Talbot, in 1918. It subsequently passed through various hands till its recent purchase by the County Council.

The west front wears an unmistakably 19th-century mien: there is indeed an original Norman doorway, but the 19th-century 'Norman' windows above, the low pitch of the roof, the tall Lombardic pinnacles, betray the hand of the early-19th-century restorer. Walking round the outside, we can enjoy the large churchyard, crammed with tombs and headstones; and across the wall to the south can gaze down on the ruins of the rest of the monastic church, which lie now outside the churchyard, inaccessible from here. The present church is but the nave, preserved as the parish church after the Dissolution. It was Thomas Mansel Talbot who restored it between 1805 and 1809.

Inside, the nave is impressive, severely Cistercian, with its long arcades of rectangular piers and plain round arches; the large early-19th-century windows in the aisles flood the church with light, the west windows are filled with glass by Morris & Co., and the east window glows with glass by Sir William Laurence; seven sanctuary lamps burn before the High Altar. In the south aisle there are four great Elizabethan or Jacobean alabaster tombs of Mansels, with the recumbent effigies of Sir Rice, Sir Edward, Sir Thomas and Sir Lewis, and their wives – a breathtaking array – and a Jacobean wall monument to Sir Thomas Bussey of Heydour in Lincolnshire, who married a Mansel. The collection of family tombs continues in the north aisle, where later Mansels are commemorated; John Ivory Talbot married the daughter of the 1st Lord Mansel, and his son John inherited Margam on the death of Bussey, 4th Lord Mansel, in 1750. The centre of the chapel is occupied by the grand tomb (by E. Armistead, R.A.) of Theodore Mansel Talbot (1876), inspired by the 13th-century tomb of Archbishop Grey in York Minster; there are other Talbot monuments, and a number of hatchments. Nearby hangs a faded photograph of Fr. Stanton, of St Alban's Holborn. It is a fascinating interior, with great atmosphere.

At the far end of the churchyard is a small museum, filled with Celtic crosses; and at the other end, outside the churchyard gate, there is a cottage which may not at first attract attention. But a garden door beside it leads into the gardens of the great house. Here the front of the cottage will be found to be an elaborate garden temple, of astonishing Renaissance workmanship, a relic of the first late-16th-century mansion of the Mansels. A garden path leads on to an even more astonishing building – the enormous 18th-century Orangery, which faces south across the park. Here for a moment the visitor may feel that he is at Versailles: a fountain plays before the grand façade, and urns and other ornaments adorn the terrace. It has been admirably restored by the County Council, and is used for concerts and exhibitions. Further on, it is possible to inspect the medieval ruins of the Abbey – fragments of the choir, transepts and chapter house – now undergoing repair. The Talbots preserved these as garden ornaments. Beyond, on the hillside, surrounded by plantations of cedars and evergreens, stands the Tudor Gothic pile of Margam Castle, built for C. R. Mansel Talbot by Thomas Hopper (1830–5). It stands at present gloomy and empty, damaged in a recent fire, but awaiting

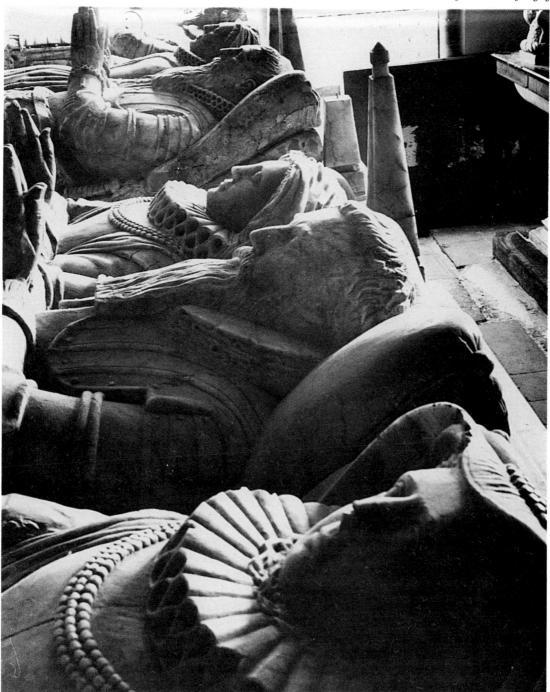

Margam Abbey: recumbent Mansels in the south aisle

restoration. With its pinnacles and lavish traceried windows, and standing in its Victorian gardens, it is Margam's final great surprise, and provides, with the other remarkable buildings nearby, an astonishing contrast to the sober austere beauty of the Cistercian church.

Ewenny Priory

Ewenny lies between Bridgend and the sea – 1¼ miles from Bridgend, 3 miles from the sea. Travelling west from Cardiff, a minor road leads from the main road to Ogmore and Ewenny. There are views across to the industry of Bridgend to the north, but our road leads south-west. Before we reach the village of Ewenny a D. o. E. signpost, EWENNY PRIORY: ANCIENT MONUMENT, directs us to the right, along a pretty country lane. Suddenly there is a clearing in the trees, and we are face to face with enormous medieval walls, a round tower, and then a gatehouse; a grand medieval barn follows, an entrance to a large farmyard with a big house behind, and then another tower. Beyond this stands a church, ancient, cruciform, with a battlemented central tower: there are arrow slits in the battlements, and all the windows everywhere are small: indeed it appears almost fortified, part of the solid walls which still almost surround the entire Priory. Such is Ewenny.

The Priory was founded in 1140 by Maurice de Londres as a cell of Gloucester for Benedictine monks. It stood in half conquered country – hence the fortifications. The nave was originally built by the founder's father William de Londres in the early years of the 12th century, before the founding of the Priory, and this has always been the parish church. At the Dissolution the eastern parts of the church, together with the monastic property, passed to Sir Edward Carne, whose descendant Frances Carne married Edward Turbervill in the 18th century. The Turbervills in course of time became Picton-Turbervills, and the family still hold the property and live here, so adding to the sense of timelessness which so powerfully infects the place today. The eastern parts of the church passed into the guardianship of the Office of Works (now D. o. E.) in 1949; the entire church is open during hours of daylight, and the nave is used regularly for worship.

Inside, there is a sturdy Norman north arcade of four bays: there is no south aisle, as the cloisters abutted here. At the east end the stone pulpitum survives, with its two doors, one on either side of the altar, which led into the monastic choir. Above this there is a wooden partition, so that there is all too little appreciation of the church as a whole; but we can enter the chancel by an outside door on the north side. Here the north transept has disappeared, but the crossing survives, with four lofty arches bearing the tower, standing on solid rectangular piers. The chancel is vaulted, and a medieval wooden screen divides the chancel from the crossing. The stone altar has been restored, though the chancel is not normally used for worship. The south transept survives: it has lost

Ewenny Priory: the south transept

its eastern chapels, but the blocked arches are there, all severe Norman work, and here and elsewhere are numerous carved fragments of early crosses or tombstones. There is the tomb of the founder: *'Ici gist Morice de Londres le fondur. Dieu le rende sun labur am'*, reads the inscription in Old French ('Here lies Maurice de Londres the Founder. God reward him for his work. Amen'). The top of the slab is adorned with a floriated cross. There is a large altar tomb of black and white marble to Edward Carne who died in 1650, and a number of attractive 18th- or early-19th-century monuments to the Turbervills.

A door on the south side opens into the ruined transept chapels. From here there is a delightful view across the private gardens of the Priory House, where peacocks strut and call. But this is a private garden, and trespassers across the ruined walls are, of course, not welcome.

The great walls, north gatehouse and round tower can all be inspected from the road; to visit the south gatehouse (which is on the far side of the garden) permission must be obtained from the Priory House. On certain occasions the gardens are open to the public for local causes, but at other times the grounds are private. The sanctity of Ewenny must be preserved.

DIOCESE OF
ST ASAPH

St Asaph Cathedral

DRIVING ALONG THE A55 from Hawarden, from Chester, from England, the countryside opens up where the road passes close to the wide estuary of the Dee; to the south is a backdrop of hills. And suddenly, on its own modest hill, appears a little town, or big village, half shrouded by trees – and a church with a big solid square tower. This is the cathedral city of St Asaph. It is a modest little town, with the countryside lapping its every street and lane. The main street climbs the hill, with the bellcoted Perp parish church at the bottom, the Cathedral at the top. Here it stands, the smallest of the ancient cathedrals of England and Wales, surrounded by smooth, spreading lawns, cruciform, with wide transepts, wide-aisled nave, the big bold castellated tower, all built of silvery

St Asaph Cathedral: 15th-century stalls in the chancel

rough-hewn stone, an aisleless chancel encased in ashlar by Gilbert Scott: coupled lancets here, larger traceried windows elsewhere.

St Asaph is one of the most ancient Christian sites in Britain: here St Kentigern (or Mungo), exiled temporarily from Scotland, established a monastery in 560 – thirty-seven years before St Augustine arrived in England. It was endowed by Cadwallon Liu, Lord of Tegeingl, nephew of St Asaph, who succeeded Kentigern as Bishop (when the latter returned to Scotland) – and gave his name to the place. These early Celtic bishops steadfastly maintained their independence of Canterbury; not till Norman times was the pattern of dioceses and parishes introduced into Wales, and the first Bishop of St Asaph to receive consecration at Canterbury was Gilbert, who was consecrated by Archbishop Theodore in 1143.

Nothing survives of the earliest cathedral – indeed what we see was largely rebuilt at the end of the 13th century, after being sacked by the soldiers of Edward I; the tower was not completed till 1385. Every possible misfortune assailed the Cathedral thereafter: burnt by Owen Glendowr, sacked again by the Roundheads, a hurricane brought down the top of the tower in 1714; the chapter house was pulled down in 1779, and much of the nave was roofless till the 19th century. The restoration by Sir Gilbert Scott took place between 1869 and 1875.

Inside, the nave is wide, with a broad low-pitched oak-panelled roof, its bosses gilded. Everything is low and wide: the nave arcades, the crossing arches, are all simply chamfered; pillars lack capitals. The clerestory is low, its windows square with simple tracery: the wooden vaulting of the crossing, the timbered chancel roof, the nave aisles – all these are wide and low. Except for the gilding in the roof, there is little colour, little decoration.

The chancel is altogether richer: here stand the 15th-century canopied stalls for Dean and canons – the seats for the choir are in the crossing – there is a Victorian bishop's throne and alabaster reredos; here the hand of Gilbert Scott is everywhere apparent: he practically rebuilt the chancel. The transepts are pleasantly furnished as chapels: the north transept is reserved for Welsh services. The only glass of note is in a window in the south transept, which contains early-19th-century heraldic glass by Eginton.

It is disappointing to find so few monuments in a church of such antiquity: one 13th-century effigy in the south aisle is perhaps the tomb of Bishop Anian (1268–93), who rebuilt the Cathedral at that time; a Victorian brass in the chancel commemorates Bishop John Owen, Chaplain to Charles I, Bishop of St Asaph 1629, 'imprisoned in the Tower of London and exiled from his see'. He died in 1651. A tablet in the south aisle is to the memory of Mrs Hemans, the poetess (d. 1835), 'whose character is best portrayed in her writings'; a seated marble figure at the west end is of William Davies Ripley, 'Dean and Chancellor of St Asaph for more than fifty years' (d. 1826), 'erected by the gentlemen, clergy and commonalty of the diocese'. There is an enormous iron chest, made by the noted smith Robert Davies of Wrexham; originally made to house the cathedral plate, it now stands near the north door as a capacious offertory box.

On display is an interesting collection of 16th-century Welsh Bibles and Prayer Books, including William Salusbury's New Testament (1567) and William Morgan's Bible (1588), which was used by the Prince of Wales at his Investiture at Caernarvon Castle in 1969. St Asaph was closely associated with a group of scholars and translators after the Reformation: they are commemorated by the imposing Translators' Monument in the churchyard, erected in 1902 and designed by Prothero, Middleton and Phillott of Cheltenham.

The Bishop's Palace, now abandoned for a new single-storey house built under the very shadow of the west wall of the churchyard, stands serene across wide lawns to the south-west. A distinguished late-18th-century stone house, with central bow and shallow dome, it was built for Bishop Bagot in 1791. Bagot was the first bishop to reside in the diocese for more than a month in the year since the early 18th century. The Cathedral Library, founded by Dean Watkin Williams at the end of the 19th century, occupies a Victorian Tudor building opposite the east end of the Cathedral; there is a small museum in the undercroft of the Registry at the north-west corner of the churchyard.

DIOCESE OF
ST DAVID'S

St David's Cathedral

WHO CAN FORGET ST DAVID'S – the rocky inlets along the coast, the craggy headlands, the cliffs, green fields, stone walls, small solitary farms, a background of purple hills, wild flowers everywhere? St David's is at the end of the world: roads from Haverfordwest, from Fishguard, reach St David's at last; only narrow lanes lead on from there to the coast, to Ramsey Sound or Whitesands Bay, lanes shaggy with long grass in summer. The sea is never far away – long stretches of sand at Newgale, the little harbour at Solva, St David's Head itself.

Who can forget the Cathedral, set in its little valley, the pinnacled tower rising unexpectedly above a poppy field, or across the ruins of the medieval Bishop's Palace, or just visible at the end of the village street? The village – it is no more than a village, albeit a cathedral city (the portentous words CITY HALL are inscribed above the entrance to the village hall, and a public house is named the City Inn – consists of stone houses surrounding a small green: an hotel or two, a bank, a shop or so: that is all. Here, at the end of the world, St David, Patron Saint of Wales, founded his little monastery and built his first church in the 6th century.

We can make our way down the sloping street to the bell tower and gatehouse which guard the approach to the Cathedral. Here we must stand and stare – at a cathedral of great antiquity and rugged beauty, set incredibly in a fold of green fields with hardly a sign of human habitation, and almost within sound of the sea. The long arm of the nave, the broad transepts, the tall central tower, the chancel and longer, lower arm of the Lady Chapel embraced by chancel aisles – it is a perfect composition built of grey, silvery, purple stone as though hewn from the local rock. Building of the present church – nave, choir, transepts – began in 1180 under Bishop Peter de Leia. Bishop Gower added the Lady Chapel, eastern chapels, and added a second storey to the tower (which had

been rebuilt a century before, after the fall of the first, low, tower) in the first half of the 14th century. Early in the 16th Bishop Vaughan, the third great building bishop, added the top storey to the tower, and (as we shall see inside) the Chapel of the Trinity.

We can descend the steep steps into the churchyard, walk round the building, cross the little stream which almost washes the west front, and survey the ruined medieval Bishop's Palace, a handful of cottages, one or two larger houses set within their garden walls, note the site of the cloisters on the north side, and Gilbert Scott's west front (1860) which was built to replace John Nash's front (1793) – picturesque but disapproved of. Then we can enter by the south porch.

The nave is broad and light, lit by the traceried Dec windows of the aisles and the smaller round-headed windows of the clerestory. It is a wonderful interior, built of that same grey, silvery purple stone: the arcades are Transitional Norman, with alternating clustered columns, octagonal or round, round arches, heavily moulded and each arch different, a triforium of narrow, paired, pointed arches with clerestory above set, with the triforium, in another smaller heavily moulded arcade. It is a remarkable composition, and it is fascinating to reflect that this solid, rough-hewn, Transitional nave is contemporary in date with the E.E. elegance of the nave at Wells. Turning east, Bishop Gower's elaborate stone pulpitum is crowned with its organ; above that a hanging rood with attendant figures (by W. D. Caroe), and above that, spanning the nave, a flat timber ceiling of wonderful workmanship with elaborate pendants connected by low arches, each pendant, each arch, intricately carved; it is the work of William Pole, Treasurer of the Cathedral 1470-1509. As we walk up the nave we shall become aware of another charm of the place: the gentle slope upwards of the nave towards the east, due to the sloping site:

St David's Cathedral, with the ruins of the Bishop's Palace, set in a fold of green fields close to the sea

there is a difference of some 14 ft between the west door and the Lady Chapel. We can admire Bishop Gower's pulpitum, with his tomb occupying the recess at the south end, and, climbing the steps through the doorway at the east end of the south aisle, ascend into the south transept, and so into the chancel.

The nave is spacious and impressive, the chancel secluded and intimate. Here pointed arches, and a clerestory of lancets above, lead the eye upward to the gaily painted and gilded 15th-century timber ceiling, and eastward to the lancets above the High Altar, with Hardman's glass above, Salviati's mosaics below. On the south side stands the rare wooden 15th-century sedilia, on the north what remains of St David's shrine, in the centre the table tomb of Edmund Tudor, father of Henry VII – originally in the Grey Friars' Church at Carmarthen, brought here at the dissolution of that monastery; and in the floor 15th-century tiles – all gold and reddish brown – perhaps made at Malvern. Turning west we enter the choir through

St David's Cathedral: the 13th-century nave, with Bishop Gower's pulpitum and Treasurer Pole's ceiling

an ancient wooden parclose screen. Here, under the tower, is a set of glorious 15th-century stalls, complete with canopies and misericords, one bearing the Royal Arms, for the Queen, like all her predecessors, is senior Prebendary of St David's; the Bishop's throne (*c.* 1500) is lofty and imposing, with three pinnacled canopies. Here and elsewhere the ancient woodwork seems to take on the colour of the stone, bleached soft brown or grey. And, above, the ceiling of the lantern tower is brightly painted in blues and reds and gold, dis-

playing the arms of bishops from the 12th century onwards.

Continuing our tour we can explore the eastern chapels, St Nicholas', St Edward's, separated from the eastern ambulatory by E.E. arcades; and in the centre is the longer Lady Chapel. This contains elaborate sedilia and canopied tombs – badly weathered after the original vault fell in during the 16th century, when these eastern parts became ruined. Oldrid Scott restored the Lady Chapel vault, and after his death W. D. Caroe continued the restoration, c. 1906. An unexpected pleasure is the Trinity Chapel, between the High Altar and the ambulatory. This was in origin an open court, until Bishop Vaughan formed the chapel in the early 16th century. On either side of the altar unglazed windows open into the ambulatory; above the altar is a 14th-century stone reredos, with panels of the Crucifixion and of four apostles. *'Ecce Agnus Dei Qui tollit peccata mundi'*, reads the inscription; beneath is a stone altar, made up of ancient fragments (by Caroe), and long shafts support a fan-vaulted roof. Facing the altar an iron grille in a small arched recess holds a casket containing the bones of St David himself, and a tiny opening in the wall gives on to the High Altar behind.

The Chapel of St Thomas Becket opens out of the north transept: it is vaulted, and above is the Cathedral Library, which is open to visitors at certain times (it is approached from the north choir aisle). On the wall of the transept, over the remains of St Caradoc's shrine, is a memorial to the composer Thomas Tomkins (d. 1656), whose father was Cathedral organist.

Outside again, we can explore the ruins of the Palace – which far exceeded in magnificence any bishop's residence in Wales or England: even as a ruin it is spectacular. The gatehouse on the north side leads into a vast open grassy courtyard. The Bishop's private apartments – chapel, solar, hall and kitchen – occupied the east side; the state apartments – Great Hall, another chapel, and so on – were on the south; and on the west there was a range of smaller and simpler domestic apartments. These are the oldest part (12th–13th century); the grander buildings followed – the Bishop's quarters in the late 13th century, the state rooms built by Bishop Gower in the 14th. Decay set in after the Reformation: the Palace was still occupied at the end of the 16th century, but a century later it was all roofless and derelict. In the 18th century a new palace was built at Abergwili, near Carmarthen; this is where the present Bishop lives. Since 1932 the ruined palace has been in the care of the Office of Works (D. o. E.), and careful restoration has been carried out. It is a pleasure to wander among the ruins, climb up into the empty chambers, or sit in the great courtyard on the garden seats.

Cardigan Priory: the 14th-century monastic chancel

Kidwelly Priory seen from the castle

Here, at the end of the world, the medieval bishops held court and entertained, debated and prayed. For us today it is a thrill to stand upon an upper parapet, or by an empty gaping window lower down, and gaze out towards the Cathedral, and the smiling countryside all around.

Cardigan Priory

The former priory church stands in a delightful position close to the River Teifi; west tower and nave were largely rebuilt in 1702, but the chancel is elaborate Perp work of the late 14th century. Cardigan was a cell of the Benedictine Abbey of Chertsey, and to this, and to its shrine of Our Lady with the Taper, Cardigan owed its fame. After the Dissolution the monastic buildings became a private house, converted in the late 18th century in cheerful Gothick taste for Thomas Johnes of Hafod; but all is now more or less submerged in the adjoining hospital.

Kidwelly Priory

An ancient port, a strategic point on the estuary of the Gwendraeth, the little town is dominated by the medieval castle – one of the grandest in

Wales – and the tall spire of the priory church. This Benedictine Priory was founded *c.* 1130 as a cell of Sherborne, and most of the church survived as the parish church after the Dissolution. A tapering 14th-century spire, a wide aisleless nave and chancel, short transepts, the interior is austere, light and impressive. Curious staircases in the thickness of the walls, and blocked doorways, speak of monastic origins; there is a 14th-century alabaster figure of the Virgin, and a handsome 18th-century organ (by Thomas Warne).

Llanbadarn Fawr Priory

Although it lies on the outskirts of Aberystwyth, this is an ancient village, dominated by the grand cruciform priory church with its central tower and

ABOVE *Llanbadarn Fawr* BELOW *Monkton Priory;*

low spire. Big black slate tombs by the south porch greet the visitor – 'So teach us to number our days'; the doorway is E.E., as is much of the church, gaunt, impressive, aisleless, with a grand austere crossing and strong monastic atmosphere; there are narrow lancets everywhere, and some good Victorian glass. The early crosses in the south transept (of *c.* 700) speak of the first Celtic monastery here; later it became a cell of the Benedictine Abbey at Gloucester, but afterwards the Celtic traditions were revived; later still the church was appropriated by the Cistercian Abbey of Vale Royal. After the Dissolution it survived as the parish church; J. P. Seddon restored it in the late 1860s – to him is due the mosaic chancel floor, the reredos, the Victorian glass. There is an array of distinguished 18th- and early-19th-century monuments to the Powells of Nanteos and the Pryses of Gogerdden.

St Clears: a small 12th- and 13th-century priory church

Monkton Priory

Pembroke Castle and Monkton Priory beckon to one another across the river: it is a magnificent sight. Monkton is a grand Benedictine cruciform church, with a tall narrow south tower, large echoing porch, and an interior of austere monastic spaciousness. The chancel with its canopied stalls and other splendid fittings is a Victorian rebuilding, as is the N.E. chapel. 'It's too big,' said the church cleaner, struggling to polish the gorgeous tiles in the sanctuary. There is an imposing Jacobean tomb to Sir Francis Meyrike (1608), and an accomplished marble monument to Sir Hugh Owen, Bt., 'the last in the direct line of the Ancient and Honourable House of Orielton', by John Bacon junior (1809).

St Clears Priory

The A40 hurries through the town, but the old street to the south leads to the priory church – which stands down its long churchyard path opposite the late-Georgian Town Hall. Originally a small Cluniac priory (the Cluniac Order was an offshoot of the Benedictine), there is a 13th-century west tower, an aisleless nave and chancel, and a grand Norman chancel arch with splendid carvings; it was suppressed as an alien priory in the reign of Henry V, but still stands in almost monastic isolation surrounded by its ample meadows, the River Taf beyond.

DIOCESE OF
ST WOOLOS

St Woolos Cathedral

ST WOOLOS STANDS on Stow Hill, overlooking the industrial town of Newport. The shopping streets, the public buildings, the railway station, lie below; endless roads of small houses climb the hill to the Cathedral – with only Victoria Place, a street lined on both sides with charming early Victorian terrace houses, worth a glance. And from its hilltop churchyard St Woolos looks down too on the River Usk, with its great Transporter Bridge

– which brings to mind that other Transporter Bridge across the Tees at Middlesbrough.

It was on this hilltop that Woolos, himself a convert to the Christian religion, founded a church early in the 6th century, a building of mud and wattle. A more permanent building followed – then a Saxon church, parts of which are the bones of the curious very narrow nave which still stands between the nave proper and the west tower. After

St Woolos Cathedral: the Norman nave, looking west to St Mary's Chapel beyond

the Conquest the larger nave was added, and the tower was built in the 15th century by Jasper Tudor, uncle of Henry VII. When the new Diocese of Monmouth was founded in 1921, St Woolos became, first, the Pro-Cathedral, then, in 1949, the Cathedral of the diocese. A new chancel, and extensions to the east end, were added in 1960.

It is that little narrow nave – called St Mary's Chapel – which forms the entrance to the church: a sloping floor, some mutilated monuments, a few tiny lancet windows – and we are face to face with a sumptuous Norman arch which leads into the nave, an arch supported on two intriguing columns with crudely carved capitals, said to have come from the Roman fort at Caerleon nearby. The view through this into the Norman nave is memorable and moving: on either side a sturdy arcade, with the plainest of round arches, cushion capitals and simple round piers – and a clerestory above of narrow Norman windows. Wider aisles and chancel were built in the 14th century, but the chancel, largely rebuilt in the 19th century, has now been replaced by the long new chancel (by Alban Caroe), dedicated in 1962. It is a modest affair, long and low and light – echoing the long low St Mary's 'nave' at the west end – and marries happily with the proportions of the rest of the church; it is built of old stone, from a demolished church at Kemys Inferior. There are simple stalls for Dean and canons, a simple throne for the Bishop, and behind the altar a high mural and small round window, filled with glass by John Piper. The mural – or marbling – forms a narrow dorsal for the altar; designed by Mr Piper, it was executed by the scenery painters of Covent Garden Opera House.

Abergavenny Priory

Spectacular countryside: the Brecon Beacons, the Black Mountains, the Sugar Loaf, Ysgyryd Fawr, the Usk, the Gavenny – a remote world which was strategic country to the Romans and the Normans, and is strategic country to the walker and tourist of today. Abergavenny is a charming town, with streets of Georgian houses and a Victorian town hall: the Castle stands on one side – once a Norman border fortress, but tamed now, and standing in the public gardens – the Priory stands on the other, its tall Perp tower clearly visible, but a stone's throw from the bottom of the main street.

Abergavenny Priory: the immense figure of Jesse in the north chapel

The Benedictine Priory was founded *c.* 1100 by Hamelin de Bohun, as a cell of the Abbey of St Vincent at Le Mans: it was originally a cruciform building, with a Lady Chapel extending beyond the present chancel; the spacious nave is a rebuilding of 1882. The site of the cloisters and other monastic buildings on the south side of the nave is now a car park, but there is still a long wing extending from the transept (used as parish rooms and so on), and an old monastic barn on the west. The church itself is imposing, with monuments and furnishings of great interest. The crossing and chancel are 14th century, and vaulted: here stand the splendid early-16th-century stalls, canopied and elaborately carved with gorgeous beasts – a lion couchant, a dragon – with the prior's stall marked with a mitre. There are good misericords, and the tracery in the backs has more than a hint of the Renaissance. In the north chapel is an even more remarkable piece of carving: an immense figure of Jesse reclining, the root, as it were, of an enormous Tree of Jesse, which once formed the reredos screen between the High Altar and the Lady Chapel. Alas, the 'trunk' has been sawn off and all the 'branches' destroyed. But Jesse's magnificent figure still lies here.

In the south chapel are the tombs of the great border family of Herbert, ancestors of the Earls of Pembroke: in the centre, Sir William (d. 1446), the sides of the chest carved with figures of the apostles, the panel at the end depicting the Annunciation; nearby is his younger son, Sir Richard, defeated by the Lancastrians at Edgecote, and beheaded (1469); in a canopied recess in the south wall is another Sir Richard (d. 1510), illegitimate son of the 1st Earl of Pembroke (of the first creation), Gentleman Usher to Henry VII and Constable of Abergavenny Castle: the back of the tomb depicts the Assumption – which has miraculously survived – with figures of angels supporting the Virgin on either side. He was father of the 1st Earl of Pembroke of the second creation, and therefore direct forebear of the present family at Wilton and, of course, of George Herbert the poet. One other tomb must be mentioned – that of David Lewis, first Principal of Jesus College, Oxford (d. 1584), in the north chapel.

There is a very large Royal Arms of Queen Anne, in a very good frame (1709).

octagonal columns, with triforium and clerestory above, this nave is extremely moving. At the west end stands the tomb of Henry, Lord Herbert of Raglan, 2nd Earl of Worcester: he and his wife lie under a canopy, wearing their coronation robes (1549); this is the best thing in the church. In 1841 wide, galleried, shallow transepts, with big 'churchwarden Norman' windows, were added, and at the end of the century a new chancel was added in a competent Gothic by Seddon and Carter; the galleries were removed in 1957. There is a Jacobean tomb in the south transept to Mrs Clayton (d. 1627), with her two husbands kneeling at her side and a brood of twelve children below.

It is a large but rather empty church, but the Norman nave is one of the grandest buildings of its date in Wales, and in its own right unforgettable.

Chepstow Priory

Over the Severn Bridge, and turn right: the signpost points to Chepstow. We are in a different world – Wales. The River Wye divides Wales from England, and a medieval castle here protected the frontier. Its venerable ruins stand on a ridge above the river. Chepstow is very much a frontier town, with part of the town walls surviving, though largely concealed from view by buildings. It is superb country, with the Wye making its incredible horseshoe bend at Tidenham, and continuing upstream to Tintern, where the ruins of the Abbey stand in a valley of supreme beauty.

The entrance to Chepstow is through the ancient West Gate: the street descends towards the Priory, which is at first hard to find, surrounded as it is by a maze of small streets.

The Benedictine Priory was founded at the end of the 11th century by William FitzOsbern, as a cell of the Abbey of Cormeilles in Normandy, which he had founded in 1060: the west front is Norman, with a grand, highly ornamented doorway set between two smaller blind arches, with a triplet above. The tower above that is a handsome and by no means incongruous addition of 1705, built from the stone of the original central tower which had fallen in 1701: no wonder – chancel and transepts were pulled down at the Dissolution, and the tower was left with little to support it. The nave, which had been used as the parish church, survived. Though shorn of its aisles, this austere 11th-century nave is magnificent. Stark and severe, with the simplest of round arches set on

Usk Priory

Usk is a delightful little town, or big village, in wonderful countryside beside the River Usk, haunt of fishermen: in local hostelries the traveller will be regaled with trout or salmon from the river, in season. A small square, with a public house or two, a shop or two, watched over by the fragment of a marcher castle, leads to the lane at the end of which stands the priory church. A medieval gatehouse on the right leads to the Priory House, built on the site of the conventual buildings after the Dissolution: the gate on the left to the church – standing in a churchyard of old tombs and headstones. A twelfth-century tower, Perp windows in nave and north aisle, and 15th-century west and north porches, almost identical, with ogee doorways and carved panelled parapets: such is the church. The walls which surround grassy enclosures at the east end are relics of the north transept and chancel.

Usk Priory was founded for Benedictine nuns c. 1135, and the tower and crossing date from this period. Nave and north aisle are like two wide parallel naves, divided by an E.E. arcade, with a wooden barrel roof. The interior is dominated by a very fine 15th-century screen, gaily painted; the east bay of the nave is the choir, and, beyond, the grand Norman crossing arches, with the rib vaulting beneath the tower, make a numinous vaulted sanctuary. There is a handsome 18th-century pulpit, and an enormous and ancient parish chest.

Chepstow Priory: the 11th-century nave arcade, austere and magnificent

Usk Priory: the 15th-century screen and the Norman arches of the crossing

GLOSSARY

Abbey	Monastic church ruled by an abbot or abbess.
Ambulatory	Processional walk round apsidal or square east end, behind the high altar.
Apse	Semi-circular or polygonal east end of church or chapel.
Ashlar	Masonry of finely finished even blocks.
Aumbry	Cupboard, usually in north wall of sanctuary, to hold the Blessed Sacrament, or sacred vessels.
Baldacchino	Canopy over altar, supported on columns.
Ballflower	Petalled globelike ornament, used as decoration in early 14th century.
Baroque	Large-scale, forceful and original treatment of Renaissance architecture, associated with Vanbrugh, Hawksmoor and Archer.
Benedictines	*see* Introduction.
Boss	Carved stone at intersection of the ribs of a vault.
Box pew	Enclosed pew with door and high partitions, much favoured in 18th century.
Broach spire	Earliest type of spire, where the tower rises direct into the spire without parapet or pinnacles; the 'broach' is the sloping triangular piece of masonry connecting the angle of the square tower with the adjacent face of the octagonal spire.
Campanile	Free-standing bell tower.
Canons	Augustinian, Secular: *see* Introduction.
Capital	The crown of a column.
Carthusians	*see* Introduction.
Cartouche	Decorative tablet for inscription or coat of arms.
Chancel	The eastern limb of a church.
Chantry chapel	Chapel endowed for the saying of Mass for the soul of a particular person or family.
Chapter	Governing body of cathedral (Dean and Chapter) or monastery.
Chapter House	The council chamber for the Chapter.
Chevet	French term denoting the radiating chapels and ambulatory of an apsidal east end.
Chevron	Inverted 'V' ornament.
Cinquefoil	Five-leafed decoration in tracery.
Cistercians	*see* Introduction.
Clerestory	Top stage of nave or chancel, lit by windows.
Coade stone	Artificial stone manufactured in the late 18th and early 19th century by the Coade family in Lambeth.
Collegiate church	Church served by college of Canons or Prebendaries.
Corbel	A block, usually of stone, projecting from a wall to support an arch or vault.

Corinthian	*see* Orders.
Cornice	Horizontal projection at the top of a wall.
Crocket	Small carved ornament on the side of a spire or pinnacle.
Crossing	The intersection of nave, choir and transepts in a cruciform church.
Crypt	Vaulted chamber below church.
Curvilinear	Later Dec tracery of flowing pattern.
Cusp	Connecting point between the arcs in Gothic tracery, constituting trefoils, quatrefoils, etc. (q.v.)
'Dec'	The Decorated style: first half of 14th century.
Diapering	Decoration of wall surface in patterned brick or stone.
Dog-tooth	Small pyramidal carved ornament in late Norman and E.E. architecture.
Doric	*see* Orders.
Dorter	Monastic dormitory.
'E.E.'	The Early English style: the earliest English Gothic (13th century).
Easter Sepulchre	Carved and usually elaborately decorated recess on the north side of a sanctuary where the Blessed Sacrament was placed on Good Friday.
Fan vault	*see* Vault.
Feretory	Space (usually behind high altar) for the shrine of a saint.
Fleche	Small timber or lead-covered spire.
Flushwork	Decorative use of dressed stone in flint walling to provide (often elaborate) patterns.
Flying buttress	Buttress in the form of an arch or demi-arch to support the thrust of a high vault.
Frater	Monastic refectory.
Frontal	Embroidered drapery to cover an altar.
Geometrical	Earliest form of Dec tracery, composed of geometrical patterns.
Gothick	Fanciful 18th-century version of Gothic.
Groined vault	*see* Vault.
Grisaille	Grey-white monochrome glass, adorned with enamelled patterning.
Hatchment	Corruption of 'achievement': painted board depicting a deceased person's coat of arms, displayed first on his house, then removed to a church.
Ionic	*see* Orders.
Lancet	Narrow pointed arched window, characteristic of E.E. architecture.
Lierne	*see* Vault.
Minster	Loosely-used term for a major church: the cathedral at York is always known as York Minster.

Misericord	Projecting ledge on underneath of hinged seat of stall, to support the occupant standing.
Narthex	Entrance vestibule.
Nave	Western limb of a church.
Newel	Retaining pillar in circular staircase; newel staircase.
Norman	Norman architecture, the English version of Romanesque.
Ogee	Design of an arch or window incorporating both convex and concave curves.
Orders	The classical orders in Greek or Roman architecture. Doric – Greek Doric: solid, often fluted, column with simple cushion capital and no base; Roman Doric: narrower column, sometimes fluted, with base and cushion capital; Tuscan Doric: a later, plain and severely designed version of Roman Doric. Ionic: elegant column, sometimes fluted, with ram's horn capital. Corinthian: graceful column, with base and elaborately carved capital of acanthus leaves.
Palladian	Architecture based on the principles of Andrea Palladio (1518–1580).
Pediment	Classical low-pitched version of the Gothic gable.
'Perp'	The Perpendicular style, the latest phase of Gothic architecture in England (c. 1350–1550).
Pilaster	Pier or pillar attached to wall.
Piscina	Recess with basin and drain, usually in south wall of sanctuary, for washing the sacred vessels.
Prebendary	Canon (q.v.); adjective, prebendal.
Premonstratensian	see Introduction.
Presbytery	Sanctuary of church, or priest's house.
Priory	Monastic church ruled by prior or prioress; subordinate to an abbey.
Pulpitum	Stone screen dividing chancel from nave in major church.
Quatrefoil	Four-leafed decoration in tracery.
Quire	Alternative name for chancel (or choir).
Quoin	Dressed corner stone.
Reredos	Carved or decorative screen behind altar; altapiece.
Retrochoir	Eastern space behind high altar.
Rib vault	see Vault.
Rococo	Exotic, extravagant flowering of Continental Baroque – a style rarely employed in England.
Romanesque	In England usually termed 'Norman'.
Rood	Crucifix; rood loft, rood screen – loft, screen, supporting a rood.
Rustication	Large blocks of ashlar, or of rough-faced stone, with sunk joints, used in classical architecture to emphasize the base of a building or other wall space.
Sacrarium	Sacristy.
Sanctuary	Space surrounding the altar.
Saxon	Pre-Conquest English architecture.
Scriptorium	Monastic library.

Sedilia	Stone or wooden seats for the officiating priests on south side of sanctuary.
Shaft	Small column attached to pier or wall.
Slype	Narrow passage room in a monastery, usually between the transept and chapter house of the church, used as a common room by the monks (or nuns), where the rule of silence was relaxed and guests could be received.
Spandrel	The triangular space between two arches, or between an arch and an adjoining pilaster.
Springers	The base stems of a vault, springing from a pillar or wall.
Stiff-leaf	Carved foliage, typical of the E.E. style.
String course	Projecting horizontal band of masonry.
Tabernacle	Receptacle for housing Blessed Sacrament.
Tabernacle-work	Traceried decoration of wall.
Tester	Canopy for altar or pulpit.
Three-decker	Three-tiered pulpit, with reading desk, stall and pulpit above one another.
Tierceron	see Vault.
Tracery	Intersecting decoration of a window; see Curvilinear; Geometrical; Perpendicular.
Transept	The north and south extending limbs of a cruciform church.
Transitional	'Transitional Norman' – the transition from Norman to Gothic.
Trefoil	Three-leafed decoration in tracery.
Triforium	Arcaded storey above the arches and below the clerestory in a major church, often containing a gallery.
Tympanum	Space between the lintel arch in a Saxon or Norman doorway, often containing elaborate carving.
Undercroft	Crypt.
Vault	Arched covering of space in stone (or brick or wood); barrel vault: a vault built in one continuous arch; groined vault: the intersection of such vaults (Norman); rib vault: the simplest form of cross-vaulting – quadripartite, employing two diagonal and two transverse ribs; sexpartite, employing an extra rib springing from the centre of the wall on each side (late Norman and E.E.); tierceron vault: employing secondary ribs, from wall to central boss (E.E.); lierne vault: the use of small decorative ribs, introduced for ornamental rather than structural purposes (Dec); fan vault: the latest phase of Gothic vaulting, where fan-shaped panelled ribs extend in equal lengths from wall to centre of roof (Perp).
Venetian window	Palladian triple window, the central opening arched.
Vesica window	Oval window, with pointed head and foot.
Voussoirs	Wedge-shaped stones used in the construction of an arch.

INDEX OF PERSONS

INDEX OF PLACES